Mastering the IT Audit

Assuring a resilient and compliant
IT landscape through effective audit

Jyothi Ramaswamy

bpb

www.bpbonline.com

First Edition 2026

Copyright © BPB Publications, India

ISBN: 978-93-65893-274

To View Complete
BPB Publications Catalogue
Scan the QR Code:

Dedicated to

My seniors and colleagues

About the Author

Jyothi Ramaswamy is a seasoned risk, security, audit, and compliance professional with over 25 years of experience in the information security domain. Her career spans a distinguished tenure at Tata Consultancy Services Ltd., where she specialized in defining, implementing, reviewing, and auditing controls across complex IT environments. Currently operating as a freelance consultant, auditor, and trainer, Jyothi brings expertise in auditing diverse facets of organizational process management, particularly in the realms of information security and data privacy. Her consulting work is rooted in global standards, with a strong focus on ISO 27001, ISO 20000, ISO 9001, ISO 27701, and CIS controls.

Jyothi is a passionate educator and a certified trainer, known for delivering impactful sessions on cybersecurity, service and quality management, and regulations. Her audit experience spans enterprise networks, firewall-segregated infrastructures, and air-gapped systems. She has played key roles in ISO audits, SSAE assessments, third-party risk evaluations, and internal audits across various business functions. A committed member of professional bodies such as ISACA, IEEE, and GCA, Jyothi actively contributes to local chapters and has led numerous awareness programs on data privacy, cyber risk, and audit methodologies. Her credentials include ISO 27001:2022 Lead Auditor, CRISC – Certified in Risk and Information Systems Control, CISM – Certified Information Security Manager, CRISP – Certified Risk Professional, BS 7799 Lead Implementer, and APMG accredited ISACA Chapter Trainer for CISM and CRISC certifications.

Known for her collaborative spirit, sharp analytical skills, and problem-solving capabilities, Jyothi continues to contribute to the future of audit and security through her thought leadership and hands-on expertise.

About the Reviewers

❖ **Nikhil Deshmukh** is a senior IT auditor and a certified information system auditor (CISA). He is currently responsible for Governance, Risk, and Compliance (GRC), cybersecurity audits, and AI audits. Nikhil is also focused on infrastructure security assessment, ensuring robust protection and compliance across IT environments. An active reader, he engages with a wide range of IT-related literature and hosts podcasts on IT audits, sharing insights and developments in the field. Additionally, Nikhil has delivered seminars on IT security and information security, contributing to the broader discourse on safeguarding digital assets and systems.

❖ **Dinesh Kumar Budagam** is a seasoned IT professional with over 15+ years of experience across diverse domains within the technology sector. His expertise spans Microsoft technologies, Hadoop-based Big Data systems, data engineering, cloud security, privacy, and cybersecurity.

Over the course of his career, Dinesh held key technical and leadership roles at prominent organizations, including IBM, where he was a core contributor, and served as a consultant to major tech leaders such as Microsoft and Meta. Dinesh began his professional journey as a developer and steadily progressed through roles including technical lead and senior technical manager.

Currently, he serves as a senior manager and senior cybersecurity consultant at VISA, where he specializes in cybersecurity and functions as a security architect. In this capacity, Dinesh led strategic initiatives aimed at protecting the organization's most critical digital assets. His responsibilities include designing and implementing advanced security frameworks and strategies for Big Data and cloud environments and focusing on ensuring these platforms remain secure, compliant, and resilient to emerging cyber threats.

Dinesh holds a bachelor of technology in electrical and electronics engineering (2005) and a master's degree in software engineering (2008), which together provide a strong foundation for his technical and analytical capabilities. Additionally, he is a certified IBM solution architect for Big Data analytics, certified cloud architect, certified system architect and is a senior IEEE member. Dinesh completed Advance CyberSecurity and Generative AI: Technology, Business, and Society Program professional certificate program from Stanford University and has published a textbook on Oracle Cloud Infrastructure Security Handbook and Journals on Cybersecurity/AI.

❖ **Sanyam Jain** is a globally recognized security engineering leader and cybersecurity thought leader, known for securing complex digital ecosystems and enhancing resilience across cloud-native environments. With deep expertise in cloud security, security operations, application security, compliance, and security automation, he helps enterprises and startups exceed their security goals through strategic foresight and technical depth.

He brings a DevSecOps-first approach, designing secure architectures, embedding security in CI/CD, and automating compliance. His technical skills span threat detection, Kubernetes security, identity and access management, encryption, and network security across AWS, Azure, and Google Cloud. Sanyam is well-versed in ISO 27001, SOC 2, SOX, HITRUST, GDPR, HIPAA, PCI DSS, and NIST CSF, enabling secure-by-design implementations that meet audit requirements. His research has appeared in Forbes, TechCrunch, ZDNet, and more. He serves as a Judge for Globee® Awards, mentors through NITI Aayog, advises startups, and supports NGOs like GDI Foundation. He reviews technical books for several publishing houses and has mentored thousands via Udacity and other platforms. Sanyam holds a Master's from BITS Pilani and is a Certified Kubernetes Administrator.

Acknowledgement

I want to express my heartfelt gratitude to those who have stood by me throughout this journey, both personally and professionally.

To my family, thank you for your unwavering support, patience, and belief in me. Your encouragement has been the quiet strength behind every milestone and every chapter of this book. I want to thank my father, who taught me to keep learning throughout life, my mother and sisters who supported me relentlessly, my husband who motivated me to take all challenges that came my way, and last but not least, my daughter who lived through my *change approver* mindset.

I am also deeply thankful to my seniors from Tata Consultancy Services Ltd. Trivandrum during my early career, who instilled the habit of excelling in all activities. They provided guidance, vision, and support throughout my professional journey. My supervisors and colleagues from the information security team and the delivery excellence team require a special mention here for helping me learn to look at the bigger picture and cultivate the habit of reviewing solutions, keeping the business context in mind. I would like to acknowledge the support from the cybersecurity service delivery team, my managers, team members, and customer managers, who have helped me in strengthening the governance mindset. The lessons I learned under your direction have echoed through every stage of my growth, and I am very grateful for your support; I will always be thankful for the lessons that you taught me. This book is, in many ways, a reflection of those early lessons and the people who helped instill them.

Preface

Throughout this book, we explain why an IT audit is important in helping an organization strengthen its IT infrastructure, mitigate potential outages in operations, and identify areas for improvement. The major steps here are risk identification and mitigation; assessment of resilience; geography and industry compliance verification; data and platform protection; and last but not least, assuring governance mechanisms through proper documentation and reporting. Audit process requires understanding of the IT landscape, perimeter setup, and various upstream and downstream connectivity. The landscape covers the various appliances, firewall, IDS and IPS, servers, network devices, their configuration, and maintenance. Capacity management, incident management and change management are the main governance activities that stitch the responsibilities of the IT team of any organization. In addition to these, the auditor has to understand the security policies, the patching practices, and the segregation of networks to manage different access levels to different teams.

Once one becomes an IT auditor, they will be able to provide value to managing the backbone of the organization by ensuring security, availability, and integrity of operations and data within their organization. This helps in career growth in the IT service, operation, strategic, and project management roles. Auditors possess a deep understanding of systems, controls, and vulnerabilities. With the right mindset and skill-building, they can evolve into engineers who design secure, efficient, and compliant systems from the ground up.

Chapter 1: IT Audit and Assurance Standards Statements- Key concepts such as auditing, deciding the criteria, and risk-based approach to audits, etc., are explained. It also covers the principles of auditing, due professional care, conflict of interest, and independence.

Chapter 2: IT Audit Defined, Charter and Criteria- Highlights the benefits of the audit process, e.g., improved management system performance, enhanced credibility and trust, better risk management, and increased organizational efficiency.

Chapter 3: Planning, Scheduling, Reporting and Follow-ups for Audit- Steps of conducting an audit: entry meeting, gathering audit evidence, document review, interview techniques, and observations, site inspections are introduced here. We will learn the process of managing an audit program for the IT department and the operations of an organization.

Chapter 4: Types of Audits- Types of audits are explained herewith, like internal audits, external audits, first-party audits, second-party audits, and third-party audits.

Chapter 5: IT Policies, Processes and SOPs- How the policies, processes and operating procedures are defined for typical tasks to be managed by the IT team. We will also get the view of the roles and their responsibilities, helping us to focus on the operational aspects of the IT operations.

Chapter 6: Risk Management and Impact Analysis- The key risk areas relevant to the systems and processes are identified. We see how common risk areas are analyzed, including cybersecurity vulnerabilities, system availability, data backups, and disaster recovery capabilities. Risk management is to be carried out based on the impact on the specific industry and business requirements.

Chapter 7: Procurement, Asset, Capacity and Cloud Service Management- IT policies have to look at the complete life cycles of the equipment, starting with procurement, configuration, defining and implementing procedures, inventorising of assets by marking critical equipment and finally managing EOL for this equipment. IT policies should also focus on interconnection of equipment, access management, monitoring usage to ensure capacity management, and build-in continuity by managing backup systems.

Chapter 8: Access Management and Acceptable Usage Policy- Access management in an organization is the virtue of how well the organization functions when it comes to the authorization of assets to users. Acceptable use policy gives the dos and don'ts and outlines the expectations for how employees and other authorized users should interact with the assets.

Chapter 9: Network, Server, Storage and End Point Management- This chapter talks about process of monitoring and maintaining network devices, servers and storage devices, to optimize the performance. This has to encompass the management of hardware, software, security, and backups to minimize slowdowns and downtime.

Chapter 10: Business Continuity and Disaster Recovery Planning- BCP and DRP provides assurance of IT infrastructure being available for delivering the required services during disruptive events, such as natural disasters, cyberattacks and communication failures, etc. Planning continuity looks at critical services and also takes inputs from asset inventory for critical assets.

Chapter 11: Organization Context and IT Services- IT operation management processes are essential to ensure meeting service requirements, and to continually improve service management. Ensuring information security becomes an integral part of managing IT operations. Business context defines how IT supports the business mission and operations, and how to plan IT strategies and initiatives.

Chapter 12: Logging and Monitoring Services- Through logging of events and activities within a system or application, user actions and error messages are captured. Monitoring helps in measuring the performance and health of a system, such as resource usage, network traffic, and error rates. This helps in designing corrective and preventive actions for process improvements.

Chapter 13: KPIs and Status Reports- This chapter talks about creating guidelines for designing, planning, implementing, continuous testing, improving the processes in an ongoing manner, and governing the complete enterprise IT architecture. Criticality of the assets give inputs to KPIs and governance measures through status reports.

Chapter 14: BCP Drills, Plans and Reports- IT team conducts simulated exercises that test the effectiveness of the business's BCP. After every BCP drill, the business continuity team analyzes and reports the effectiveness of continuity measures. The learnings from drills go as feedback to the various operating procedures.

Chapter 15: Configuration and Change Management- This helps in ensuring that changes to an organization's technical environment are documented and managed in a structured manner. In change management, changes to applications and hardware are tracked, while configuration management focuses on how the physical attributes of application or systems are consistently maintained and managed.

Chapter 16: IT Audit Frameworks ISO 20000 and ITIL– This chapter focuses on how IT audits begins with deciding the audit framework, identifying the aims and benefits of framework, understand the compliance requirements, benefits of audits, etc. The difference between ITIL as a framework and ISO as a certification will also be covered here.

Chapter 17: Organizations, People, Data and Technology Processes– During an IT audit, auditors have to focus on the effectiveness, reliability, and security of an organization's IT infrastructure, systems, and processes. IT audit comprises a review of asset safeguarding practices, namely, data, application systems, technology, and people.

Chapter 18: Partners, Value Streams and Processes- Partner audit focuses on assessing the partner or vendor's past project performance, technical expertise, compliance with industry standards, and financial stability in ensuring uninterrupted services. Value stream analysis can help evaluate the current way of working, identify new requirements, and propose improvements.

Chapter 19: Scope of Audit, and Audit Plan- Audit planning should define the role and responsibilities of an auditor, and also should include all the entities in the enterprise landscape, including external stakeholders. The apex processes of the organization like information security and quality management systems, need to be included in audit process along with IT policies and operation processes, to ensure IT processes are in alignment. Data at rest and in transit has to be checked for the sensitivity, to see whether the processes around them are adequate.

Chapter 20: Review of Policy and Controls- Purpose of the audit function is to evaluate and test the design (ToD) and execution of controls implemented for effectiveness (ToE) by processes surrounding the business operations. Scope of the audit has to be defined either to the entire enterprise or to a specific entity within the enterprise ad all relevant policies surrounding the operations of IT team has to be reviewed along with the governance mechanism in place.

Chapter 21: Interviews, Site Visits and Technical Testing- Status reports and actions on any deviation from threshold has to be given adequate importance as this provides inputs to ToE. Site visits to data centre, support systems like UPS, power backup, access control and CCTV monitoring area etc give inputs to effectiveness of processes put in place. Conflict of interest is another area to be checked thoroughly for ensuring ToE.

Chapter 22: Audit Findings and Actionable Audit Report- An audit report must be well-written to effectively stand out, capture interest, and promote changes. Audit report should illustrate non-conformities, outline positives, call out opportunities for improvement, and should be translatable to actions to close non-conformities.

Chapter 23: Evolving with the Audit Landscape- This chapter provides a conclusion to all areas that have been covered in the book, along with some guidelines on how to plan the audit and prepare a proper audit report with actionable observations. This will also mention how the remediation can be planned on audit observations, and verification audit has to be conducted to cross check the reediation measures taken as a result of audit.

Coloured Images

Please follow the link to download the
Coloured Images of the book:

https://rebrand.ly/32e9bb

We have code bundles from our rich catalogue of books and videos available at https://github.com/bpbpublications. Check them out!

Errata

We take immense pride in our work at BPB Publications and follow best practices to ensure the accuracy of our content to provide an indulging reading experience to our subscribers. Our readers are our mirrors, and we use their inputs to reflect and improve upon human errors, if any, that may have occurred during the publishing processes involved. To let us maintain the quality and help us reach out to any readers who might be having difficulties due to any unforeseen errors, please write to us at:

errata@bpbonline.com

Your support, suggestions and feedback are highly appreciated by the BPB Publications' Family.

At www.bpbonline.com, you can also read a collection of free technical articles, sign up for a range of free newsletters, and receive exclusive discounts and offers on BPB books and eBooks. You can check our social media handles below:

Instagram

Facebook

Linkedin

YouTube

Get in touch with us at: business@bpbonline.com for more details.

Piracy

If you come across any illegal copies of our works in any form on the internet, we would be grateful if you would provide us with the location address or website name. Please contact us at business@bpbonline.com with a link to the material.

If you are interested in becoming an author

If there is a topic that you have expertise in, and you are interested in either writing or contributing to a book, please visit www.bpbonline.com. We have worked with thousands of developers and tech professionals, just like you, to help them share their insights with the global tech community. You can make a general application, apply for a specific hot topic that we are recruiting an author for, or submit your own idea.

Reviews

Please leave a review. Once you have read and used this book, why not leave a review on the site that you purchased it from? Potential readers can then see and use your unbiased opinion to make purchase decisions. We at BPB can understand what you think about our products, and our authors can see your feedback on their book. Thank you!

For more information about BPB, please visit www.bpbonline.com.

Join our Discord space

Join our Discord workspace for latest updates, offers, tech happenings around the world, new releases, and sessions with the authors:

https://discord.bpbonline.com

Table of Contents

CHAPTER 1

IT Audit and Assurance Standards Statements

Introduction

In this chapter, key concepts such as auditing, deciding the criteria, and a risk-based approach to audits are explained. It also covers the principles of auditing, due professional care, conflict of interest, independence, etc. IT audits and assurance statements are vital tools for ensuring that IT systems are secure, reliable, and compliant. They empower organizations to build a resilient IT infrastructure, safeguard their data, and earn the trust of their stakeholders in an increasingly digital world.

In today's interconnected world, **information technology (IT)** is the backbone of almost every business operation. However, with its benefits come risks, such as data breaches, system failures, and compliance challenges. This is where IT audits and assurance statements play a critical role. By prioritizing IT audits, organizations can navigate the complex IT landscape with confidence and turn potential risks into opportunities for growth and improvement.

An IT audit is a detailed evaluation of an organization's IT systems, infrastructure, policies, and operations. Its purpose is to ensure alignment with business goals while complying with relevant regulations. These audits are essential for identifying vulnerabilities, managing risks, and maintaining data security.

Through IT audit learning, one gains skills in various process frameworks, the ability to assess risks systematically, and expertise in tools used for auditing IT environments. Staying updated on compliance requirements and developing actionable solutions for audit findings are also critical outcomes. IT auditing is vital in today's rapidly evolving digital landscape to ensure efficiency, security, and regulatory adherence.

Structure

The chapter covers the following topics:

- Key concepts
- Components of IT management
- Core standards for IT audits
- Assurance statements
- Regulatory compliance requirements

Objectives

This chapter aims to introduce the readers to the concept of the IT audit process and take them through the basic components of IT management, core standards for IT audits, and regulatory compliance requirements. The components of IT management will help the auditor to have a critical look at how the organization's structure is set up, and the standards allow the auditor to decide the applicable controls that need to be checked during the audit. The regulatory compliance requirements are the driving factor for setting up controls and the periodicity of the audit process. Together, all these will create an environment which functions well, is managed well and is subjected to periodic reviews. We will see how these will help in addressing the credibility requirements for an organization.

This chapter contains an introduction to the audit process for first-time auditors and helps them to visualize the audit being conducted. We will also see the outcome of audits, i.e., the assurance statements obtained from different types of audits. By the end of this chapter, we will have obtained an introduction to what an audit is, why an audit is required, who is audited, and what the outcome of an audit is.

Key concepts

The main areas of focus in an IT audit include IT governance, which examines how the organization aligns its IT strategy with business objectives, and risk management, which evaluates safeguards against cybersecurity threats and ensures the effectiveness of disaster recovery plans. Compliance plays a significant role in ensuring adherence to related regulations. Technical infrastructure is reviewed for performance, while access controls are assessed to prevent unauthorized use of sensitive systems.

An audit for IT audits focuses on evaluating whether an organization's IT processes, systems, and controls align with international standards, for information security management or for IT service management. These audits are conducted to ensure compliance, enhance operational efficiency, and build stakeholder trust in the organization's ability to manage risks and protect sensitive information. Audits assess the organization's adherence to policies, procedures, and controls outlined in the relevant standards.

The audit process typically involves a detailed review of documentation, interviews with staff, and inspection of IT systems to verify compliance and identify areas for improvement. The ultimate goal is to demonstrate the organization's commitment to best practices in IT management, security, and compliance.

Auditing is a systematic process of examining, evaluating, and verifying an organization's financial records, operational processes, or IT systems to ensure accuracy, compliance, and effectiveness. It plays a critical role in governance, accountability, and risk management across industries and domains. The IT department is the core that connects your company's networks, systems, applications and data in one central spot to ensure they are functioning properly. It is through an IT system that a business, whether large or small, is able to remain competitive. Different areas of IT include sales, invoicing, accounting, taxes, marketing, HR, customer development and retention, and product development. It supports all the departments of every business. IT service management involves overseeing an organization's IT operations, resources, and infrastructure to ensure technology is effectively leveraged and aligned with the overall business strategy. Professionals in IT implement policies, practices, and procedures essential for managing the maintenance and utilization of hardware, software, and networks, regardless of the industry or business environment. IT management is a salient feature in every organization, and is evident in the following areas:

- **Proper IT management supports business operations**: IT lies at the core of almost all business activities.

- **Brings efficiency and productivity**: IT management ensures that a business's information technologies are secure, optimized, and performing efficiently.

- **Manages risks**: IT systems are to be subjected to business impact assessments and risk analysis, which will help in identifying controls to minimize the impact due to any outages and risks caused by the impact.

- **Improves data management**: IT management improves data management by implementing mechanisms for all users to collaborate, transfer data as required, and store and protect confidential and sensitive data.

- **Plays a strategic role in business growth**: IT management needs a shift in the placeholder from BAU maintenance/management activities to strategic/tactical activities by aligning with the organization's strategic goals, fostering innovation, managing risks, and allocating resources.

Components of IT management

Depending on the business needs and organizational structure, IT management can be broken down into several key components. Typical components are given as follows:

- **IT governance**: Aligning the IT investments and operations with the organization's strategies, followed by the required risk management practices. This leads to the establishment of a framework for decision-making, risk management, and accountability.

- **IT financial management**: Embedding strategic planning, budgeting, tracking, and managing the costs, benefits, and risks of IT investments, in a way to keep the performance metrics at an acceptable level. It includes costing, ROI analysis, accounting, and cost-tracking activities.

- **IT service management (ITSM)**: Focuses on delivering IT support to end-users to meet the needs of the business. ITSM includes service support along with service delivery.

- **IT operations management**: Involves overseeing and managing daily activities, processes, and infrastructure needs of a typical organization, by being responsible for delivering value to the business through technology support.

- **IT project management**: Defines project scopes, budgets, timelines, and resources. It ensures all IT initiatives reach their designated goals in a timely manner and within budget.

- **IT security management**: Protects the organization's data assets and systems from threats and ensures compliance with relevant regulations and standards by implementing security measures and monitoring vulnerabilities to ensure business continuity.

The general responsibilities of the IT managers and the IT team are as follows:

- Managing IT procurement budget and configuration/monitoring costs.

- Determining IT systems/controls that are required for achieving company goals.

- Monitor compliance and integrity of the complete landscape.

- Control network security and ensure zero breach in the organization with proper **operating level agreements (OLAs)**.

- Roll out and administer new software, hardware, and relevant data systems.

- Provide technical or service desk support to employees with proper **service level agreements (SLAs)**.

It is clear that IT managers and professionals within the IT management field need to have subject matter expertise on all things technical, and also have a solid understanding of what goes into business operations. It is up to the IT team to ensure that business operations are using technology to support all aspects of the company strategy and its goals. At the end of the day, the IT leaders at your business will be the problem solvers as your business implements new technologies and systems within its network.

Auditing is an essential process in verifying that organizations comply with **International Organization for Standardization** (**ISO**) standards. ISO auditors must follow specific guidelines to ensure audits are thorough, objective, and aligned with the requirements of the relevant ISO standard.

Core standards for IT audits

IT audits play a critical role in ensuring the security, efficiency, and compliance of IT systems, which form the backbone of any organization. The IT audit and assurance process involves conducting specific procedures to provide reasonable assurance regarding the subject matter. Practitioners undertake assignments that deliver varying levels of assurance, ranging from reviews to attestations or examinations.

Each IT audit or assurance assignment must comply with established standards, ensuring that individuals are qualified to perform the work, the procedures are appropriately executed, the scope of work is clear, and findings are reported accurately based on the assignment's nature and results.

For engagements carried out by a single individual, they must have the necessary skills and knowledge to complete the assignment. In cases where a team is involved, the collective expertise and knowledge of the team must meet the requirements to effectively execute the work.

ISO/IEC 20000 and **Information Technology Infrastructure Library** (**ITIL**) are closely related frameworks that provide best practices and standards for **IT service management** (**ITSM**). Organizations use ITIL as a roadmap to implement ITSM processes and achieve operational excellence. Once processes are established, they can pursue ISO/IEC 20000 certification to demonstrate compliance and validate their ITSM practices.

ISO 20000 outlines the requirements for organizations to establish, implement, maintain, and continuously enhance a **service management system** (**SMS**). The standard covers the planning, design, transition, delivery, and improvement of services to meet organizational needs and deliver value effectively.

ITIL has been a cornerstone of the ITSM industry, offering guidance, training, and certification programs. It has transformed traditional ITSM practices by incorporating customer experience, value streams, and digital transformation. ITIL also embraces modern methodologies such as Lean, Agile, and DevOps. ITIL is currently at version 4 and equips organizations to tackle emerging service management challenges and leverage modern technology. It provides a flexible, coordinated, and integrated framework for the governance and management of IT-enabled services.

ITIL and ISO 20000 framework together help an organization to achieve the following:

- **Integrated service management framework**: Combines standardization with practical implementation.

- **Improved service delivery**: Consistent, reliable, and high-quality IT services.

ITIL is a set of best practices and guidelines for ITSM that originated in the United Kingdom. It provides a framework for aligning IT services with business needs and focuses on continuous improvement. ITIL covers various aspects of ITSM, including service strategy, design, transition, operation, and continual service improvement.

ISO 20000 is an international standard for IT service management. It outlines best practices and requirements for the effective management of IT services. ISO 20000 focuses on improving the quality of IT service delivery, enhancing customer satisfaction, and ensuring continuous service improvement. It is a formal and structured framework with specific requirements that organizations must adhere to in order to achieve certification.

To summarize, the comparison between ITIL and ISO 20000 is as follows:

Aspect	ITIL	ISO/IEC 20000
Nature	Best practice framework	International standard
Focus	Guidance for IT service management	Certification of organizations
Audience	Individuals (IT Professionals)	Organizations
Approach	Flexible and adaptable	Mandatory (auditable) requirements
Purpose	Service management best practices	Formal compliance and certification

Table 1.1: Comparison of ITIL framework and ISO 20000 standard

ISO standard provides the approach to compliance through a layered approach in documenting the auditable requirements in alignment with the business objectives and the compliance requirements. At the first level, the policies are drafted, which highlight what all processes have to be addressed for obtaining compliance, then come the control objectives, which provide the best practices from the industry. This is followed by procedures, which capture the methods of carrying out the objectives that are captured in the policies. There will be guidelines that are provided for information on how the activities are to be carried out to address the policies.

The following figure explains the layered approach:

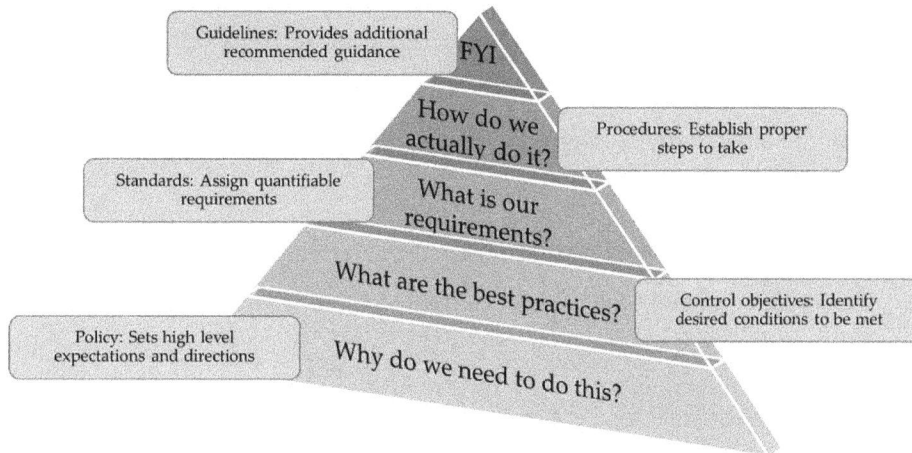

Figure 1.1: *Layered approach as per ISO standard*

Some widely recognized core standards and frameworks used in IT audits are as follows:

- **ISACA's IT Assurance Framework (ITAF):** ITAF provides guidelines, standards, and tools for performing IT audits. Its key areas include audit planning, execution, and reporting.

    ISACA's **Information Technology Audit Framework (ITAF)** is a comprehensive IT audit framework that establishes standards that address IT audit and assurance practitioners' roles and responsibilities, ethics, expected professional behavior, and required knowledge and skills; provides guidance and techniques for planning, performing, and reporting of IT audit and assurance engagements. Based on ISACA's material, ITAF provides a single source for IT audit and assurance to practitioners to obtain guidance on the performance of audits and the development of effective audit reports.

- **COBIT Framework: Control Objectives for Information and Related Technologies (COBIT)** is a globally recognized framework developed by ISACA for managing and governing enterprise IT. It provides a comprehensive set of guidelines, principles, and best practices for aligning IT processes with business objectives, ensuring effective governance, risk management, and compliance. COBIT enables organizations to achieve strategic goals by optimizing the value derived from IT investments while managing risks and ensuring resource efficiency. It supports stakeholders in ensuring IT operations are secure, reliable, and aligned with organizational priorities. The framework is widely used across industries to enhance IT governance and improve decision-making.

The six principles of COBIT 2019 provide a foundation for effective governance and management of enterprise IT. These principles ensure that the framework aligns IT processes with business goals while addressing governance and operational needs.

The principles are as follows and will be elaborated in subsequent chapters:

o　Provide stakeholder value

o　Holistic approach

o　Dynamic governance systems

o　Governance distinct from management

o　Tailored to enterprise needs

o　End-to-end governance system

- **ISO/IEC 27001**: ISO/IEC 27001 is the international standard for establishing, implementing, maintaining, and continuously improving an **Information Security Management System (ISMS)**. It provides a comprehensive framework for managing sensitive information, ensuring its confidentiality, integrity, and availability. For IT audits, ISO 27001 serves as a critical benchmark to assess an organization's information security practices. It has the following benefits:

  o　Evaluates the organization's risk assessment processes, including identification, analysis, and treatment of risks, especially for IT assets.

  o　Establishes ISMS.

  o　Supports audits focused on confidentiality, integrity, and availability of information assets.

  o　Evaluates management's role in ensuring the availability and right functioning of the IT landscape, review of ISMS performance, and implementation of timely corrective actions to address any malfunctions.

ISO/IEC 27001 provides a robust foundation for conducting IT audits, ensuring that an organization's information security practices are resilient, compliant, and aligned with business objectives. Auditors can use the standard to evaluate existing controls, identify vulnerabilities, and recommend improvements, ultimately strengthening the organization's overall security posture.

- **NIST Cybersecurity Framework**: NIST **Cybersecurity Framework (CSF)**, developed by the *National Institute of Standards and Technology*, provides a comprehensive set of best practices, guidelines, and standards for managing cybersecurity risks. It is widely used by organizations to establish, implement, and maintain effective cybersecurity practices. For IT auditing, the NIST CSF offers a structured approach to evaluate and ensure the security and resilience of IT systems.

The NIST framework provides comprehensive guidance for managing and reducing cybersecurity risks. It consists of five core functions: Identify, Protect, Detect, Respond, and Recover, and all these phases are interconnected through the major step: Govern.

Govern phase ensures that every control that is implemented in each of the five phases is aligned to the business objectives and also managed using a **Plan, Do, Check, Act (PDCA)** cycle, so that the process improvement is built in along with the implementation. Refer to the following figure:

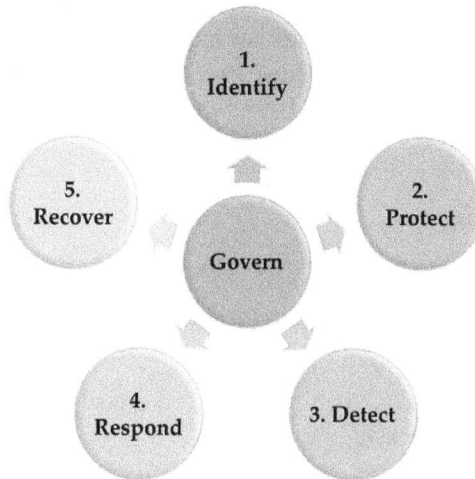

Figure 1.2: NIST Cybersecurity Framework

The benefits of using NIST CSF in IT audit are as follows:

- **Comprehensive coverage**: Addresses all aspects of cybersecurity, from asset identification to incident recovery.

- **Risk-based approach**: Focuses on identifying and managing risks in alignment with organizational objectives.

- **Standardization**: Provides a common language and structure for cybersecurity audits, facilitating communication with stakeholders.

- **Scalability**: Applicable to organizations of all sizes and industries.

- **Improvement-oriented**: Helps organizations prioritize and continuously enhance their cybersecurity posture.

NIST Cybersecurity Framework is an invaluable tool for IT auditing, providing a structured methodology to assess cybersecurity practices and identify areas for improvement. By leveraging the framework, organizations can strengthen their defenses, enhance compliance, and ensure resilience against cyber threats. For auditors, the NIST CSF offers a standardized approach to deliver actionable insights that align the IT operations with best practices.

Audit standards

An audit is a systematic, independent examination of an organization's operations and processes to ensure accuracy, compliance, and efficiency. It involves collecting and evaluating evidence to determine whether the organization's operations comply with established criteria, such as laws, regulations, and internal policies.

ISO auditors must follow specific guidelines to ensure audits are thorough, objective, and aligned with the requirements of the relevant ISO standard. **ISO/IEC 19011:2018** is a standard that outlines the principles and guidelines for auditing management systems, which can include IT management systems (such as those based on ISO 20000 for IT service management systems and ISO 27001 for ISMS or other IT-related standards).

The focus areas of ISO/IEC 19011 include the following:

- **Principles of auditing**:
    - **Integrity**: Auditors should demonstrate honesty and fairness in their work.
    - **Fair presentation**: Audit findings should reflect the true results of the audit process.
    - **Due professional care**: Auditors must exercise professional judgment and care during the audit process.
    - **Confidentiality**: Auditors should respect confidentiality during and after the audit process.
    - **Independence**: Auditors must be independent from the activities they audit to ensure objectivity.
    - **Evidence-based approach**: Audit conclusions should be based on verifiable evidence.
- **Managing an audit program:** Creating guidelines to help organizations manage and plan audit programs, ensuring that audits are consistent, objective, and effective.
- **Audit process**: Defines the processes of preparing, conducting, and reporting audits, ensuring transparency and consistency. The audit process includes the following steps:
    1. Initiating the audit
    2. Planning the audit
    3. Conducting the audit
    4. Reporting audit findings
    5. Follow-up and verification
- **Competence and evaluation of auditors**: Ensures that auditors are properly trained and capable of carrying out audits effectively.

- **Audit techniques**: ISO/IEC 19011 provides insight into different auditing techniques and methodologies, including interviews, observation, sampling, and document review, which are applicable to IT audits as well.

As mentioned earlier, ISO/IEC 19011 is often used in conjunction with ISO 20000 for IT service management practices and ISO/IEC 27001, and information security management practices, when conducting audits of the IT landscape. It can also be used when auditing other IT-related management systems, such as ISO/IEC 22301 (business continuity management), to ensure effective governance, risk management, and compliance.

Assurance statements

Assurance is a process for independently ensuring the accuracy of an audit. Assurance typically occurs after an audit and provides a second opinion on the financial data, solidifying its validity. Organizations may conduct assurance processes to ensure an auditor's report is accurate and includes all necessary information. This process can be useful for providing additional assurance to investors, business owners and managers that their auditing and financial reporting processes are factual and reliable. Assurance statements for IT audits are formal declarations made by auditors to provide confidence and credibility regarding the reliability and accuracy of an organization's IT systems and processes.

Data breaches and cyberattacks pose significant risks in today's business environment. Implementing robust IT management strategies is essential for protecting organizations from these threats. Businesses aiming to maintain long-term competitiveness must prioritize the efficient and responsible integration of IT management tools into their operations. In the context of an IT audit, assurance statements are formal declarations issued by auditors after assessing an organization's IT systems, existing controls, and processes. These statements serve as a way for auditors to communicate their professional judgment about the effectiveness of the IT systems in meeting specified standards, regulations, and organizational requirements.

A successful IT audit will result in providing the information and data needed to ensure that the infrastructure, policies, and operations are all exactly where they are required to be. These audits are your way of knowing that the controls in place are working to protect the company's assets and the integrity of the data, and remain in line with the objectives of the company. It is just one more way you can work to keep all sensitive data locked. Assurance statements are particularly important in the areas of information security, risk management, and compliance.

Importance of assurance statements in IT audits

Assurance statements have a lot of significance in IT audits.

Let us look at the major outcomes of obtaining assurance statements:

- **Confidence in IT governance**: Assurance statements help management, regulators, and other stakeholders understand the effectiveness of the organization's IT governance, risk management, and security practices.

- **Compliance**: Many regulatory frameworks (e.g., GDPR, SOC 2, HIPAA, PCI-DSS) require assurance on the effectiveness of IT controls. Assurance statements help demonstrate compliance.

- **Risk management**: Assurance statements highlight potential risks in the IT environment, enabling organizations to address vulnerabilities before they can be exploited.

- **Internal improvement**: By providing insights into the strength of IT controls, assurance statements allow organizations to identify areas for improvement and optimize their IT security posture.

- **Third-party confidence**: In business relationships, assurance statements from external auditors can build trust with partners, customers, and other stakeholders, showing that the organization's IT systems are properly secured and compliant.

Organizations will have to comply with several regulatory frameworks based on the line of business of the organization. One major entity that will get scrutinized during such regulatory compliance verifications is the IT landscape of the organizations to ensure that their information systems, processes, and controls meet specific security, privacy, and operational standards mandated by regulatory bodies. These regulations vary by industry, region, and type of data being handled, etc.

Regulatory compliance requirements

The following is a list of typical regulatory compliance requirements that mandate IT audits:

- **General Data Protection Regulation (GDPR)**: European Union; **California Consumer Privacy Act (CCPA)**: United States (California); **Data Protection and Digital Privacy (DPDP) Act**: India; **Personal Data Protection Act (PDPA)**: Singapore; **Personal Information Protection and Electronic Documents Act (PIPEDA)**: Canada; **Personal Data Protection Law (PDPL)**: Saudi Arabia

  o Organizations that process personally identifiable data are required to implement appropriate technical and organizational measures to ensure data security.

  o IT audit focus for compliance will be data handling practices, breach response, access control, encryption protocols, etc.

- **Health Insurance Portability and Accountability Act (HIPAA)**: United States

  o Organizations that handle **Protected Health Information (PHI)**, including healthcare providers, insurers, and business associates, and service organizations providing support to the listed companies.

  o IT audit's focus will be on system security, data access controls, user authentication, encryption, breach detection mechanisms, etc.

- **Sarbanes-Oxley Act (SOX):** United States

  o Publicly traded companies in the United States to ensure the accuracy and reliability of financial reporting and service organizations providing support to the listed companies.

  o IT audit focuses on financial data integrity, access controls, logging, and data retention.

- **Payment Card Industry Data Security Standard (PCI DSS):**

  o Organizations that store, process, or transmit credit card/payment card information and service organizations providing support to these organizations.

  o IT audit focuses on network security, encryption, access controls, vulnerability management, monitoring systems, etc.

- **ISO/IEC 27001**: International

  o Organizations globally, regardless of industry, that seek to establish, implement, maintain, and improve the ISMS.

  o IT audit focus will be on risk assessments, control effectiveness, monitoring, and incident management.

- **Service Organization Control 2 (SOC 2)**: United States/Global

  o Service organizations that store or process data pertaining to their customers (e.g., IT service providers, IT enabled service providers, cloud service providers, SaaS providers).

  o Regular IT audits are required to assess compliance with the *Trust Services Criteria* to give assurance on system security, data handling, privacy protection, incident response, etc.

- **Gramm-Leach-Bliley Act (GLBA)**: United States

  o Financial institutions, including banks, insurance companies, and securities firms and service organizations providing services to these organizations.

  o IT audits focus on compliance with the security and privacy provisions of GLBA by ensuring proper access control, encryption, monitoring, and information disposal.

Organizations are mandated to ensure that their IT systems and controls align with the regulatory requirements to protect sensitive data, mitigate risks, and maintain business operations. IT audits are required for providing evidence on various regulatory compliance frameworks and standards that focus on risk management, data security, privacy, financial integrity, and more. They help verify that the required technical controls are in place, especially for data protection, access control, encryption, and incident management.

Conclusion

In this chapter, we looked at the core standards for IT audits and learned that assurance statements are fundamental to ensuring robust governance, risk management, and compliance within an organization. By adhering to globally recognized standards, such as those outlined by ISACA, ISO, and other regulatory bodies, organizations can maintain transparency, mitigate risks, and safeguard critical information systems. We also covered the pivotal role of assurance statements in providing stakeholders with confidence in the reliability, security, and effectiveness of IT operations and controls. These statements, grounded in rigorous audit methodologies, validate the organization's commitment to accountability and continuous improvement. By integrating these standards and assurance practices into their IT frameworks, organizations can enhance decision-making, build stakeholder trust, and align IT operations with strategic objectives, fostering a secure and efficient technological environment.

In the next chapter, we will be looking at the advantages of the audit process, such as improved performance of management systems, strengthened credibility and trust, enhanced risk .management, and greater organizational efficiency emphasizes the organization efficiency and credibility.

Join our Discord space

Join our Discord workspace for latest updates, offers, tech happenings around the world, new releases, and sessions with the authors:

https://discord.bpbonline.com

CHAPTER 2
IT Audit Defined, Charter and Criteria

Introduction

As seen in *Chapter 1, IT Audit and Assurance Standards Statements*, an IT audit is a systematic evaluation of an organization's IT systems, processes, and controls to ensure they operate securely, efficiently, and in compliance with regulatory and organizational requirements. It provides assurance on the effectiveness of IT governance, risk management, and operational performance. The IT audit charter is a formal document outlining the purpose, authority, scope, and responsibilities of the audit function, serving as a guide for conducting independent and objective evaluations. Audit criteria are the standards, policies, regulations, and best practices against which the IT systems are assessed, ensuring consistent and reliable evaluations. Together, these elements form the foundation for effective IT audits that enhance organizational resilience and alignment with strategic goals.

Structure

This chapter covers the following topics:

- Key concepts
- Defining an audit charter
- Benefits of getting audited
- Audits and governance

Objectives

As mentioned in *Chapter 1, IT Audit and Assurance Standards Statements*, ISO 19011 is essential for any organization that needs to conduct internal audits or manage external audits of its management systems, which includes its IT systems. ISO 19011 provides a standardized approach to auditing by establishing consistent processes, terminology, and methodologies. It offers comprehensive guidance on audit principles, procedures, and techniques, enabling organizations to manage audit programs effectively. The standard also includes criteria for auditor competence, as well as guidance on their evaluation and development, ensuring a robust framework for auditing activities and personnel management. This foundational approach ensures that IT audits are conducted systematically, delivering actionable insights to enhance an organization's IT governance and risk management practices.

Key concepts

An **audit charter** is a formal document that outlines the purpose, authority, responsibilities, and scope of an audit function within an organization. It serves as a foundational guide for internal or external auditors and is a critical element for ensuring that the audit process aligns with the organization's objectives, compliance requirements, and governance standards. Let us look at some of the key terms:

- **IT audit**: An IT audit is a systematic evaluation of an organization's information technology infrastructure, applications, data, policies, procedures, and related processes to ensure that IT systems operate efficiently, securely, and align with organizational goals, regulatory requirements, and industry standards. IT audits assure that risks are managed effectively, systems are reliable, and data integrity is preserved.

- **IT audit charter**: An IT audit charter is a comprehensive and authoritative document that serves as the cornerstone for defining the structure and operation of an organization's IT audit function. It is typically approved by senior management or the audit committee to formalize the role and authority of the audit team. The charter establishes the framework within which the IT audit team operates, ensuring alignment with organizational goals and industry standards.

- **IT audit criteria**: IT audit criteria are the benchmarks, standards, or requirements against which an organization's IT systems, processes, and controls are evaluated during an audit. They form the foundation for assessing the effectiveness, security, and compliance of IT operations. Well-defined criteria ensure that audits are conducted systematically, consistently, and objectively, enabling organizations to identify gaps, risks, and areas for improvement.

Using ISO 19011 provides organizations with a robust framework to:

- Adopt auditing best practices established through international consensus.

- Enhance credibility and demonstrate auditing capability to customers and stakeholders.

- Drive improvements in management systems and processes through structured and systematic audits.

- Satisfy customer and regulatory audit requirements efficiently.

- Ensure consistent training, evaluation, and development of auditors.

Auditors must be well-versed in the seven principles of auditing and apply them throughout the audit process. These principles serve as a guiding framework, ensuring professionalism, objectivity, and ethical conduct. With the introduction of ISO 19011:2018, a risk-based approach was added to align with the increasing emphasis on risk management across management system standards.

The principles of auditing are as follows:

- **Integrity**: Upholding honesty and ethical behavior.

- **Fair presentation**: Reporting findings truthfully, accurately, and objectively.

- **Due professional care:** Exercising diligence and competence during audits.

- **Confidentiality**: Protecting sensitive information and maintaining discretion.

- **Independence**: Ensuring impartiality and avoiding conflicts of interest.

- **Evidence-based approach**: Basing conclusions on verifiable and reliable evidence.

- **Risk-based approach**: Considering risks to focus audits on areas of greatest significance.

Applying these principles ensures that audits are conducted to the highest standards, emphasizing integrity, risk awareness, and evidence-based evaluations. This approach not only enhances audit credibility but also ensures that audits effectively achieve their intended objectives.

Defining an audit charter

An **audit charter** is a formal document that outlines the purpose, authority, and responsibilities of the audit function within an organization. According to ISO 19011, which provides guidelines for auditing management systems, the development of an audit charter should adhere to the principles and structure.

A well-defined IT audit charter helps set clear expectations, promotes accountability, and supports the effective management of risk and compliance within the organization.

The key components of an IT audit charter are as follows:

- **Purpose and mission**: Defines why the IT audit function exists, emphasizing objectives like risk management, compliance, and operational improvement.

- **Authority**: Grants auditors the necessary access to systems, personnel, and records to perform their duties effectively.

- **Scope of work**: Specifies areas to be audited, such as IT governance, cybersecurity controls, data protection measures, and IT asset management.

- **Responsibilities**: Outlines the roles of the IT audit team, including planning, executing, reporting, and following up on audit findings.

- **Independence**: Highlights the importance of objectivity and independence in the audit process, ensuring freedom from undue influence.

- **Compliance standards**: Reference applicable frameworks like ISO 27001, **Control Objectives for Information and Related Technology (COBIT)**, **Information Technology Infrastructure Library (ITIL)**, and **National Institute of Standards and Technology (NIST)** for audit activities.

IT audit criteria serves as the benchmark for evaluating an organization's IT systems, processes, and controls during an audit. These criteria ensure that the audits are conducted consistently, objectively, and effectively, allowing auditors to assess whether the IT infrastructure aligns with regulatory requirements, industry standards, and organizational goals. The sources of IT audit criteria are diverse and provide a solid foundation for establishing performance standards, compliance requirements, and risk management practices.

The common sources of IT audit criteria are as follows:

- **Internal policies and procedures**: Organization-specific guidelines, security protocols, and operational workflows.

- **Industry standards**: Frameworks like ISO/IEC 27001, NIST Cybersecurity Framework, COBIT, and ITIL.

- **Regulatory requirements**: Laws such as GDPR, HIPAA, SOX, and PCI DSS that mandate specific controls and compliance measures.

- **Best practices**: Widely recognized practices in IT management and cybersecurity.

- **Audit objectives**: Criteria are selected based on the goals of the audit, such as ensuring data confidentiality, system integrity, or operational efficiency.

The purpose of criteria in IT audits is to provide a clear and objective framework for evaluating an organization's IT systems, processes, and controls. These criteria serve as the standards against which the audit will measure the effectiveness, security, and compliance of the IT infrastructure. By establishing consistent benchmarks and criteria, ensure that audits are performed systematically and yield actionable insights.

The purpose of the criteria in IT audits is as follows:

- **Establishing a baseline for evaluation**: Criteria offers a set of predefined standards that auditors use to assess whether the organization's IT systems meet regulatory, operational, and security requirements.

- **Ensuring consistency and objectivity**: Using standardized criteria ensures that audits are conducted in a fair, unbiased manner, regardless of the auditor or the area being assessed.

- **Promoting compliance**: Audit criteria help organizations determine whether they are adhering to applicable laws, regulations, and industry standards, ensuring compliance and reducing the risk of penalties.

- **Identifying risks and gaps**: By evaluating IT systems against well-defined criteria, auditors can identify potential vulnerabilities, inefficiencies, and areas of non-compliance, providing organizations with valuable insights for risk mitigation and process improvement.

- **Facilitating continuous improvement**: Audit criteria help identify opportunities for enhancing IT operations, security controls, and governance processes, promoting ongoing improvement and alignment with organizational goals.

- **Providing accountability and transparency**: Clear criteria enhance the accountability of the audit process, allowing stakeholders to understand how conclusions were reached and what actions are necessary for improvement.

Criteria in IT audits are essential for guiding auditors in delivering objective, meaningful, and consistent evaluations that help organizations improve their IT systems, mitigate risks, and ensure compliance with regulatory standards.

Sample IT audit charter

A sample audit charter will have the following sections, and the information on the date of creation and version of the document. All ISO standards require evidence of **Senior Leadership Commitment,** and hence the charter should be approved by the head of the audit team and the head of operations, i.e., CEO/COO. Let us look at the essential sections of an audit charter:

- **Purpose and mission**: The purpose of the IT audit function is to provide independent, objective assessments of the organization's information technology systems, processes, and controls to ensure they are operating effectively, securely, and in compliance with relevant laws, regulations, and organizational policies. The mission of IT auditing is to support risk management, improve operational efficiency, and protect organizational assets through systematic evaluations.

- **Authority**: The IT audit function is authorized by the board of directors and senior management to:

  o Access all necessary records, systems, personnel, and processes relevant to the audit scope.

  o Carry out audits without any interference from the management or operational areas being audited.

- o Report findings directly to senior management and the audit committee, ensuring independence and transparency.

- **Scope of work**: The IT audit function will evaluate and audit the following areas:

  - o **IT governance**: Ensuring that IT strategies, policies, and objectives align with business goals.

  - o **Information security**: Assessing the effectiveness of controls designed to protect sensitive data and prevent unauthorized access.

  - o **Compliance**: Verifying compliance with legal, regulatory, and contractual obligations, including data privacy laws (e.g., GDPR, HIPAA) and industry standards (e.g., ISO 27001, PCI DSS).

  - o **Risk management**: Evaluating the identification, management, and mitigation of IT risks.

  - o **System performance**: Auditing the efficiency, reliability, and availability of IT systems.

  - o **Business continuity**: Ensuring the robustness of disaster recovery and business continuity plans.

  - o **Change management**: Reviewing processes for managing system and software changes to avoid vulnerabilities.

- **Responsibilities**: The IT audit function is responsible for:

  - o **Planning**: Developing audit plans based on risk assessments and organizational priorities.

  - o **Execution**: Conducting audits, evaluating IT systems, and collecting evidence through interviews, system reviews, and documentation analysis.

  - o **Reporting**: Communicating audit findings to management, including risks, gaps, and improvement opportunities.

  - o **Follow-up**: Monitoring the implementation of corrective actions in response to audit findings.

  - o **Continuous improvement**: Evaluating and enhancing audit methodologies to stay aligned with best practices and organizational needs.

- **Independence and objectivity**: The IT audit function must remain independent of the areas being audited to ensure objectivity and integrity. Auditors should not be involved in the design or implementation of IT systems or controls that they audit. They must conduct audits impartially, providing unbiased reports based on facts and evidence.

- **Compliance with standards and frameworks**: The IT audit function will comply with relevant auditing standards, including:

  o **ISO 19011**: Guidelines for auditing management systems.

  o **ISO/IEC 27001**: Information Security Management System standards.

  o **COBIT**: Framework for IT governance and management.

  o **NIST Cybersecurity Framework**: Guidelines for improving the cybersecurity posture.

  The IT audit function will also adhere to regulatory standards, industry best practices, and organizational policies.

- **Reporting and communication:**

  o **Audit reports**: All findings, conclusions, and recommendations will be communicated in written audit reports, which will be provided to senior management and relevant stakeholders.

  o **Frequency**: Reports will be issued at the conclusion of each audit, and periodic updates will be given on ongoing audit activities.

  o **Escalation**: In cases of significant risks or non-compliance, the IT audit function is authorized to escalate issues directly to senior management and the audit committee.

- **Resources and planning**: The IT audit function will be allocated sufficient resources (personnel, time, tools) to perform audits effectively. The **chief audit executive (CAE)** will ensure that the audit team has the necessary training and skills to carry out audits competently and that adequate planning is conducted to prioritize audits based on risk assessments.

- **Review and updates**: This IT audit charter will be reviewed annually or as needed to ensure it remains relevant and aligned with the organization's goals, risk environment, and regulatory requirements. Any amendments will be approved by senior management and the audit committee.

This sample IT audit charter provides a comprehensive framework to guide the IT audit function within an organization, ensuring it operates independently, focuses on key risk areas, and delivers value through clear and actionable audit findings.

Benefits of getting audited

An audit provides organizations with a systematic evaluation of their processes, systems, and controls. Beyond compliance, audits offer significant advantages that contribute to overall efficiency, risk management, and strategic growth.

Implementing a structured audit process within an organization offers a wide range of benefits. These advantages not only enhance internal controls and ensure regulatory compliance but also contribute to long-term organizational success. Let us look at the benefits in detail:

- **Enhanced compliance**:
  - o Ensures adherence to legal, regulatory, and contractual requirements.
  - o Helps demonstrate conformity with industry standards such as ISO 27001, GDPR, HIPAA, or PCI DSS.
  - o Reduces the risk of penalties or legal actions due to non-compliance.

- **Improved risk management:**
  - o Identifies vulnerabilities and risks in processes, systems, and controls.
  - o Provides actionable recommendations to mitigate risks effectively.
  - o Encourages proactive identification and management of potential threats.

- **Increased operational efficiency:**
  - o Highlights inefficiencies and areas for improvement within processes.
  - o Drives optimization of workflows and resource utilization.
  - o Supports continuous improvement initiatives.

- **Strengthened security and data protection**
  - o Validates the effectiveness of security measures and controls.
  - o Identifies weaknesses in protecting sensitive data and systems.
  - o Enhances trust by safeguarding information assets.

- **Credibility and stakeholder confidence:**
  - o Builds trust with customers, investors, and business partners by demonstrating accountability and transparency.
  - o Provides assurance to stakeholders that the organization's systems and processes are reliable.

- **Strategic alignment:**
  - o Ensures that IT and operational goals align with organizational objectives.
  - o Helps organizations stay competitive by adhering to best practices.

- **Facilitated certification and market advantage:**
  - o Simplifies achieving international standard certifications such as ISO/SOC2.
  - o Enhances marketability and provides a competitive edge in securing contracts.

- **Better decision-making:**
  - o Provides management with accurate and reliable insights for strategic decisions.
  - o Supports data-driven improvements across the organization.
- **Cultural shift toward accountability:**
  - o Encourages a culture of accountability and continuous improvement.
  - o Increases awareness of compliance, security, and operational standards among employees.
- **Cost savings:**
  - o Identifies inefficiencies and waste, enabling cost reductions.
  - o Mitigates potential financial losses from non-compliance or security breaches.

By embracing the audit process, organizations not only ensure compliance but also unlock opportunities for growth, efficiency, and improved governance.

In summary, implementing an audit process provides a range of strategic, operational, and financial benefits. It helps organizations enhance risk management, ensure compliance, drive operational efficiencies, build trust with stakeholders, and foster continuous improvement, contributing to long-term success and sustainability.

Audits and governance

ISO 19011 is the international standard that provides guidance on auditing management systems. It focuses on ensuring that audits are conducted systematically and effectively while aligning with the governance framework of an organization.

The following is an outline of how audits relate to governance under ISO 19011:

- **Role of audits in governance**:
  - o **Accountability**: Audits promote accountability by providing assurance that the organization's management systems and processes are aligned with its governance objectives.
  - o **Risk management**: Audits identify risks, assess controls, and ensure mitigation strategies are in place, supporting governance efforts to safeguard organizational assets.
  - o **Performance evaluation**: Through structured audits, organizations can evaluate the effectiveness of their management systems and how well they align with governance frameworks.
  - o **Compliance assurance**: Audits verify adherence to laws, regulations, and internal policies, ensuring governance principles are maintained.

- **Key governance concepts addressed by ISO 19011**:

    o **Principles of auditing**: The standard emphasizes seven principles (e.g., integrity, independence, evidence-based approach) to ensure audits align with governance values like transparency, accountability, and fairness

    o **Alignment with strategic objectives**: Audits conducted per ISO 19011 ensure management systems support the organization's overall strategic and governance goals

    o **Stakeholder communication**: ISO 19011 emphasizes clear reporting, which fosters trust and accountability with stakeholders, a critical component of governance

- **Integration of governance in the audit process:** ISO 19011 highlights the integration of governance aspects throughout the audit lifecycle:

    o **Planning stage:**

        ▪ Establishing audit objectives that reflect governance priorities such as risk management, regulatory compliance, and ethical conduct

        ▪ Considering the governance framework when defining the scope and criteria of the audit

    o **Execution stage**:

        ▪ Evaluating whether governance policies, processes, and controls are effectively implemented.

        ▪ Gathering evidence to ensure the organization's practices align with its governance principles.

    o **Reporting stage**:

        ▪ Providing insights into how well governance structures are functioning.

        ▪ Offering recommendations for improving governance-related aspects of management systems.

- **Risk-based approach**: ISO 19011 introduces a risk-based approach to auditing, which aligns closely with governance principles. This approach emphasizes the following:

    o **Prioritization of risks**: Directing audit resources toward areas that pose the highest governance risks to the organization.

    o **Proactive identification**: Helping organizations address potential governance failures before they become significant issues.

    o **Decision-making support**: Enabling leaders to make informed decisions that align with governance frameworks.

- **Ensuring auditor competence in governance:** The standard underscores the importance of auditor competence, particularly regarding governance:

  o Auditors must understand the organization's governance framework, including its policies, regulations, and ethical standards.

  o Training and continuous development ensure auditors can evaluate governance-related aspects effectively.

- **Governance improvement through auditing**:

  o **Feedback loop**: Audit findings serve as inputs for enhancing governance structures.

  o **Continuous improvement**: Audits identify areas where governance policies or practices may need revision or strengthening.

  o **Stakeholder trust**: By aligning audits with ISO 19011, organizations demonstrate their commitment to governance principles, fostering trust with stakeholders.

Audits conducted under the guidance of ISO 19011 play a vital role in supporting and enhancing organizational governance. By ensuring that audits are systematic, risk-based, and aligned with the governance objectives, organizations can achieve greater accountability, transparency, and strategic alignment, thereby strengthening their overall management systems and stakeholder trust.

Governance defined by COBIT in the audit process

COBIT defines six principles for a governance framework that can be used to build a governance system for the enterprise. The framework is depicted in the following figure:

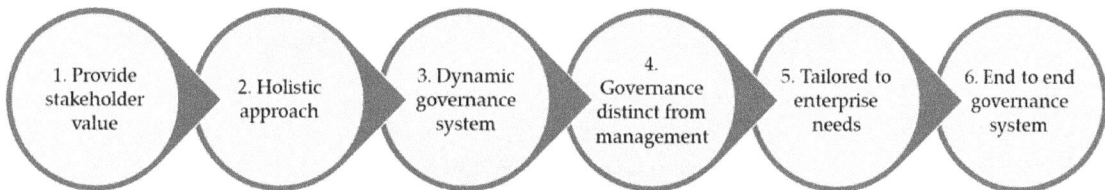

Figure 2.1: COBIT governance framework

Let us look at these principles in detail:

- Each enterprise needs a governance system to satisfy stakeholder needs and to generate value from the use of IT. Value reflects a balance among benefits, risk and resources, and enterprises need an actionable strategy and governance system to realize this value.

- A governance system for enterprise IT is built from a number of components that can be of different types and that work together in a holistic way.

- A governance system should be dynamic. This means that each time one or more of the design factors are changed (e.g., a change in strategy or technology), the impact of these changes on the enterprise governance system must be considered. A dynamic view of enterprise governance will lead toward a viable and future-proof governance system.

- A governance system should clearly distinguish between governance and management activities and structures.

- A governance system should be tailored to the enterprise's needs, using a set of design factors as parameters to customize and prioritize the governance system components.

- A governance system should cover the enterprise end to end, focusing not only on the IT function but on all technology and information processing the enterprise puts in place to achieve its goals, regardless of where the processing is located in the enterprise.

COBIT also defines the components of a governance system as illustrated in the following figure:

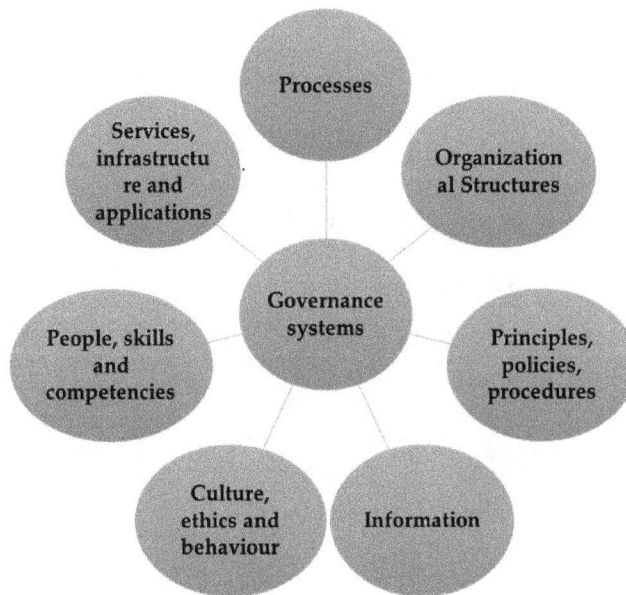

Figure 2.2: COBIT governance system

Each enterprise needs to establish, tailor and sustain a governance system built from a number of components to satisfy governance and management objectives. The components interact with each other, resulting in a holistic governance system for IT. Let us look at them in detail:

- Processes describe an organized set of practices and activities to achieve certain objectives and produce a set of outputs that support the achievement of overall IT-related goals.

- Organizational structures are the key decision-making entities in an enterprise.

- Principles, policies and frameworks translate desired behavior into practical guidance for day-to-day management.

- Information is pervasive throughout any organization and includes all information produced and used by the enterprise. COBIT focuses on information required for the effective functioning of the governance system of the enterprise.

- Culture, ethics and behavior of individuals and of the enterprise are often underestimated as factors in the success of governance and management activities.

- People, skills and competencies are required for good decisions, execution of corrective action and successful completion of all activities.

- Services, infrastructure and applications include the infrastructure, technology and applications that provide the enterprise with the governance system for I&T processing.

The ITIL framework for **IT service management (ITSM)** emphasizes aligning IT services with business objectives. Within ITIL, audits and governance play crucial roles in ensuring accountability, compliance, and the effective management of IT services. Governance in ITIL refers to the framework and processes that ensure IT services are managed effectively and align with organizational objectives. It encompasses oversight, decision-making, and accountability for IT service management.

The key aspects of ITIL governance include the following:

- **Strategic alignment**: Ensuring IT services support the organization's strategic goals.

- **Accountability**: Defining roles and responsibilities for managing IT services and decision-making.

- **Risk management**: Identifying, assessing, and mitigating risks associated with IT services.

- **Policy enforcement**: Establishing and maintaining policies for IT service delivery, security, and compliance.

Audits and governance are interconnected within ITIL, as both contribute to the continuous improvement and accountability of IT services. Their integration ensures that governance principles are adhered to and that audit findings are used to enhance governance structures:

- **Audit findings inform governance**: Results from audits provide valuable insights into governance effectiveness and highlight areas for policy or control improvements.

- **Governance directs audits**: Governance frameworks define the objectives, scope, and priorities for audits based on organizational goals and risk appetite.

- **Continuous feedback loop**: Governance reviews and adapts based on audit outcomes, fostering a culture of accountability and ongoing enhancement.

Benefits of audits and governance in ITIL

The benefits of audits and governance are as follows:

- **Improved accountability**: Clear governance structures and regular audits foster accountability among IT teams.

- **Enhanced compliance**: Ensures adherence to internal policies, external regulations, and contractual obligations.

- **Increased efficiency**: Audits identify inefficiencies, while governance enforces streamlined processes.

- **Better risk management**: Proactively identifies and addresses risks, reducing the likelihood of service disruptions.

- **Continuous improvement**: Both audits and governance drive iterative enhancements to IT services and processes.

As per ITIL, audits and governance work together to ensure IT services are effectively managed, compliant, and aligned with organizational goals. The audits provide critical insights into process performance and adherence to governance frameworks, while governance establishes the principles and policies that guide IT service management. Together, they enable organizations to deliver high-quality, reliable, and secure IT services that meet both business and stakeholder expectations.

Audits and governance are closely interconnected in ISO 20000, with each supporting the other to ensure the effectiveness of the **service management system**. Let us look at how they are connected:

- **Governance driving audits**: Governance mechanism in an organization establishes the objectives, scope, and frequency of audits. It ensures that audit results are reviewed at the management level and that corrective actions are implemented.

- **Audits supporting governance**: Audits provide objective insights into the effectiveness of governance structures and processes. They highlight gaps, risks, or inefficiencies, enabling governance improvements.

Benefits of audits and governance in ISO 20000

The combination of audits and governance delivers several benefits to organizations implementing ISO 20000, mentioned as follows:

- **Enhanced compliance**: Ensures adherence to the standard's requirements, regulatory obligations, and SLAs.

- **Improved service quality**: Regular audits and effective governance drive continuous improvement in service delivery.

- **Risk reduction**: Identifies and mitigates risks associated with IT services, ensuring business continuity.

- **Operational efficiency**: Streamlines processes through audit insights and governance policies.

- **Stakeholder trust**: Demonstrates accountability and transparency, enhancing trust among customers and stakeholders.

- **Certification readiness**: Internal audits prepare organizations for successful certification or recertification under ISO 20000.

The key processes where audits and governance play a role are:

- **Service level management**: Ensures SLAs are monitored, reported, and reviewed for compliance.

- **Change management**: Audits ensure that changes are managed effectively with minimal disruption.

- **Incident and problem management**: Governance ensures structured resolution processes, and audits evaluate their effectiveness.

- **Risk management**: Governance establishes risk policies, while audits verify their implementation.

- **Continuous improvement**: Audits provide insights, and governance ensures implementation of improvements.

In ISO 20000, audits and governance form the backbone of an effective IT service management system. Governance provides the structure, policies, and oversight to manage IT services effectively, while audits offer objective evaluations to ensure compliance, performance, and continuous improvement. Together, they help organizations deliver reliable, efficient, and high-quality IT services that align with business objectives and customer needs.

ISO/IEC 27001 is the international standard for **Information Security Management Systems (ISMS)**, focusing on protecting the confidentiality, integrity, and availability of information. Within ISO 27001, audit and governance are critical components that ensure the ISMS is effectively implemented, monitored, and continually improved to address information security risks and meet compliance requirements.

Governance in ISO 27001 provides the overarching framework for managing and overseeing the ISMS. It ensures that security practices align with the organization's objectives, regulatory requirements, and risk tolerance.

The key components of governance in ISO 27001 are as follows:

- **Leadership and commitment**: Top management is responsible for setting the direction of the ISMS and ensuring its alignment with business goals and establishing and endorsing an information security policy.

- **Roles and responsibilities**: Governance defines clear roles, responsibilities, and accountabilities for managing and maintaining the ISMS.

- **Risk management oversight**: Governance includes the continuous review and approval of the risk management framework, ensuring effective risk mitigation.

- **Policy and objective setting:** Governance establishes policies, objectives, and measurable targets for information security aligned with organizational needs.

- **Performance monitoring**: Regular management reviews evaluate the ISMS's effectiveness, based on audit results, KPIs, and changes in risk or business context.

- **Regulatory compliance**: Governance ensures compliance with applicable laws, regulations, and contractual obligations related to information security.

The key processes where audit and governance intersect in ISO 27001 are as follows:

- **Risk assessment and treatment:** Governance ensures the risk framework is robust, while audits evaluate its effectiveness.

- **Control monitoring and evaluation**: Governance defines control objectives, and audits verify their implementation and efficiency.

- **Incident management**: Governance oversees the incident response process, while audits assess the handling and documentation of incidents.

- **Policy review and update**: Governance ensures policies remain relevant, and audits verify adherence to these policies.

- **Management review**: Governance involves periodic reviews, incorporating audit results to enhance decision-making.

ISO 27001 emphasizes the **Plan-Do-Check-Act (PDCA)** cycle, where audits and governance play crucial roles, as mentioned as follows:

- **Plan**: Governance establishes policies, objectives, and risk management strategies.

- **Do**: Implementation of the ISMS, with governance overseeing resource allocation and accountability.

- **Check**: Internal and external audits evaluate performance, compliance, and effectiveness.

- **Act**: Governance ensures corrective actions and improvements are implemented based on audit findings.

In ISO 27001, audits and governance are indispensable for the effective management of an ISMS. Governance provides the strategic oversight needed to align information security with organizational goals, while audits deliver objective evaluations of the ISMS's performance and compliance. Together, they ensure that the ISMS remains robust, resilient, and capable of addressing evolving security challenges.

The ISO 20000 standard and ITIL framework can be related as per *Figure 2.3*. The implementation of processes begins with aligning to the ITIL framework and capturing the business requirements and related evidence. Once this is done, the 6 pillars will be defined and once all documentation and evidence are recorded, the organization can go for assessment to obtain the ISO 20000 certification.

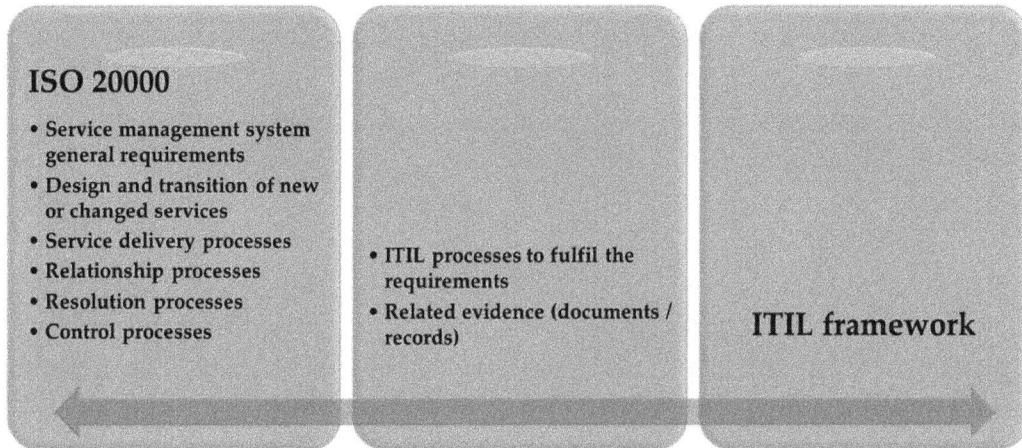

Figure 2.3: ISO and ITIL processes

Conclusion

An IT audit is a critical tool for organizations to assess the effectiveness, security, and compliance of their information technology systems and processes. It helps identify risks, ensures regulatory adherence, and promotes operational efficiency. The audit charter serves as a foundational document that clearly defines the scope, purpose, authority, and responsibilities of the audit function, ensuring that audits are conducted with integrity, independence, and objectivity. Meanwhile, audit criteria, which include internal policies, industry standards, regulatory requirements, and best practices, provide the benchmark for evaluating IT systems and controls. By adhering to these principles, organizations can enhance their governance, improve risk management, and continuously improve their IT infrastructure to meet strategic goals and compliance obligations.

Audit and governance are foundational elements in ensuring the effectiveness, accountability, and continuous improvement of organizational systems and processes. While governance provides the structure, policies, and oversight required to align operations with strategic goals, audits offer a systematic, evidence-based approach to evaluate compliance, performance, and risk management. Together, they establish a robust framework that fosters transparency, enhances stakeholder confidence, and drives operational excellence. By integrating audits with governance practices, organizations can not only meet regulatory and industry standards but also proactively identify opportunities for innovation and improvement, ensuring long-term resilience and success.

Moving forward, we will explore the process of planning IT audits and examine the typical responsibilities of auditees. Additionally, we will discuss how IT policies can be reviewed to ensure alignment with the business objectives. The next chapter highlights the importance of gathering evidence to validate the step-by-step procedures followed by the IT team in implementing organizational policies and adhering to industry best practices.

Join our Discord space

Join our Discord workspace for latest updates, offers, tech happenings around the world, new releases, and sessions with the authors:

https://discord.bpbonline.com

CHAPTER 3

Planning, Scheduling, Reporting and Follow-ups for Audit

Introduction

The audit process is a structured approach that ensures the effective evaluation of organizational systems, processes, and controls. It begins with audit planning, where objectives, scope, and resources are defined to align the audit with organizational goals. Audit scheduling ensures that audits are conducted at appropriate intervals, taking into account risk levels, regulatory requirements, and operational priorities. Reporting provides clear and actionable insights into audit findings, highlighting areas of compliance, non-conformance, and opportunities for improvement. Finally, follow-up ensures that corrective actions are implemented, verified, and sustained over time, driving continuous improvement and maintaining the integrity of systems and processes. Together, these components form a comprehensive framework for conducting audits that are systematic, objective, and aligned with organizational success.

Structure

This chapter covers the following topics:

- Key concepts
- Audit plan
- Auditee responsibilities
- Review of policy and gathering evidence

Objectives

The primary objective of audit planning, scheduling, reporting, and follow-up is to establish a systematic and efficient process for evaluating organizational systems, controls, and processes. This ensures that audits are conducted in a structured, objective, and timely manner.

Specific objectives include audit planning, scheduling of the audit, reporting, and follow-up mechanisms. Through this, we can define the scope, objectives, and methodology of the audit to ensure alignment with organizational goals, risks, and compliance requirements. The steps to organize and allocate resources effectively by determining appropriate audit intervals and prioritizing areas of high risk or significance are clearly defined. Reports are to be drafted capturing transparent, accurate, and actionable insights into audit findings, including areas of compliance, non-conformance, and opportunities for improvement. Proper follow-up has to be done to ensure that identified issues are addressed, corrective actions are implemented and verified, and the effectiveness of changes is sustained over time.

By achieving these objectives, the audit process not only ensures compliance but also fosters continuous improvement, risk mitigation, and the overall strengthening of organizational governance.

Key concepts

Audit planning, scheduling, and follow-ups are essential for ensuring a thorough and effective audit process.

In audit planning, it is crucial to define the audit objectives, determine the scope, assess risks, allocate resources, establish the methodology, and consider regulatory requirements. A well-structured plan helps streamline the audit process and ensures its effectiveness.

The audit schedule involves developing a timeline, coordinating with stakeholders, allowing flexibility for adjustments, and regularly reviewing progress. Setting realistic deadlines and ensuring cooperation from all involved parties can make the audit more efficient.

Follow-ups after an audit include reviewing findings, implementing corrective actions, continuously monitoring progress, and integrating lessons learned into future audit cycles. This ensures that identified issues are addressed and improvements are sustained over time.

Audit plan

The scope of ISO 19011 covers the entire auditing process, from planning and conducting audits to reporting findings and following up on corrective actions. It emphasizes key auditing principles such as integrity, fair presentation, due professional care, confidentiality, and independence. Adhering to these principles ensures that auditors provide unbiased assessments and deliver reliable audit outcomes.

ISO 19011 adopts a risk-based approach, enabling auditors to prioritize areas of significant importance and potential impact. By focusing on risks and opportunities within an organization's management systems, this approach enhances the efficiency and effectiveness of audits.

The implementation of ISO 19011 offers numerous benefits. It provides a structured framework for evaluating and improving management system performance, identifying nonconformities, and ensuring compliance with standards and regulations. Organizations that follow ISO 19011 guidelines can strengthen their credibility, trust, and reputation among stakeholders, both internally and externally.

ISO 19011 is applicable to a variety of audit types, including internal audits conducted by organizations, external audits by customers or regulatory bodies, and third-party certification audits performed by independent certification bodies. By offering a standardized framework and common language, ISO 19011 promotes consistency and comparability in audit practices across diverse sectors and industries.

ISO 19011 is designed to provide auditors and audit teams with the knowledge and skills necessary to perform audits effectively and in alignment with the standard's guidelines. It encompasses essential concepts, auditing principles, planning and execution of audits, reporting findings, and managing corrective action follow-ups. Through interactive case studies, exercises, and discussions, participants will gain practical experience and enhance their auditing proficiency.

By adopting ISO 19011 and conducting audits in accordance with its framework, organizations can consistently monitor and refine their management systems. This approach drives improved performance, increased customer satisfaction, and sustainable success in today's dynamic and competitive business landscape.

Audit planning is a crucial phase in the audit process, serving as the foundation for a successful and effective audit. ISO 19011 guidelines for auditing management systems offers a structured approach to audit planning, ensuring audits are conducted systematically and aligned with organizational objectives.

Clause 5 of the standard provides guidance on the audit program management function, which auditors should reference when assessing internal audit requirements.

Those responsible for managing the audit program should ensure the following:

- The audit program is properly established and planned.
- Risks and opportunities related to the audit program are identified.
- Audit program objectives are clearly defined.
- The competence of the audit team aligns with the audit scope and objectives for each audit within the program.
- Sufficient resources are available for all audits in the program.

- Individual audits are monitored for the ongoing evaluation and improvement of the audit program.

It is important to distinguish that managing an audit program is not the responsibility of an individual auditor. Audit program management differs from the planning and execution of audits, which are separate processes (although in smaller organizations, one person may perform both tasks).

Preparing for an audit can be taken up as follows:

1. **Audit planning**: This section explains the steps involved in planning an audit, including defining the audit criteria, determining audit scope, selecting the audit team, and establishing the audit schedule.

2. **Establishing audit criteria**: Defining audit criteria is essential for conducting effective audits. This section provides guidance on establishing audit criteria based on applicable standards, regulations, and organizational requirements.

3. **Developing an audit program**: An audit program helps ensure that audits are conducted systematically and efficiently. This section covers the development of an audit program, including the identification of audit activities, resources, and timelines.

4. **Audit resources and competence**: This section discusses the resources required for conducting audits, such as competent auditors, access to relevant information, and appropriate audit tools. It also emphasizes the importance of auditor competence and continuous professional development.

The key components of audit planning, as outlined in ISO 19011, include the following:

1. **Establishing audit objectives**: Defining the purpose and scope of the audit is essential. Audit objectives should align with the organization's goals, requirements, and expectations. Clear and well-defined objectives guide the audit team, ensuring the audit delivers valuable insights and achieves its intended outcomes.

2. **Determining audit criteria**: Audit criteria are the benchmarks against which the management system will be evaluated. These may include internal policies, applicable laws and regulations, industry standards, and customer requirements. Clear and relevant audit criteria help focus the audit on key areas and enable objective evaluations.

3. **Selecting the audit team**: A competent audit team is critical for effective assessments. Team members should possess the required knowledge, skills, and experience to evaluate various aspects of the management system. When forming the audit team, consider the expertise needed for different areas to ensure a balanced and capable composition.

4. **Defining audit scope**: The audit scope establishes the boundaries and extent of the audit. It specifies the functions, processes, locations, and organizational units that

are included or excluded. A clearly defined scope ensures the audit team focuses on relevant areas and provides an accurate assessment of the management system under review.

5. **Determining audit schedule and resources**: The audit schedule outlines the timeline for audit activities, considering the availability of auditors, organizational requirements, and necessary resources. Allocating adequate personnel, information, and tools ensures the audit proceeds smoothly and enables the collection of sufficient, relevant evidence.

6. **Conducting document review**: A document review is a vital step in audit planning. This process involves examining policies, procedures, records, and past audit reports to understand the management system, identify areas of concern, and prepare for on-site activities.

7. **Developing the audit plan**: The audit plan serves as a roadmap, detailing the approach, methodologies, and specific activities to be performed. It includes audit objectives, scope, criteria, schedule, resource allocation, methods, and activity sequences. A well-structured audit plan ensures consistency, efficiency, and alignment with organizational goals.

By adhering to ISO 19011's guidance on audit planning, organizations can prepare audits that are systematic, well-targeted, and insightful. By following these principles, organizations can ensure their audits are efficient, targeted, and valuable in driving continuous improvement and compliance.

Proper planning lays the foundation for effective audits that evaluate management systems, foster continuous improvement, and contribute to achieving organizational objectives.

Defining the audit scope is a vital aspect of audit planning, as it establishes the boundaries and extent of the audit. ISO 19011 offers clear guidance on determining the audit scope to ensure the audit focuses on relevant areas and provides an accurate assessment of the audited management system.

The key factors to consider when defining the audit scope include the following:

- **Organizational context**: Understanding the organization's context is essential, including its objectives, size, structure, processes, and industry sector. This insight helps establish the boundaries of the management system being audited and identifies the critical functions, processes, locations, or organizational units to include within the audit scope.

- **Audit objectives**: Clearly defined audit objectives are crucial for determining the scope. These objectives should align with the organization's goals, requirements, and expectations. They provide direction to the audit team, ensuring the audit delivers meaningful insights and fulfils its intended purpose. The scope should be structured to support the achievement of these objectives.

- **Applicable requirements**: Identify all applicable requirements that the audited management system must meet. These may include internal policies, external standards, legal and regulatory obligations, customer expectations, and contractual commitments. The audit scope should cover the areas and processes subject to these requirements to ensure a comprehensive compliance assessment.

- **Risk-based approach**: Adopt a risk-based approach to define the audit scope. Evaluate the risks and opportunities associated with the audited management system to pinpoint areas of significant importance or potential impact. Prioritize high-risk areas within the scope to ensure the audit addresses the most critical aspects of the management system effectively.

- **Meeting stakeholder expectations**: Consider the expectations of stakeholders such as customers, regulators, employees, and other interested parties. Understand their concerns, requirements, and focal points. Incorporating these expectations into the audit scope ensures the audit provides valuable insights and addresses stakeholder concerns.

- **Practical constraints**: Account for practical limitations, including time, resources, and feasibility. Assess available resources such as auditors, expertise, documentation, and access to relevant information. Define a scope that can be realistically executed within the available resources and allocated timeframe.

- **Management system boundaries**: Clearly identify the boundaries of the audited management system. Determine the specific functions, processes, locations, or organizational units to be included or excluded. A well-defined scope eliminates ambiguity and ensures the audit team remains focused on the intended areas of assessment.

Clearly documenting the audit scope in the audit plan is essential to ensure a shared understanding among the audit team, auditees, and other stakeholders. Effective communication of the defined audit scope is crucial to aligning audit activities with the intended scope and objectives. By adhering to the guidance provided by ISO 19011, organizations can establish a well-defined audit scope that facilitates focused and effective audits of their management systems.

The audit plan should include audit procedures defined through the strategy, along with the intended scope and objectives. Audit strategy will outline the overall approach for the audit, including the resources required, timelines, and key audit areas. Audit procedures will detail the specific procedures to be performed, such as tests of controls, substantive tests, and analytical procedures.

The overall audit approach will determine the nature, timing, and extent of audit procedures. Resource allocation is another activity that helps in identifying the necessary resources, including the audit team, required expertise (IT specialists, ISO experts), tools (workflow tracking tools), etc.

Audit timeline and milestones are to be established as part of the audit plan. Auditees should be provided a detailed timeline that includes key milestones, deadlines for each audit phase (planning, fieldwork, reporting), and a final completion date. As part of the test of controls, the design and operating effectiveness of internal controls will be evaluated to determine the institutionalization of the proactive and reactive controls.

A key aspect of documenting audit results or evidence is clearly defining the audit objective. The audit objective specifies the purpose of auditing a particular key business process. For example, in the case of change management, the objective of auditing change control management is to ensure that all changes are implemented appropriately. This involves verifying that changes are first reviewed, documented, and approved before they are executed. Consequently, the objective of the audit test being conducted would be to confirm that all changes are properly documented and approved prior to implementation.

Auditee responsibilities

Internal auditing is a critical element of an organization's risk management framework. It acts as a safeguard, ensuring compliance with regulations, ethical standards, and best practices.

Audit charter, as discussed in *Chapter 2, IT Audit Defined, Charter and Criteria*, mandatorily documents IT audit and assurance functions. Audit charter should be defined to ensure the following:

- Independence, code of ethics, and standards.

- Purpose, responsibility, authority, and accountability.

- Protocols that the IT audit and assurance practitioner will follow in the performance of engagements, including but not limited to communication and escalation.

- Roles and responsibilities of the auditee during the IT audit or assurance engagement.

The audit process involves both the auditors, who carry out the audit, and the auditee, who is responsible for providing the required information and cooperation. A clear understanding of these roles and responsibilities is crucial for ensuring the audit is effective and efficient. Additionally, setting a timeline for the various stages of the audit helps maintain the process's momentum and ensures its timely completion.

The typical responsibilities of an auditee include the following:

- Notifying staff within the organization about the audit to ensure their availability.

- Providing necessary resources to the audit team, such as interview rooms, communication facilities, and clerical support.

- Offering guidance to the audit team, if required.

- Presenting objective evidence when requested by the auditor.

- Cooperating with the audit team throughout the process.

- Identifying and initiating corrective actions if a non-conformity is found.

An auditee refers to an organization, or specific functions of it, being audited. We are referring to the audit of the IT function and its operations here.

An auditee's role in the audit is as follows:

- **Cooperation**: The auditee plays a key role in the internal audit process by fully cooperating with auditors. This includes providing access to relevant documents, systems, and personnel. Auditees must be open and transparent, as this contributes to a smooth and efficient audit process.

- **Preparation**: Auditees should be well-prepared for the audit by thoroughly understanding its objectives, scope, and methodology. This preparation enables auditees to provide accurate and comprehensive information to the auditors.

- **Documentation**: Auditees should maintain organized and up-to-date documentation of their processes, policies, and procedures. This serves as evidence of compliance and helps address any findings or recommendations from auditors. Auditees must be able to present these documents when requested during the audit.

- **Communication**: Effective communication is essential for a successful internal audit. Auditees should promptly share any concerns, issues, or changes that could impact the audit. They should actively engage with auditors, clarifying questions and providing additional insights to ensure a thorough understanding of the audited area.

- **Self-assessment**: Auditees should regularly assess their processes, risks, and controls. Proactive self-assessments help identify potential risks or areas for improvement before auditors raise them. This demonstrates a commitment to continuous improvement and proactive risk management.

- **Follow-up**: After the audit, auditees should follow up on the recommendations or findings provided by the auditors. This involves implementing corrective actions and monitoring their effectiveness. By addressing identified weaknesses, auditees contribute to the improvement of internal controls.

Auditees play a crucial role in facilitating the audit process, ensuring its accuracy and effectiveness. The success of the audit is not solely the responsibility of the auditors.

Auditees have to work in a collaborative mode along with auditors to ensure the following:

- **Provide access to relevant information**: The auditee must grant auditors unrestricted access to necessary documents, records, and systems.

- **Cooperate with audit team**: Auditees should establish a cooperative relationship with the audit team, ensuring open communication and collaboration throughout the audit.

- **Identify risks and weaknesses**: As those closest to the internal processes and controls, auditees are best positioned to identify potential risks and weaknesses.

- **Maintain a complete and accurate audit trail**: This involves providing organized documentation, ensuring proper filing, and maintaining clear records of any changes made during the audit.

- **Collaborate in developing remediation plans**: Auditees can contribute valuable insights by working with the audit team to develop practical, effective remediation actions that align with organizational goals.

- **Implement corrective actions**: Following the audit, auditees are responsible for implementing corrective actions and improvements. Timely execution of these actions enhances the effectiveness of the audit and supports the organization's ongoing growth and stability.

In the context of ISO standards, the auditee (the organization or part of it being audited) plays a crucial role in ensuring the audit process is effective and efficient. Their responsibilities include the following:

- **Preparation for audit**:
  - o Be familiar with the audit scope, objectives, and criteria.
  - o Ensure that relevant personnel are available for the audit and are prepared to provide necessary information.
  - o Organize and make all relevant documents, records, and evidence readily accessible for review.

- **Providing information and access**:
  - o Grant access to facilities, processes, systems, and records relevant to the audit to the auditors.
  - o Be transparent in sharing information and provide clear and truthful responses to auditor queries.
  - o Facilitate interviews with personnel and support observations of processes.

- **Cooperation with the audit team**:
  - o Establish a collaborative relationship with the auditors to ensure a smooth audit process.
  - o Address the auditors' requests promptly and provide clarification as needed.
  - o Avoid obstructing or delaying the audit process.

- **Demonstrating compliance**:
  - o Present evidence of conformity with requirements, including quality and service management processes, documented information, and records.
  - o Showcase how the organization fulfils customer and statutory/regulatory requirements.

- **Engagement in findings and feedback**:
  - o Actively participate in discussions regarding nonconformities or areas of improvement identified by the auditors.
  - o Provide additional insights or context when necessary to ensure findings are well understood.

- **Follow-up on audit outcomes**:
  - o Address any nonconformities or observations by developing and implementing corrective actions.
  - o Monitor the effectiveness of corrective actions and ensure they are aligned with the organization's quality objectives.
  - o Use audit feedback as an opportunity for continual improvement of the quality and **service management system (SMS)**.

The responsibilities of the auditee are critical to the success of any audit process. By fulfilling their roles effectively, auditees not only facilitate the audit but also contribute to the continuous improvement of processes and systems within the organization.

Auditee should also imbibe the following characteristics:

- **Collaboration and transparency**: Auditees must cooperate fully with auditors by providing access to relevant information, documents, and personnel. Transparency during the audit process ensures the accuracy of findings.

- **Preparation and documentation**: Proper preparation, including maintaining organized and up-to-date records, enables auditees to provide evidence of compliance and effective operations. This streamlines the audit process and helps address any findings or non-conformities promptly.

- **Commitment to improvement**: The auditee's willingness to address audit findings, implement corrective actions, and embrace continuous improvement demonstrates a proactive approach to strengthening systems and processes.

- **Shared responsibility**: While auditors lead the process, the success of the audit heavily depends on the auditee's engagement, preparedness, and cooperation. This shared responsibility ensures that the audit objectives are achieved and that organizational goals are supported.

Review of policy and gathering evidence

Policy management involves the creation, communication, implementation, and maintenance of policies within an organization. This process includes developing a comprehensive framework that defines the rules and procedures governing various business areas, such as compliance, employee conduct, privacy, data security, and operational practices.

A well-structured policy management plan enables employees to quickly adapt to changes and stay informed about the latest regulations, supporting them in effectively performing their duties.

The review of policies involves assessing the effectiveness and relevance of existing policies to ensure they align with current business needs, regulatory requirements, and industry standards. This process helps identify any gaps or outdated provisions that may need revision or updating.

Gathering evidence during this review is essential for validating that the policies are being properly implemented and adhered to. This includes collecting documentation, records, and other relevant data that demonstrate the policy's effectiveness and compliance. The evidence can be used to verify that the organization's policies are functioning as intended and provide insights into areas for improvement.

Review of organization policy/process/procedure is called the **Test of Design (ToD)**, and this is a crucial initial step in assessing the effectiveness of the internal controls within an organization. It ensures that controls are not only conceived but also properly implemented within the operational framework. This test is essential for establishing a solid foundation for effective internal control systems.

In this section, the detailed approach to the ToD will be examined, highlighting the systematic process used to evaluate and confirm the structural integrity and adequacy of a company's internal controls. The initial audit, which does the ToD, comprises the following:

- **Verification of control existence**: The main objective of the review of policy is to confirm that a control is actually in place as claimed by the organization. This involves a comprehensive review of the control's structure and its integration into the operational process. Ensure that the necessary IT service management controls, such as incident management, change management, and service continuity, are designed and implemented as required by ISO 20000.

- **Evaluation of control adequacy**: This involves comparing the control's design to the risks and requirements it is meant to manage. Assess whether the design of each control is sufficient to mitigate the risks related to IT services, such as downtime, security breaches, or service failures. The design should align with the specific needs of the organization and its IT services.

- **Identifying design flaws**: Review of policy aims to uncover any inherent design flaws that could compromise the control's effectiveness, regardless of how well it is executed. Potential issues could include unclear objectives, inadequate risk coverage, or impractical implementation. Examine whether the design of the ITSM processes and controls is effective or if there are any flaws, such as incomplete processes, unclear procedures, or a lack of coverage for key service areas.

- **Alignment with ISO 20000 requirements**: Evaluate whether the controls are in place to meet the key ISO 20000 requirements, such as service delivery, governance, monitoring, and continual improvement.

- **Integration into business operations:** Review how the ITSM processes are integrated with other business functions and ensure that the design supports operational objectives and compliance with relevant industry standards and regulations.

By conducting the ToD, organizations can ensure that their IT SMS under ISO 20000 is designed to achieve the expected results and meet the framework's standards, providing a solid foundation for effective and efficient service delivery.

Key principles of gathering evidence in ISO 19011 require capturing the objective and reliable evidence. Evidence should be based on facts, observations, interviews, and documentation. The evidence gathered must be relevant to the audit objectives and criteria. Auditor's findings and conclusions should be supported by the evidence gathered. It should be sufficient in quantity and quality to support the audit's conclusions.

The evidence gathered during the audit provides the basis for the following:

- Determining conformity with the audit criteria.

- Identifying non-conformities or areas for improvement.

- Supporting audit findings and conclusions.

- Demonstrating the credibility and objectivity of the audit process.

Evidence is gathered through interviews, review of documents and records, observation of processes, sampling, etc.

Audit checklists and tools can help guide the process of evidence collection and ensure consistency across audits.

Collected evidence should be systematically documented and organized to facilitate review and analysis. This includes noting the source, nature, and relevance of the evidence.

In the context of ISO 20000, the review of policies is a critical aspect of maintaining an effective SMS. Policies, such as the service management policy, guide the organization in achieving its objectives, ensuring service quality, and meeting business and customer requirements. Regular reviews ensure that policies remain relevant, effective, and aligned with the organization's goals and the evolving needs of its stakeholders.

ISO 20000 specifies the following key considerations for reviewing policies:

- **Alignment with organizational objectives:**

  o   Verify that policies support the organization's purpose, strategic direction, and goals for IT service management.

  o   Assess whether policies are consistent with the business and service objectives.

- **Compliance with ISO 20000 requirements:** Ensure policies are aligned with the standard's requirements, including the organization's commitment to continual improvement, customer satisfaction, and adherence to statutory and regulatory obligations.

- **Effectiveness and applicability:**

  o   Evaluate whether the policies are effectively implemented and remain applicable to current services, processes, and operational needs.

  o   Check if the policies are driving desired outcomes, such as improved service delivery and enhanced customer satisfaction.

- **Integration with the SMS:**

  o   Ensure that the policies are integrated into the SMS and reflected in the organization's processes, procedures, and practices.

  o   Confirm that policies provide clear direction for setting objectives, managing risks, and addressing opportunities.

- **Performance evaluation and feedback:**

  o   Use performance metrics, audit findings, and customer feedback to assess whether the policies are effective in achieving their intended purpose.

  o   Analyze any service performance issues, incidents, or nonconformities that may indicate the need for policy updates.

- **Stakeholder engagement:**

  o   Engage stakeholders, including customers, employees, and partners, during the policy review to ensure their needs and expectations are addressed.

  o   Validate that the policies are understood and followed by all relevant parties.

- **Documented information and control:**

  o   Confirm that policies are documented, controlled, and communicated effectively to ensure consistency across the organization.

  o   Review documented versions of the policies to ensure they are up to date and accessible to those who need them.

- **Continual improvement:**
  - o Ensure that the policies reflect the organization's commitment to continual improvement.
  - o Update policies to address new risks, opportunities, or changes in technology, business processes, or customer requirements.

While reviewing policies, the policies should be evaluated, gaps/improvements should be identified, revisions should be made as necessary, revisions should be approved, delta changes should be communicated, and relevant records for the rationale of changes should be documented/retained.

Evidence gathered during audits or assessments directly informs the policy review process, highlighting gaps, risks, or inefficiencies that may necessitate policy updates. In turn, updated policies guide future practices, ensuring alignment with organizational goals and standards like ISO 9001, ISO 20000, or ISO 27001.

Conclusion

The processes of scheduling audits, reporting findings, and conducting follow-up actions are integral to a successful audit cycle. Audit scheduling ensures that audits are conducted at appropriate intervals, prioritizing high-risk areas and aligning with organizational and regulatory timelines. Reporting provides clear, actionable insights into compliance, performance, and improvement opportunities, fostering transparency and informed decision-making. Follow-up ensures that corrective actions are implemented effectively, verifying their impact and sustaining improvements over time. Together, these components create a structured framework that drives accountability, enhances organizational performance, and supports continuous improvement in line with strategic objectives.

Auditees play an essential role in enabling an efficient and meaningful audit. Their active involvement not only ensures the audit process runs smoothly but also reinforces a culture of accountability, compliance, and continuous improvement within the organization. This, in turn, supports the achievement of business objectives and enhances overall organizational performance.

By systematically reviewing policies and collecting evidence, organizations can maintain robust governance structures, enhance operational efficiency, and drive continual improvement. These practices ensure sustained compliance with standards, improve stakeholder confidence, and contribute to the organization's long-term success.

In the upcoming chapters, we will learn about how to plan for the different types of audits based on the business and regulatory requirements.

CHAPTER 4
Types of Audits

Introduction

In the earlier chapters, we saw that audits are essential tools for assessing the effectiveness, compliance, and performance of an organization's processes, systems, or controls. They provide valuable insights into areas that require improvement, helping organizations align with regulatory requirements, industry standards, and internal goals.

In this chapter, we look at the different types of audits. Audits are categorized into different types based on their purpose, scope, and the parties involved. Each type of audit serves a unique function, contributing to a comprehensive understanding of an organization's operations. Each of the audits provides different insights and focuses on distinct aspects of an organization. Understanding these types enables organizations to select the appropriate audit approach based on their objectives, risks, and compliance needs.

Structure

The chapter covers the following topics:

- Key concepts
- Types of internal audits
- Types of external audits

Objectives

In this chapter, we will look at the audits as vital tools for evaluating and improving an organization's performance, compliance, and risk management. The classification of audits into various types, such as internal, external, compliance, operational, and specialized audits, allows organizations to take a focused approach in addressing specific areas of concern, ensuring a comprehensive evaluation of their processes and systems.

By the end of this chapter, the reader will have learned to separate audits into distinct types, serving several critical purposes, and ensuring that the organizations can tailor their approach to meet specific goals and achieve meaningful outcomes. Each type of audit focuses on different areas, stakeholders, and objectives, which helps organizations efficiently manage risks, ensure compliance, and drive improvement. Roles of auditees can be defined clearly based on the type of audit. The management can evaluate the operational effectiveness of the different functions through different types of audits.

Key concepts

Through defining different types of **information technology (IT)** audits, the following objectives can be met:

- **Clarity of purpose**: Different audits, such as operational, compliance, or IT audits, address unique aspects of an organization. Separating them ensures that the scope and goals of each audit are well understood and targeted. Separation allows audits to align with organizational priorities.

- **Specialized expertise:** Different audits require distinct expertise. Any IT audit needs technology specialists as well as process experts. Categorizing audits ensures the right expertise is applied.

- **Targeted risk assessment:** Internal operational audits identify inefficiencies, and external audits are for certification or regulatory compliance. Separating audits allows organizations to address risks in a focused and systematic way.

- **Improved resource allocation:** Categorizing audits helps organizations plan better and deploy resources where they are most needed, reducing redundancy and optimizing efforts.

- **Enhanced stakeholder confidence:** External audits are for acquiring certifications and compliance audits assure regulators. Distinguishing audit types allows organizations to address the concerns of different stakeholders effectively.

- **Compliance with standards and regulations**: Standards such as **ISO 9001** (quality management), **ISO 27001** (information security), or **Sarbanes-Oxley (SOX)** require specific types of audits. Separating audits ensures compliance with these requirements.

- **Facilitating continuous improvement**: Operational audits focus on efficiency, while IT audits enhance cybersecurity. Separating audits ensures continuous improvement in targeted domains.

- **Supporting certification and accreditation**: Many standards and frameworks, such as those from the **International Organization for Standardization (ISO)**, **System and Organization Controls (SOC)**, or **General Data Protection Regulation (GDPR)**, require specific types of audits. Categorizing audits helps organizations meet these requirements systematically.

Types of internal audits

Internal audits in the context of IT focus on evaluating the effectiveness, efficiency, and compliance of an organization's IT systems, controls, and processes. They are an essential component of risk management and ensure that IT operations align with organizational goals, regulatory requirements, and industry standards.

The key objectives of internal IT audits are as follows:

- **Evaluate IT controls**:

  o Assess design and operational effectiveness of IT controls (e.g., access control, data protection, and disaster recovery).

  o Identify control gaps or vulnerabilities in IT systems.

- **Ensure compliance**:

  o Verify adherence to IT-related regulatory requirements and standards, such as GDPR, HIPAA, or ISO 27001.

  o Confirm compliance with the organization's IT policies and procedures.

- **Mitigate IT risks**:

  o Identify and assess risks related to cybersecurity, data breaches, system failures, and unauthorized access.

  o Recommend strategies for mitigating these identified risks.

- **Enhance IT governance**:

  o Review the effectiveness of IT governance frameworks, including IT strategy alignment with business objectives.

  o Ensure accountability for IT decision-making and resource allocation.

- **Optimize IT processes**:

  o Evaluate the efficiency and performance of IT operations, such as system maintenance, software development, and incident management.

  o Identify opportunities for process improvement and cost optimization.

- **Assess IT security**:
  - o Review measures for protecting sensitive information from unauthorized access, theft, or loss.
  - o Test incident response plans and disaster recovery capabilities.

The scope of internal IT audits can be defined based on a wide range of areas, namely:

- **Access management**: Reviewing user access controls, role-based permissions, and authentication mechanisms.
- **Cybersecurity**: Evaluating firewalls, intrusion detection systems, and anti-malware solutions.
- **Data protection**: Ensuring compliance with data privacy regulations and the effectiveness of encryption and backup strategies.
- **Disaster recovery and business continuity**: Assessing plans and capabilities to recover operations after disruptions.
- **IT asset management**: Reviewing the inventory, usage, and lifecycle management of hardware and software assets.
- **IT change management**: Evaluating how changes to IT systems are planned, tested, and implemented.
- **Third-party vendor management**: Ensuring that IT service providers comply with security and performance requirements.

Benefits of internal audit

An internal audit schedule is a comprehensive plan that outlines when, where, and how internal audits will be conducted within an organization. It ensures that audits are systematic, well-coordinated, and cover all critical areas to comply with standards like ISO 9001, ISO 27001, ISO 20000, or any other applicable frameworks.

The benefits of an **internal audit schedule** are systematic coverage, resource optimization, proactive risk management, improved compliance, enhanced transparency, etc.

An internal IT audit is a critical component of an organization's **governance, risk management, and compliance (GRC)** framework. By assessing IT processes, systems, and controls, an internal IT audit provides actionable insights that help organizations optimize operations, ensure regulatory compliance, and protect their digital assets.

The following are the key benefits of conducting internal IT audits:

- **Enhanced risk management**:
  - o Identifies vulnerabilities in IT systems and processes.
  - o Helps prioritize and mitigate risks based on their potential impact on the organization.

- **Improved IT governance**:
  - o Ensures that IT policies and procedures align with the organization's overall goals and objectives.
  - o Promotes accountability by clearly defining roles and responsibilities within the IT function.
- **Regulatory compliance:** Verifies adherence to industry regulations, standards, and legal requirements, such as ISO 27001, SOC 2, GDPR, or HIPAA.
- **Strengthened internal controls**:
  - o Evaluates the effectiveness of existing IT controls and recommends improvements to address gaps or weaknesses.
  - o Ensures critical systems and data are safeguarded against threats.
- **Cost optimization**: Identifies inefficiencies in IT processes or systems, helping to reduce waste and optimize resource allocation.
- **Improved data security**:
  - o Assesses the effectiveness of cybersecurity measures, including firewalls, intrusion detection systems, and encryption protocols.
  - o Ensures sensitive data is protected from unauthorized access or cyber threats. Sensitive data can be protected from being lost, accessed without authorization, or shared inappropriately by using **data loss prevention (DLP)** tools.
    - ▪ DLP solutions are used across three primary areas. They secure **data at rest** by protecting stored information in databases, devices, or backups from unauthorized access or theft. They monitor and safeguard **data in transit** as it travels through networks, email systems, or file transfers, preventing interception or leakage. Additionally, they ensure the secure handling of **data in use**, protecting sensitive information while files are being edited or shared.
- **Business continuity and resilience**:
  - o Reviews disaster recovery and business continuity plans to ensure the organization can respond effectively to disruptions.
  - o Validates backup systems and recovery processes to minimize downtime during crises.
- **Informed decision-making**:
  - o Provides management with reliable data and insights about IT performance, enabling better strategic decisions.

      o   Offers recommendations to align IT initiatives with the organization's long-term goals.

- **Increased stakeholder confidence**:

      o   Demonstrates a commitment to strong IT governance and proactive risk management.

      o   Builds trust among stakeholders, including customers, investors, and regulators, by showcasing robust IT practices.

- **Facilitation of continuous improvement**:

      o   Encourages regular reviews and updates to IT systems, processes, and policies.

      o   Promotes a culture of continuous learning and improvement within the IT team.

By conducting regular internal IT audits, organizations can ensure their IT environment is secure, efficient, and aligned with their strategic objectives, while also safeguarding their reputation in an increasingly digital world.

Developing an internal audit schedule

An internal audit schedule is essential for maintaining an organized, systematic approach to auditing. It ensures that audits are conducted effectively, focusing on critical areas and aligning with organizational priorities. By following the schedule, organizations can improve risk management, compliance, and continuous improvement efforts.

The steps to develop an internal audit schedule are as follows:

1. **Conduct risk assessment**: Identify high-priority areas based on risk levels, criticality, and past audit results.

2. **Consult stakeholders**: Engage process owners, department heads, and management to determine audit needs.

3. **Prioritize audits**: Focus on areas with significant risks, compliance requirements, or frequent issues.

4. **Align with business goals**: Ensure the audit schedule supports organizational objectives and operational timelines

5. **Create a calendar**: Plot the audits on a calendar, ensuring proper distribution and adequate time for follow-ups.

6. **Monitor and revise**: Regularly review the schedule to incorporate changes in risks, processes, or regulations.

An example of an internal audit schedule in a typical IT services organization is as follows:

Audit area	Audit objective	Frequency	Planned date	Duration	Auditor (s)	Criteria
Information security	Compliance with ISO 27001	Quarterly		2 Days		ISO 27001 annex A controls
Change management	Evaluate change processes	Biannually		1 Day		Internal IT CM policy
Data protection	GDPR compliance	Annually		3 Days		GDPR articles 5–32
Quality management	ISO 9001 compliance	Annually		2 Days		ISO 9001:2015 clauses
IT asset management	Efficiency and control	Biannually		1 Day		ITAM policy and procedures

Table 4.1: Sample internal audit schedule

Maintaining a comprehensive audit schedule for internal audits can have several beneficial outcomes for an organization, namely, improved compliance, enhanced risk management practices, increased efficiency, increased confidence in internal controls, etc. This will lead to improved stakeholder confidence through demonstrating commitment to regular and periodic assessments, which further leads to continuous improvement.

By consistently following a comprehensive audit schedule, an organization can achieve better governance, increased accountability, and overall improved performance.

Types of external audits

External IT audits are conducted by independent third parties to evaluate an organization's IT systems, controls, processes, and overall compliance with regulations, standards, and industry best practices. These audits provide an unbiased assessment of IT-related risks, security, and performance, which can help organizations maintain compliance, enhance credibility, and improve operational efficiency.

External IT audits are conducted to provide an independent and unbiased assessment of an organization's IT systems, processes, and controls. These audits serve as a cornerstone for ensuring compliance, mitigating risks, and enhancing the efficiency and security of IT operations.

The following are the key objectives of conducting external IT audits:

- **Ensure regulatory compliance**: Validate the organization's adherence to applicable laws, regulations, and standards related to IT systems.

- **Evaluate IT security posture**: Assess the effectiveness of IT security measures in protecting data, systems, and networks from cyber threats.

- **Mitigate IT-related risks**: Identify and address potential risks to IT systems, such as operational failures, data breaches, and unauthorized access.

- **Validate IT governance practices**: Evaluate the organization's IT governance framework to ensure alignment with business objectives and industry standards.

- **Verify data integrity and accuracy**: Confirm that data stored, processed, and transmitted by IT systems is accurate, complete, and reliable.

- **Assess IT operational efficiency**: Identify inefficiencies in IT processes and recommend improvements for operational performance.

- **Strengthen business continuity and disaster recovery**: Evaluate the organization's preparedness for handling IT disruptions and ensuring business continuity.

- **Improve third-party governance**: Assess third-party IT service providers and vendors to ensure compliance with contractual agreements and security standards.

- **Provide assurance to stakeholders**: Enhance the confidence of stakeholders, including customers, investors, and regulators, in the organization's IT systems and controls.

- **Support certification or accreditation efforts**: Help organizations achieve certifications such as ISO 27001, SOC 2, or ISO 20000 by evaluating compliance with required standards.

- **Enhance decision-making and strategic planning**: Provide insights into IT performance and risks to support management in making informed decisions.

The competence of an auditor is a very important factor in carrying out an effective audit process. An auditor's ability to evaluate systems, processes, and controls critically and independently ensures that audit findings are accurate, reliable, and actionable. Competent auditors not only bring technical knowledge and skills but also uphold professional ethics and maintain objectivity throughout the audit process.

Auditor competence is particularly critical in specialized fields, such as IT audits, where technical expertise and an understanding of standards, frameworks, and risks are essential. Organizations depend on the auditor's qualifications, experience, and judgment to ensure compliance, improve processes, and mitigate risks effectively.

ISO 19011 emphasizes the importance of auditor competence while planning external audits, including the following:

- **Knowledge of standards**: Familiarity with the standards being audited (e.g., ISO 20000, ISO 27001).

- **Technical expertise**: Understanding of the organization's industry, processes, and risks.

- **Audit skills:** Proficiency in planning, conducting, and reporting audits.

- **Interpersonal skills:** Effective communication, conflict resolution, and cultural sensitivity.

Audit preparation

A pre-audit is a crucial preparatory phase that helps organizations ensure readiness for an external audit. A pre-audit involves assessing the readiness of an organization's IT systems, processes, and documentation to ensure a smooth and efficient audit process. It provides an opportunity to identify gaps, address potential non-conformities, evaluate the effectiveness of systems, and confirm compliance with applicable standards.

In the context of external IT audits, the pre-audit phase plays a vital role in ensuring the organization is fully prepared to meet the audit requirements and achieve its objectives.

Pre-audit helps to:

- **Evaluate readiness**: Assess the organization's preparedness for the external audit.

- **Identify gaps**: Highlight areas of non-compliance or weaknesses in policies, procedures, and processes.

- **Address non-conformities**: Provide time to implement corrective actions before the formal audit. Pre-audits help in systematically evaluating documentation, security controls, risk management practices, and operational workflows. This will result in uncovering gaps that might lead to major non-conformities during a formal audit. This early detection enables corrective actions, minimizing compliance risks.

- **Familiarize teams**: Ensure employees understand the audit requirements and processes.

Typical pre-audit activities are as follows:

- **Define the scope of audit**: Confirm the scope, objectives, and criteria for the external audit.

- **Review documentation**: Conduct an internal review of key documents such as policies, procedures, risk assessments, and SLAs.

- **Process verification**: Validate that key processes are being followed as documented (e.g., incident management, change management) and perform walkthroughs or mock audits to assess process compliance.

- **Evidence collection**: Gather evidence such as records, logs, reports, and meeting minutes that demonstrate compliance and ensure that evidence is complete, accurate, and readily accessible during the audit.

- **Staff awareness**: Conduct training sessions to prepare employees for auditor interviews and communicate the importance of transparency and honesty during the audit process.

- **Ensure internal audits are conducted**: Perform a focused internal audit and document findings.

- **Prepare a detailed pre-audit report**: Compile a report summarizing the results of the pre-audit activities, including non-conformities/action plans, and share the report with relevant stakeholders for review/approval and action before the external audit.

Conducting pre-audits will result in improved compliance due to the identification/rectification of non-conformities in advance, and enhanced confidence for the auditees in their readiness to face the audit.

There are various types of external IT audits, each tailored to specific goals and compliance needs. Understanding these types is essential for selecting the right audit based on organizational requirements.

Key types of external IT audits

The key types of an external audit are as follows:

- **Compliance audits**: To ensure that the organization complies with the applicable laws, regulations, and standards related to IT.

  A compliance audit is a formal review conducted to evaluate whether an organization adheres to external regulations, internal policies, and industry standards. These audits are crucial for ensuring that an organization operates within the legal and ethical boundaries defined by regulatory bodies, contractual obligations, or organizational policies.

  Objectives of compliance audits include assurance in adherence to regulations, namely, GDPR, HIPAA, SOX, or PCI DSS, evaluation of design and effectiveness of IT controls and processes, timely mitigation of risks that could lead to penalties, reputational damage, or operational disruptions, etc.

- **Certification audits**: To validate the organization's compliance with a specific certification standard.

  A certification audit is a formal process conducted by an independent, accredited auditor/firm to evaluate whether an organization meets the criteria for certification under a specific standard or framework and provide external validation of an organization's compliance with industry standards, demonstrating its commitment to quality, security, or other operational benchmarks. Common certification standards include ISO 20000, ISO 27001, SOC 2, ISO 9001, and PCI DSS, etc., depending on the business operations of the organization.

Objectives of compliance audits include validation of compliance with the specific requirements of the certification standard (ISO 27001 for information security), showcase demonstration of industry best practices, provide stakeholder assurance, and gain a competitive edge by demonstrating certified excellence.

- **Cybersecurity audits:** To assess the organization's cybersecurity posture, identify vulnerabilities, and ensure protection against cyber threats.

  A cybersecurity audit is a systematic evaluation of an organization's information systems, controls, and processes to assess their effectiveness in protecting the confidentiality, integrity, and availability of their applications, assets and data processed within the applications, against cyber threats. These audits help identify vulnerabilities, evaluate compliance with security standards, and ensure that the organization's cybersecurity practices align with industry best practices and regulatory requirements.

  Cybersecurity audits focus on assessing the security posture in organization's ability to prevent, detect, and respond to cyber threats, identifying vulnerabilities to uncover weaknesses in systems, networks, or processes that could be exploited by attackers, ensuring compliance to relevant regulations and frameworks (e.g., NIST Cybersecurity Framework, ISO 27001) by enhanced incident response practices, timely mitigation of risks, etc.

- **Financial IT audits**: To ensure the accuracy, security, and integrity of IT systems used for financial reporting, such as a SOX audit to ensure the IT systems supporting financial reporting comply with Sarbanes-Oxley Act requirements.

  A Financial IT audit focuses on evaluating the IT systems, controls, and processes that support an organization's financial operations and reporting. These audits ensure the reliability, accuracy, and security of financial data by examining the IT infrastructure, applications, and controls that drive the financial systems. Financial IT audits play a critical role in maintaining compliance with financial regulations, safeguarding sensitive financial information, and ensuring that the organization's financial reporting is accurate and trustworthy.

  This type of external audit verifies that the financial data is accurate, complete, and free from unauthorized modifications, helps in evaluating IT controls supporting financial reporting (especially for listed organizations to ensure correctness of business results), confirms compliance to financial regulations, such as **Sarbanes-Oxley Act (SOX)**, GDPR, or other relevant laws, by implementing the right risk mitigation practices, improving the operational efficiency, etc.

- **Operational IT audits**: To evaluate the efficiency and effectiveness of IT operations and processes.

  Operational IT audit evaluates the efficiency, effectiveness, and reliability of an organization's IT systems, processes, and controls that support day-to-day operations.

It focuses on assessing how well IT systems align with and support the organization's business objectives, ensuring the expected performance and value-added services delivery.

Operational IT audits provide actionable inputs to help organizations optimize resources, improve service delivery, and achieve strategic goals. This is achieved by evaluating IT system performance, optimization of resource utilization, enhancing operational effectiveness, mitigation of operational risks, assurance in alignment with business objectives, etc.

- **Data protection and privacy audits**: To assess the organization's data protection and privacy practices, such as a HIPAA audit, to ensure the security and privacy of healthcare data.

Data protection audit is a systematic examination of an organization's policies, procedures, and systems to ensure compliance with different data protection laws, such as the GDPR, **California Consumer Privacy Act (CCPA)**, and best practices. It focuses on evaluating how an organization collects, stores, processes, shares, and secures personal and sensitive data. Data breaches and privacy violations are the most impactful challenges faced by any organization. Data protection audits are essential for safeguarding sensitive information, maintaining customer trust, and mitigating legal and financial risks.

Data privacy audits lead to transparency in information to all stakeholders about how their data is collected, used, and protected, resulting in providing support to accountability and governance and enhancing data management practices. By systematically assessing data handling processes, identifying vulnerabilities, and implementing improvements, these audits help organizations safeguard sensitive information, mitigate risks, and build stakeholder trust. Regular data protection audits not only ensure legal compliance but also foster a culture of accountability and continuous improvement in managing and protecting data.

- **Third-party vendor audits**: To evaluate IT services provided by third-party vendors to ensure compliance with organizational policies and standards such as a SOC 2 Type II audit for a vendor providing IT hosting services.

A third-party vendor audit is a systematic evaluation of the practices, processes, and controls of an organization's external vendors, suppliers, or service providers. These audits assess whether vendors meet the organization's security, compliance, and operational requirements, especially when handling sensitive data, delivering critical services, or accessing the organization's systems.

In today's interconnected business landscape, organizations increasingly rely on third-party vendors to support operations. However, this reliance introduces risks, such as data breaches, regulatory non-compliance, and operational disruptions, stemming from vendor vulnerabilities. The third-party vendor audit should focus on the complete supply chain so as to ensure vendors adhere to the required standards and best practices.

Objectives of third-party vendor audits include assessment of security practices implemented to protect data, systems, and processes from unauthorized access or cyber threats, risk mitigation practices in identifying potential risks, such as data breaches, operational inefficiencies, or compliance gaps, that could impact the organization, support business continuity for the complete operation by addressing availability of all entities in the supply chain.

- **Energy and environmental IT audits**: To assess IT operations for energy efficiency and environmental impact.

  An energy and environmental audit is a full-fledged evaluation of an organization's energy consumption, resource usage, and environmental impact. The primary aim of such audits is to identify opportunities to optimize energy efficiency, reduce waste, comply with environmental regulations, and support sustainability goals.

  Environmental, social, and governance (ESG) principles have become an important criterion of modern business operations, reflecting the growing emphasis on sustainability. ESG in operations focuses on embedding sustainable practices, fostering employee well-being, maintaining ethical supply chains, and ensuring transparent governance across all aspects of an organization's activities. By doing so, companies enhance their resilience, improve their reputation, and meet the demands of investors, regulators, and consumers. These audits not only help reduce operational costs but also enhance responsibility towards environmental sustainability and improve an organization's reputation as a responsible corporate entity.

External audit approach

As covered in an earlier section, external IT audits are essential for ensuring compliance with regulatory requirements, identifying vulnerabilities, and enhancing overall operational efficiency. To achieve these objectives, external IT audits follow a structured approach, comprising multiple key phases that guide the audit process from start to finish. Each phase of an external IT audit serves a specific purpose, from understanding the organization's IT environment to validating the effectiveness of implemented controls.

Conducting external audits for IT systems is a vital practice for ensuring the security, compliance, and efficiency of an organization's technology infrastructure. These audits provide an objective assessment of IT controls, processes, and systems, helping organizations identify vulnerabilities, address compliance gaps, and align operations with regulatory and industry standards. By engaging external independent auditors, organizations can gather valuable inputs on potential risks and areas for improvement, institutionalizing accountability and trust among stakeholders. External IT audits not only safeguard critical assets but also enhance IT governance, operational resilience, and overall business performance.

The systematic progression through these phases ensures a thorough and objective evaluation, enabling organizations to address risks, improve IT governance, and align with industry best practices. The essential phases of an external IT audit comprise planning, fieldwork, reporting, and follow-up, highlighting their significance and contributions to a successful audit process.

The external IT audit typically involves multiple key phases, given as follows:

1. **Planning and preparation**: Understand the organization, the IT environment, and the scope of the audit. The steps are as follows:

    a. Define the audit scope and objectives.

    b. Understand the organization's business, IT systems, and relevant processes.

    c. Identify risks, controls, and compliance requirements (e.g., GDPR, SOC2, ISO 27001).

    d. Develop an audit plan, including timelines, resources, and methodologies.

    e. Communicate with stakeholders about the audit process and requirements.

2. **Risk assessment**: Identify and assess risks within the IT environment. The steps are as follows:

    a. Perform risk assessments on critical IT assets, data, and processes.

    b. Review the organization's risk management framework.

    c. Assess current IT controls and their effectiveness in mitigating risks.

    d. Evaluate compliance with applicable laws and regulations.

    e. Identify potential vulnerabilities in IT systems.

3. **Data collection and evaluation**: Gather and evaluate evidence to assess the effectiveness of IT controls. Refer to the following steps:

    a. Review IT policies, procedures, and documentation.

    b. Perform technical assessments, such as network scans, vulnerability assessments, or penetration testing.

    c. Interview key IT staff and other relevant personnel.

    d. Evaluate the design and operational effectiveness of IT controls.

    e. Test the functionality and security of IT systems (e.g., access controls, disaster recovery, change management).

4. **Analysis and evaluation**: Analyze the collected data and determine whether IT controls are operating as intended. The steps are as follows:

    a.   Assess whether the IT environment aligns with industry best practices.

    b.   Identify gaps or weaknesses in controls.

    c.   Determine the potential impact and likelihood of identified risks.

    d.   Review any past audit findings or remediation actions.

5. **Reporting**: Document the audit findings and provide recommendations for improvement. Refer to the following steps:

    a.   Summarize audit findings, including strengths and weaknesses of IT controls.

    b.   Provide a risk-based assessment of the organization's IT environment.

    c.   Offer recommendations for improvements in IT processes and controls.

    d.   Prepare an audit report tailored to both management and technical audiences.

    e.   Discuss findings with management and clarify any concerns.

6. **Follow-up**: Ensure that the organization addresses audit findings and recommendations. The steps are as follows:

    a.   Monitor the implementation of corrective actions.

    b.   Conduct follow-up audits or reviews to assess progress on remediation.

    c.   Evaluate whether the proposed changes effectively mitigate identified risks.

Each of these phases helps to ensure that the audit process is thorough, objective, and aligned with best practices, delivering value to the organization by identifying risks and recommending improvements to IT governance, controls, and security. By following this phased approach, organizations can achieve a clear understanding of their IT strengths and vulnerabilities, address compliance gaps, and implement best practices to safeguard their systems and data. A well-executed audit not only mitigates risks but also empowers organizations to drive continuous improvement in their IT operations, fostering resilience and long-term success in an increasingly complex and dynamic digital landscape.

Defining an external audit schedule for IT audits involves several key steps to ensure thoroughness and effectiveness. Business impact analysis on the IT systems for the effectiveness of controls on establishing the confidentiality, integrity, and availability of business operations will help in the creation of the audit frequency for different functions of the organization. The schedule has to be arrived at after assessing the IT environment and identifying the critical systems and applications that need to be audited.

Once this is done the audit objectives have to be defined by including steps towards assessing compliance with IT security standards, evaluating the effectiveness of IT controls, and identifying potential vulnerabilities. Keeping all these in view, an audit plan can be developed by specifying the areas to be audited and the criteria for the evaluation.

External IT audits provide a framework for organizations to address a broad spectrum of risks and compliance needs. By leveraging different types of external IT audits, organizations can enhance trust with stakeholders, secure their IT environments, and ensure their IT practices align with regulatory and business objectives.

The objectives of external IT audits extend beyond compliance to include risk mitigation, operational efficiency, and strategic alignment of IT systems. By addressing these objectives, external audits play a vital role in enhancing the security, reliability, and performance of an organization's IT environment while building stakeholder confidence.

Conclusion

We saw how each type of audit serves a unique purpose, contributing to a broader understanding of organizational effectiveness. Internal audits enhance process efficiency and drive continuous improvement, while external audits provide impartial assessments to meet regulatory or certification requirements. Compliance audits ensure adherence to laws and standards, operational audits identify inefficiencies, and IT audits safeguard digital infrastructure and data security. Specialized audits further address specific needs, such as environmental or energy efficiency.

Ultimately, a well-conducted external audit empowers organizations to mitigate threats, uphold data integrity, and adapt to the evolving technological landscape, laying a strong foundation for sustainable growth and success in the digital age.

In summary, the separation of audits into types enables organizations to optimize resources, ensure focused evaluations, and achieve strategic and operational objectives effectively. A well-planned and executed audit program, encompassing various audit types, fosters a culture of accountability, compliance, and resilience, ultimately contributing to long-term success.

In the upcoming chapters, we will look into how to define the different types of documentation required for capturing the operational practices in managing the IT landscape of the organization. The operating practices can be defined into policies, processes, and **standard operating procedures** (**SOPs**). The suite of documentation, along with applicability statements, will provide the required governance mechanisms and the scope of audits.

Join our Discord space

Join our Discord workspace for latest updates, offers, tech happenings around the world, new releases, and sessions with the authors:

https://discord.bpbonline.com

CHAPTER 5

IT Policies, Processes and SOPs

Introduction

In this chapter, we will be discussing the various types of documentation, such as policy, process, and **standard operating procedure** (**SOP**). In today's globalized and interconnected business landscape, the reliance on robust IT infrastructure is very critical for continuous operational efficiency, assurance of data security, and compliance with business regulations. This interconnectedness brings forth both opportunities and challenges, leading to the development of comprehensive frameworks to establish boundaries and ensure secure, streamlined operations.

Organizations must proactively define and enforce clear boundaries around their IT environments to protect sensitive data, prevent unauthorized access, and mitigate cyber risks. These boundaries include setting up network segmentation, enforcing access controls, and defining protocols for data flow across internal and external networks. Such measures not only enhance security but also align with regulatory requirements and industry standards.

The foundation of a secure and efficient IT ecosystem lies in the clear delineation of roles and responsibilities. By assigning specific tasks and accountabilities to both the IT team and broader organizational units, businesses can ensure that all critical functions, including system administration, incident response, and compliance management, are effectively managed.

Practices for access provisioning, deprovisioning, and acquiring privileged access pose a significant security risk if not managed effectively. Clearly defined roles and responsibilities are vital for verifying the need for privileged access by documenting the accountability for each task. Organizations should maintain detailed logs of privileged access requests and approvals, enabling traceability and audit readiness.

Structure

This chapter addresses the following topics:

- Key concepts

- IT policy and processes

- Standard operating procedures

- Roles and responsibilities

- Eliminating conflict of interest

Objectives

In the field of IT service management, well-defined processes and SOPs are essential for ensuring consistency, efficiency, and security. To effectively implement and maintain these processes, it is crucial to establish clear policies and procedures that guide the IT team in understanding and executing their roles. All standards, especially the ISO standards, mandate that the roles have to be clearly defined, and the responsibilities and authorities have to be specifically documented. This helps in creating a clear organizational structure, showing the reporting relationships also. Bringing visibility to the reporting relationship helps in implementing the policies and conducting operations using the SOPs.

By the end of this chapter, readers will understand how the policies, processes, and SOPs are defined for a typical IT team. We will also get the view of the roles and their responsibilities. These will enable us to focus on the operational aspects of the IT operations and thus become adept IT auditors.

Key concepts

IT policies, processes, and SOPs are crucial for organizations to manage and secure their information technology infrastructure effectively. Let us look at some of the key concepts:

- **IT policies**: Policies are drafted focusing on the importance of technology and infrastructure in achieving the business objectives of any organization. Policies facilitate guidelines to protect data and IT resources from unauthorized access, breaches, and other security threats. Policies assure adherence to regulatory requirements and industry standards. Correctly documented policies improve the efficiency and reliability of IT operations. Policy definition begins with the identification and mitigation of potential

IT risks. User accountability and user responsibilities are clearly documented, and users are educated on acceptable use of IT resources.

- **IT processes**: Processes around IT systems are created to optimize IT workflows to enhance productivity and reduce delays in delivering services. Processes are developed for handling IT incidents that otherwise will result in downtime of operations. Processes for managing changes across the environment are implemented to ensure a structured approach to managing changes in IT systems and infrastructure. Processes lead to high-quality delivery of IT services and mandate regular assessment of IT process performance. Assessing performance through the right **key performance indicators** (**KPI**) will lead to process improvements, which will result in achieving better KPIs.

- **IT procedures**: IT procedures are documented step-by-step instructions that guide the execution of IT-related tasks, ensuring consistency, security, and compliance across an organization's technology environment. They define how IT operations, security controls, and administrative tasks should be performed to align with business objectives, regulatory requirements, and industry standards. Key IT procedure areas are security procedures, operations and infrastructure procedures, service management procedures, compliance and audit procedures, etc.

- **Standard operating procedures (SOPs) for IT operations**: SOPs are created with a focus on achieving consistent execution of tasks and processes. SOPs are in place for onboarding and induction training. They provide clear instructions for training new employees. SOPs help in maintaining reliability by high standards of quality in all instances of IT operations. SOPs help in achieving compliance with policies and regulatory requirements through documented procedures and institutionalized processes to save time and resources.

In an era where technology is the backbone of business operations, the importance of well-defined IT policies, processes, and SOPs cannot be overstated. These frameworks serve as the foundation for secure, efficient, and compliant IT environments, ensuring that an organization's technological resources align with its strategic goals.

The primary purpose of IT policies is to establish rules and guidelines for the use, management, and protection of IT systems. Processes and SOPs, on the other hand, provide step-by-step instructions to ensure consistent implementation of these policies across the organization. Together, they empower businesses to navigate the complexities of modern IT ecosystems while addressing critical challenges such as cybersecurity threats, regulatory compliance, and operational inefficiencies.

Key objectives of IT policies, processes, and SOPs include establishing governance, enhancing data security, mitigating risks, standardizing operations, and promoting regulatory compliance. They also play a pivotal role in managing access controls, supporting continuous improvement, and fostering a culture of accountability and awareness across the organization.

The objectives can be described as follows:

- **Governance and accountability**: Governance measures include defining clear **roles and responsibilities (R and R)** across the organization for IT management, establishing a structured framework for decision-making, accountability, and enforcement of IT practices, aligning IT operations with the organization's overall strategic goals.

- **Data security and privacy**: Controls or securing sensitive data are to be implemented to safeguard sensitive organizational, employee, and customer data against unauthorized access, breaches, or misuse. Policies should align with data protection regulations such as **General Data Protection Regulation (GDPR), Health Insurance Portability and Accountability Act (HIPAA)**, and **California Consumer Privacy Act (CCPA)**, by creating procedures for secure handling, storage, and disposal of data.

- **Resilience by right risk mitigation practices**: Practices should lead to identification, assessment, and mitigation of IT-related risks, including cybersecurity threats, system failures, and human errors. This requires incident handling procedures in establishing mechanisms to respond to and recover from incidents quickly, minimizing downtime and business disruptions.

- **Standardize IT operations**: Create repeatable and consistent workflows for IT-related tasks and activities. Document procedures (SOPs) to ensure uniformity in how IT operations are performed across teams and locations. Enhance efficiency, reduce errors, and improve coordination among stakeholders.

- **Control access and secure critical systems**: Enforce the principle of least privilege to restrict access to critical systems and data. Define processes for managing privileged access requests, approvals, and reviews. Prevent insider threats, unauthorized access, and potential misuse of IT resources.

- **Support continuous improvement and scalability**: Enable regular reviews and updates of IT policies and processes to adapt to evolving business needs and technological advancements. Foster a culture of continuous improvement through monitoring, feedback, and optimization. Ensure scalability to accommodate organizational growth or changes in IT infrastructure.

- **Enhance user awareness and responsibility**: Promote a security-first mindset across the organization by training employees on IT policies, cybersecurity best practices, and their responsibilities. Establish clear communication channels for reporting incidents, suspicious activities, or violations of policies. Reduce human error, which is a leading cause of security breaches, through education and awareness.

- **Support strategic IT alignment**: Ensure IT policies and processes align with the organization's mission, vision, and long-term objectives. Optimize resource utilization to balance operational needs, security, and cost-effectiveness. Foster innovation by allowing IT teams to focus on strategic initiatives rather than reactive problem-solving.

To summarize, the complete documentation to represent IT operations, namely, IT policies, processes, and SOPs, together create a secure, compliant, and efficient IT environment that supports the organization's overall success.

IT policy and processes

IT audits play a crucial role in evaluating an organization's IT systems, controls, and practices to ensure they meet regulatory, operational, and security requirements. Central to the success of any IT audit are the policies and processes that define how IT operations are governed, managed, and executed. These elements serve as the foundation upon which compliance, efficiency, and security are built.

Policies and processes are indispensable for IT audits, serving as the backbone of a secure, compliant, and efficient IT ecosystem. They provide the structure and documentation needed to demonstrate adherence to regulatory requirements, reduce risks, and ensure the consistent execution of IT operations. By investing in robust IT policies and processes, organizations not only enhance their audit readiness but also foster trust, accountability, and resilience in their IT environments.

ISO standards, including ISO 20000 for **Information Security Management Systems** (**ISMS**), provide clear guidance on the definition of policies and processes. As we saw in the earlier chapters, ISO/IEC 20000 is the international standard for **IT service management** (**ITSM**). It specifies requirements for establishing, implementing, maintaining, and continually improving a **service management system** (**SMS**).

In the **Information Technology Infrastructure Library** (**ITIL**), policies are high-level principles, rules, and guidelines established by management to govern decisions and ensure consistent actions. They provide a framework for setting objectives and guide process design and implementation.

ISO 20000 emphasizes that IT policies should:

- **Support strategic objectives**: Align with the organization's overall business objectives and IT service management goals.

- **Provide direction and framework**: Guide the establishment and operation of the SMS in achieving the business objectives.

- **Include commitments**: Clearly elaborate how service requirements will be addressed, how continual improvement will be embedded, and specify how compliance with applicable requirements will be achieved.

- **Be documented and communicated**: The policy must be clearly and unambiguously documented, communicated to all relevant stakeholders, and available to stakeholders as appropriate.

- **Be reviewed and updated**: It should be periodically reviewed to ensure it remains relevant and effective.

ISO 20000, service management policy, specifies that top management must establish a service management policy that:

- Is appropriate to the business objective of the organization.

- Provides a framework for setting service management objectives.

- Includes a commitment to satisfy applicable requirements.

- Includes a commitment to continual improvement of the SMS.

- Is maintained as documented information.

- Is communicated within the organization and available to interested parties.

ISO standard requires a planning activity, which serves as the basis for planning the SMS, including establishing objectives and determining the necessary processes.

In short, the IT policy is strategic, aligned with business objectives, and sets the direction for IT service management. The policy supports the implementation and continual improvement of the SMS and is backed by senior management's commitment.

Examples of policies are information security policy, access management policy, configuration management policy, change management policy, incident management policy, service level policy etc.

ISO 20000 defines IT processes as structured activities designed to achieve specific service management objectives. These processes ensure consistent, reliable, and effective delivery of IT services.

Key requirements for IT processes

In today's technology-driven world, effective IT processes are essential for ensuring the stability, security, and efficiency of an organization's operations. These processes provide a structured approach to managing IT services, infrastructure, and resources while aligning with business goals. To achieve this, organizations must establish robust IT processes that adhere to industry best practices and regulatory requirements.

IT processes in ISO 20000 are designed to ensure effective and consistent service delivery. They must be integrated within the SMS and aligned with the service management policy. Continuous monitoring and improvement are essential for maintaining process effectiveness.

In ITIL, processes are structured sets of activities designed to achieve specific objectives, transform inputs into outputs, and deliver value to the customer. These processes provide a systematic approach to managing and delivering IT services, ensuring consistency, efficiency, and alignment with business needs. They define *what* needs to be done, *how* it should be done, *who* is responsible, and *when* it should be done. Let us look at the characteristics of IT processes:

- **Aligned with service management policy**: Processes should support the overall service management policy and objectives.

- **Documented and controlled**: Critical processes must be documented, controlled, and maintained as part of the SMS.

- **Consistent and repeatable**: Processes should provide consistency and repeatability in service delivery.

- **Defined roles and responsibilities**: All the players get clearly assigned roles and responsibilities for process execution and accountability.

- **Performance measurement and improvement**: Ensures all activities are monitored, measured, and analyzed for implementing improvement mechanisms.

- **Integration and interaction**: Processes should be integrated and interact effectively with each other within the SMS.

ISO 20000 requires organizations to establish, implement, maintain, and continually improve an SMS, which includes defining necessary processes and their interactions. ISO also defines the operation of the SMS by specifying the operational planning and control of processes required to meet service requirements and achieve service management objectives. Performance evaluation through monitoring, measuring, and evaluating processes to ensure they achieve intended outcomes is an important aspect of ISO standards.

ISO 20000 standard specifies several key processes, including:

- **Service delivery processes**:
  - Service level management
  - Service reporting
  - Service continuity and availability management
  - Budgeting and accounting for services
  - Capacity management
  - Information security management

- **Relationship processes**:
  - Business relationship management
  - Supplier management

- **Resolution processes**:
  - Incident management
  - Problem management

- **Control processes**:
    - o Configuration management
    - o Change management
- **Service transition processes**:
    - o Service asset and configuration management
    - o Release and deployment management

The key differences between policy and process in the ISO context are given as follows:

- **Policy**: High-level, strategic, and principle-based, sets direction and intent, policy answers to what has to be done.

- **Process**: Detailed, operational, and action-oriented, describes how, who, and when to achieve the policy's objectives, the process gives the steps of realizing the *what* that has been defined in policy.

ITIL brings out the difference in a slightly different way, given as follows:

- **Policy**: High-level strategic direction, guides decision-making and behavior, provides broad steps in scope, and is less detailed.

- **Process**: Provides detailed, operational execution, defines activities, roles, inputs, outputs, and KPIs, specific and action-oriented.

IT procedures

IT procedures under ISO 20000 define how these IT services are planned, implemented, delivered, and continuously improved while maintaining compliance with the standard's requirements. These procedures help organizations establish a structured ITSM framework, enhancing service quality, incident response, change management, and risk mitigation. IT procedures under ISO 20000 provide a structured approach to managing IT services, improving efficiency, and ensuring regulatory compliance. By following these standardized processes, organizations can enhance IT service delivery, minimize risks, and achieve operational excellence.

The key IT procedures aligned with ISO 20000 are as follows:

- **Service management procedures**: Defines and documents available IT services and their dependencies, establishes **service level agreements (SLAs)** and monitors compliance, ensures IT resources meet business demand and performance expectations, and implements measures to maintain IT service uptime and reliability.

- **Incident and problem management procedures**: Defines how IT teams log, categorize, investigate, and resolve incidents within SLA timelines, focuses on identifying and resolving the root cause of recurring incidents to prevent future disruptions, and handles user requests for IT support, access, and system modifications efficiently.

- **Change and release management procedures**: Governs the assessment, approval, and implementation of IT changes with minimal risk, and ensures smooth rollout of software updates, patches, and system upgrades while maintaining service continuity.

- **Asset and configuration management procedures**: Tracks hardware, software, and IT infrastructure throughout their lifecycle, maintains a **configuration management database** (**CMDB**) for tracking IT components and their relationships.

- **Security and risk management procedures**: Ensures secure access, data protection, and vulnerability management, defines backup strategies and recovery plans for IT systems, and conducts internal audits and risk assessments to ensure ISO 20000 compliance.

- **Continual service improvement procedures**: Measures KPIs, SLAs, and customer satisfaction for continuous improvement, evaluates past incidents to improve future response strategies, and enhances ITSM procedures based on feedback and evolving business needs.

ITIL defines procedures, best practices, and workflows to improve IT service efficiency, reduce risks, and enhance customer satisfaction. ITIL-based IT procedures focus on service lifecycle stages, covering incident response, change management, asset tracking, service delivery, and continual improvement. IT procedures based on ITIL ensure standardized IT operations, improved service delivery, and risk mitigation. By adopting ITIL best practices, organizations can enhance efficiency, compliance, and customer satisfaction while aligning IT services with business goals.

Both ISO 20000 and ITIL focus on ITSM, but they differ in approach, scope, and implementation. ISO 20000 is a formal standard, while ITIL is a best practice framework. Refer to the following table:

IT procedure area	ISO 20000	ITIL
Service management	Requires documented procedures for service delivery, SLA management, and IT governance.	Provides best practices for managing IT services but allows customization.
Incident and problem management	Requires a structured approach for incident logging, categorization, resolution, and review.	Recommends best practices like **root cause analysis** (**RCA**) and using a **known error database** (**KEDB**).
Change and release management	Mandates formalized change management procedures, risk assessments, and approvals.	Suggests using the **change advisory board** (**CAB**) and risk-based change planning.

IT procedure area	ISO 20000	ITIL
Asset and configuration management	Requires strict CMDB procedures.	Encourages CMDB use but does not enforce specific methodologies.
Service request fulfilment	Standardizes request handling, ensuring timely approvals and tracking.	Recommends automating service request workflows for efficiency.
Capacity and performance management	Requires documented procedures to monitor, report, and optimize IT capacity.	Suggests using performance metrics, forecasting, and reporting tools.
Security and risk management	Emphasizes formal risk assessment, compliance audits, and security controls.	Aligns with IT security best practices like access control, vulnerability management, and data protection.
IT continuity and disaster recovery	Defines strict business continuity and disaster recovery (BCP and DRP) procedures.	Provides guidelines for IT continuity planning but does not mandate specific policies.
Continual service improvement	Requires ongoing improvement through audits and performance reviews.	Uses the **Plan-Do-Check-Act** (**PDCA**) to refine ITSM processes.

Table 5.1: Comparison of IT procedures between ISO 20000 and ITIL

In summary, ISO 20000 focuses on structured, process-driven IT procedures that organizations must follow to achieve compliance, and ITIL encourages adaptability, allowing organizations to select relevant procedures based on business needs. The decision on which framework has to be used for strengthening IT processes and compliance for the enterprise has to be taken based on the criteria in the next section. If an organization wants a formal, auditable certification, ISO 20000 provides mandatory IT procedures for compliance. If an organization prefers flexible ITSM best practices, ITIL provides guidelines that can be tailored.

Standard operating procedures

In the context of ISO 20000, SOPs are detailed, step-by-step instructions designed to ensure consistent execution of IT service management processes. They provide operational guidance and support compliance with the SMS.

In ITIL, SOPs are documented to ensure consistency, efficiency, and compliance with ITIL best practices.

The purpose and importance of IT SOPs are as follows:

- **Consistency and efficiency**: Ensure consistent execution of tasks across different instances of operations and various departments, giving importance to reducing errors and inefficiencies.

- **Compliance and control**: Support compliance with ISO 20000 requirements, ITL requirements, other quality/security requirements, and internal controls as defined in the processes.

- **Knowledge transfer and training**: Facilitate training and knowledge transfer through proper documentation to new or temporary staff.

- **Audit and accountability**: Provide a documented trail on what/how/when/by whom for audits and accountability.

- **Operational continuity**: Ensure continuity of operations during staff turnover or emergencies by making the operational guidelines available for the team taking over responsibilities.

The requirements for IT SOPs in ISO 20000 can be listed as follows:

- **Alignment with processes and policies**: SOPs should align with IT processes defined in the SMS and support the service management policy. They provide detailed instructions for implementing policies and processes.

- **Documented information**: ISO 20000 requires maintaining documented information to support the effective operation of the SMS. SOPs are part of this documented information, detailing how to perform specific tasks.

- **Control of documents**: SOPs must be controlled documents, ensuring they are:

  o **Approved and authorized**: Before use, to bring in visibility of operations.

  o **Accessible and available**: To all relevant staff based on their roles.

  o **Updated and reviewed**: Regularly updated for accuracy and relevance, reviewed to keep the business objectives.

  o **Retained as evidence**: Of operational consistency and compliance to be made available during reviews and audits.

- **Communication and training**: SOPs must be communicated to relevant personnel based on their roles and responsibilities, and training must be provided as needed to ensure proper execution.

Typical IT SOPs required by ISO 20000 are:

- **Service delivery SOPs**:
  - o Service level management procedures.
  - o Service reporting guidelines.
  - o Capacity and availability management SOPs.
  - o Information security procedures.
- **Change and configuration management SOPs**:
  - o Change request and approval process.
  - o Configuration item identification and control.
- **Incident and problem management SOPs**:
  - o Incident logging and resolution procedures.
  - o Problem identification and root cause analysis.

The key points to remember here are given as follows:

- SOPs provide detailed operational guidance to support the implementation of IT processes.
- They minimize risks, enhance accountability, and support business continuity.
- SOPs contribute to continuous improvement and overall service quality in IT operations.
- SOPs should be regularly reviewed and updated to remain relevant and effective.

Roles and responsibilities

In IT operations, clearly defined roles and responsibilities are essential for ensuring accountability, efficiency, and compliance. They help in streamlining workflows, reducing conflicts, and enhancing communication within IT teams. Roles and responsibilities may vary depending on the specific IT process (e.g., incident management, change management), but there are common roles applicable across various IT functions.

ISO 20000 does not prescribe specific job titles but outlines responsibilities required to meet the standard's requirements. Roles may vary depending on the organization's size, structure, and service management complexity.

ITIL defines various roles to support its service lifecycle stages: service strategy, service design, service transition, service operation, and continual service improvement.

ISO provides guidelines on organizational roles, responsibilities, and authorities. These guidelines require roles, responsibilities, and authorities to be assigned and communicated to ensure:

- management system conforms to ISO requirements.

- processes deliver intended outcomes.

- performance is reported to top management for review and improvement.

- awareness of roles and responsibilities is promoted throughout the organization.

Service strategy roles

These roles focus on defining the overall service strategy, aligning IT with business goals, and managing financials:

- **Business relationship manager**:
  o Acts as the primary liaison between IT and business units.
  o Identifies business needs and ensures IT services meet those needs.
  o Maintains a positive relationship with customers.

- **Service portfolio manager**:
  o Manages the service portfolio, ensuring services align with business requirements.
  o Evaluates new service proposals and decides on service retirements.
  o Monitors service investments and returns.

- **Financial manager**:
  o Manages IT budgets, accounting, and charging for IT services.
  o Ensures cost efficiency and effective financial planning.

- **Demand manager**:
  o Analyzes and predicts demand for IT services.
  o Works with capacity management to ensure services meet demand.

Service design roles

These roles are responsible for designing IT services, including architecture, security, and service continuity:

- **Service design manager**:
  o Oversees the design of new or changed services.
  o Ensures designs meet business requirements and service strategies.

- **Service level manager**:
  - o Defines, negotiates, and monitors SLAs.
  - o Ensures services meet agreed-upon service levels.
- **Availability manager**:
  - o Ensures IT services are available according to SLAs.
  - o Monitors and improves service availability and reliability.
- **Capacity manager**:
  - o Ensures IT infrastructure meets current and future capacity needs.
  - o Balances performance, cost, and capacity.
- **IT service continuity manager**:
  - o Manages risks to IT services to ensure continuity during disasters.
  - o Plans and tests disaster recovery strategies.
- **Information security manager**:
  - o Protects confidentiality, integrity, and availability of data.
  - o Ensures compliance with security policies and standards.
- **Supplier manager**:
  - o Manages supplier relationships and performance.
  - o Negotiates and maintains contracts and agreements.

Service transition roles

These roles focus on managing change, release, and deployment to minimize disruption to live services:

- **Service transition manager**:
  - o Ensures smooth transition of new or changed services into operations.
  - o Coordinates activities across transition processes.
- **Change manager**:
  - o Controls the lifecycle of changes to minimize risk and impact.
  - o Chairs CAB meetings for change approvals.

- **Release and deployment manager**:
  - o   Plans, schedules, and controls releases and deployments.
  - o   Ensures successful deployment of new or updated services.

- **Configuration manager**:
  - o   Manages and maintains the CMDB.
  - o   Ensures the integrity and accuracy of **configuration items** (**CIs**).

- **Knowledge manager:**
  - o   Maintains the **knowledge management system** (**KMS**).
  - o   Ensures accurate and accessible knowledge for decision-making.

Service operation roles

These roles ensure day-to-day operational stability, incident management, and service fulfillment:

- **Service desk**:
  - o   Single point of contact for users for incidents, service requests, and queries.
  - o   Logs, categorizes, prioritizes, and resolves or escalates tickets.

- **Incident manager**:
  - o   Manages the incident lifecycle to restore service quickly.
  - o   Ensures incidents are resolved within SLAs.

- **Problem manager**:
  - o   Identifies and manages the root causes of incidents.
  - o   Minimizes the impact of incidents by implementing permanent fixes.

- **Technical manager**:
  - o   Oversees technical resources and infrastructure management.
  - o   Ensures availability, performance, and recovery of IT systems.

- **Application manager**:
  - o   Manages and supports business applications throughout their lifecycle.
  - o   Works with development teams for application changes and improvements.

- **IT operations manager**:
  - o Oversees IT operations, including batch jobs, backups, and monitoring.
  - o Ensures day-to-day operational stability and efficiency.

Continual service improvement roles

These roles focus on assessing and improving IT services and processes:

- **CSI manager**:
  - o Identifies and manages improvement opportunities.
  - o Monitors and reports on performance metrics and KPIs.
- **Process owner**:
  - o Accountable for a specific process's effectiveness and efficiency.
  - o Ensures process documentation, training, and continuous improvement.

RACI matrix

A **Responsible, Accountable, Consulted, Informed (RACI)** matrix helps clarify roles and responsibilities. RACI Matrix is a responsibility assignment tool used in project management, process design, and operations management to clearly define roles and responsibilities. It helps identify who is Responsible, Accountable, Consulted, Informed for each task or activity within a project or process.

RACI calls out the responsibilities for the roles given as follows:

- **Responsible**:
  - o The person(s) who actually perform the work or task.
  - o They are responsible for getting the job done.
  - o There can be multiple Responsible parties for a task.
- **Accountable**:
  - o The person who owns the task or decision and is ultimately answerable for its completion.
  - o This role has the authority to approve the work.
  - o There must be only one Accountable person for each task to avoid confusion.
- **Consulted**:
  - o Person(s) whose input, feedback, or expertise is required before the task is completed.

- o   They provide guidance and advice.
- o   This role is typically two-way communication.
- **Informed**:
  - o   Person(s) who are kept up to date on progress, decisions, or outcomes.
  - o   They do not contribute directly, but need to be aware.
  - o   This role is typically one-way communication.

The benefits of using a RACI matrix in IT teams are as follows:

- **Clarifies responsibilities**: Prevents role conflicts and duplication of effort.
- **Improves accountability**: Ensures tasks are completed as designated.
- **Enhances communication**: Establishes clear reporting lines and escalation paths.
- **Streamlines decision-making**: Identifies who is responsible for approvals and decisions.
- **Facilitates collaboration**: Encourages cross-functional teamwork and knowledge sharing.

The following table is an example of RACI for a typical IT team:

Tasks	IT manager	System admin	Network engineer	Helpdesk tech	Security analyst	DBA	App support
IT strategy and planning	A	C	C	I	C	C	C
System deployment and configuration	I	R/A	C	I	I	C	C
Network design and maintenance	I	C	R/A	I	C	I	I
User support and incident handling	I	C	C	R/A	C	I	C
Security monitoring and incident response	I	C	C	I	R/A	I	I
Patch management and updates	I	R	C	I	C	C	C
Data backup and recovery	I	R	C	I	I	A	C
Database administration	I	C	I	I	C	R/A	I

Tasks	IT manager	System admin	Network engineer	Helpdesk tech	Security analyst	DBA	App support
Application maintenance and support	I	C	C	C	I	C	R/A
Change management	A	R	C	I	C	C	C
Access control and user permissions	I	R	C	I	R/A	I	C
Incident escalation and resolution	I	R	C	C	C	C	R
IT audits and compliance reporting	A	C	C	I	R	C	C

Table 5.2: RACI matrix

The key points to note from the RACI matrix are as follows:

- **A (Accountable)**: Only one role should be marked accountable per task to avoid confusion.

- **R (Responsible)**: Multiple roles can be responsible for performing tasks. SOPs will provide guidance on what each role has to do.

- **C (Consulted)**: Input is required from these roles for decision-making. This is generally the management team and the finance or legal team.

- **I (Informed)**: These roles are kept updated about the status of tasks, but are not actively involved in operations to complete the tasks.

A RACI matrix can be defined easily if the organization has documented clear roles and responsibilities guided by the policies and SOPs. Capturing the RACI matrix helps in achieving the following:

- Clear roles and responsibilities enhance accountability, efficiency, and communication.

- This helps in minimizing role conflicts and ensuring proper escalation and decision-making.

- RACI matrices provide clarity on stakeholder involvement in each process activity.

- Roles should be regularly reviewed and updated as part of continuous improvement.

Eliminating conflict of interest

The international standards for ITSM assure that IT services are delivered effectively, efficiently, and consistently. One of the key aspects of maintaining service integrity and trust is the elimination of conflicts of interest.

A conflict of interest will be created when personal interests or relationships could improperly influence or appear to influence professional judgment or decisions related to IT services. In IT service management, conflicts of interest can impact objectivity, impartiality, and service quality, leading to biased decisions, compromised security, or unfair service practices.

Although the ISO 20000 standard does not explicitly mention *Conflict of Interest*, it implies the need to eliminate it through several clauses, including leadership and governance, planning, support (people and competence), and operation.

Conflict of interest in ITSM occurs in the following functions:

- **Vendor selection**: An employee selecting a vendor who is a family member or close friend.

- **Incident resolution**: An incident manager favors specific users or departments for faster incident resolution.

- **Change approval**: Approving a change that benefits the approver's interests or investments.

- **Access control**: Granting privileged access to individuals without proper justification or review.

Consequences of conflict of interest

As we learned in the previous section, conflicts of interest arise when an individual's interests and their professional duties and responsibilities interfere with each other. These conflicts can compromise one's ability to make impartial decisions and ultimately jeopardize the integrity and credibility of their organization.

Conflicts of interest in IT operations can have several significant consequences:

- **Compromised objectivity**: When personal interests interfere with professional duties, it can lead to biased decision-making, affecting the fairness and integrity of operations.

- **Erosion of trust**: Even the perception of a conflict of interest can damage trust within an organization, leading to a lack of confidence in leadership and processes.

- **Legal and ethical issues**: Conflicts of interest can result in legal repercussions and ethical violations, potentially leading to fines, sanctions, or damage to the organization's reputation.

- **Reduced efficiency**: When conflicts of interest are present, they can create inefficiencies and distractions, diverting attention from the organization's primary goals and objectives.

Addressing conflicts of interest proactively by fostering a culture of transparency and ethical behavior can help mitigate these negative outcomes.

Best practices for eliminating conflict of interest

Eliminating conflicts of interest is challenging, but implementing best practices can help minimize their occurrence and impact. Organizations can adopt practices for helping in proactively managing and mitigating conflicts of interest, thereby safeguarding their integrity, reputation, and long-term success.

The best practices for eliminating conflict of interest in ITSM are:

- **Policy and governance**: Develop and communicate a clear policy defining conflicts of interest and actions to avoid or resolve it, including guidelines for disclosure, review, and mitigation of potential conflicts.

- **Code of conduct**: Establish a code of conduct promoting ethical behavior and transparency, including consequences for non-compliance.

- **Segregation of duties (SoD)**: Separate conflicting roles, such as incident resolution and incident approval, change request submission and change approval, vendor selection and vendor management, etc.

- **Independent review and approval**: Implement independent reviews for key decisions, such as procurement, change management, and incident closures.

- **Disclosure mechanisms**: Require employees to disclose any personal relationships or financial interests that could lead to conflicts of interest, maintain a conflict of interest register to document disclosures and actions taken.

- **Decision-making transparency**: Document and communicate decision-making processes and criteria, especially for supplier selection and change management.

- **Internal audits and reviews**: Regularly audit ITSM processes to identify potential conflicts of interest, review compliance with the conflict of interest policy, and other ethical guidelines.

- **External audits**: Engage independent auditors to provide impartial assessments of ITSM practices.

- **Employee training**: Educate employees on identifying and managing conflicts of interest, conduct regular training on ethical decision-making, and reporting mechanisms.

Controls to mitigate conflict of interest

Controls to mitigate conflict of interest include mechanisms for implementing objective decision criteria, namely, the use of predefined, transparent criteria for incident prioritization, change approvals, and supplier selection, and strengthening approval processes by maintaining transparent records of decisions, justifications, and approvals.

The controls that can be implemented are as follows:

- **Access controls and approvals**: Enforce **role-based access control (RBAC)** to limit access to sensitive information and systems.

- **Rotation and job transfers**: Implement role rotation to reduce familiarity and bias.

- **Supplier and vendor management processes**: Conduct impartial vendor evaluations and audits.

We have seen previously that conflicts of interest in IT operations can have serious repercussions on the integrity, efficiency, and trust within an organization. They can lead to biased decision-making, damage to reputation, and potential legal consequences. By proactively identifying and managing these conflicts through transparent policies, ethical behavior, and continuous monitoring, organizations can mitigate the risks and maintain a fair and productive work environment. Ultimately, fostering a culture of integrity and accountability is key to ensuring the long-term success of IT operations.

Conclusion

In any IT organization, the establishment and effective implementation of IT policies, processes, and SOPs are essential for ensuring smooth, secure, and efficient operations. They serve as the foundation for delivering high-quality IT services, maintaining compliance, and managing risks. The policies, processes, and SOPs form the backbone of an organization's IT governance framework. We have seen in this chapter that to maintain robust ITSMS, IT organizations need to establish clear and comprehensive IT policies, well-structured IT processes, and detailed SOPs.

Well-defined IT policies, such as an information security policy, change management policy, and acceptable use policy, are essential for protecting the organization's IT infrastructure and ensuring alignment with organizational goals. Clearly defined IT processes (such as incident management, problem management, and service level management) ensure that tasks are executed in an organized manner, mitigating the risk of errors and improving overall service quality. SOPs (such as those for system backups, patch management, or user access control) are crucial for ensuring tasks are executed correctly, efficiently, and consistently, especially in complex or highly regulated environments.

The success of IT operations depends on the effective integration of these components, driving both operational excellence and risk management. By formalizing and continuously improving these aspects, IT organizations can create an environment of accountability, security, and efficiency, ultimately ensuring value delivery and stakeholder satisfaction.

By establishing well-defined boundaries, clear R and R structures, and robust mechanisms for managing different levels of access, organizations can mitigate risks, ensure operational continuity, and build a secure and resilient IT environment. This holistic approach empowers enterprises to navigate the complexities of today's interconnected world confidently.

In the next chapter, we will look at how operating controls will be defined, considering the potential risks that may create an impact on the day-to-day operations. We will learn that the relationship between security controls and risk impact is central to a typical risk management framework. Security controls are measures and safeguards put in place to protect information systems and data from threats, vulnerabilities, and other potential risks.

Join our Discord space

Join our Discord workspace for latest updates, offers, tech happenings around the world, new releases, and sessions with the authors:

https://discord.bpbonline.com

CHAPTER 6
Risk Management and Impact Analysis

Introduction

This chapter introduces the risk management process that has to be the starting point in defining the processes, policies, and the organization structure itself. When we speak of risk management, the process involves identifying risks and conducting risk assessment. Assessing a risk can be done through an impact analysis process, where the risk will be simulated, and the after effects will be documented as the impact of the risk.

Risk is often viewed as something to avoid due to its connection with threats. However, risk is also linked to opportunity, and failing to seize opportunities can be a risk in itself. For instance, missing out on underserved markets or unmet customer demand can pose significant opportunity costs. Implementing strategic changes often involves updating the product and service portfolio, which requires careful risk management to navigate the uncertainties and opportunities that come with such changes.

An organization's portfolio of products and services can be aligned with an underlying portfolio of risks that need to be managed. When service management is effective, the products and services listed in the service catalogue and pipeline represent opportunities to create and capture value for customers, the organization, and other stakeholders. Conversely, if not managed well, these products and services can become threats, as they carry risks related to demand fluctuations, resource commitments, and operational costs.

By embedding risk management at the beginning of the IT process definition, organizations can create a solid foundation that enhances security, compliance, and overall efficiency. This proactive approach not only mitigates potential risks but also supports the long-term success and stability of the organization.

Structure

This chapter covers the following topics:

- Key concepts
- Risk management
- Risk identification and categorization
- Risk impact analysis
- Risk mitigation processes

Objectives

By the end of this chapter, we will understand that risk management is the process of identifying, assessing, and controlling threats to an organization's capital and earnings. These threats, or risks, could stem from a variety of sources, including financial uncertainties, legal liabilities, strategic management errors, accidents, and natural disasters. It also encompasses the protection of data and the organization's reputation.

We will also learn in this chapter that impact analysis, often referred to as **business impact analysis (BIA)**, is a crucial component of risk management. It involves assessing the effects of disruptions to business operations and identifying critical functions and systems. By the end of this chapter, we will see that effective risk management in IT management is crucial for maintaining the integrity, security, and availability of an organization's IT assets. By proactively addressing IT risks, organizations can ensure smooth operations, protect sensitive data, and achieve long-term success.

Key concepts

Risk management involves making informed decisions by quantitatively evaluating uncertainties and their potential impact on an organization's objectives. It emphasizes using quantitative methods, such as decision trees, influence diagrams, and probabilistic modelling, to evaluate alternatives and determine the most effective risk mitigation strategies.

Risk is an inherent part of every action and decision we make. In today's fast-paced business landscape, organizations encounter various risks, including economic, financial, strategic, and operational challenges. To navigate these uncertainties effectively, a structured approach to identifying, analyzing, and mitigating risks is essential. This is where risk assessment becomes crucial.

Risk is defined as *the effect of uncertainty on objectives* as per ISO 31000. In every organization, uncertainties arise and, as a consequence, there is the potential for events that constitute opportunities for benefit or threats to success. Risk management is popularly accepted as being concerned with both positive and negative aspects of risk. **Information Technology Infrastructure Library** (ITIL) describes IT risks, in a very comprehensive manner, as *potential threats or vulnerabilities that could disrupt the delivery of IT services, impacting business operations, and can include issues like hardware failure, software defects, cyberattacks, data breaches, human error, natural disasters, regulatory non-compliance, and inadequate staffing, all of which need to be identified, assessed, and mitigated through a proactive risk management process.* ISO 20000, defines risk management *as a systematic process where an organization identifies, analyses, and takes action to mitigate potential risks within their* **IT service management** (ITSM) *processes, ensuring continuous monitoring and improvement to minimize disruptions and optimize service delivery.* In short, this is about proactively identifying and addressing potential issues that could impact the quality and reliability of IT services delivered to customers.

As a first step for initiating risk assessment, a baseline *normal* operating state has to be established. Management and the IT team have to collaborate to assess the systems, applications, and services as well as scripts that may run in the IT environment under scope.

This chapter provides an overview of risk assessment, highlighting its significance in business and examining the different types of risks organizations face.

As a first step for addressing the risk management process, we should understand that in today's digital age, organizations heavily rely on their IT infrastructure for daily operations, data management, and communication. This reliance leads to exposure to various risks that can disrupt these systems, leading to significant financial, operational, and reputational damage.

IT risk management involves identifying, assessing, and mitigating these risks to ensure the smooth and secure functioning of IT systems. Risk identification and assessment depend on a scientific impact analysis, where potential risks have to be simulated to understand the impact that may be caused to the operations. Risk management can be defined as follows:

- **Identify risks**: Recognize potential threats and uncertainties that could impact the organization's operations, finances, security, and compliance.

- **Assess and analyze risks**: Evaluate the likelihood and impact of risks using qualitative and quantitative methods.

- **Prioritize risks**: Rank risks based on their potential impact and likelihood, ensuring focus on the most critical threats.

- **Develop risk mitigation strategies**: Implement measures to reduce, transfer, avoid, or accept risks effectively.

- **Enhance decision-making**: Use data-driven and objective risk assessments to guide business strategies and operations.

- **Ensure business continuity**: Minimize disruptions by integrating risk management into **business continuity planning (BCP)**.

- **Comply with regulations and standards**: Align with industry best practices and frameworks such as ISO 27001, ISO 20000, SOC 2, and other regulatory requirements.

- **Improve organizational resilience**: Strengthen the organization's ability to adapt to changes and uncertainties.

- **Monitor and review risks continuously**: Regularly assess the effectiveness of risk controls and update strategies as needed.

- **Foster a risk-aware culture**: Promote risk awareness and accountability across all levels of the organization.

Risk assessment is a vital process that enables businesses to identify and manage potential threats that could disrupt their operations. It involves analyzing risks, assessing their likelihood, and determining the severity of their impact. However, errors in risk assessments can lead to either underestimating or overestimating risks, resulting in ineffective risk management. To facilitate capturing all dimensions and aspects of risk management, we need to document the following, keeping the business objectives in view:

- **Identify critical business functions**: Determine essential operations that must be maintained for business continuity.

- **Assess the consequences of disruptions**: Evaluate financial, operational, reputational, and regulatory impacts of potential incidents.

- **Establish recovery priorities**: Prioritize systems, processes, and services based on their importance to the organization.

- **Determine recovery time objectives (RTO) and recovery point objectives (RPO)**: Define acceptable downtime and data loss limits for key functions.

- **Analyze dependencies and interconnections**: Identify relationships between business processes, technology, and third-party services.

- **Optimize resource allocation**: Ensure effective use of personnel, technology, and infrastructure for rapid recovery.

- **Support BCP**: Provide essential data for developing contingency plans and resilience strategies.

- **Enhance decision-making during crisis**: Equip leadership with data-driven insights to respond effectively to disruptions.

- **Ensure compliance with regulatory requirements**: Align impact analysis with frameworks like ISO 22301 (Business Continuity), ISO 27001, and ISO 20000.

- **Improve long-term organizational resilience**: Strengthen the ability to anticipate, respond to, and recover from disruptions efficiently.

Information systems face various threats, including equipment malfunctions, environmental disruptions, human or technical errors, and intentional attacks that are often sophisticated, strategic, well-coordinated, and well-funded. If successful, these attacks can cause significant or even catastrophic harm to an organization's operations, assets, individuals, other organizations, and even national security. Consequently, it is crucial for organizations to stay vigilant. Senior executives, leaders, and managers must understand their roles and responsibilities and be held accountable for protecting organizational assets and managing risk effectively.

Risk management

All organizations have a legal and ethical responsibility to ensure a standard of diligence that protects employees and representatives from foreseeable risks of harm.

It is crucial for the IT management team to keep track of the probable threats that are commonly included in risk assessment. Depending on the systems, stakeholders, and environments, additional threats may become applicable. This dynamic nature has to be thought through during the risk management phase. Risk management encompasses mainly three processes: risk assessment, risk mitigation, and risk assessment.

To fulfill this duty of diligence, organizations must:

- **Identify and assess risks**: Organizations must demonstrate that they have identified and evaluated all foreseeable risks associated with a specific location or activity. Risk assessments should be regularly reviewed, updated, and documented.

- **Implement mitigation measures**: Reasonable steps must be taken to manage risks effectively. This includes maintaining up-to-date policies, procedures, and mechanisms to address identified risks. Adhering to local community standards helps demonstrate awareness of best practices among other organizations operating in the same area.

- **Develop emergency plans**: Comprehensive response plans, including assistance measures, must be in place to address emergencies involving staff, regardless of location.

- **Ensure informed consent**: Employees must be aware of and acknowledge the risks they may face, as well as the measures in place to manage them. A documented process should confirm their understanding, though such documentation does not serve as a legal waiver in court.

- **Enhance risk awareness**: Staff should receive regular updates, guidance, and training on potential risks and the appropriate responses to them.

- **Provide support and protection**: Organizations must ensure that adequate support systems and insurance coverage are available to assist employees affected by incidents.

NIST definition

There are seven steps in the risk management process as per the **National Institute of Standards and Technology** (**NIST**) and these are essential for the successful execution of the risk management process. These steps are given as follows:

1. **Prepare**: System-level perspective by establishing a context and priorities for managing security and privacy risk.

2. **Categorize**: Clearly categorize the system and the information handled by the system based on an analysis of the impact of any loss.

3. **Select:** Select an initial set of controls for the system based on industry best practices and customize the controls as needed to manage risk.

4. **Implement**: Implement the controls and document processes and SOPs to describe how the controls are operationalized within the system and its environment.

5. **Assess:** Assess the controls to determine if the controls are implemented correctly, functioning as intended, and resulting in the desired outcomes.

6. **Authorize**: Authorize the system controls based on the threshold of risk that is acceptable for the organization.

7. **Monitor**: System and the associated controls are to be monitored on an ongoing basis to assess control effectiveness.

The risk management process involves identifying, describing, and analyzing risks, followed by risk evaluation, treatment, and continuous monitoring. It also includes residual risk reporting, threat and opportunity management, and formal audits, all aligned with the organization's strategic objectives.

Risk management is conducted at every level within an organization. Strategic risk management addresses long-term risks that could affect the organization's ability to achieve its mission. Program and project risk management focuses on risks that might influence medium-term goals and objectives. Operational risk management is concerned with risks impacting short-term goals and objectives. At all levels, risk management is guided by the strategic direction set by the organization's leadership, aligning with the business objectives of the organization.

Risk capacity is determined by the organization's governance. Risk management efforts must ensure that risks are kept within this capacity. If the level of risk within an organization exceeds its risk capacity, it could severely impact the organization's ability to operate. Risk capacity refers to the maximum level of risk that an organization can withstand, typically considering factors such as reputational damage, asset loss, and other critical impacts.

Risk appetite is established by the organization's governance and guides decision-making and risk management activities. While some organizations are willing to take significant risks to achieve substantial gains, others prefer to minimize risks, which can also limit their opportunities. An organization's risk appetite represents the level of risk it is willing to accept. It should always be lower than the organization's risk capacity.

The flow chart provided in *Figure 6.1* outlines the basic steps in the risk management process and how these are related to each other. The figure also shows how the output of the audit can provide feedback to the risk management process for process improvement:

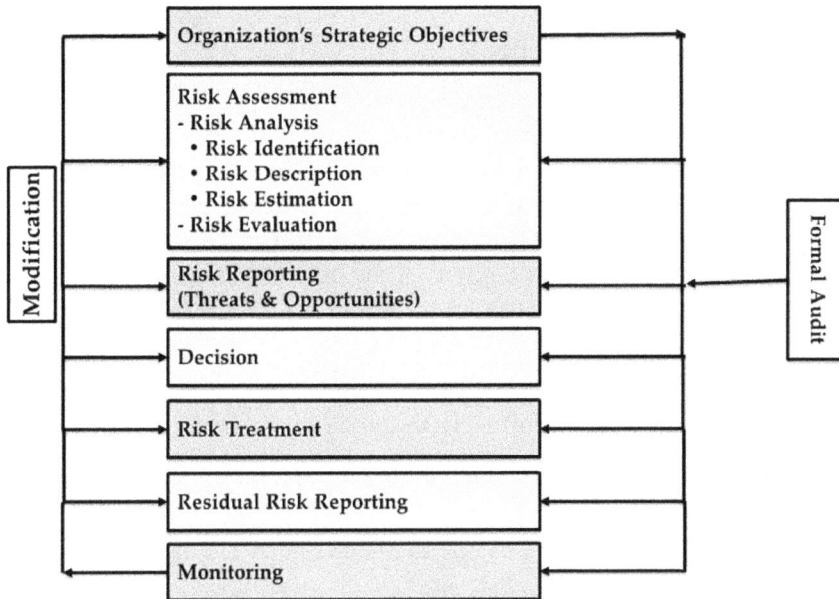

Figure 6.1: *Risk management process*

Risk management methodology

Risk assessment is the initial step in the risk management methodology. Organizations utilize this process to gauge the potential threats and associated risks to an IT system throughout the life cycle. The results of a risk assessment help in identifying appropriate controls for risk treatment, namely, mitigating or eliminating risks. Risk is determined by the probability of a specific threat source exploiting a potential vulnerability and the resulting impact of that adverse event on the organization.

Risk management safeguards and enhances the value of an organization and its stakeholders by supporting the achievement of organizational objectives through the following:

- Establishing a framework that enables consistent and controlled execution of future activities.

- Enhancing decision-making, planning, and prioritization by providing a comprehensive and structured understanding of business activities, uncertainties, and potential opportunities or threats.

- Contributing to more efficient allocation of capital and resources within the organization.

- Reducing volatility in non-critical areas of the business.

- Protecting and strengthening assets and the organization's reputation.

- Developing and nurturing the organization's talent and knowledge base.

- Maximizing operational efficiency.

An organization's risk management policy should clearly outline its approach to risk, its risk appetite, and its overall risk management strategy. It should also define the roles and responsibilities for risk management across the organization. The policy should reference any legal requirements relevant to policy statements, such as those related to health and safety regulations. To support the risk management process, an integrated set of tools and techniques should be used throughout the different stages of the business process.

For the risk management process to be effective, it requires:

- Commitment from the chief executive and executive management.

- Clear assignment of responsibilities within the organization.

- Allocation of adequate resources for training and fostering a culture of risk awareness among all stakeholders.

Risk management involves making informed decisions by quantitatively assessing uncertainties and their potential impact on an organization's objectives. It emphasizes using quantitative methods, such as decision trees, influence diagrams, and probabilistic modeling, to evaluate alternatives and determine the most effective risk mitigation strategies.

Risk identification and categorization

Risk identification is the process of systematically recognizing potential risks that could impact an organization's objectives. It is the first step in the risk management process and involves identifying both threats and opportunities that may influence strategic, operational, financial, or compliance goals.

Risk identification aims to pinpoint an organization's exposure to uncertainty. This necessitates a deep understanding of the organization, the market it operates in, and the legal, social, political, and cultural environment it exists within. Additionally, it involves developing a comprehensive grasp of the organization's strategic and operational objectives, including factors critical to its success and the associated threats and opportunities.

Effective risk identification is crucial for proactive risk management, as it enables organizations to anticipate potential issues, minimize negative impacts, and capitalize on opportunities. It sets the foundation for the next steps in the risk management process, including risk analysis, evaluation, and treatment.

The purpose of risk identification is:

- To create a comprehensive list of risks that could affect the organization.

- To understand the sources and causes of risks.

- To provide a foundation for risk analysis and evaluation.

Risk identification should be conducted methodically to ensure all significant activities within the organization are identified, and the risks arising from these activities are clearly defined. It is important to identify and categorize all related volatilities.

Risk identification techniques are methods used to systematically recognize potential risks that could impact an organization's objectives. These techniques help organizations identify threats and opportunities across strategic, operational, financial, and compliance areas.

Effective risk identification techniques help organizations to proactively address risks before they materialize, enhance decision-making by understanding potential uncertainties, allocate resources efficiently to mitigate significant risks, identify opportunities that can be leveraged for strategic advantage, etc.

Organizations use different risk identification techniques at different stages, and these can be defined as follows:

- **Brainstorming**: Collaborative sessions with stakeholders to identify potential risks.

- **Checklists**: Using predefined lists of common risks for reference.

- **SWOT analysis**: Assessing *strengths, weaknesses, opportunities, and threats*.

- **Interviews with experts**: Consulting with **subject matter experts** (**SMEs**) or experienced team members.

- **Historical data analysis**: Reviewing past incidents and lessons learned.

- **Scenario analysis**: Considering different scenarios to explore potential risks.

- **Root cause analysis**: Identifying underlying causes of potential risks.

- **Workshops and meetings**: Engaging cross-functional teams for a broad perspective.

Risk register

The primary outcome of risk identification is a **risk register**, which has to be maintained as a centralized document for identify, assess, and manage risks within an organization. It serves as a key tool in the risk management process, helping organizations track potential threats and opportunities that could impact their objectives.

A risk register is an integral part of the risk management process in all organizations, which typically includes:

- **Risk description**: Detailed explanation of the risk event.

- **Risk category**: Classification (e.g., strategic, operational, financial).

- **Risk cause**: Root cause or source of the risk.

- **Potential impact**: Possible consequences if the risk occurs.

- **Likelihood**: Estimated probability of occurrence.

- **Risk owner**: Person or team responsible for managing the risk.

Classification of organizational risks

In risk management, risks are generally classified into five main categories: strategic risk, operational risk, financial risk, compliance risk, and reputation risk. Each of these categories has unique characteristics and requires specific mitigation strategies. IT risks encompass a range of potential threats to an organization's IT systems, including strategic, operational, and compliance risks. Let us look at each of them:

- **Strategic risks**: Strategic risk refers to the potential losses a business may face due to poor decision-making, changing market conditions, or failure to adapt to competition. These risks often arise from external factors such as technological advancements, shifts in consumer behavior, or economic downturns.

- **Operational risks**: Issues arising from day-to-day IT operations, such as system outages, network failures, and application errors. Can be caused by human mistakes caused by employees, business process failures or inefficiencies, supply chain disruptions impacting business continuity, leading to system failures or disrupting operations.

- **Financial risks**: Financial risk refers to the potential loss of assets, revenue, or financial stability due to market fluctuations, poor financial decisions, or economic crises. This type of risk affects businesses, investors, and even individuals.

- **Compliance risks**: Compliance risk arises when businesses fail to adhere to legal, regulatory, or industry-specific requirements. Failing to comply with laws can lead to fines, reputational damage, or even a business being wound up.

- **Knowledge management risks**: These relate to the effective management and control of knowledge resources, including their production, protection, and communication. External factors may include unauthorized use or abuse of intellectual property, regional power failures, and competitive technology, while internal factors could involve system malfunctions or the loss of key staff.

- **Reputational risks**: Reputational risk is associated with negative public perception, loss of trust among stakeholders, media and public relations impact, and potential financial losses mainly due to failure of IT systems.

- **Environmental risks**: These include natural disasters or environmental changes that can impact IT infrastructure functioning expectedly.

Sources of risk

Understanding the sources of IT risks can help organizations develop effective strategies to mitigate them and ensure the resilience of their IT systems.

Causes of IT risks are the underlying factors or events that can lead to potential threats affecting an organization's IT systems and operations. Understanding these causes is essential for effective risk management, as it helps organizations proactively identify, assess, and mitigate risks before they materialize.

The causes of IT risks can be diverse and multifaceted. These IT risks mostly arise from the following sources:

- **Cybersecurity threats**: Threats like data breaches, identity theft, and financial fraud resulting from malware attacks, phishing scams, and unauthorized access to sensitive data.

- **Hardware failure**: Issues with physical components like servers, hard drives, or network devices that can lead to data loss or downtime.

- **Software defects**: Bugs or weaknesses in software applications that can be exploited by attackers.

- **Data loss**: Accidental deletion of critical data, data corruption.

- **Natural disasters**: Earthquakes, floods, and power outages impacting IT infrastructure.

- **Human error**: Mistakes by IT staff, incorrect configuration settings.

- **Third-party vendor risks**: Security vulnerabilities within services provided by external vendors.

- **Outdated technology**: Using legacy systems or software that are no longer supported or secure.

- **Lack of employee training**: Insufficient training on IT security and best practices, leading to unintentional security breaches.

- **Regulatory and compliance issues**: Failure to comply with legal or regulatory requirements, resulting in penalties and reputational damage.

Origination of IT risks refers to the sources or triggers that give rise to potential threats affecting an organization's IT systems and operations. Understanding where IT risks originate is crucial for effective risk management, as it helps organizations anticipate vulnerabilities and implement proactive measures to mitigate them. IT risks can originate from internal or external sources and may be intentional or unintentional.

By understanding the origins of IT risks, organizations can build more resilient IT systems and better safeguard their critical assets and data. Understanding and clearly calling out origins of IT risks helps the risk committee proactively identify and address potential vulnerabilities, enhances risk assessment by understanding how risks are interconnected, enables targeted implementation of controls and preventive measures, and improves incident response by identifying the root causes of IT risks.

Best practices

The best practices followed by many organizations in the identification and categorization of risks are as follows:

- Involve stakeholders from all levels of the organization for a comprehensive view. Most of the organizations have a risk committee with representatives from all departments.

- Review and update the risk register regularly to capture emerging risks. The risk committee has to meet periodically to review and revise the risk evaluation. Any change in business objectives should be immediately followed by a comprehensive review of risks.

- Use multiple techniques as explained previously to ensure thorough risk identification.

- Align risk identification with organizational objectives and strategy. Different categories of risks have different impacts, and risk review has to be aligned with business goals.

Risk impact analysis

Understanding an organization's cyber risk profile and vulnerabilities is crucial for evaluating the effectiveness of risk management, controls, standards, and prioritizing actions. To comprehend risks, organizations must identify what is valuable to them, which varies across different entities. This could include data, reputation for uninterrupted operations, physical assets and infrastructure, or revenue dependent on a single asset, such as a website. Identifying and assessing risks necessitates understanding the organizational context.

As technology evolves, so do cyber risks. Organizations should review their cyber risks and controls when introducing new technology, new suppliers, or changing existing technology. If an organization has an established risk management process, it can be beneficial to utilize this existing framework for identifying, assessing, and recording risks, for example, on a risk register.

Effectively managing cyber risks is a crucial aspect of good governance. Threats such as data breaches, extortion, and cyber-related operational disruptions, lead to financial, legal, operational, and reputational consequences for every type of operations. Risk assessment is defined in ISO 31000 as the overall process of risk identification, risk analysis, and risk evaluation.

Risk simulation is a quantitative method used to model the uncertainty of risks and their potential impact on objectives. This provides a probabilistic view of potential impacts, helping organizations understand the likelihood of different risk scenarios and make informed decisions. Risk impact analysis is the process of evaluating the consequences of identified risks on an organization's objectives, and this is done based on the outcome of risk simulation, which provides the likelihood of risks materializing. Risk impact analysis helps in prioritizing risks based on their severity and helps in determining the most effective risk mitigation strategies.

The resources needed to implement the organization's risk management policy must be clearly defined at every management level and within each business unit. Those involved in risk management should have their roles in coordinating risk management policy and strategy explicitly outlined, in addition to their other operational responsibilities. The same level of clarity is required for individuals responsible for auditing and reviewing internal controls and facilitating the risk management process. Risk management should be ingrained within the organization through strategy and budget processes. It should be emphasized in induction programs, training and development sessions, and integrated into operational processes, such as product and service development projects.

Risk simulation enhances risk impact analysis by providing a more detailed and probabilistic view of potential impacts, rather than relying on static estimates. By using risk simulations, organizations can move from qualitative impact assessments to more data-driven, quantitative evaluations. Risk simulation exercise helps assess the uncertainty and variability of impacts, giving a comprehensive understanding of risk exposure.

The two terms, risk simulation and risk impact analysis, can be understood through analyzing the different aspects of both these processes. The aspects that we need to look at are the focus of both these processes, the approach to be taken, the outcome of each of these, and the purpose of both. Refer to the following table:

Aspect	Risk simulation	Risk impact analysis
Focus	Examines the probability distribution of outcomes	Assesses the severity of consequences
Approach	Quantitative (probabilistic modelling)	Qualitative or quantitative evaluation
Outcome	Range of possible scenarios and their likelihoods	Prioritization of risks by impact severity
Purpose	To explore uncertainty and variability	To understand the magnitude of impact

Table 6.1: Comparison of risk simulation and risk impact analysis

Risk simulation provides a dynamic, probabilistic view of risks, while risk impact analysis focuses on scientifically evaluating the severity of consequences. These two techniques have to be used together, and they offer a powerful approach to understanding risks and making data-driven decisions.

To estimate the likelihood of an adverse event, threats to an IT system must be evaluated in conjunction with its vulnerabilities and the existing controls. Impact refers to the degree of harm that could result from a threat exploiting a vulnerability. The level of impact is influenced by the potential impacts to the mission of the organization. It assigns a relative value to the IT assets and resources affected, such as the criticality and sensitivity of IT system components and data.

Risk impact analysis should include three things:

- **Mission**: Mission of the complete system, including the processes implemented by the system.

- **Criticality**: Importance of the availability of the system, determined by its value and the value of the data processed by this system to the organization.

- **Sensitivity:** Nature of the system and the data processed in the system.

Assessing the likelihood and impact of risks in decision-making involves the following steps:

1. **Collect data**: Gather relevant data from various sources, such as historical information, expert opinions, industry benchmarks, and external factors that may influence the likelihood and impact of risks.

2. **Represent probability or frequency**: Fit the collected data to appropriate probability distributions based on the nature of the risks. For instance, use the Bernoulli distribution for binary events, the Poisson distribution for the number of occurrences within a fixed time frame, or the Weibull distribution for time-related events with varying failure rates.

3. **Model impact as distributions**: Express the potential impact of risks as distributions, capturing the range of possible outcomes and their associated probabilities. Fit the data to a distribution or use distributions like PERT to represent expert forecasts.

4. **Perform quantitative analysis**: Apply suitable quantitative methods, statistical analysis, or decision trees, to estimate the likelihood and potential impact of the identified risks. This enables organizations to prioritize risks based on their potential effect on objectives and allocate resources effectively.

ISO 20000 provides a well-defined standard outlining how an organization should function amidst uncertainties and risks. It recognizes risks as foundational elements of IT service management, significantly impacting daily operations. Risk management under ISO 20000 is essential for a service-oriented IT organization to assess risks and address potential incidents before they affect business operations.

Risk register

Risk register, as explained in the earlier section, forms a crucial aspect of this detailed requirement of managing risk and documenting the complete details of risk management. It is designed to consolidate the identification and assessment of uncertainties, risks, and opportunities. A risk register makes it easier for the IT team and the rest of the organization to record, track, manage, and evaluate the risks. This documentation is a requirement for ISO 20000 compliance and encapsulates large amounts of data for in-depth assessment and evaluation.

For each risk, the register has a set of general information, such as:

- A detailed description of the risk.
- Specification of risk type (operational, strategic, compliance, etc.).
- Likelihood of occurrence of risk.
- Severity of the effect of risk.
- Risk value, product of likelihood and severity.
- Measures taken to prevent, mitigate, or transfer the risk.
- Risk owner, individual or department responsible for managing the risk.
- Current status of the risk.
- Additional controls required to treat risk to bring it under the risk appetite value.
- Timelines for implementing additional controls.

Risk assessment reports can vary in detail and complexity, ranging from intricate and comprehensive to straightforward outlines of risks and suggested controls. The format and content of the report should be tailored to the audience's level of expertise in information security and what will best highlight potential risks. The primary goal of a risk assessment is to identify and document organizational risks and devise a strategy to address them, ensuring that the organization is well-prepared to manage potential threats. Refer to the following figure:

Risk ID	Risk description	Risk category	Risk cause	Potential impact	Impact (1-3)	Likelihood (1-3)	Risk level (Impact * likelihood)	Risk owner	Risk treatment controls	Balance residual risk
R-001	Data breach due to phishing attack	Cybersecurity	Human error, social engineering	Data theft, financial loss, Reputational damage	3 - High	3 - High	9 - Critical	IT Security Manager	Implement MFA, Employee phishing awareness training	Medium
R-002	System outage due to hardware failure	Operational	Aging hardware, Lack of maintenance	Operational disruption, Loss of productivity	3 - High	2 - Medium	6 - High	IT Infrastructure Lead	Implement redundant hardware, Regular maintenance and monitoring	Low
R-003	Non-compliance with new data privacy regulations	Compliance	Regulatory changes, Lack of awareness	Legal penalties, Reputational damage	3 - High	2 - Medium	6 - High	Compliance Officer	Update data handling policies, Conduct staff training on new regulation	Medium
R-004	Supply chain disruption impacting IT services	Operational	Third-party dependency, Vendor issues	Service delays, financial impact	3 - High	1 - Low	3 - Medium	Procurement Manager	Diversify suppliers, Establish backup agreements	Low
R-005	Ransomware attack on critical systems	Cybersecurity	Malicious external threat	Data loss, Operational downtime, financial loss	3 - High	3 - High	9 - Critical	CISO (Chief Information Security Officer)	Implement advanced threat detection, Regular backups, Incident response plan	Medium

Figure 6.2: Sample risk register

Risks impacting the availability of assets, operation of enterprises can be identified and addressed with BCP and **disaster recovery planning** (**DRP**). These are critical components of risk assessment that help organizations prepare for, respond to, and recover from disruptive events. Both strategies aim to minimize the impact of incidents on business operations, ensuring organizational resilience and continuity of services.

BCP is the process of creating systems and procedures that enable an organization to continue operating during and after a disruption. It focuses on maintaining essential business functions regardless of the nature of the incident. DRP focuses specifically on the recovery of IT systems, data, and infrastructure after a disaster or significant disruption. It aims to restore technology systems as quickly as possible to minimize downtime and data loss. We will learn more about BCP and DRP in *Chapter 10, Business Continuity and Disaster Recovery Planning.*

Risk mitigation processes

Risk mitigation or treatment is the process of choosing and implementing actions to manage risks. It primarily involves risk control or mitigation, but also includes other strategies such as risk avoidance, risk transfer (e.g., outsourcing to third-party suppliers), risk acceptance (choosing to tolerate the risk without further action), etc.

Any system of risk treatment should provide the following characteristics at a minimum:

- Effective and efficient operation of the organization.
- Effective internal controls.
- Compliance with laws and regulations.

The risk analysis process enhances the organization's operational effectiveness and efficiency by pinpointing risks that demand management's attention. This analysis is taken as the input to the risk mitigation process, by the creation of controls that will reduce the impact or likelihood of risks, thereby reducing the risk value. The risk committee must then work on prioritizing risk control actions based on their potential benefits to the organization and recommend the mitigation actions to management. The effectiveness of internal controls is measured by the extent to which the proposed measures can eliminate or reduce the identified risks. The cost-effectiveness of internal controls is evaluated by comparing the implementation cost against the anticipated risk reduction benefits.

Risk mitigation in the ITIL standard involves identifying, assessing, and implementing measures to reduce the impact and likelihood of risks affecting IT services. In ITIL, risk mitigation is integrated across various service management practices to ensure continuity, security, and reliability of IT services.

Risk mitigation is a continuous process in ITIL that ensures IT services are resilient, secure, and aligned with business needs. By integrating risk management into each phase of the ITIL lifecycle, organizations can proactively address potential threats, minimize their impact, and maintain high service availability and security.

When proposing controls, it is essential to evaluate the potential economic impact of taking no action versus the cost of implementing the proposed measures. This analysis often requires detailed information and assumptions that may not be readily available.

The first step is to determine the cost of implementation. This should be calculated as accurately as possible since it serves as the baseline for evaluating cost-effectiveness. Next, an estimate of the potential loss if no action is taken must be made. By comparing these two figures, management can make an informed decision on whether to proceed with the risk control measures.

Compliance with laws and regulations is mandatory, not optional. Organizations must be aware of the relevant legal requirements and implement appropriate controls to ensure compliance. In rare cases, some flexibility may be considered if the cost of reducing a risk is completely disproportionate to the risk itself.

Risk treatment should address both technical and human risks, considering threats from both external attacks and internal errors or malicious actions. The control framework should incorporate preventative, detective, and corrective controls to manage risks effectively. Additionally, risk treatment involves mitigation and recovery strategies.

It is not feasible to list all potential controls, but some key strategies include:

- **Security and privacy by design**: Integrating cybersecurity considerations early in the planning and development stages of technical changes and product development to safeguard the security and privacy requirements of the data. This proactive approach reduces the need for last-minute risk acceptance or significant redesigns.

- **Threat intelligence**: Gaining a comprehensive understanding of the threat landscape to anticipate and prepare for potential risks.

- **Zero trust security**: Implementing **roles-based access controls** (**RBAC**) to ensure access to information and data is granted only to those who need it.

- **Cybersecurity policies**: Establishing policies as part of the cybersecurity program, including guidelines for data classification, technology usage, and asset management and maintenance.

- **Access controls**: Managing access to sensitive information by promptly revoking access rights when a user's role changes or they leave the organization.

- **Background checks**: In compliance with legal requirements, conducting background checks and obtaining clearances for employees and contractors.

- **Human risk controls**: Providing regular training and testing to enhance awareness and resilience against social engineering attacks.

- **External testing**: Conducting security assessments such as penetration testing to evaluate the effectiveness of security measures.

- **Detection controls**: Utilizing systems like **intrusion detection systems (IDS)** to monitor and identify suspicious activities.

- **Risk mitigation and transfer**: Implementing incident response plans to minimize the impact of security incidents. Additionally, organizations can transfer risks through solutions like cyber insurance.

These controls form a comprehensive approach to risk treatment, ensuring organizations are well-prepared to prevent, detect, respond to, and recover from cybersecurity threats.

Effective risk management necessitates a structured reporting and review process to ensure that risks are appropriately identified and assessed, and that suitable controls and responses are in place. Regular audits of policy and standards compliance should be conducted, and performance against standards should be reviewed to identify opportunities for improvement. It is important to remember that organizations are dynamic and operate within dynamic environments. Consequently, changes within the organization and its operating environment must be identified, and necessary adjustments made to systems.

The monitoring process should provide assurance that there are adequate controls in place for the organization's activities and that procedures are understood and followed.

Additionally, any monitoring and review process should determine whether:

- The measures adopted achieved the intended outcomes.

- The procedures and information gathered for the assessment were appropriate.

- Enhanced knowledge could have led to better decision-making and identified lessons for future risk assessment and management.

The following principles are fundamental to effective risk management:

- **Risk is an inherent part of business**: Organizations must appropriately manage risks, recognizing that not all risks should be avoided. Risk-taking is essential for long-term sustainability. However, risks must be identified, understood, and evaluated against the organization's risk appetite, then managed and monitored accordingly.

- **Consistency in risk management**: Effective risk management requires a holistic approach to maintain consistency throughout the organization. This involves continuous stakeholder consultation and flexibility to accommodate the unique needs of different organizational units or customer scenarios. This tailored approach ensures that risk management procedures are relevant and effective across all areas.

- **Risk management culture and behaviors**: A strong risk management culture is crucial for sustainability and achieving business goals. This culture should be reflected in behaviors and beliefs, including:

  o Recognizing the importance of effective risk management for organizational success.

- o Demonstrating proactive risk management behaviors.

- o Maintaining transparency and clarity in risk management procedures, roles, responsibilities, and accountabilities.

- o Encouraging the reporting of risks, incidents, and opportunities, with appropriate follow-up actions.

- o Designing remuneration structures that support positive behaviors, avoiding penalties for reporting incidents, and discouraging excessive reporting.

- o Promoting learning and growth in risk management maturity by leveraging experiences from within the organization and other entities.

Conclusion

Risk management and impact analysis are vital components of effective business strategy and operational resilience. In today's dynamic and uncertain environment, organizations face a variety of risks, including financial, strategic, operational, and cybersecurity threats. By systematically identifying, assessing, and mitigating these risks, businesses can protect their assets, maintain operational continuity, and enhance decision-making.

Impact analysis complements risk management by evaluating the potential consequences of disruptions, helping organizations prioritize critical functions and develop robust recovery strategies. Together, these practices ensure a proactive approach to risk, enabling organizations to adapt to challenges, safeguard stakeholder interests, and achieve long-term sustainability.

As organizations continue to navigate complex risks, adopting a structured, data-driven approach to risk management and impact analysis will be crucial. This involves continuous monitoring, improvement, and alignment with industry standards such as ISO 27001, ISO 20000, and ITIL processes.

ISO 31000, which is a specific risk management framework, provides a comprehensive framework for risk management that is designed to help organizations identify, assess, and manage risks effectively. It emphasizes that risk management is an integral part of organizational processes, supporting the achievement of strategic and operational objectives.

The standard highlights the importance of a structured and comprehensive approach to risk management that is customizable to an organization's specific needs and context. It promotes a holistic view of risk, considering both threats and opportunities, thus enabling organizations to make informed decisions that enhance value creation and protection.

By following ISO 31000, organizations can enhance resilience, optimize risk-taking, and improve performance, thus achieving a balanced approach to risk and opportunity management. This standard provides a flexible and dynamic framework that supports sustainable growth, stakeholder confidence, and strategic success.

In the upcoming chapters, we will look at how the different IT processes can be defined, keeping risk management as the guiding factor.

Join our Discord space

Join our Discord workspace for latest updates, offers, tech happenings around the world, new releases, and sessions with the authors:

https://discord.bpbonline.com

CHAPTER 7

Procurement, Asset, Capacity, and Cloud Service Management

Introduction

In this chapter, we will be discussing the different processes that are part of the overall IT process or the IT policy for an enterprise.

The IT asset procurement process involves acquiring hardware and software assets required by an organization. We need to look at identifying the needs of an organization and getting the required budget approved by management. Vendor selection is followed next and then initiating purchase from the selected vendor. Once procured, assets need to be installed and configured, and the **standard operating procedures** (**SOPs**) for the assets are to be documented.

The **IT asset management** (**ITAM**) process involves tracking and managing the lifecycle of IT assets. We need to create an inventory for all the assets and the complete lifecycle of migrating the assets to production up to retirement, and maintaining the performance of the assets.

The capacity management process involves ensuring that IT resources are adequate to meet current and future demands. The capacity management is closely coupled with performance management practice, and this encompasses service performance and capacity analysis, and planning.

Cloud service management process is another important IT process that defines how cloud services can be utilized for the IT services provided by the organization to the end customers. As organizations increasingly adopt cloud-based services and technologies, it is crucial to identify and define supporting contract clauses and principles to ensure clear and documented cybersecurity expectations. Cybersecurity clauses and principles are essential service components that should be integrated with foundational contract elements, such as **service level agreements (SLAs)**, task orders, and governing standards.

Structure

This chapter covers the following topics:

- Key concepts
- IT asset procurement process
- Asset management process
- Capacity management process
- Cloud service management process

Objectives

In today's rapidly evolving digital landscape, effective management of IT resources is crucial for organizations striving to maintain operational efficiency, security, and cost-effectiveness. This lesson introduces four fundamental IT processes that form the backbone of a well-organized and secure IT environment.

The IT asset procurement process elaborated the foundation of acquiring the right technology resources to support business needs while ensuring cost efficiency and compliance. The ITAM process helps in maintaining a central, accurate inventory of IT assets. This asset management process ensures optimal utilization, minimizes security risks, and facilitates efficient lifecycle management from acquisition to retirement or disposal. The asset lifecycle includes capacity management process which ensures that IT infrastructure is adequately scaled to meet current and future business demands without compromising on performance or cost-efficiency. Ongoing monitoring of the assets' utilization helps in managing the expected performance of the applications against the available capacity of the assets.

Capacity management is the process of ensuring that an organization's IT infrastructure, applications, and services have the necessary resources to meet current and future business demands efficiently and cost-effectively. It involves monitoring, analyzing, and optimizing the performance and utilization of IT resources to prevent over-provisioning, underutilization, and performance bottlenecks.

Cloud services refer to the delivery of computing resources, such as storage, processing power, and applications, over the internet. By leveraging remote servers hosted on the internet, businesses can access computing resources on-demand, enabling flexibility, scalability, and cost-efficiency, paying only for what they use. Cloud service process involves monitoring, provisioning, securing, and optimizing cloud resources to support dynamic business needs.

By the end of this chapter, the readers will gain a comprehensive understanding of these processes, their significance, and best practices to implement them effectively. By mastering these foundational concepts, IT professionals can contribute to the strategic goals of their organizations while enhancing operational resilience and security.

Key concepts

Understanding the previously mentioned processes can help organizations effectively manage their IT operations, ensuring efficient resource utilization, compliance, and scalability.

ITAM typically covers all software, hardware, networking equipment, cloud services, and client devices. In some instances, it may also include non-IT assets, such as buildings or information, if they have financial value and are necessary for delivering IT services. Asset management is a well-established discipline that involves acquiring, operating, maintaining, and disposing of organizational assets, particularly critical infrastructure.

ITAM is a specialized area of asset management that focuses on managing the lifecycle and total costs of IT equipment and infrastructure. A key component of ITAM is **software asset management** (**SAM**), which deals specifically with the acquisition, development, release, deployment, maintenance, and retirement of software assets. SAM processes ensure effective management, control, and protection of software assets.

The capacity management practice typically focuses on managing service performance and the performance of the underlying resources it relies on, including infrastructure, applications, and third-party services. In many organizations, this practice also extends to overseeing the capacity of supporting personnel. Service performance plays a crucial role in meeting the expectations and requirements of customers and users, greatly influencing their satisfaction and perceived value of the services they use. Analyzing and planning for capacity and performance supports service planning and development, as well as continuous service delivery, assessment, and enhancement.

In **IT service management** (**ITSM**), cloud computing transforms service architecture and redefines the distribution of responsibilities among service consumers, service providers, and their partners. This shift is particularly significant for in-house service providers, such as an organization's internal IT departments. When adopting a cloud computing model, some infrastructure previously managed by the IT team provider is replaced by a partner's cloud service and the need for infrastructure management expertise and resources is reduced or eliminated. New security and compliance risks and requirements emerge, impacting both the IT team, compliance team, and the cloud service partner. On the flip side, cloud services rely on internet connectivity, and hence, network latency can impact the speed of data transfers and application performance.

IT asset procurement process

IT procurement is the organized process of identifying, acquiring, and managing technology resources, including hardware, software, cloud services, and IT infrastructure, to meet business needs. It ensures that IT assets are sourced efficiently, cost-effectively, and in compliance with organizational policies and security standards. It involves careful vendor selection, thorough contract management, and a deep understanding of hardware and software lifecycles. Although the specifics may differ across industries, the primary goals are to maximize efficiency and minimize risk.

The process extends beyond the initial purchase to include maintenance and, eventually, the disposal or repurposing of assets. As assets reach the end of their useful life, the procurement cycle starts again. A properly defined asset procurement process helps with the following:

- Ensure cost-effective and efficient acquisition of IT resources.

- Align IT purchases with business and operational needs.

- Maintain compliance with security, legal, and regulatory requirements.

- Manage vendor relationships and contract negotiations effectively.

- Optimize IT asset lifecycle management from procurement to disposal.

Procurement process

According to ISO 20000, the IT procurement process involves a structured approach to acquiring IT services or goods, including clearly defining requirements, evaluating vendor capabilities, managing contracts, and monitoring performance, all while adhering to the principles of SLAs and ensuring alignment with business needs; essentially focusing on a controlled and documented process to procure IT solutions that meet the organization's service management objectives. The IT procurement process consists of the following steps:

1. **Assessment and planning**:

   a. Identify business requirements for IT assets (hardware, software, services).

   b. Define specifications, budget, and procurement strategy.

   c. Ensure alignment with IT governance and compliance policies.

2. **Vendor selection and evaluation**:

   a. Research and shortlist potential vendors.

   b. Assess vendors based on reliability, security, compliance, and cost.

   c. Conduct **request for proposal (RFP)** or **request for quotation (RFQ)** processes.

3. **Vendor quotation and proposal review**:

   a. Evaluate vendor proposals based on technical and financial criteria.

   b. Compare pricing, SLAs, and contract terms.

   c. Select the most suitable vendor.

4. **Contract negotiation and approval**:

   a. Negotiate terms, pricing, warranties, and SLAs.

   b. Ensure compliance with regulatory and cybersecurity requirements.

   c. Obtain internal approvals before finalizing the contract.

5. **Procurement and acquisition**:

   a. Issue **purchase orders** (**POs**) to selected vendors.

   b. Track order fulfillment, shipping, and delivery schedules.

   c. Ensure received assets match agreed specifications.

6. **Implementation and deployment**:

   a. Install, configure, and integrate acquired IT assets.

   b. Conduct testing and security assessments before deployment.

   c. Provide necessary training for end-users.

7. **Ongoing management and maintenance**:

   a. Monitor IT asset usage, performance, and security compliance.

   b. Manage software licenses, updates, and support agreements.

   c. Track maintenance schedules and renewal timelines.

8. **Disposal and decommissioning**:

   a. Identify obsolete or redundant IT assets.

   b. Ensure secure data erasure before disposal or repurposing.

   c. Comply with environmental and regulatory disposal standards.

Benefits of the procurement process

An effective IT procurement process not only optimizes costs and resources but also ensures that the organization remains compliant, secure, and aligned with its strategic goals. The benefits of an effective IT procurement process are as follows:

- Reduces IT costs through strategic vendor management and negotiations.

- Enhances operational efficiency by acquiring the right technology.

- Ensures compliance with security, legal, and industry regulations.

- Improves IT asset lifecycle management and resource optimization.

- Strengthens vendor relationships and ensures better service quality.

Vendor management process

Vendor management is a critical aspect of IT asset procurement. It involves the process of evaluating, selecting, and overseeing vendors to ensure that they deliver the necessary products and services efficiently and effectively. Along with the aforementioned steps on vendor selection, vendor evaluation, and contract negotiation, vendor onboarding is a very important activity, which comprises integrating vendors into the organization's processes and providing training and orientation for vendors on the organization's policies, procedures, and expectations. Another important process is monitoring the performance of vendors through defining proper **key performance indicators** (**KPIs**) and metrics, and conducting regular performance reviews to assess vendors' adherence to SLAs and contractual obligations.

Vendor relationship management is another important process that leads to fostering a collaborative environment where vendors are treated as partners and work together to achieve common goals. Vendors are to be subjected to continuous risk assessment and monitoring, such as supply chain disruptions and cybersecurity threats. Monitoring compliance in an ongoing manner for compliance with regulatory and contractual requirements is also a very important aspect of managing vendor services.

Effective vendor management in IT asset procurement ensures that the organization acquires high-quality IT assets, maintains strong vendor relationships, and achieves cost efficiency and compliance.

IT procurement process

The IT procurement process plays a critical role in ensuring that IT operations run efficiently, securely, and cost-effectively. By carefully selecting, acquiring, and managing IT assets, organizations can enhance performance, reduce risks, and improve resource utilization.

The key benefits of documenting all steps of IT procurement in IT operations are as follows:

- **Cost optimization and budget control**: Helps in reducing IT expenses by ensuring the best value from vendors, avoiding overspending on unnecessary or redundant technology, leveraging bulk purchasing, vendor discounts, and contract negotiations, etc.

- **Improved IT asset lifecycle management**: Ensures that IT assets are procured, deployed, maintained, and decommissioned efficiently, prevents issues like hardware obsolescence and software non-compliance, and enables predictable refresh cycles for IT infrastructure and devices.

- **Vendor management and strategic partnerships**: Enables better vendor selection through competitive bidding and evaluation, strengthens relationships with trusted technology providers for long-term support, ensures **service level agreements (SLAs)** are met, and improves reliability.

- **Enhanced IT security and compliance**: Ensures that IT assets meet security, data protection, and regulatory requirements (ISO 27001, GDPR, SOC 2, etc.), reduces risks associated with unauthorized or non-compliant software and hardware, and implements vendor risk assessments to minimize supply chain vulnerabilities.

- **Increased IT efficiency and performance**: Ensures that hardware, software, and cloud resources meet performance needs, helps IT teams deploy and scale infrastructure efficiently to support business demands, and reduces downtime by ensuring timely procurement of replacement parts and services.

- **Support for digital transformation and innovation**: Facilitates the adoption of new technologies like AI, cloud computing, and automation, aligns IT investments with business growth and technological advancements, and enables agility and scalability by integrating modern IT solutions.

- **Risk mitigation and business continuity**: Ensures redundancy and backup solutions are in place to prevent operational disruptions, reduces reliance on single-source vendors, mitigates supply chain risks, and supports disaster recovery planning by securing IT assets needed for resilience.

Thus, a well-defined process for procurement of IT assets ensures that IT operations are cost-effective, secure, and aligned with business goals. By optimizing asset acquisition and management, organizations can enhance IT performance, mitigate risks, and drive innovation.

Asset management process

The purpose of the ITAM practice is to plan and manage the full lifecycle of all IT assets, to help the organization maximize value, control costs of operation, manage risks, support decision-making about purchase, re-use, retirement, disposal of assets, and meet regulatory and contractual requirements.

ITAM is a critical component of ISO 20000, focusing on the lifecycle management of IT assets, including hardware, software, cloud services, and infrastructure. It ensures that IT assets are tracked, maintained, and optimized to support service delivery.

The key aspects of ITAM in ISO 20000 are:

- **Asset identification and inventory**: Keeping and maintaining an up-to-date record of all IT assets which are part of the IT operations is the primary task in the ITAM. Assets need to be classified based on type, criticality, and business impact in the inventory.

- **Asset lifecycle management**: Manage IT assets from procurement to disposal is an important part of ITAM. This helps in ensuring that assets are used efficiently and securely throughout their lifecycle.

- **Software asset management**: As part of the SAM process, third-party software licenses are to be tracked, and compliance with vendor agreements has to be verified at all steps. Keeping the SAM inventory helps in preventing unauthorized software installations and license violations.

- **Configuration and relationship management**: Asset dependencies are to be captured in a proper **configuration management database** (**CMDB**). CMDB helps in ensuring accurate mapping of assets to IT services.

- **Cost and risk optimization**: Asset inventory helps in controlling IT expenses by optimizing asset utilization. This also helps in reducing security risks by managing outdated or vulnerable assets.

- **Compliance and regulatory alignment**: ITAM helps ensure IT assets comply with security, legal, and regulatory requirements. It also helps in maintaining audit trails for IT asset transactions and changes.

- **Integration with IT service management** (**ITSM**): ITAM can be aligned with other ITSM processes like incident, problem, and change management processes. A proper ITAM leads to the right business continuity and disaster recovery plans.

Software asset management

SAM is the practice of managing and optimizing the purchase, deployment, maintenance, usage, and disposal of software applications within an organization. It ensures compliance with licensing agreements, minimizes security risks, and reduces unnecessary software costs. SAM is a key component of ITAM and aligns with standards like ISO 19770 (ITAM) and ISO 27001 (information security), along with ISO 20000 and ITIL.

Technology risk management (**TRM**) is the process of identifying, assessing, mitigating, and monitoring risks associated with IT infrastructure, software, cloud services, data, and emerging technologies. It ensures that organizations can maintain security, compliance, business continuity, and operational resilience in the face of evolving cyber threats, system failures, and regulatory requirements. TRM is an area focused on all regulations due to the magnitude of incidents that can be caused by outdated software being used in the enterprise network.

The key objectives of SAM are:

- Ensure compliance with software licensing and vendor agreements.

- Optimize software usage and costs by preventing over-purchasing or underutilization.

- Mitigate security risks from unauthorized or outdated software.

- Improve IT governance by maintaining visibility and control over software assets.

- Support business continuity with well-managed software lifecycle processes.

SAM is a subset of ITAM that specifically deals with software lifecycle management, licensing compliance, and security. ITAM covers a broader scope, including hardware, networking, cloud, and software assets, focusing on overall IT resource efficiency. Both have to work together to ensure cost-effective, secure, and compliant IT operations.

SAM lifecycle can be explained as follows:

- **Software procurement and licensing**:
  - o Evaluate business requirements and select appropriate software solutions.
  - o Ensure compliance with vendor licensing models (perpetual, subscription, **Software as a Service (SaaS)**, etc.).
  - o Maintain a centralized record of licenses, purchase agreements, and usage rights.

- **Software deployment and installation**:
  - o Distribute software securely and efficiently across the organization.
  - o Use automated deployment tools to streamline software installation.
  - o Ensure proper configuration and access control settings are in place.

- **Software usage and monitoring**:
  - o Track software usage and license consumption across all devices.
  - o Identify unused or underutilized software to optimize costs.
  - o Detect unauthorized installations that may pose security risks.

- **Software maintenance and compliance management**:
  - o Ensure timely updates, patches, and renewals to reduce vulnerabilities.
  - o Conduct regular software audits to verify compliance with licensing agreements.
  - o Avoid legal and financial penalties due to non-compliance.

- **Software retirement and decommissioning**:
  - o Identify and remove obsolete, unsupported, or redundant software.
  - o Ensure secure data erasure before disposal or reallocation.
  - o Update asset records to reflect license reallocation or termination.

Benefits of the asset management process

ITAM, including SAM, significantly contributes to the service value chain by being integrated into the design and transition, as well as the obtain/build value chain activities. The benefits of ITAM in ISO 20000 can be captured as follows:

- **Improved IT service delivery**: Ensures IT assets are aligned with service requirements.

- **Cost savings**: Reduces unnecessary expenditures on redundant or underutilized assets.

- **Compliance assurance**: Helps meet licensing, regulatory, and security requirements.

- **Risk mitigation**: Prevents security vulnerabilities from unmanaged or outdated assets.

- **Operational efficiency**: Enhances IT visibility, control, and decision-making processes.

Capacity management process

Capacity management is the process of ensuring that an organization's IT infrastructure, resources, and services can meet current and future business demands efficiently. It focuses on balancing performance, cost, and scalability while preventing underutilization or over-provisioning of IT resources. Capacity management is a core component of ITSM and aligns with frameworks like ITIL, ISO 20000, and ISO 27001. Effective capacity management is proactive, not reactive. The organizations doing well at capacity management make sure that business and service needs are met with a minimum of IT resources.

Capacity management focuses on minimizing the risk of slowdowns or outages while preventing waste from overprovisioning. Effective capacity management processes are essential for delivering the highest quality service at the lowest possible cost. This is initiated with inputs from performance management, which involves data collection, performance monitoring, performance analysis, reporting, and performance tuning. The real advantages are realized when capacity planning is implemented, incorporating predictive analytics and financial analysis to ensure IT is optimized from a business-relevant perspective.

The key objectives of capacity management are as follows:

- Ensure that IT resources meet business demands without performance degradation.

- Optimize resource utilization to prevent over-provisioning and reduce costs.

- Forecast future capacity needs based on business growth and usage trends.

- Improve service performance, reliability, and availability.

- Align IT capacity with budgetary constraints and business goals.

In ITIL, the capacity management lifecycle entails an ongoing process of monitoring, forecasting, and managing an organization's IT resources to ensure they meet current and future business demands. This process includes stages such as defining capacity requirements, capacity planning, performance monitoring, capacity optimization, and reviewing and updating capacity plans.

The key components of the ITIL capacity management lifecycle are as follows:

- **Business capacity management**: Understanding business needs and translating them into IT capacity requirements, forecasting IT resource needs based on business growth and service demand.

- **Service capacity management**: Analyzing the capacity of individual services to ensure they meet SLAs, monitoring application response times, database performance, and service availability to meet the scope of services offered.

- **Component capacity management**: Assessing the capacity of individual IT components, such as servers, network devices, and storage, tracking CPU, memory, storage, and network utilization to prevent resource bottlenecks throughout the service life cycle.

Capacity management lifecycle

The ultimate goal of the capacity management process is to ensure that the right amount of IT capacity is available at the right time to deliver services efficiently. The capacity management lifecycle can be elaborated as follows:

- **Capacity planning**:
  - o Identify business needs and expected workload demands.
  - o Define performance requirements and scalability objectives.
  - o Develop a capacity plan that aligns with business growth and IT strategy.

- **Monitoring and performance analysis**:
  - o Continuously monitor system performance, resource usage, and trends.
  - o Use tools for application performance monitoring and network monitoring.
  - o Identify bottlenecks and potential performance degradation.

- **Capacity modeling and forecasting**:
  - o Analyze historical data and trends to predict future capacity needs.
  - o Use techniques like trend analysis, workload simulation, and predictive analytics.
  - o Plan for scalability in on-premises, cloud, and hybrid environments.

- **Resource optimization and tuning**:
  - o Right-size IT resources to avoid waste and improve efficiency.

- o   Implement load balancing, caching, and tuning techniques.

- o   Ensure that cloud and on-premise resources scale dynamically based on demand.

- **Incident and problem resolution**:

  - o   Address capacity-related issues (e.g., slow performance, downtime, resource contention).

  - o   Implement **root cause analysis (RCA)** for recurring capacity problems.

  - o   Optimize capacity to prevent future incidents.

- **Continuous improvement**:

  - o   Regularly review and update capacity plans.

  - o   Implement automation and AI-driven analytics for proactive capacity management.

  - o   Align capacity goals with business and IT strategy.

Benefits of capacity management

Effective capacity management ensures that IT resources are used efficiently, performance is optimized, and business operations run smoothly. It plays a crucial role in supporting organizational growth, reducing costs, and enhancing service quality. The benefits of capacity management can be captured as follows:

- **Optimized resource utilization**: Ensures that IT resources such as servers, storage, and network bandwidth are used optimally, reducing waste and preventing overprovisioning. By avoiding overprovisioning and underutilization, organizations can save on unnecessary expenditures and reduce operational costs.

- **Improved performance**: By proactively monitoring and managing capacity, organizations can prevent performance bottlenecks, slowdowns, and outages, ensuring smooth and reliable IT operations. Ensures that IT services consistently meet performance expectations and SLAs, leading to higher customer satisfaction.

- **Scalability**: Capacity management allows organizations to scale IT resources up or down based on demand, ensuring that they can handle peak loads and avoid resource shortages. Helps organizations plan for future growth and changes in demand, ensuring that IT infrastructure can support business expansion and new initiatives.

- **Strategic decision-making**: Provides valuable insights into resource usage, performance trends, and capacity needs, enabling informed decision-making. Utilizes predictive analytics to forecast future capacity requirements, helping organizations plan and budget for IT investments strategically.

- **Business continuity**: Reduces the risk of unexpected downtime by ensuring that IT resources are adequately provisioned and monitored. Enhances disaster recovery planning by ensuring that sufficient capacity is available to support critical business functions during and after disruptions.

- **Compliance and governance**: Ensures that IT capacity management processes comply with industry regulations and standards, reducing the risk of non-compliance and associated penalties. Supports IT governance by providing a structured approach to managing IT resources and aligning them with business objectives.

- **Improved stakeholder communication**: Provides clear and transparent communication to stakeholders about capacity planning, resource utilization, and performance. Ensures that IT capacity management aligns with the overall business strategy, fostering collaboration between IT and business units.

- **Enhanced efficiency**: Implements automated capacity management tools and processes, reducing manual efforts and improving efficiency. Promotes continuous improvement by regularly reviewing and updating capacity plans based on performance data and changing business needs.

Capacity management ensures that IT resources are aligned with business demands, preventing performance bottlenecks and resource wastage. A strong capacity management process enables businesses to scale seamlessly, manage costs effectively, and support strategic growth. Together, asset management and capacity management play a vital role in maintaining a well-optimized IT infrastructure, supporting business continuity, and driving innovation.

As elaborated earlier, in ITSM, capacity management ensures that IT services and infrastructure are sufficient to meet current and future business needs without over- or under-provisioning resources. Some real-life examples of capacity management are as follows:

- **Monitoring website traffic**: Capacity management has to be done for predicting the surge in traffic and ensuring that servers, databases, and network bandwidth are scaled appropriately. Failure to manage capacity can lead to website crashes or slow performance, causing customer dissatisfaction.

- **Cloud resource scaling**: During product launches or marketing campaigns, organizations need to temporarily increase virtual machines or storage capacity to handle spikes in demand. ITSM capacity management ensures seamless scaling without interrupting service delivery.

- **Handling email servers**: Capacity management ensures email servers have adequate storage, processing power, and network capacity to accommodate peak usage periods.

- **Data centers**: Data centers process, store, and manage vast amounts of information. Capacity management ensures they operate efficiently by forecasting the hardware and software requirements, cooling systems, and energy usage to meet organizational demands without waste.

Continuous monitoring is essential in capacity management because it ensures that IT systems and resources remain optimized, responsive, and cost-effective while adapting to changing demands. By monitoring resource usage in real time, organizations can detect potential slowdowns or capacity limitations before they cause system failures. Capacity-related issues, like slow applications or server crashes, directly impact users. Continuous monitoring ensures services remain smooth, fast, and reliable, leading to higher customer satisfaction.

Cloud service management process

NIST defines cloud computing as: *Cloud computing is a model for enabling ubiquitous, convenient, on-demand network access to a shared pool of configurable computing resources (e.g., networks, servers, storage, applications, and services) that can be rapidly provisioned and released with minimal management effort or service provider interaction.*

ISO defines cloud computing as: *Paradigm for enabling network access to a scalable and elastic pool of shareable physical or virtual resources with self-service provisioning and administration on-demand.* A cloud environment can encompass a wide range of computing resources, from fundamental infrastructure components such as processors, memory, and networks to advanced software resources like databases and applications.

Characteristics of cloud computing

Cloud computing can be defined through six essential characteristics that differentiate it from traditional hosting services. Understanding these characteristics is crucial for maximizing cloud computing benefits and strategically planning cloud adoption:

- **Resource pooling**: Cloud providers consolidate physical and virtual resources to serve multiple **cloud service customers** (**CSCs**) using a multi-tenant model. Resources such as storage, processors, memory, and network bandwidth are dynamically allocated and reassigned based on demand.

- **Broad network access**: Cloud services are accessible over a network via web browsers or specialized applications, enabling seamless use across various client platforms, including servers, mobile devices, laptops, IoT devices, and tablets.

- **Rapid elasticity**: Cloud resources can be scaled up or down quickly, often automatically, to meet fluctuating demands. From the CSC's perspective, these capabilities appear unlimited and can be acquired in any quantity at any time.

- **Measured service**: Cloud platforms automatically monitor, control, and optimize resource usage through metering mechanisms tailored to the service type (e.g., storage, bandwidth, or active user accounts). This enables transparent reporting and pay-as-you-go billing, promoting cost efficiency and accountability.

- **On-demand self-service**: CSCs can request and provision cloud resources independently, such as computing power and storage, without requiring manual intervention from the **cloud service provider** (**CSP**).

- **Multi-tenancy**: Unlike resource pooling, multi-tenancy ensures that multiple CSCs share cloud resources securely and efficiently, with proper isolation mechanisms to maintain privacy, security, and performance consistency.

By understanding these essential characteristics, organizations can effectively plan cloud adoption, optimize resource management, and enhance operational efficiency.

Categories of cloud-based services

CSPs are entities that deliver cloud services to consumers or end-users. They offer various components of cloud computing, allowing consumers to purchase a wide range of services. There are several categories of cloud-based services, including:

- **IaaS providers**: In the **infrastructure as a service (IaaS)** model, CSPs offer infrastructure components that would typically exist in an on-premises data center. These components include servers, networking, storage, and the virtualization layer.

- **SaaS providers**: In the SaaS model, vendors provide a wide array of business technologies, such as **human resources management (HRM)** software and **customer relationship management (CRM)** software. The SaaS vendor hosts and delivers these services over the internet.

- **PaaS providers**: In the **platform as a service (PaaS)** model, vendors offer cloud infrastructure and services that can perform numerous functions. PaaS is primarily used in software development and provides more services than IaaS. PaaS providers deliver the operating system, middleware, and application stack, along with the underlying infrastructure.

Cloud computing offers various deployment models to meet different business needs. The following table gives an overview of the three primary types: public cloud, private cloud, and hybrid cloud:

Factors	Public cloud	Private cloud	Hybrid cloud
Resources	Resources are shared among multiple customers.	Resources are shared with a single organization.	It is a combination of public and private clouds, based on the requirement.
Tenancy	Data from multiple organizations is stored in the public cloud.	Data of a single organization is stored in a private cloud.	Data is stored in the public cloud, and provides security through the public cloud.
Pay model	Pay as per usage.	Have a variety of pricing models depending on services.	It can include a mix of public cloud pay-as-you-go pricing and private cloud fixed pricing. It has other pricing models such as consumption-based, subscription-based, etc.

Factors	Public cloud	Private cloud	Hybrid cloud
Operated by	Third-party service provider.	Specific organization.	It can be a combination of both.
Scalability and flexibility	Has more scalability and flexibility.	It has predictability and consistency.	It has scalability and flexibility by allowing organizations to use a combination of public and private cloud services.
Expensive	Less expensive.	More expensive.	It can be more expensive, but it can also be less expensive, depending on the specific needs and requirements of the organization.
Availability	The general public (over the internet).	Restricted to a specific organization.	It can be a combination of both.

Table 7.1: Comparison of different types of clouds

Cloud service governance

Managing your cloud begins with choosing the right platform. There are various solutions available from cloud management platform vendors, including PaaS and IaaS. These platforms provide a unified dashboard that allows you to view and manage all your workloads and cloud resources. A cloud management platform assists the IT organization in managing cloud services, optimizing resources, virtualizing servers, and ensuring compliance. Many of these platforms are built on open source cloud software, which helps you avoid dependencies on a vendor.

Cloud service management includes all of the service-related functions that are necessary for the management and operation of those services required by or proposed to cloud consumers. When evaluating cloud service models, organizations should focus on several key areas. While these aspects are typically addressed through specific contract clauses with CSP, they serve as essential considerations for categorizing and determining the necessary cloud services. The primary areas of focus include:

- Incident management
- Privileged access management
- Cryptographic assurance
- Data protection and sovereignty
- **Identity and access management (IAM)**
- Secure development, security testing, and validation

- Network and communications security

- Logging, auditing, and continuous monitoring

Each of these areas plays a critical role in ensuring the security, compliance, and operational efficiency of cloud services within an organization. As cloud computing continues to evolve, organizations must adopt a strategic approach to cloud service management, focusing on continuous improvement, adaptability, and integration with overall IT and business objectives. By doing so, businesses can fully leverage the benefits of cloud computing while maintaining control and efficiency.

Risk assessment

Supply chain risks involve threat actors exploiting vulnerabilities within the supply chain to compromise the integrity of system components and achieve their broader objectives. To mitigate these threats, organizations must include supply chain security considerations in their contractual agreements, encompassing points of manufacturing, transportation, integration, and operation. As part of the cloud service procurement process, your organization should conduct supply chain risk assessments and request that CSPs provide information on their supply chain risk management plans, ownership details, subsidiary relationships, and third-party relationships.

Cloud-based IAM models present unique security challenges due to their shared responsibility structure. Managing user accounts, system services, and entities, including their identification, authentication, and permission rights, often requires coordination among multiple stakeholders, such as the customer, CSP, and **identity provider** (**IDP**). To mitigate risks, service contracts should clearly define account management responsibilities for all parties involved. They should also outline measures to prevent unauthorized access, whether from non-privileged or privileged users and systems. The federation of identities and credentials should be limited to agreed trust frameworks to reduce exposure. Additionally, unauthorized third-party access to an organization's cloud instance or data must be strictly controlled.

Contracts should mandate comprehensive access logging with retention periods long enough to support audit and incident response. Furthermore, agreements must specify the CSP's obligations regarding application backdoors and unauthorized system-based access.

Connectors to cloud-based applications

Application programming interfaces (**APIs**) are critical for integrating applications, services, and systems in cloud environments. Proper API management ensures security, performance, scalability, and compliance while enabling seamless connectivity between cloud services, third-party applications, and enterprise systems. Effective API management in the cloud enhances security, scalability, and performance while ensuring compliance with governance policies. Organizations should implement robust security measures, lifecycle management, and monitoring to maintain reliable and secure API ecosystems.

APIs are the backbone of cloud services, enabling seamless integration, automation, and scalability across applications, platforms, and ecosystems. They facilitate interoperability between cloud environments, allowing businesses to leverage hybrid, multi-cloud, and serverless architectures effectively. By implementing robust API management practices, organizations can ensure secure, efficient, and scalable cloud operations. Key aspects such as security enforcement, access control, performance optimization, monitoring, and compliance play a crucial role in maintaining API reliability and protecting cloud-based assets.

With well-designed APIs, businesses can accelerate digital transformation, enhance user experience, and drive innovation, making cloud services more agile and responsive to market demands. However, proper governance, version control, and security policies are essential to mitigate risks and ensure long-term API sustainability in cloud environments.

Technology risk management

TRM is a critical component of **cloud service management** (**CSM**), ensuring that cloud environments remain secure, resilient, and compliant with regulatory standards. As organizations increasingly rely on cloud services, managing technology risks becomes essential to mitigate security threats, operational disruptions, and regulatory non-compliance. TRM plays a vital role in CSM, ensuring that cloud environments are secure, compliant, and resilient against evolving threats. By integrating risk assessment, security controls, compliance frameworks, and incident response strategies, organizations can minimize cloud-related risks while optimizing performance and business continuity.

To effectively manage technology risks in cloud environments, organizations should implement a structured cloud risk management framework that aligns with industry best practices and regulatory standards. A cloud risk assessment is crucial for identifying and mitigating potential risks in cloud service management. Common cloud risk areas are given as follows:

- **Data security risks**: Data leakage, unauthorized access, and lack of encryption.
- **Operational risks**: Downtime, system failures, poor service reliability.
- **Regulatory and compliance risks**: Non-compliance penalties, audit failures.
- **Cyber threats**: Ransomware, phishing, insider threats, misconfigured security settings.
- **Patching of cloud infrastructure and applications**: Vulnerabilities due to outdated infrastructure, operating systems, and legacy applications.

Benefits of cloud services

Integrating cloud services into IT operations brings numerous advantages, enhancing scalability, flexibility, security, and cost-efficiency. Organizations leveraging cloud computing can streamline IT management, improve performance, and support business growth.

The key benefits of cloud services in IT operations are as follows:

- **Scalability and flexibility**: Easily scale resources up or down based on demand to support business growth without significant infrastructure investment and enables rapid deployment of new applications and services.

- **Cost efficiency and optimized IT spending**: Reduces **capital expenditures (CapEx)** on hardware and data centers, operates on an **operational expenditure (OpEx)** model, paying only for what is used (pay-as-you-go). Also minimizes maintenance costs as cloud providers manage infrastructure.

- **Improved business continuity and disaster recovery (BC/DR)**: Ensures data redundancy and backups across multiple locations, provides automated failover mechanisms for high availability, and helps in reducing downtime with quick recovery options.

- **Enhanced security and compliance**: Cloud providers offer robust security controls, including encryption, IAM, and compliance with various regulations, regular security updates and patches, minimizing vulnerabilities, and advanced threat monitoring and incident response services.

- **Increased collaboration and remote work enablement**: Allows employees to access data and applications from anywhere, supports remote and hybrid work models with cloud-based collaboration tools, and enables real-time file sharing, document editing, and video conferencing.

- **Faster innovation and deployment**: Cloud platforms provide access to AI, ML, and automation tools, speeds up application development and deployment using agile methodologies, and enables rapid testing of new technologies and business models.

- **Better IT resource utilization and management**: Frees up IT teams from hardware maintenance and routine system management, improves resource allocation by dynamically adjusting computing power, and provides centralized monitoring and management via cloud dashboards.

Adopting cloud services in IT operations enhances scalability, security, cost-efficiency, and agility while improving collaboration and disaster recovery capabilities. Organizations can focus on innovation, streamline IT management, and respond faster to market demands by leveraging cloud solutions.

Conclusion

In this chapter, we learned that an effective IT procurement is not just about purchasing the right technology; it also involves strategic planning, continuous evaluation, and alignment with business goals. As technology evolves, organizations must remain agile, adapting their procurement strategies to meet emerging needs while maintaining security, compliance, and cost-effectiveness. We saw how effective asset management and capacity management are for organizations to maximize the value of their IT resources while minimizing risks and costs. A well-structured asset management and capacity management process not only improves financial planning but also supports sustainability by ensuring proper asset disposal or repurposing. Cloud service management is essential for organizations to effectively utilize cloud resources while ensuring security, cost-efficiency, and performance optimization. A well-managed cloud environment ensures seamless service delivery, compliance with security standards, and cost control through resource optimization.

In the next chapter, we will be learning about access management policy and acceptable usage policy. Onboarding applications and users to the enterprise network, in the right manner, is the focus of access management. Acceptable usage policy is part of user education and helps users understand the dos and don'ts steps while addressing the role-based responsibilities. The upcoming chapters help us to learn the remaining IT processes, which will help us become efficient IT auditors. *Chapter 20, Review of policy and controls* and *Chapter 21, Conducting interviews, site visits and technical testing,* will elaborate on the checks we have to do as IT auditors to verify the effectiveness of controls in all these IT processes.

Join our Discord space

Join our Discord workspace for latest updates, offers, tech happenings around the world, new releases, and sessions with the authors:

https://discord.bpbonline.com

CHAPTER 8

Access Management and Acceptable Usage Policy

Introduction

In the earlier chapters, we learned about the importance of IT policies, processes and standard operating procedures, how risk management and impact analysis are done for an enterprise, and the major processes for managing assets, namely, procurement, asset, capacity management and cloud service management processes. In this chapter, we will learn about the importance of access management, which is a crucial aspect of cybersecurity that involves controlling and monitoring who has access to the information and resources within an organization. The process ensures that only authorized individuals can access specific data and systems, safeguarding sensitive information from unauthorized use or breaches. We will also discuss how the users are to be clearly instructed on how they can use the organizational assets and access.

Structure

The chapter covers the following topics:

- Key concepts
- Identity and access management
- User and domain management process
- Acceptable usage policy

Objectives

In this chapter, we will learn how proper access control is the focus of implementing security controls to all organizational assets. Access management ensures that access control policies are well-defined, documented, and enforced in alignment with regulatory and organizational requirements. Acceptable usage policy promotes ethical and professional behavior in the use of IT resources, fostering a culture of accountability and security awareness.

Key concepts

Access management is the process of controlling and monitoring who has access to specific resources, systems, or data within an organization. Its primary goals are to ensure that authorized users have the right access to perform their tasks, and unauthorized access is prevented to protect sensitive information.

Key components of access management can be explained as follows:

- **Identification**: Determining who is requesting access (e.g., username or ID).

- **Authentication**: Verifying the identity of the user (e.g., passwords, biometrics).

- **Authorization**: Granting permissions based on the user's role or need-to-know basis.

- **Accountability**: Logging and monitoring activities to ensure compliance and traceability.

Access management is vital for maintaining security and mitigating risks like data breaches or unauthorized system usage.

The efficient management of the user access lifecycle, including timely provisioning, modification, and revocation of access, is crucial to maintaining security and operational efficiency. Additionally, this process focuses on the segregation of duties to minimize fraud risks and prevent conflicts of interest by implementing RBACs. Employee awareness and training programs are essential to ensure that users understand and follow access management best practices. Access management plays a critical role in supporting incident response by enabling swift action in cases of unauthorized access, credential compromise, or privilege escalation.

Along with provisioning access on a *need-to-know* basis, users should be provided with the details on dos and don'ts about how the access has to be utilized. AUP comes in here and is a document that outlines the rules and guidelines for how users can interact with an organization's resources, such as its computers, networks, and data. Its purpose is to ensure proper use to minimize risks.

Key aspects of an AUP can be captured as follows:

- **Permitted uses**: Clearly defines what is allowed (e.g., work-related activities).

- **Prohibited activities**: Specifies what is forbidden (e.g., downloading pirated software, using systems for illegal purposes).

- **Monitoring and enforcement**: States how usage will be tracked and the consequences for violations.

- **Security measures**: Includes guidelines like protecting passwords and avoiding malware.

The objective of access management is to ensure that only authorized users, applications, and systems have appropriate access to resources based on business needs and security principles. It aims to enforce the principle of least privilege by granting only the minimum access required to perform specific tasks, reducing security risks. Strong authentication and authorization mechanisms, such as **multifactor authentication** (**MFA**), are implemented to enhance security and prevent unauthorized access. Continuous monitoring, logging, and auditing of access activities help detect anomalies, unauthorized access attempts, and policy violations.

The objective of ensuring an **acceptable usage policy** (**AUP**) is created for all users, is to define the appropriate and responsible use of an organization's information systems, networks, and resources to ensure security, compliance, and efficiency. It establishes clear guidelines on how different types of users like, employees, contractors, and other authorized users, should access, handle, and protect company data, preventing misuse, unauthorized activities, and security threats. By outlining permissible and prohibited activities, the policy helps mitigate risks such as data breaches, malware infections, and insider threats while ensuring compliance with regulatory and legal requirements.

AUPs are important for protecting organizational integrity and ensuring legal compliance. The AUP also supports business continuity by preventing actions that could disrupt operations, degrade system performance, or compromise sensitive information. In addition, the policy serves as a foundation for enforcing disciplinary actions against violations and ensures that all users understand their responsibilities regarding cybersecurity, data privacy, and acceptable internet, email, and system usage. By aligning with industry standards and organizational objectives, the AUP helps create a secure, efficient, and compliant working environment.

The process ensures that only authorized individuals can access specific data and systems, safeguarding sensitive information from unauthorized use or breaches.

Identity and access management

Identity and access management (**IAM**) is a fundamental component of cybersecurity that ensures the right individuals and systems have appropriate access to the right resources at the right time. It encompasses policies, processes, and technologies designed to manage digital identities, authenticate users, and enforce access controls, minimizing security risks while enabling seamless business operations.

IAM is critical for protecting sensitive data, applications, and IT infrastructure from unauthorized access, insider threats, and cyberattacks. By implementing IAM frameworks, organizations can enforce the principle of least privilege, ensuring users have only the permissions necessary to perform their job functions. Key IAM capabilities include user provisioning and deprovisioning, MFA, **single sign-on (SSO)**, **role-based access control (RBAC)**, and continuous monitoring of access activities.

As per **International Standards Organization (ISO)** standards, policies and controls for managing both physical and logical access to information and related assets should be defined and enforced in accordance with business needs and information security requirements. Access control rules should be established by defining and aligning appropriate access rights and restrictions with relevant entities. Entities can include both human users and technical or logical elements, such as machines, devices, or services. To streamline access control management, specific roles can be assigned to groups of entities.

When defining and implementing access control rules, the following considerations are essential:

- Ensuring alignment between access rights and the classification of information.

- Maintaining consistency between access rights and the security needs of the physical perimeter.

- Taking into account all types of connections in distributed environments to ensure entities are granted access only to information and assets (including networks and services) they are authorized to use.

- Addressing how dynamic access control factors or elements can be incorporated effectively.

Access control is often guided by fundamental principles, with two of the most commonly applied being:

- **Need-to-know**: Access to information is granted only when necessary for an entity to perform its assigned tasks. Different roles and responsibilities require access to different types of information, leading to distinct access profiles.

- **Need-to-use**: Access to IT infrastructure is provided only when a clear and justifiable need exists.

When defining access control rules, careful consideration should be given to:

- Establishing rules based on the principle of least privilege, following the approach of *everything is generally forbidden unless explicitly permitted,* rather than the less secure alternative of *everything is generally permitted unless explicitly forbidden.*

- Access to information, many a time, depends on the data classification and ISO mandates process on information classification and labelling. Rules have to be defined to manage changes in information labels, whether triggered automatically by information processing systems or manually adjusted by users.

- Handling modifications to user permissions, whether initiated by the system automatically or by an administrator.

- Defining and regularly reviewing the approval process to ensure access rights remain appropriate and aligned with security requirements.

IAM definitions in industry standards

In the **Information Technology Infrastructure Library** (**ITIL**), access management is defined as a key process within the operational service phase. As mentioned previously, this focuses on granting authorized users the appropriate level of access to IT services, systems, and data while preventing unauthorized access. Access management process ensures that security policies, defined in **information security management**, are properly enforced and that users only receive access based on business needs and security principles.

The primary goal of access management in ITIL is to protect organizational data and services by ensuring that only authorized individuals can access them. It supports **confidentiality, integrity, and availability** (**CIA**) by enforcing defined access rights based on roles and responsibilities. The process also involves managing user authentication, authorization, monitoring access activities, and ensuring compliance with security policies.

Key activities in ITIL access management are as follows:

- **Requesting access**: Users submit access requests, which are validated against predefined policies.

- **Verification and authorization**: Requests are reviewed based on user roles, business needs, and security principles like least privilege.

- **Provisioning and granting access**: Approved access rights are assigned to users based on established guidelines.

- **Monitoring and logging**: User access is continuously monitored to detect anomalies, unauthorized attempts, or policy violations.

- **Periodic review and revocation**: Access rights are regularly reviewed and updated to ensure that only active and authorized users retain necessary access.

In ISO 20000, access control is not explicitly addressed as a dedicated section but is recognized as a critical component of service management. It is integrated within broader concepts like **service level agreements** (**SLAs**) and security management, ensuring that only authorized individuals can access specific IT services based on their roles and permissions. Managing access to critical systems and data effectively is essential for maintaining both service quality and security.

The access management process has to work closely with identity management, information security management, and incident management processes to ensure security compliance and swift action against unauthorized access attempts. It also integrates with **IT service management** (**ITSM**) functions to handle access-related service requests and issues efficiently. While not explicitly outlined as a standalone clause, access control principles play a key role in enabling effective service management, aligning with best practices for data protection and system security. Service portfolio establishes clear access requirements based on service offerings and user roles. SLAs include access control measures specified within service level agreements with customers. For enhanced security measures, organizations can adopt the specific access control requirements outlined in ISO 27001 to complement ISO 20000.

Implementing access control within ISO 20000 requires explicit steps to address the following:

- **Define access policies**: Develop clear guidelines specifying who can access specific systems and data based on job roles.

- **User identification and authentication**: Use robust mechanisms like passwords, MFA, or biometrics to verify identities.

- **Authorization controls**: Assign access levels based on roles and adhere to the principle of least privilege.

- **Access monitoring and logging**: Regularly track user activity and log access attempts to identify potential security risks.

- **Periodic reviews and updates**: Regularly review and update access permissions to align with evolving business needs.

Physical access management

Physical access controls are also to be implemented to safeguard the organization against unauthorized entry for the safe upkeep of the assets, including IT assets. Security perimeters are to be defined and used to protect areas that contain information and other associated assets as part of the physical security process. IT processes should focus on areas where the physical environment of systems is crucial, processes, including IT processes, ensure compliance with established standards.

Physical security breaches occur when unauthorized individuals gain access and may:

- Steal devices and equipment.

- Plant unauthorized devices, endangering the availability of services.

- Access confidential information in physical form.

A common form of physical security breach is sabotage, which involves intentional acts of destruction or disruption targeting data centre operations. Additionally, the theft of physical servers, hard drives, or other equipment can lead to the compromise and loss of sensitive information.

Physical premises should be monitored using surveillance systems, which may include security personnel, intruder alarms, video monitoring solutions such as **closed-circuit television** (**CCTV**), and physical security information management software. These systems can be managed internally or outsourced to a monitoring service provider. Monitoring systems must be secured against unauthorized access to prevent surveillance data, such as video feeds, from being accessed by unauthorized individuals or the system from being remotely disabled. Any monitoring and recording systems should be implemented in compliance with local laws and regulations, including data protection and **personally identifiable information** (**PII**) protection laws. Special attention should be given to the monitoring of personnel and the retention periods for recorded video.

Importance of identity and access management

User access in IT refers to the process of managing and controlling who within an organization can access specific applications, data, and systems. This ensures that only authorized individuals have the necessary permissions based on their roles and responsibilities, helping to prevent unauthorized access and maintain data security.

Securing access to an organization's resources involves two key components: identity management and access management.

Identity management, the primary function of IAM, is responsible for verifying login attempts against an identity database, which maintains an up-to-date record of individuals authorized to access the organization's systems. This database is continuously updated as employees join or leave, change roles, or take on new projects. It typically contains details such as employee names, job titles, reporting structures, mobile numbers, and personal email addresses. The process of validating a user's login credentials against their stored identity is known as authentication. To enhance security, many organizations implement **multifactor authentication** (**MFA**), also referred to as **two-factor authentication** (**2FA**). MFA adds an extra layer of verification beyond just a username and password. Common methods include sending a one-time code to a registered mobile phone or email address, which must be entered within a specified time frame.

Access management, the second part of IAM, determines which resources a verified user or system can access. Organizations define different levels of access based on factors like job title, seniority, security clearance, and project involvement. Once authentication confirms a user's identity, authorization ensures they are granted the appropriate level of access to resources. **User access management** (**UAM**) defines and enforces access to resources within an organization's IT infrastructure. It manages user permissions and privileges, ensuring that access is restricted based on job roles and security policies.

Components of UAM can be defined as follows:

- **Authentication**: Authentication is the process of verifying the identity of a person or system to confirm they are who or what they claim to be. Authentication technology enforces access control by comparing a user's credentials against a database of authorized users or an authentication server. Authentication enables organizations to keep their networks secure by permitting only authenticated users or processes access to protected resources. This can include personal computers, wireless networks, wireless access points, databases, websites, and other network-based applications and services.

- **Authorization**: Once authentication is complete, the next step is authorization, which grants users permission to perform specific actions. After logging into a system, a user may attempt to execute certain commands. The authorization process verifies whether they have the necessary permissions to do so. In simple terms, authorization enforces access policies by defining what activities, resources, or services a user is allowed to access. Authorization and authentication work together within the **authentication, authorization, and accounting** (**AAA**) model. First, the user is authenticated, and only then are they authorized for specific actions or access levels.

- **Accounting**: Accounting tracks and records the resources a user consumes during a session, such as system usage time and the volume of data sent or received. It logs session details and usage metrics, which are essential for managing authorization controls, billing, trend analysis, resource utilization, and capacity planning.

- **Provisioning**: Assigns appropriate access rights when a new employee joins the organization. User provisioning involves the process of establishing, managing, updating, and removing user accounts and their access across various applications and systems simultaneously, whether they are on-premises, cloud-based, or a hybrid of both.

- **Deprovisioning**: Revokes access when an employee leaves the company to prevent unauthorized entry. This involves the removal of privileges or access from an account triggered by events such as an internal transfer to another department or the departure of an employee from the organization. Access to critical files and applications is either deactivated or entirely deleted.

The primary goal of IAM systems is to ensure that authentication and authorization are executed securely for every access attempt. IAM plays a crucial role in cybersecurity by helping IT departments balance security and accessibility. It ensures that sensitive data and systems remain protected while allowing authorized employees and devices to access the resources they need.

Without a tool based IAM system, organizations must manually track every entity with access to their systems, along with how and when that access is used. This makes auditing a complex, time-consuming, and labour-intensive task. IAM solutions automate these processes, significantly streamlining auditing and reporting while ensuring organizations can easily demonstrate proper access governance, an essential requirement in many contracts and legal regulations. As explained earlier, IAM plays a crucial role in addressing various regulatory and compliance obligations. Many laws, regulations, and contractual agreements mandate strict data access governance and privacy management, which IAM systems are specifically designed to support.

IAM solutions help organizations verify and manage identities, detect suspicious activity, and generate compliance reports. These capabilities are essential for meeting regulatory requirements such as **know your customer** (**KYC**), transaction monitoring for suspicious activity, etc. Additionally, data protection laws like the **General Data Protection Regulation** (**GDPR**) in Europe and U.S. regulations such as the **Health Insurance Portability and Accountability Act** (**HIPAA**) and the **Sarbanes-Oxley Act** (**SOX**) impose stringent security standards. Implementing a robust IAM system simplifies compliance with these regulations, helping organizations maintain security while reducing operational and regulatory risks.

With the increasing adoption of cloud computing, remote work, and hybrid IT environments, IAM has evolved to support identity federation, Zero Trust security models, and adaptive authentication. Compliance with regulatory frameworks also relies on strong IAM controls to protect data privacy and ensure auditability.

A well-implemented IAM strategy enhances security, improves operational efficiency, and supports business agility by enabling secure collaboration while reducing the risk of credential-based attacks and unauthorized access. As cyber threats become more sophisticated, organizations must continuously refine their IAM practices to stay ahead of emerging risks and evolving compliance requirements. Thus, by effective access management, organizations can maintain a secure IT environment, reduce security risks, and ensure regulatory compliance while enabling seamless and controlled access to critical IT resources.

Access control rules can incorporate dynamic elements, such as functions that assess past access patterns or specific environmental factors. These rules can be implemented at varying levels of granularity, from broad restrictions covering entire networks or systems to more detailed controls down to specific data fields. Factors like user location and the type of network connection used for access may also be considered. The complexity and granularity of access control directly impact costs, with stricter rules and finer control typically leading to higher expenses. Therefore, access control rules and their level of granularity should be defined based on business requirements and risk assessments to ensure an optimal balance between security and cost efficiency.

User and domain management process

User management is a vital component of enterprise IT, focusing on regulating and overseeing user access to networks and systems. This process is essential for ensuring security, compliance, and organizational efficiency. It involves tasks such as defining access levels, verifying user identities, managing permissions, and monitoring user activities. Without an effective user management system, organizations face risks like security breaches, data exposure, and operational inefficiencies.

User management is part of IAM plays a critical role in enhancing security, ensuring regulatory compliance, and boosting operational efficiency. By implementing automated user provisioning, enforcing the principle of least privilege, and maintaining comprehensive audit trails, organizations can fortify their cybersecurity defenses while facilitating seamless and secure access for users.

Beyond safeguarding against security risks, user management also boosts productivity by simplifying access to resources, ensuring that authorized individuals have timely access to the right tools and data. It enhances accountability by tracking user activities and providing a comprehensive audit trail for troubleshooting, compliance, or investigations.

Let us look at the reasons user management is essential in the IAM process:

- **Enhanced security and access control**: Effective user management ensures that only authenticated users receive appropriate permissions aligned with their roles and responsibilities, minimizing the risks of insider threats and external breaches.

- **Regulatory compliance**: Compliance with regulations such as GDPR, HIPAA, and ISO 27001 mandates strict access controls and identity verification. Robust IAM solutions support compliance by enforcing security policies and maintaining detailed audit trails.

- **Streamlined user provisioning and deprovisioning**: Automating user provisioning accelerates the process of granting appropriate access to new employees, boosting productivity. Similarly, prompt deprovisioning ensures immediate revocation of access when an employee exits, reducing security risks from lingering permissions. (User onboarding is the alternate term used for user provisioning and user offboarding for user deprovisioning).

- **Reduction in human errors and insider threats**: Manual UAM can lead to misconfigurations or over-provisioning. IAM solutions automate these processes to guarantee consistent policy enforcement and reduce vulnerabilities.

- **Role-based and attribute-based access control (RBAC/ABAC)**: IAM enables the implementation of RBAC and ABAC models, granting users permissions strictly tied to their job roles or attributes, thereby upholding the principle of least privilege.

- **Enhanced user experience features**: Features like single sign-on and multifactor authentication simplify authentication, improving usability while maintaining stringent security standards.

- **Scalability and operational efficiency**: As organizations expand, manual user management becomes impractical. IAM solutions scale alongside growth, automating lifecycle management and periodic access reviews to maintain a secure environment for large user bases.

- **Comprehensive auditability and reporting**: IAM systems generate detailed logs of user activities, access attempts, and policy changes, facilitating thorough security audits, anomaly detection, and governance enforcement.

As a focus area of enterprise IT management, user management protects sensitive systems and data by ensuring access is strictly limited to authorized users, thereby maintaining the security and integrity of organizational resources.

RBAC assigns access permissions to users based on predefined roles within an organization. A role represents a job function or responsibility (e.g., tester, developer, administrator, HR manager, finance analyst). ABAC grants access based on attributes (i.e., characteristics or properties) of the user, the resource, or the environment. Attributes can include user job roles, location, department, time of access, device type, and more. E.g.: Any employee working in the "Finance" department is allowed to access sensitive financial data only when using a corporate device within office hours.

Organizations often combine RBAC and ABAC for optimal access control. For example, RBAC might define broad roles, while ABAC refines access by adding situational or contextual constraints.

Key differences between RBAC and ABAC can be captured as follows:

Aspect	RBAC	ABAC
Basis for access	User roles or job functions	Attributes of the user, resource, or environment
Flexibility	More rigid, role based permissions	Highly flexible, dynamic policies
Management effort	Easier to implement and maintain	Requires more effort to define and manage attributes
Granularity	Role-level granularity	Attribute-level granularity, allowing more precision

Table 8.1: Comparison of RBAC and ABAC

Domain access management

Domain access management involves overseeing and regulating user access to domain resources, systems, and services within an organization's IT framework. It ensures that only authorized individuals can interact with domain-based assets, safeguarding security, ensuring compliance, and enhancing operational efficiency.

Key aspects of domain access management are as follows:

- **User authentication and authorization**: Identity verification is required before accessing domain resources. Methods include passwords, MFA, and SSO. Authorization defines user permissions using RBAC or ABAC.

- **Domain controller and Active Directory management**: **Domain controllers (DCs)** store data for authentication and authorization. **Active Directory (AD)** is often used to manage users, groups, and policies within a domain. Group policies help implement security settings and access restrictions organization wide.

- **Privileged access management (PAM)**: Restricts and monitors access for high-level administrative accounts. **Just-in-time (JIT)** access and least privilege principles are employed to minimize unnecessary permissions. Tracks and audits privileged accounts to mitigate misuse.

- **Single sign-on (SSO) and federation**: SSO enables users to log in once and access multiple domain services without repeated authentication. Federation facilitates secure access across multiple domains or organizations.

- **Access controls and policies**: Implements RBAC to allocate precise permissions to users. Enforces account lockout settings, strong password policies, and session timeouts. Manages service accounts and automated system access securely.

- **Monitoring, auditing, and compliance:** Logs and monitors access activities to detect unauthorized behavior. Conducts routine access reviews and audits to adhere to regulations like GDPR, ISO 27001, etc. Utilizes **security information and event management (SIEM)** tools for real-time monitoring and threat detection.

- **User lifecycle management**: Provisioning ensures new users have appropriate access at onboarding. Access is adjusted for users transitioning roles or departments. Immediate deprovisioning prevents risks from inactive accounts when users exit the organization.

Effective AD management ensures streamlined network operations, strong security, and compliance with organizational policies. By centralizing identity and access control, organizations can reduce administrative overhead while protecting sensitive data and resources.

PAM is a security framework designed to control, monitor, and protect access to accounts with elevated permissions, often referred to as privileged accounts. These accounts provide significant control over critical systems, applications, and sensitive data, making them a prime target for potential misuse or cyberattacks. PAM enforces strict protocols to ensure that only authorized individuals can access privileged accounts and that such access is limited to what is necessary for specific tasks. By implementing tools and processes like RBAC, MFA, JIT access, and session monitoring, PAM reduces the risks associated with excessive or unnecessary permissions and enhances an organization's overall cybersecurity posture.

Federation in domain access refers to the establishment of trust relationships between multiple domains or organizations, enabling secure and seamless access to shared resources. It allows users from one domain to authenticate and access resources in another domain without needing separate credentials for each domain. Key features of federation in domain access include SSO, which allows users to authenticate once and gain access to multiple domains or services without repeated logins. Trust Relationships are established using protocols like **security assertion markup language (SAML)**, OAuth, or WS-Federation, ensuring secure authentication and authorization between domains. Identity federation enables users to authenticate via their home domain's identity provider, leveraging the trust relationship to access resources in partner domains. Centralized identity management reduces administrative complexity and enhances security by consolidating user identity management across domains.

The user life cycle in domain access involves various stages, beginning with user account creation when a new employee, contractor, or partner joins an organization. At this stage, access rights are provisioned based on the user's role, responsibilities, and department. Following this, user authentication and authorization processes verify identities through methods like passwords, MFA, or biometrics, ensuring that users have access only to resources relevant to their responsibilities.

As users transition roles or responsibilities, their access permissions are updated to reflect their new needs. User activities are continuously monitored to detect unauthorized behavior, and logs are maintained for compliance and security purposes. When a user temporarily no longer requires access, such as during a leave of absence, their account is deactivated or suspended to prevent misuse. Upon a user's departure from the organization, account deprovisioning ensures all access rights are revoked, and access to systems, applications, and data is removed to prevent lingering permissions.

Periodic access reviews are conducted to confirm that user access remains appropriate and aligns with their current roles, maintaining security and compliance throughout the user life cycle. This comprehensive approach ensures that access to domain resources is systematically controlled and managed.

Domain access management is fundamental for maintaining the security of an organization's IT environment. By applying robust authentication methods, enforcing precise access control policies, monitoring activities, and managing privileged accounts, organizations can enhance their cybersecurity posture, ensure compliance, and optimize operational efficiency.

In the context of ISO 20000, IAM, user access, domain access, and the AUP are integral to ensuring effective ITSM and security. IAM is not explicitly addressed as a standalone section in ISO 20000 but is embedded within broader service management practices. It plays a critical role in managing user identities and access to IT services, ensuring that only authorized individuals can access specific resources. This aligns with ISO 20000's focus on maintaining service quality and security. User access is managed through processes that ensure permissions are granted based on roles and responsibilities, adhering to the principle of least privilege. This is essential for protecting sensitive information and maintaining compliance with SLAs outlined in ISO 20000. Domain access, while not explicitly mentioned, is indirectly supported through the standard's emphasis on secure and efficient management of IT resources. It involves controlling access to domain-specific systems and services, ensuring that access aligns with organizational policies and security requirements.

Acceptable usage policy

An AUP is a document that defines the guidelines and rules for the proper use of an organization's resources, including IT systems, networks, and data. It ensures users understand their responsibilities while minimizing risks like security breaches, legal liabilities, and misuse of resources. This policy typically outlines what is considered appropriate behavior and usage, such as accessing systems for authorized purposes, maintaining strong passwords, and safeguarding sensitive information. It also specifies prohibited activities, such as downloading pirated software, sharing passwords, or using the network for illegal or unethical purposes. Additionally, an AUP often covers the consequences of violating the policy, monitoring practices, and the organization's right to restrict access or take disciplinary action. By clearly defining these terms, an AUP helps maintain security, protect organizational resources, and support compliance with legal and regulatory requirements.

Data classification refers to the process of organizing data into categories based on its sensitivity, importance, and intended use. This helps organizations determine the level of protection required for different types of data. Common classification levels include public, internal, confidential, and restricted. The classification ensures that sensitive data is appropriately handled, stored, and shared according to its risk level. Data classification should always be followed by data labelling. Data labelling is the practice of assigning clear, visible labels to data based on its classification. These labels act as identifiers that communicate the data's sensitivity and handling requirements. For example, a document marked *confidential* would indicate that only authorized personnel can access it, whereas a *public* label implies no restrictions on sharing. Labelling is crucial for enforcing data protection policies and ensuring compliance with regulations. The AUP helps ensure that data is used responsibly and aligns with the organization's security policies while protecting its resources from misuse or breaches. Together, data classification and labelling work in harmony with the AUP to safeguard sensitive information, ensure compliance, and promote accountability in data handling.

The information life cycle consists of distinct stages that data undergoes, from creation to disposal. It begins with the creation or collection of information, where data is generated or gathered from various sources. The next stage is storage, where the information is securely stored in physical or digital formats, often with backups to ensure availability. Following this, the usage stage involves accessing and processing the information for specific purposes while maintaining strict access controls to ensure security. Once the data is in use, it may need to be shared or distributed, which requires secure methods to prevent unauthorized exposure, particularly in compliance with various regulations. After its active use, information enters the retention stage, where it is preserved based on regulatory or business requirements. When the data is no longer actively needed but must be kept for legal or archival purposes, it moves to the archival stage. Finally, the disposal or deletion stage ensures that information is securely destroyed when no longer required to prevent unauthorized recovery and mitigate risks. Proper management throughout this life cycle safeguards security, compliance, and the effective use of resources. Individuals, including both internal personnel and external parties, who access or utilize an organization's information and related assets should be made aware of the information security requirements for safeguarding and handling these resources. They must take responsibility for their use of any information processing facilities.

The organization should establish and communicate a topic-specific policy on the acceptable use of information and associated assets to all users. This policy should provide clear guidance on how individuals are expected to handle and interact with information and assets, outlining:

- Acceptable and unacceptable behavior from an information security perspective.

- Permitted and prohibited uses of information and associated assets.

- Monitoring activities conducted by the organization.

Acceptable use procedures should be defined for the entire information lifecycle, taking into account its classification and associated risks. These procedures should address:

- Access restrictions based on classification levels to ensure appropriate protection.

- Maintenance of an authorized user record for information and associated assets.

- Protection of both temporary and permanent copies of information in alignment with the security level of the original data.

- Storage of assets in accordance with manufacturer specifications.

- Clear labelling of all storage media (both electronic and physical) for proper identification by authorized recipients.

- Authorization and secure deletion methods for the disposal of information and associated assets.

Additionally, in cases of public cloud services, where assets do not belong to the organization, appropriate controls should be established. The use of third-party assets and any organizational resources linked to them (e.g., information, software) should be properly identified and managed through agreements with cloud service providers. Special considerations should also be made when operating within a collaborative working environment to ensure information security is maintained.

Return of assets and access deprovisioning should also be part of the AUP. Personnel and relevant parties must return all organizational assets in their possession when their employment, contract, or agreement is altered or terminated. The process of change or termination should be formalized to ensure the return of all physical and electronic assets previously issued or entrusted to the individual by the organization.

AUP complements these practices by defining the rules for how users should interact with IT systems and resources. It ensures that usage aligns with organizational objectives and security policies, reducing the risk of misuse or breaches.

Conclusion

We saw how IAM, user access, domain access, and the AUP are interrelated components essential for maintaining the security, compliance, and efficiency of an organization's IT infrastructure. IAM provides the overarching framework for managing and securing user identities and their access to organizational resources. It enforces principles like least privilege, strong authentication, and lifecycle management to minimize security risks while ensuring operational efficiency.

User access focuses on the allocation and control of permissions, ensuring that individuals have appropriate access to systems and data based on their roles and responsibilities. Effective management of user access is crucial for safeguarding sensitive information and preventing unauthorized activities. Domain access extends these principles within an organization's IT environment, enabling secure and efficient management of user access to domain-specific resources and services. It incorporates mechanisms like centralized authentication, SSO, and federation to streamline access and enhance user productivity while maintaining robust security controls.

The AUP complements these practices by setting clear expectations for how users should interact with organizational resources. It defines acceptable and prohibited behaviors to protect systems, data, and networks, promoting accountability and reducing the risk of misuse or breaches.

Together, these elements form a cohesive strategy for managing identities, access, and responsibilities within an organization, helping to ensure a secure and efficient operating environment while aligning with regulatory and operational requirements.

In the next chapter, we will be learning about network, server, storage and end point management processes. These are critical areas of IT infrastructure management that ensure smooth operation, security, and efficiency of an organization's technology ecosystem. The IT management team interacts with the non-IT business team through these processes when service requests are raised, asking for support from the IT team. These processes make the IT team visible to the entire organization.

Join our Discord space

Join our Discord workspace for latest updates, offers, tech happenings around the world, new releases, and sessions with the authors:

https://discord.bpbonline.com

CHAPTER 9

Network, Server, Storage and Endpoint Management

Introduction

In the earlier chapters, we learned about the major IT processes and access management processes. In this chapter, we will learn about the importance of network, server, storage, and endpoint management, which are essential in modern IT environments, for maintaining security, performance, and availability. These components form the foundation of IT operations, supporting business applications, data processing, and communication. Effective management of these elements enhances operational efficiency, strengthens cybersecurity, and ensures business continuity.

Network management involves monitoring, maintaining, and securing network infrastructure, including routers, switches, firewalls, and communication protocols. It ensures optimal connectivity, bandwidth allocation, and security policies to protect against cyber threats and unauthorized access.

Network, server, storage, and endpoint management are fundamental to maintaining a secure and efficient IT infrastructure. A well-integrated management strategy ensures high availability, security, and compliance while minimizing risks and optimizing performance. Organizations must adopt proactive monitoring, automated security enforcement, and efficient resource allocation to maintain a resilient IT environment.

Structure

The chapter covers the following topics:

- Key concepts
- Network management
- Server management
- Storage management
- Endpoint management

Objectives

In this chapter, we will learn about network, server, storage, and endpoint management for IT auditors, focusing on equipping them with the ability to evaluate and enhance the efficiency, security, and compliance of IT infrastructures. IT auditors should develop a comprehensive understanding of network architecture, server configurations, storage systems, and endpoint devices, along with their roles and interconnections, even though they have not worked in IT teams. They must gain the ability to assess the effectiveness of security controls, including firewalls, intrusion detection systems, and endpoint protection measures, ensuring these align with organizational policies and regulatory requirements.

A critical objective is learning to analyze logs from network devices, servers, and endpoints to detect anomalies and security threats. IT auditors must also assess the robustness of backup and disaster recovery processes to ensure the integrity and availability of organizational data. Endpoint management, including patch management and **mobile device management** (**MDM**), is another crucial area to ensure devices are configured securely and meet compliance standards. Evaluating network performance and resilience strategies like redundancy and failover mechanisms is essential to ensure service continuity.

This helps us in improving our ability to identify vulnerabilities and risks across IT infrastructures and recommend effective mitigation strategies. Verification in network, server, storage, and endpoint management is crucial to ensure security, reliability, and compliance with organizational policies and industry regulations. Regular verification processes help detect vulnerabilities, prevent unauthorized access, and maintain the integrity and performance of IT infrastructure.

Key concepts

The objectives of learning network, server, storage, and endpoint management focus on building a comprehensive understanding of IT infrastructure and its role in maintaining security, performance, and business continuity. Learners should be able to design, implement, monitor, and secure these critical components to support organizational needs effectively.

Server management focuses on provisioning, configuring, and maintaining both physical and virtual servers that host applications and process data. It includes regular security patching, resource optimization, and ensuring that CPU, memory, and storage are utilized efficiently. Backup and disaster recovery strategies are crucial in preventing data loss and system failures, ensuring that servers remain available and operational.

Key aspects include monitoring network traffic, managing access control and security policies, optimizing performance, and implementing firewall and intrusion prevention systems to safeguard the organization's infrastructure. This includes the ability to configure and manage network devices such as routers, switches, and firewalls while implementing security measures like **virtual private network** (**VPN**), access controls, and intrusion prevention systems.

Another important goal is to develop the skills necessary for managing servers, both physical and virtual. This involves provisioning, configuring, and maintaining servers while ensuring proper resource utilization, system performance, and security. Learners should be able to implement patch management, backup and disaster recovery strategies, and troubleshoot server-related issues to ensure availability and reliability.

Storage management is a critical aspect of IT infrastructure, and learners should gain proficiency in handling different storage architectures, including cloud, on-premise, and hybrid solutions. Understanding data backup, disaster recovery, encryption, and access control mechanisms is essential for ensuring data integrity and security while also learning how to plan for scalable storage solutions.

Endpoint management focuses on securing and controlling devices such as desktops, laptops, mobile devices, and IoT endpoints. It is critical in securing and controlling devices such as laptops, desktops, mobile devices, and **Internet of Things** (**IoT**) endpoints. Learners should be able to implement endpoint security strategies, configure device management policies, monitor remote endpoints, and ensure compliance with security standards. This includes provisioning and configuring devices securely, deploying endpoint security measures such as antivirus and firewalls, managing patch updates to mitigate vulnerabilities, and enabling remote monitoring and management to maintain security and compliance. The ability to manage patch updates, detect vulnerabilities, and enforce security policies across all endpoints is crucial for minimizing risks associated with cyber threats. By achieving these objectives, learners will develop the skills needed to manage and secure IT infrastructure components effectively. They will be able to implement best practices in network, server, storage, and endpoint management to enhance operational efficiency, improve security posture, and support organizational IT goals.

Analyzing logs from network devices, servers, and endpoints is essential for identifying anomalies and potential security threats. Log formats, log retention policies, and tools like **security information and event management** (**SIEM**) to aggregate and analyze data are to be reviewed in detail to see the effectiveness of **IT service management** (**ITSM**) practices. Review should also focus on processes required in recognizing patterns, detecting unusual activity such as unauthorized login attempts, and correlating events across systems to highlight potential breaches or vulnerabilities.

When assessing the robustness of backup and disaster recovery processes, diligence should be given to the practices ensuring backups are conducted regularly, securely stored, and tested periodically for reliability. This includes evaluating infrastructure availability and data availability to ensure they align with organizational requirements and minimize downtime. Special attention should be given to encryption during the storage and transmission of backup data to prevent unauthorized access.

Endpoint management is another critical area, as endpoints are often entry points for cyberattacks. Processes should be in place to ensure that devices are patched promptly to fix vulnerabilities and are configured to comply with organizational security policies. This involves verifying MDM systems for centralized control over endpoints, checking for secure configuration baselines, and verifying the implementation of anti-malware tools and other endpoint protection measures.

Network performance and resilience strategies, including redundancy and failover mechanisms, are vital for maintaining uninterrupted service. Checks should include the effectiveness of these strategies through reviewing network architecture, testing failover scenarios, and ensuring that redundancy systems are operational and properly configured. Checks should be in place to assess bandwidth management, latency metrics, and the capability to handle unexpected network traffic surges, ensuring the infrastructure remains robust under varied conditions.

These aspects are interconnected, and addressing them thoroughly ensures a secure, compliant, and resilient IT environment.

Network management

A network management service enhances value for its users by delivering precise and reliable information regarding an organization's active network connections and usage patterns, enabling adjustments to its network bandwidth capacity as needed. Network management refers to the process of administering, maintaining, and securing an organization's network infrastructure to ensure optimal performance, availability, and security. It includes tasks such as configuring network devices, maintaining connectivity, troubleshooting issues, and ensuring network security. Effective network management ensures the smooth operation of communication systems, supports business-critical applications, and minimizes downtime or disruptions. It often leverages tools to monitor traffic, detect anomalies, and enforce policies to protect data and maintain performance.

Every information system carries inherent risks to an organization, and determining whether those risks are acceptable is ultimately a decision for the business to make. Implementing measures such as firewalls, resource isolation, robust system configurations, authentication mechanisms, access control systems, and encryption can help reduce identified risks to levels deemed acceptable.

Key focus areas of network management are:

- **Network security**: Firewalls, **intrusion detection/prevention systems (IDS/IPS)**, VPNs, encryption.

- **Network performance**: Bandwidth optimization, uptime monitoring, load balancing.

- **Configuration management**: Version control, change management, network device updates.

- **Access control and authentication**: User permissions, **role-based access control (RBAC)**, **multifactor authentication (MFA)**.

- **Incident response and monitoring**: SIEM, log analysis, anomaly detection.

Effective network management ensures regulatory compliance, security threat prevention, optimal network performance, operational risk reduction, effective incident investigation, etc.

A network audit evaluates the effectiveness of an organization's network security, performance, and compliance. Audit includes evaluation of security controls like firewall rules, network segmentation, IDS/IPS effectiveness, in addition to assessing regulatory compliance. Analyzing network performance and availability, through monitoring **service level agreement (SLA)**, and ensuring service availability through proper redundancy and failover mechanisms, etc., are also assessed during IT audits. Other checks that are part of network management review are verification of access control measures and inspection of incident response capabilities.

The IT audit checklist for network management covers the following domains:

- **Security controls audit**: Review of firewall configurations and rule sets, assessment of IDS/IPS deployment and logging mechanisms, verify VPN security configurations and remote access policies.

- **Compliance audit**: Ensure compliance with industry regulations and security frameworks, verification of encryption standards for data transmission and storage.

- **Access control and authentication audit**: Review user account management and privilege assignment, enforcing least privilege access and RBAC, and verification of MFA implementation.

- **Network performance and availability audit**: Analyzing bandwidth usage and network congestion, monitoring uptime and redundancy measures, assessing failover and disaster recovery preparedness.

- **Incident response and log management audit**: Evaluate SIEM implementation for centralized log management, ensuring the presence of anomaly detection mechanisms, review process for incident tracking and effectiveness of response time.

Network management is ensured in various enterprises using the following tools:

- **SIEM solutions**: Splunk, IBM QRadar

- **Network monitoring tools**: SolarWinds, Nagios

- **Firewall and IDS/IPS management**: Palo Alto, Cisco Firepower, Snort

- **Vulnerability scanners**: Nessus, Qualys, OpenVAS

- **Configuration and change management**: ManageEngine, ServiceNow

A network diagram is a visual representation of an organization's IT infrastructure, including devices, connections, and topology. A network diagram illustrates the layout of network devices, namely, routers, switches, firewalls, servers, workstations, cloud services, VPNs, internet connections, and links. Keeping this diagram updated is crucial for security, troubleshooting, compliance, and network efficiency. An up-to-date network diagram is essential for security, troubleshooting, compliance, and disaster recovery. Regularly updating and maintaining it ensures that IT teams can effectively manage, secure, and scale enterprise networks.

Internet links

Internet link management involves overseeing and optimizing the use of internet connections to ensure consistent and efficient network performance. Internet link management is a critical function within ITSM, ensuring the reliability, performance, and security of an organization's internet connectivity. This includes balancing bandwidth across multiple internet links, monitoring link uptime and latency, and implementing failover systems to maintain connectivity in case one link fails. Organizations often use load balancing and link aggregation techniques to distribute traffic evenly and enhance reliability. Effective internet link management ensures uninterrupted access, reduced downtime, and improved user experience. Configuring internet links is a critical aspect of network management that ensures high availability, security, and performance for users and business applications. Effective management of these links aligns with ITSM best practices, ensuring that internet services meet business needs while maintaining high availability and security.

A dedicated point-to-point private connection between two locations is often used for secure data transfer. Key features of a leased line are that it is private and secure as the bandwidth is dedicated to the said enterprise, stable latency and high uptime as this service is often backed by stringent SLAs, and customizable speeds due to the availability of scalable bandwidth options. Large enterprises, data centers, etc., use leased line connectivity.

Multi-protocol label switching (**MPLS**) is another popular way of networking wherein a private, high-performance network is used for secure enterprise connectivity across multiple locations. Key features of MPLS are high security and reliability, as this is not directly exposed to the public internet, prioritization of critical traffic, which is ideal for **voice over IP** (**VoIP**) services, video conferencing, and cloud applications, and scalability required for large enterprise networks with multiple branch offices. Business setups like banking, healthcare, and government agencies require multi-location businesses to use MPLS networks.

By selecting the right connectivity strategy, businesses can enhance network performance, improve security, and ensure seamless operations. Configuring internet links effectively is essential for network reliability, security, and performance. By following best practices, using redundant links, and securing firewalls and routers, organizations can ensure seamless and secure internet connectivity.

In the service strategy phase, organizations define their internet requirements, selecting service providers based on cost, reliability, and performance. Business continuity planning plays a key role in this phase, ensuring that redundancy measures such as multiple **internet service providers** (**ISPs**) and failover mechanisms are in place to ensure continuity of services.

During service design, network architecture is planned, incorporating features such as load balancing, **quality of service** (**QoS**), and security controls like firewalls and VPNs. The objective is to create a resilient internet infrastructure that aligns with business needs while minimizing downtime risks. In the service transition phase, in case of any changes in network design, changes to internet links are managed through structured change control processes. Implementing new connections, upgrading bandwidth, or modifying routing policies must go through proper testing and approval workflows to avoid disruptions. Proper documentation, including network diagrams and configuration details, is maintained to support future troubleshooting and audits.

Service operation focuses on the day-to-day monitoring and maintenance of internet links. Network monitoring tools track performance metrics such as latency, packet loss, and bandwidth utilization. Incident management processes handle connectivity issues promptly, ensuring minimal impact on business operations. When issues arise, root cause analysis is conducted to prevent recurrence and improve stability. Continual service improvement ensures that internet link management evolves to meet changing business demands. Regular performance reviews, contract evaluations with ISPs, and proactive optimization of traffic management contribute to long-term efficiency.

Network redundancy ensures that traffic continues to flow seamlessly by providing multiple pathways, even if a failure occurs. In essence, greater redundancy enhances reliability and facilitates distributed site management. If one device fails, another can take over automatically, reducing the risk of a complete network outage with minimal added complexity. However, complexity can also undermine reliability. Increased complexity makes systems more complicated to understand, raising the likelihood of human errors or software bugs introducing new points of failure. Therefore, when designing a network, it is crucial to strike a balance between achieving redundancy and managing complexity. Organizations should implement redundancy by using multiple ISPs or failover solutions to avoid single points of failure. Traffic prioritization should be enforced through QoS policies to ensure critical applications receive the necessary bandwidth. Regular performance monitoring helps detect and resolve potential issues before they impact operations. Security measures, including firewalls, IPS, and encryption, must be enforced to protect internet traffic from cyber threats.

Managing internet links within ITSM ensures that connectivity remains reliable, secure, and efficient. By integrating ITSM processes such as change management, incident response, and continuous improvement, organizations can optimize their internet infrastructure. Proactive monitoring, security enforcement, and redundancy planning are key to maintaining seamless business operations in an increasingly digital world.

Firewalls

Firewalls serve as the first line of defense against cyber threats by filtering incoming and outgoing traffic based on predefined security rules. Firewall management is a critical aspect of ITSM that ensures secure and controlled access to an organization's network. Proper firewall management is essential for maintaining compliance, protecting sensitive data, and preventing unauthorized access. Firewall management entails configuring, monitoring, and maintaining firewalls to ensure they provide robust protection for a network. This process includes establishing rules to permit or deny specific types of traffic, routinely auditing these rules, and analyzing logs to identify and respond to potential security threats. Proper firewall management addresses vulnerabilities, mitigates risks, and ensures the network remains secure and operates without disruption.

Effective firewall management is essential for safeguarding a network's security and integrity. As introduced previously, firewalls serve as a protective barrier between internal systems and external threats, filtering traffic to block unauthorized access and cyberattacks. Maintaining them properly ensures they remain effective and up to date against evolving threats. Neglecting firewall management can lead to vulnerabilities. Outdated configurations and rules may fail to address emerging risks, exposing the network to potential breaches. For instance, obsolete or conflicting firewall rules can be exploited by attackers, jeopardizing the entire system. Regular audits and updates are crucial to eliminating these weaknesses and reinforcing network defenses.

Firewall management is a multifaceted process that is crucial for maintaining network security. Effective firewall management involves:

- **Policy control**: Establishing rules that specify which traffic is permitted or denied, using criteria such as source and destination IP addresses, port numbers, and communication protocols.

- **Configuration**: Configuring rules and parameters to govern how the firewall manages both incoming and outgoing network traffic. The firewall configuration process includes securing the firewall, designing firewall zones and IP address structure, implementing **access control lists** (**ACL**), activating additional services and logging, testing the configuration, ongoing monitoring and management, etc.

- **Rule management**: Focuses on identifying and eliminating outdated or unnecessary rules to improve performance and strengthen security. Regular reviews and optimization ensure that firewall rules remain aligned with current security policies and effectively address new threats. Consistent management of these rules helps maintain the firewall's optimal performance.

- **Change management**: Regular updates with the latest patches to address identified vulnerabilities. This process is a key part of change management, which ensures that firewall software remains up-to-date and effective against emerging exploits and threats. By reducing security risks, effective change management plays a critical role in maintaining robust network security.

- **Compliance**: Complying with industry regulations and standards is a crucial aspect of effective firewall management. Ensuring that firewall configurations and policies align with regulatory requirements helps organizations safeguard sensitive data and avoid compliance breaches. Conducting regular audits and reviews is essential to maintaining compliance and identifying any gaps in security practices.

- **Performance optimization**: Involves continuous maintenance and optimization to ensure the firewall functions effectively. This process includes addressing any issues that could affect network security or data throughput.

- **Monitoring**: Vital components of maintaining network security and managing firewalls. Examining firewall logs and activities provides valuable insights to network and security administrators, helping them understand security trends and assess the effectiveness of policies.

- **Automation**: Enhances the efficiency of firewall management. It enables the analysis of traffic patterns, provides recommendations for rule optimization, and ensures uniformity across multiple firewalls.

Each component plays a vital role in protecting against evolving threats.

Effective firewall management is crucial for maintaining network security, making it essential to determine the right team for the job. Ensuring firewalls are correctly configured, maintained, and monitored requires assigning responsibilities to skilled professionals. Firewall management is a collaborative effort involving multiple roles within an organization. The IT and network security team plays a central role, handling configuration, monitoring, and incident response to protect the network from potential threats.

For organizations lacking in-house expertise, outsourcing to **managed security service providers** (**MSSP**) is a viable option. MSSPs offer specialized knowledge and 24/7 monitoring, ensuring proactive threat detection and response. This approach allows organizations with limited IT and security staff to focus on core business functions while maintaining robust network protection.

Challenges of firewall management

Like all network security activities, firewall management presents several challenges. However, with the right strategies, these obstacles can be effectively addressed. Most network administrators agree that managing firewall rules, implementing changes, and controlling user access are among the most significant hurdles:

- **Navigating complex firewall rules**: One of the primary challenges in firewall management is handling the complexity of rule sets. Firewalls often contain hundreds or even thousands of rules, making oversight difficult. Over time, these rules can become outdated, redundant, or even conflict with one another, potentially weakening security and causing performance issues. To maintain an efficient firewall, regular rule audits and optimizations are essential. This process ensures that rules remain relevant, streamlined, and free from unnecessary complexity that could hinder security or network performance.

- **Adapting to dynamic network environments**: Modern networks are highly dynamic, with constantly evolving traffic patterns, applications, and user behaviors. Firewalls must be configured to adapt to these changes without compromising security. Network and security teams must continuously monitor and adjust firewall rules to align with current network conditions. Failing to do so can result in outdated configurations that either block legitimate traffic or expose vulnerabilities. Implementing automated tools for real-time rule updates can help manage these rapid changes more effectively.

- **Balancing security with user access needs**: Managing user access is one of the most challenging aspects of firewall administration. Firewalls must regulate access for both internal and remote users, including those with privileged credentials. The key challenge lies in striking the right balance between security and accessibility. Firewalls should grant legitimate users seamless access to necessary resources while preventing unauthorized entry. Implementing MFA and RBAC strengthens security while ensuring users can perform their tasks without unnecessary restrictions.

Regularly monitoring user activities and reviewing access logs further enhances security by identifying potential misuse or unauthorized access attempts. By maintaining a proactive approach, organizations can ensure their firewalls provide both strong protection and operational efficiency.

Switches

Switches are key building blocks in a network. They exist to connect multiple devices (like wireless access points, servers, computers, and printers) on the same network, usually within a campus or building. Switches allow connected devices to communicate with each other and share information.

A switch management policy defines how network switches are configured, secured, and maintained, adhering to best practices for security, performance, and compliance. It also includes processes for managing configuration changes and monitoring.

The key aspects of such a policy can be categorized as follows:

- **Security**: Usage of secure protocols for remote management. ACLs help restrict access based on roles or network segments. Port security measures, such as limiting MAC addresses per port and disabling unused ports, enhance safety. Strong authentication, including two-factor methods, should be used for administrative access. **Virtual local area networks (VLANs)** should segment traffic for improved security and performance, while firmware updates ensure vulnerabilities are addressed. Logging and auditing provide activity tracking to identify and address potential threats.

- **Configuration management**: A Structured change management process ensures that modifications to switch configurations are documented, tested, and reversible. Templates help maintain consistency when configuring multiple switches, and regular backups secure switch configurations against data loss. Standardized naming conventions and thorough documentation make troubleshooting and management easier.

- **Performance and monitoring**: Usage of tools to track overall switch performance and to identify potential issues. Monitoring individual port traffic, utilization, and errors enables swift resolution of problems. Setting threshold alerts for high utilization or errors provides proactive issue management, while broadcast storm detection mechanisms protect against network overloads. Network segmentation further optimizes traffic flow and performance.

- **Compliance**: Configure switches to comply with industry standards and regulations. Regular audits help identify vulnerabilities and ensure compliance with applicable policies and guidelines.

- **Other considerations**: Determine whether managed or unmanaged switches suit their needs. Switch management tools can simplify configuration, monitoring, and troubleshooting. Vendor documentation should be consulted for model-specific features and recommendations.

Effective switch management is essential for maintaining a stable, secure, and efficient network infrastructure. A well-structured management process ensures optimal performance, minimizes downtime, and enhances security. By implementing standardized procedures for configuration, monitoring, and troubleshooting, organizations can prevent network disruptions and improve overall reliability.

Effective network management

Network configuration focuses on managing a network and its devices by applying the right set of policies, controls, and configurations. It encompasses activities from device discovery to configuration backups for efficient network administration. Key areas of network configuration are as follows:

- **Device discovery and management**: Configuration management plays a vital role in identifying and managing devices within a network. It automatically discovers network devices and stores critical details such as port configurations and interface settings in a centralized inventory. Maintaining an up-to-date inventory simplifies device management and allows for quick report generation using filters like device type, vendor, or location, ensuring efficient network operations.

- **Configuration backup and restoration**: Network disruptions can occur at any time, making regular configuration backups essential. Routine backups ensure that organizations can quickly restore stable device settings in case of equipment failure or unexpected incidents. Having readily available backups minimizes downtime and supports business continuity by enabling fast recovery.

- **Change management**: Accurate change tracking helps organizations identify which network engineers made specific configuration modifications. While this may not directly prevent network issues, it significantly speeds up troubleshooting and resolution. Standardized change management practices ensure that all modifications are well-documented, traceable, and implemented in a controlled manner, reducing potential risks.

- **Policy management and compliance audits**: Before implementing configuration changes, network administrators must establish clear security policies to meet compliance requirements for various frameworks. Regular compliance audits help ensure device configurations adhere to these standards, strengthening overall network security and regulatory alignment.

- **Network automation**: Automating routine network tasks such as device backups, firmware updates, and access control modifications enhances efficiency and reduces human error. By eliminating repetitive manual processes, automation improves network team productivity and ensures consistency in configuration management practices.

Regular maintenance, firmware updates, and proactive monitoring play a crucial role in identifying potential issues before they impact business operations. Proper access control and security policies help protect network switches from unauthorized changes and cyber threats. Additionally, maintaining up-to-date documentation simplifies troubleshooting, compliance audits, and future network expansions.

Automation and centralized management tools further streamline switch administration. Through the switch management process, organizations can achieve a resilient and scalable network that supports business growth while ensuring operational efficiency and security.

Network segregation

Network segregation is a critical security measure that enhances an organization's ability to protect sensitive data, reduce attack surfaces, and enforce access control policies. By segmenting networks based on security needs, organizations can limit unauthorized access, prevent lateral movement of threats, and ensure compliance with regulatory requirements.

Key techniques for network segregation include:

- **VLAN**: Logical separation of networks within the same physical hardware.

- **Firewalls**: Controlling traffic between different network segments.

- **Air-gapping**: Completely isolating a network from external or unsecured networks.

Adequate network segregation ensures that even if one part of the network is compromised, the rest remains secure.

Network segregation offers several advantages that enhance security, efficiency, and manageability. Some of the key benefits are as follows:

- **Improved security**: By isolating sensitive data or critical systems, segregation limits the impact of potential breaches. An attacker compromising one segment cannot easily access other parts of the network.

- **Better performance**: Segmented networks reduce congestion as traffic flows are limited within each segment, leading to faster and more reliable communication.

- **Enhanced control**: Admins can establish specific rules and policies for different segments, tailoring access and permissions according to the needs of users or devices.

- **Reduced scope of threats**: Malware or cyber-attacks can be contained within a segment, minimizing their spread across the network.

- **Compliance support**: Many regulatory standards require data separation. Network segregation helps organizations meet compliance requirements more effectively.

- **Easier troubleshooting**: Identifying issues is more straightforward in a segregated network since problems are often limited to specific segments.

- **Efficient resource allocation**: Resources can be dedicated to specific segments to ensure critical systems are well-supported.

Adequate network segregation requires a strategic approach, including proper classification of assets, implementation of firewalls and VLANs, and continuous monitoring for anomalies. While it adds complexity to network management, the security benefits far outweigh the operational challenges. Ultimately, adopting a well-structured network segregation strategy strengthens an organization's cybersecurity posture, minimizes risks, and supports a robust defense-in-depth approach.

Challenges

Conducting a network management audit is essential for ensuring security, compliance, and operational efficiency. However, various challenges can make the auditing process complex and time-consuming. Typical network management audit challenges are as follows:

- **Lack of documentation**: Incomplete or outdated network topology diagrams and security policies.

- **Misconfigured security controls**: Weak firewall rules, unnecessary open ports, unpatched vulnerabilities.

- **Unauthorized access and privilege creep**: Excessive access permissions granted to users over time.

- **Ineffective incident response**: Lack of real-time monitoring, delayed detection of security breaches.

- **Poor network visibility**: Lack of centralized logging and automated monitoring tools.

Network management audits play a crucial role in strengthening security, ensuring compliance, and improving network efficiency. However, challenges such as outdated documentation, compliance complexities, security gaps, and resource limitations can hinder the auditing process. To overcome these obstacles, organizations should invest in automated auditing tools, implement strong change management processes, maintain updated documentation, and ensure continuous monitoring of network activity. By addressing these challenges, organizations can enhance the effectiveness of their network audits and improve overall security and compliance.

Best practices

Network auditing is essential for maintaining security, ensuring compliance, and optimizing performance. The following best practices help organizations identify vulnerabilities, enforce policies, and enhance network reliability:

- Maintain updated network diagrams and security documentation.

- Enforce strong access control measures (RBAC, MFA).

- Implement continuous network monitoring and anomaly detection.

- Use automated compliance and security tools for real-time threat detection.

- Conduct regular penetration testing and vulnerability assessments.

Implementing best practices in network auditing enhances security, ensures compliance, and optimizes network performance. By maintaining up-to-date documentation, leveraging automation, enforcing strong policies, and conducting regular assessments, organizations can proactively identify and mitigate risks while strengthening their overall network infrastructure.

Server management

Server management is a critical IT function that ensures the reliability, security, and performance of an organization's servers. It involves monitoring, maintaining, and optimizing both physical and virtual servers to support business operations and IT services. A well-structured server management process helps organizations minimize downtime, enhance security, and improve overall efficiency.

The process encompasses key activities such as server provisioning, configuration, security management, performance monitoring, patching, backup and recovery, and incident response. Effective server management ensures that hardware and software resources are utilized adequately while maintaining compliance with industry standards and security best practices.

With the increasing complexity of IT environments, including on-premises, cloud, and hybrid infrastructures, automated tools and centralized management solutions have become essential for maintaining control over servers. Organizations that implement a proactive server management approach can reduce risks, optimize resource allocation, and ensure business continuity.

Server management is a structured approach to overseeing the operation, maintenance, security, and performance of servers within an IT environment. The server management process includes the following key stages:

1. **Server provisioning**: This is the initial phase where servers are set up and configured according to business and technical requirements. It includes selecting the appropriate server type (physical, virtual, or cloud-based), installing the operating system (Windows, Linux, or macOS), configuring hardware and software components and assigning appropriate network configurations.

2. **Server configuration and optimization**: After provisioning, servers must be fine-tuned for optimal performance and security. This includes setting up storage, memory, and processing power according to workload requirements, configuring security settings such as firewalls, encryption, and access controls, and enforcing standard configurations using automation tools.

3. **Server security management**: Ensuring security is a top priority in server management. Key security measures include implementing user access controls with RBAC, enforcing MFA for administrative access, configuring firewalls, IDS/IPS, and VPNs, regularly applying security patches and software updates, and monitoring for unauthorized access and security threats using SIEM tools.

4. **Performance monitoring and optimization**: Continuous monitoring ensures that servers operate efficiently without performance degradation. Best practices include tracking CPU, memory, disk usage, and network bandwidth, implementing monitoring tools, setting up alerts for unusual activity or performance bottlenecks, and analyzing logs and performance metrics to proactively identify and resolve issues.

5. **Patch management and updates**: Keeping software and firmware up to date prevents vulnerabilities and ensures compatibility. This includes regularly updating operating systems, drivers, and applications, automating patch deployment using tools,

and testing patches in a controlled environment before full deployment to prevent disruptions.

6. **Backup and disaster recovery**: A comprehensive backup and recovery plan is essential for business continuity. This involves setting up regular automated backups (full, incremental, or differential), using cloud-based and off-site storage for redundancy, implementing disaster recovery solutions such as failover clusters and replication, and conducting regular backup testing to verify data integrity and recovery speed.

7. **Incident response and troubleshooting**: Quick response to incidents minimizes downtime and mitigates risks. Effective incident management includes setting up an incident response plan with predefined escalation procedures, using log analysis and forensic tools to investigate security breaches, resolving hardware failures, software crashes, and network issues promptly, documenting incident resolutions for future reference and process improvement.

8. **Server decommissioning**: When a server reaches the end of its lifecycle, it must be decommissioned securely. The process includes migrating workloads and data to a new server, securely wiping or destroying sensitive data, and physically disposing of or recycling old hardware according to compliance standards.

A structured server management process is essential for maintaining system stability, security, and efficiency. By following best practices in provisioning, configuration, security, monitoring, patching, and backup management, organizations can ensure their servers operate reliably while minimizing risks. Automation and proactive management further enhance efficiency, reducing downtime and operational costs while ensuring compliance with industry regulations.

Server administration

Server administration involves managing, configuring, securing, and maintaining servers to ensure they run efficiently and securely. It covers a wide range of responsibilities, from installing and updating software to monitoring performance and enforcing security measures. Proper server administration is essential for minimizing downtime, improving security, and ensuring compliance with required standards.

Key aspects of server administration are as follows:

- **Installation and configuration**: Setting up physical or virtual servers based on organizational needs, choosing the right operating system (Linux, Windows Server, etc.), configuring network settings, including static IPs, **domain name system** (**DNS**), and firewalls, and installing and configuring essential software and security tools, etc.

- **Security and access control**: Implementing firewalls like Windows Defender, enforcing **secure shell** (**SSH**) security, applying security patches and updates regularly, setting up IDS/IPS, and managing user access through proper RBAC.

- **User and authentication management**: Creating and managing user accounts and groups, implementing authentication mechanisms like **Lightweight Directory Access Protocol (LDAP)**, **Active Directory (AD)**, or **identity access management (IAM)** solutions, enforcing password policies and **multifactor authentication (MFA)**, and monitoring login activities and failed login attempts.

- **Performance monitoring and optimization**: Tracking system performance, managing system resources and tuning configurations for efficiency, identifying and resolving performance bottlenecks, and automating performance monitoring with tools.

- **Backup and disaster recovery**: Implementing automated backup solutions, setting up off-site and cloud-based backup strategies, developing and testing disaster recovery plans, and ensuring data integrity through regular backup verification.

- **Patch and update management**: Keeping the OS and applications up to date, like Windows Update, automating patch deployment with tools like **Windows Server Update Services (WSUS)**, or **System Center Configuration Manager (SCCM)**, and conducting pre-deployment testing to avoid system failures.

- **Virtualization and containerization**: Managing virtual machines using VMware, deploying and managing containerized applications with Kubernetes, and optimizing resource allocation in virtualized environments.

- **Log management and troubleshooting**: Analyzing system logs to detect security threats and operational issues, using centralized log management tools like Splunk, and troubleshooting server issues and optimizing configurations.

- **Compliance and best practices**: Ensuring compliance with security frameworks like ISO 27001, conducting regular security audits and risk assessments, and implementing best practices for data protection and risk management.

Server management

Windows Server provides a variety of tools that help administrators integrate applications, networks, and web services within an infrastructure. Some of these tools, such as the Windows Server **Microsoft Management Consoles (MMC)**, may already be familiar to you. However, understanding the full range of management tools available in Windows Server is crucial for selecting the most suitable option for your organization.

These management tools are designed to function cohesively within Windows Server environments, addressing the intricate and interconnected demands of on-premises, hybrid, and cloud-native infrastructures.

The four primary tools for managing your Windows Server infrastructure are:

- Azure Arc
- Windows Admin Center

- System Center

- Local management tools

This ensures administrators can streamline operations while meeting specific infrastructure requirements.

The use of Linux, as a server operating system, has seen rapid growth in enterprises, gaining recognition as an alternative to traditional operating systems due to its ease of installation and user-friendly nature. Linux server management is an integration of cybersecurity and business objectives. Linux server management at scale is a vastly different activity from interacting with a terminal on one machine. The best Linux server management tools universally offer a server management GUI within a web browser. Its flexibility for custom configurations and status as an open-source operating system are key factors driving its widespread adoption. For administrators, one of the most time-consuming tasks is managing all the computers within a network. Linux management tools are available, which address this challenge by enhancing efficiency through the automation of desktop management tasks and providing a unified console for managing diverse operating systems.

The Linux server management ecosystem is built on three foundational pillars:

- **Reactive solutions**: Focused on resolving existing issues promptly.

- **Organizational solutions**: Establishing policies for users, networks, and devices to ensure structured management.

- **Preventive solutions**: Designed to mitigate or avoid potential problems before they arise proactively.

Windows and Linux server management differ significantly in terms of features, user experience, and administrative control. Here is a comparison:

Aspect	Windows Server management	Linux Server management
Ease of use	User-friendly interface; ideal for administrators new to servers.	Steeper learning curve; suited for experienced admins.
Customization	Limited flexibility; predefined settings and tools.	Highly customizable with open-source tools and configurations.
Security	Regular patches and updates from Microsoft; centralized policies.	Frequent updates and an open-source nature allow deep control.
Cost	Licensing fees apply.	Free (open source) but may involve costs for enterprise support.
Third-party integration	Seamless integration with Microsoft services and software.	Wide compatibility with third-party tools; requires manual configuration in some cases.

Aspect	Windows Server management	Linux Server management
Automation	Built-in tools like PowerShell for scripting and task automation.	Rich scripting options like Bash, Python, and other tools.
Scalability	Designed for enterprise environments with robust scalability.	Equally scalable; depends on configurations and hardware.
Community support	Microsoft support forums and enterprise-grade assistance.	Extensive community forums and support from open-source contributors.

Table 9.1: Comparison of Windows and Linux server management

Each platform has its strengths, and the choice between them often depends on your organization's needs, budget, and expertise. Windows Server offers simplicity and integration, while Linux servers provide flexibility and customization.

Effective server administration is essential for maintaining system security, stability, and efficiency. By proactively monitoring performance, securing access, and ensuring compliance, administrators can minimize risks and enhance operational resilience. Leveraging automation and best practices further optimizes server management, reducing downtime and improving overall efficiency.

Storage management

Storage management involves the processes and practices used to organize, maintain, and optimize data storage systems, ensuring accessibility, security, and efficiency. It is a critical aspect of both personal computing and enterprise IT infrastructure.

Brief overview of its components and goals are given as follows:

- **Capacity planning**: Ensuring adequate storage to meet current and future needs.
- **Data organization**: Structuring and categorizing data for efficient access.
- **Backup and recovery**: Safeguarding data against loss by creating copies and providing mechanisms for restoration.
- **Performance optimization**: Monitoring and enhancing storage system speed and reliability.
- **Security**: Protecting data from unauthorized access and breaches.
- **Storage virtualization**: Pooling storage resources to simplify management and enhance scalability.

Effective storage management is essential for maintaining data integrity, security, and performance. By leveraging best practices such as tiered storage, encryption, backups, and automation, organizations can ensure that their storage infrastructure remains scalable, secure, and compliant with industry regulations.

Storage can be categorized based on its architecture, purpose, and access method. The following are the primary types of storage used in IT infrastructure:

- **Local storage**: Hard drives and direct-attached storage devices like internal or external hard drives.

- **Network storage**: **Network attached storage (NAS)** and **storage area networks (SAN)** for shared access.

- **Cloud storage**: Scalable and accessible solutions like Microsoft Azure or AWS.

Choosing the right storage type depends on factors such as speed, cost, scalability, and security. Organizations often use a combination of storage types to meet their operational and compliance needs.

Storage management under ISO 20000 ensures that data is stored securely, efficiently, and is accessible when needed while supporting business continuity and compliance.

Key steps in the storage management process are as follows:

1. **Planning and defining storage requirements**: Identify requirements for storage capacity, performance, and availability, and define storage policies, including backup, retention, and security controls.

2. **Storage provisioning and configuration**: Allocate storage resources based on service needs, implement logical storage management, and configure access controls to restrict unauthorized data access.

3. **Performance monitoring and capacity management**: Continuously monitor storage usage and performance using tools, and plan for future storage needs based on growth trends and service demands.

4. **Security and data protection**: Implement encryption for data-at-rest and data-in-transit, configure access control mechanisms, ensure compliance with data protection regulations, and regularly review storage logs and security incidents.

5. **Backup and disaster recovery**: Implement backup strategies, store backups in secure off-site locations or cloud storage for redundancy.

6. **Incident and problem management**: Detect and respond to storage-related incidents using an ITSM ticketing system, perform **root cause analysis (RCA)** for recurring storage issues, and implement corrective actions to prevent storage failures.

7. **Compliance and auditing**: Conduct regular audits and assessments to verify storage compliance, maintain records of storage performance, failures, and remediation actions, and ensure alignment with business continuity and ITSM policies.

The storage management process in ISO 20000 ensures efficient, secure, and compliant handling of data. By aligning storage management with ITSM best practices, organizations can improve data availability, security, and performance while supporting business continuity. Effective storage management helps ensure data availability, reduces downtime, and improves resource utilization.

Auditing the storage management process ensures that storage resources are used efficiently, securely, and in compliance with industry standards like ISO 20000, ISO 27001, etc. A structured audit helps identify risks, inefficiencies, and potential security vulnerabilities while ensuring business continuity and regulatory compliance. A storage management audit helps organizations enhance security, optimize performance, and maintain regulatory compliance. Regular audits ensure that storage systems remain efficient, resilient, and secure against data loss, cyber threats, and operational failures.

Endpoint management

Endpoint management process refers to the systematic approach of managing, securing, monitoring, and maintaining all endpoint devices (such as desktops, laptops, mobile devices, and servers) within an organization's IT infrastructure. It ensures that all endpoints are correctly configured, updated, and protected against security threats while maintaining compliance with IT policies and regulatory standards.

Key aspects of endpoint management can be defined as follows:

- **Device provisioning and configuration**: Ensuring endpoints are deployed with the correct security policies, software, and configurations.

- **Security and compliance**: Implementing antivirus, encryption, firewalls, and access controls to protect endpoints.

- **Patch and update management**: Regularly updating OS and software to fix vulnerabilities and improve performance.

- **Remote monitoring and troubleshooting**: Using tools like MDM, **remote monitoring and management (RMM)** for proactive maintenance.

- **Incident response and risk management**: Detecting and responding to endpoint-related threats and vulnerabilities.

- **Decommissioning and secure disposal**: Safely wiping and disposing of obsolete endpoints following security and compliance requirements.

The goals of endpoint management processes are to enhance security, ensure compliance, optimize performance, and minimize downtime by maintaining centralized control over all endpoint devices.

Endpoint detection and response (EDR) is an advanced security solution that monitors, detects, and responds to threats on endpoint devices (laptops, desktops, servers, mobile devices). EDR provides real-time visibility, threat intelligence, and automated response capabilities to mitigate cyber threats such as malware, ransomware, and insider attacks. EDR is a critical layer of endpoint security that enhances visibility, detection, and automated response against cyber threats.

Best practices for endpoint security are given as follows:

- **Asset management**: Maintain a classified and updated endpoint inventory.

- **Access control**: Restrict endpoint access based on roles and responsibilities.

- **Patch management**: Automate OS and software updates to mitigate vulnerabilities.

- **Data encryption**: Apply encryption for data at rest and for data in transit.

- **Incident response**: Implement a SIEM system for real-time threat detection on endpoints.

To summarize, endpoint management plays a crucial role in ensuring the security, efficiency, and functionality of an organization's IT infrastructure. It allows administrators to centrally monitor, manage, and secure all endpoints, including desktops, laptops, mobile devices, and servers. By leveraging tools like patch management, asset tracking, software deployment, and remote-control capabilities, organizations can enhance productivity while minimizing vulnerabilities and compliance risks. Effective endpoint management not only streamlines routine administrative tasks but also fortifies the overall defense against cyber threats in today's dynamic IT environments.

Infrastructure management

A robust network management framework facilitates effective communication, defends against cyber threats, and ensures optimal bandwidth utilization. Server management focuses on the seamless delivery of applications and services, emphasizing performance optimization, timely patching, and disaster recovery readiness. Storage management is essential for protecting vital data, deploying scalable storage systems, and enforcing strict data security measures. Endpoint management plays a crucial role in securing the organization's devices, addressing risks such as unauthorized access, malware, and data breaches.

A holistic approach to network, server, storage, and endpoint management integrates configuration, security, compliance, performance optimization, and automation across IT infrastructure, depicted as follows:

IT component	Key focus areas	Best practices
Network management	Performance, Security, Connectivity	VLAN segmentation, Zero Trust, Network Monitoring
Server management	Uptime, Configuration, Security	Patch Management, Hardening, Load Balancing

IT component	Key focus areas	Best practices
Storage management	Capacity, Data Integrity, Backup	**Redundant Array of Independent Disks (RAID)**, Encryption, Data Lifecycle Management
Endpoint management	Compliance, Security, Monitoring	EDR, MDM, Access Control

Table 9.2: Integrated IT infrastructure management

The table summarizes the focus areas and best practices to be followed in all aspects of infrastructure management:

Conclusion

In this chapter, we saw how the understanding of network, server, storage, and endpoint infrastructure, configuration, and day-to-day management of all IT devices and storage media is vital to becoming an IT auditor. Efficient management of network, server, storage, and endpoint infrastructure is critical for maintaining a secure, dependable, and high-performing IT environment. These elements serve as the foundation of an organization's digital operations, guaranteeing consistent connectivity, data availability, and system security.

In the next chapter, we will look at business continuity and disaster recovery planning. This will help us to know whether the access management, network, server, storage management processes are sufficient to address the availability commitment provided to end customers.

By adopting best practices, leveraging automation, and implementing proactive monitoring, organizations can improve operational efficiency, minimize downtime, and enhance cybersecurity. A holistic approach to managing networks, servers, storage, and endpoints not only ensures business continuity but also prepares organizations to respond effectively to evolving technological and security demands. This comprehensive management strategy enables organizations to remain flexible, robust, and ready to meet future challenges.

Join our Discord space

Join our Discord workspace for latest updates, offers, tech happenings around the world, new releases, and sessions with the authors:

https://discord.bpbonline.com

CHAPTER 10

Business Continuity and Disaster Recovery Planning

Introduction

In the earlier chapters, we learned about the major **IT service management** (**ITSM**) processes, namely server management, network management and storage management. This chapter looks at ensuring the availability of ITSM through setting up alternate assets as backup and with auto-failover.

Business continuity planning (**BCP**) and **disaster recovery planning** (**DRP**) are critical components of ITSM that ensure organizations can maintain continuous operations and recover from disruptions. BCP focuses on the overall strategy for sustaining business functions during and after an incident, while DRP specifically addresses the restoration of IT services and infrastructure. Together, they help organizations mitigate risks, minimize downtime, and ensure compliance with industry standards such as ISO 20000, ITIL, etc. Effective BCP and DRP frameworks involve risk assessment, impact analysis, recovery strategies, testing, and continuous improvement to enhance resilience against cyber threats, system failures, and natural disasters. These plans align IT services with business objectives, ensuring seamless service delivery and operational continuity in the face of unexpected disruptions.

Service continuity management complements the broader framework of **business continuity management** (**BCM**) and planning by ensuring the restoration of IT and services within agreed timeframes following a disaster or crisis. It is activated when a service disruption or organizational risk surpasses the entity's capacity to address it through standard response and recovery practices like incident and major incident management. Such significant occurrences are typically classified as disasters. Organizations must clearly identify what constitutes a disaster in their specific context. This definition should be established beforehand, both at the organizational level and for individual services, through a business impact analysis.

Structure

The chapter covers the following topics:

- Key concepts
- Business impact analysis
- Business continuity management framework
- Disaster recovery framework
- Business continuity and disaster recovery drills

Objectives

In this chapter, we will learn how service continuity management addresses events deemed critical enough to qualify as disasters. BCP and DRP are essential frameworks for organizations to ensure resilience in the face of disruptions. Understanding BCP and DRP is essential for auditors to assess an organization's preparedness for disruptions and ensure effective risk management. By the end of this chapter, we will have understood how auditors can provide valuable insights into an organization's ability to withstand and recover from disruptions, ensuring operational stability and strategic resilience. This lesson on BCP and DRP will cover key concepts that help organizations prepare for and respond to disruptions effectively.

Key concepts

A business continuity plan outlines the critical requirements necessary for sustaining business operations and incorporates strategies to minimize disruptions for customers and employees. Its primary focus is on enabling effective crisis management. The primary objective of BCP is to maintain business operations during and after a crisis. It focuses on identifying critical functions, assessing risks, and implementing strategies to minimize downtime. BCP ensures that essential services continue, allowing the organization to recover efficiently and maintain customer trust. DRP, on the other hand, specifically addresses the restoration of IT systems and data following an incident. Its goal is to reduce the impact of disruptions by having a structured recovery plan in place. DRP focuses on backup strategies, alternative system setups, and testing procedures to guarantee rapid recovery.

Acquiring knowledge about BCP and DRP equips individuals and organizations with a systematic approach to addressing IT disruptions and promoting service resilience. The key aim is to learn how to design, implement, and sustain strategies that reduce downtime and mitigate the impact of unexpected events such as cyberattacks, system outages, or natural disasters. This understanding enables IT professionals to evaluate risks, carry out business impact analyzes, define recovery methods, and assign clear responsibilities for crisis management. Furthermore, expertise in BCP and DRP supports adherence to industry standards like ISO 20000, ITIL, and ISO 27001, ensuring IT services meet regulatory demands. Regular testing and ongoing improvements of these plans enhance an organization's capacity for swift recovery and smooth operations.

BCPs and DRPs help organizations prepare for unexpected disruptions that may temporarily limit access to essential resources. The initial step in disaster preparedness involves assessing current business operations to identify critical functions, as well as hardware and software components that could be vulnerable. It is equally important to evaluate staff capabilities to ensure they can effectively lead recovery efforts and restore operations efficiently. Both frameworks work together to safeguard an organization against unforeseen events, protect assets, and uphold business continuity.

Objectives of BCP and DRP are centered around ensuring operational resilience and minimizing disruptions during unforeseen events.

Key differences between BCP and DRP are as follows:

- **BCP**: Focuses on maintaining business operations during a disruption, considering the business impact of downtime.

- **DRP**: Concentrates on the technical aspects of recovering IT systems and data after a disaster.

As we can see, technically, BCP refers to how loss of business may be avoided and it ought to define the business requirements for continuity of operations. BCP defines the business requirements for a DRP as well, in case a disaster occurs. We learnt in the previous chapter about how the network, server, and storage configurations focus on the continuity of ITSM.

BCP focuses on maintaining essential business functions, reducing the impact of disruptions on productivity and revenue, establishing proactive strategies to mitigate risks, providing assurance to customers, employees, and partners, and complying with regulatory requirements.

Objectives of DRP can be defined as restoring IT systems efficiently, protecting critical data assets, enabling seamless failover, mitigating financial losses, and ensuring cybersecurity resilience.

The key components of BCP and DRP ensure organizations can effectively respond to disruptions and recover with minimal impact. BCP includes risk assessment to identify potential threats, business impact analysis to prioritize critical functions, response strategies to maintain essential operations, and communication plans to ensure coordination during crises. Regular testing and updates help refine the plan and improve preparedness. DRP focuses on IT recovery, including data backup solutions, system restoration procedures, alternative infrastructure setups, and cybersecurity measures to protect against data loss. Documentation and drills ensure teams are ready to execute recovery protocols efficiently. Together, BCP and DRP strengthen an organization's ability to withstand and recover from unexpected events.

Business impact analysis

Business impact analysis (BIA) is a crucial process in organizational planning that identifies and evaluates the effects of disruptions to business operations. Its primary goal is to determine critical business functions, assess potential risks, and quantify the impact of those risks in terms of financial losses, legal implications, customer satisfaction, etc.

Key steps involved in a BIA include:

1. **Identifying critical functions**: Recognizing core business activities and processes essential for operation.

2. **Assessing risks**: Pinpointing potential threats, such as cyberattacks, natural disasters, or supply chain disruptions.

3. **Quantifying impact**: Analyzing how interruptions would affect aspects like revenue, compliance, and reputation.

4. **Setting priorities**: Establishing recovery priorities to ensure the most critical functions are restored first.

5. **Defining recovery requirements**: Determining the resources, timeframes, and strategies necessary for recovery.

A BIA is foundational to BCP and DRP, as it provides the data needed to develop effective recovery strategies. Each step in the BIA process builds upon the previous one, resulting in a clear and actionable plan for managing potential disruptions.

The BIA provides a clear understanding of critical business functions and their recovery priorities, which form the foundation of BCP. It helps define **recovery time objectives (RTOs)** and **recovery point objectives (RPOs)**, ensuring that the continuity plan aligns with the organization's tolerance for downtime and data loss. RTO is the maximum allowable downtime for a business process or system after a disruption before its impact becomes unacceptable. RPO refers to the maximum amount of data loss that an organization can tolerate in case of a disruption. It indicates how far back in time data restoration must go.

Based on the risks and impacts identified in the BIA, BCP outlines strategies to ensure uninterrupted operations during emergencies. For example, BCP looks at relocating critical operations to backup facilities, utilizing alternative communication channels, activating pre-established supply chain arrangements, etc.

The technical requirements for recovering IT systems and data (e.g., hardware, software, and network dependencies) identified in the BIA lead to the definition of the DRP. The DRP uses

BIA results to prioritize recovery steps for IT infrastructure and services, ensuring critical systems are restored first. It helps define resources such as backup solutions, data replication methods, and cloud recovery services to meet the organization's recovery objectives.

Regular testing of BCP and DRP is conducted using scenarios based on the risks and impacts identified in the BIA. For example, simulated cyberattacks, power outages, or natural disasters test the organization's readiness. Testing ensures that plans are practical, up-to-date, and effective in meeting recovery objectives.

Insights from the BIA allow organizations to adapt and refine their continuity and recovery strategies as business operations evolve or as new risks emerge. In essence, BIA acts as a blueprint that guides both BCP and DRP, ensuring the organization is well-prepared to handle disruptions efficiently.

When conducting the BIA, it is essential to evaluate potential risks that could negatively impact your business. These risks will vary depending on the industry, and it is crucial to create swift and effective strategies to mitigate them. Key risks to consider include the following:

- **Customer risks**: Changes in customer behavior and needs, such as widespread order cancellations, payment difficulties, or project delays. Additionally, you may need to handle a sudden surge in demand or adapt to producing an entirely new range of products.

- **Employee risks**: During a pandemic, managing infections remains a top priority.

- **Supply risks**: Disruptions caused by the impact of supply interruptions due to issues at the supplier's end. It is vital to explore alternative suppliers or other contingency measures.

- **Financial risks**: In a crisis, maintaining cash flow is critical.

The primary challenge is organizing and prioritizing these risks to allocate resources effectively toward mitigating the most significant ones. This process lies at the heart of creating a comprehensive business continuity plan and ensuring effective management.

Business continuity management framework

A BCP is essential for building a resilient business that can adapt to an ever-changing environment and withstand potential disruptions. The ability to recover quickly from incidents such as floods or fires and resume operations seamlessly is crucial. Safeguarding the future of a business, regardless of its size, should be a top priority. For smaller businesses, having a contingency plan is even more critical, as any disruption, no matter how minor, can impact operations and profitability. Even small businesses should have measures in place to ensure continuity in the event of theft, natural disasters, IT failures, or utility outages.

A **business continuity management system** (**BCMS**) is a structured framework that helps organizations identify, assess, and mitigate risks to ensure the continuity of critical business operations. It aligns with international standards like ISO 22301, ensuring resilience against disruptions such as cyberattacks, natural disasters, system failures, and operational crises. This BCMS framework follows a **Plan-Do-Check-Act** (**PDCA**) cycle, integrating business continuity into daily operations. ISO standard for BCP is ISO 22301, titled *Security and resilience – Business continuity management systems – Requirements*. This standard provides a framework for organizations to establish, implement, maintain, and improve a BCMS. It focuses on enhancing organizational resilience and ensuring continuity of operations during disruptions. ISO 22301 outlines key aspects such as risk assessment, BIA, continuity strategies, testing and maintenance, etc.

The BCMS framework follows the PDCA cycle, integrating business continuity into daily operations. This includes the following steps:

1. **BIA**: Identifies critical business functions, dependencies, and potential impacts of disruptions.

2. **Risk assessment**: Evaluates threats, vulnerabilities, and the likelihood of disruptions to prioritize response measures.

3. **Business continuity strategy**: Defines recovery objectives, alternative work arrangements, and IT disaster recovery plans.

4. **Incident response and crisis management**: Establishes response teams, communication protocols, and escalation procedures.

5. **BCP and DRP development**: Documents business continuity and disaster recovery procedures, ensuring rapid response and recovery.

6. **Testing and training**: Conducts BCP drills, tabletop exercises, and awareness programs to validate plan effectiveness.

7. **Monitoring and continuous improvement**: Regularly reviews and updates the BCMS to address evolving risks and compliance requirements.

The most important step in implementing BCMS is establishing governance and acquiring leadership commitment. This requires securing top management support, establishing a business continuity steering committee and appointing a business continuity manager.

Next comes the definition of the BCMS scope and objectives, which involves identifying the business functions, services, and locations included within the system. This step ensures that BCMS objectives are aligned with the organization's overall goals and any applicable regulatory requirements. Additionally, **key performance indicators** (**KPIs**) are established to assess the effectiveness of the BCMS.

BCMS framework ensures compliance with regulatory requirements such as ISO 22301, ITIL, ISO 20000, and ISO 27001. A well-implemented BCMS enhances resilience, minimizes downtime, and ensures an organization is prepared for unforeseen disruptions. By following a structured approach, organizations can safeguard critical operations, protect data, and maintain customer trust. Continuous improvement and proactive testing are key to ensuring long-term success.

Acceptable downtime

BCP is designed to ensure the continuity of an organization's mission-critical processes during and after a disruption. A BCP can focus on processes within a specific business unit or cover the entire organization. Its scope may also be limited to prioritizing essential functions. For long-term recovery, a BCP can work alongside the **continuity of operations plan** (**COOP**), gradually restoring additional functions as resources and time become available. Since mission-critical processes often rely on information systems, business continuity planners must collaborate with system owners to align the BCP's goals with the capabilities of these systems.

COOP prioritizes the restoration of an organization's essential functions at an alternate location, allowing these functions to operate for up to a minimum defined number of days before transitioning back to regular operations. Additional functions, including those at a field office level, are generally managed through BCP. Minor disruptions or threats that do not necessitate relocation to an alternate site are usually outside the scope of a COOP plan.

The business continuity manager should analyze mission-critical business processes. This analysis should be conducted in collaboration with process owners, leadership, and business managers. Together, they must determine the acceptable downtime in case a process or specific system data is disrupted or becomes unavailable. Downtime can be identified in several ways:

- **Maximum tolerable downtime** (**MTD**): Refers to the maximum duration that a system owner or authorizing official can tolerate for a mission-critical process to be disrupted, factoring in all potential impacts. Defining MTD is crucial to provide contingency planners with clear guidance on selecting suitable recovery methods and determining the necessary level of detail for developing recovery procedures, including their scope and content.

- **Recovery time objective** (**RTO**): Represents the maximum duration a system resource can remain unavailable before causing unacceptable consequences for other system resources, mission-critical processes, or the MTD. Establishing RTO for an information system resource is essential for choosing technologies that effectively align with the MTD. If meeting the RTO immediately is not possible and the MTD cannot be adjusted, a plan of action and timelines of action should be created to document the issue and outline mitigation steps.

- **Recovery point objective** (**RPO**): Refers to the specific point in time before a system outage or disruption to which mission-critical data can be restored, based on the most recent backup. Unlike RTO, RPO is not directly linked to the MTD; rather, it reflects the extent of data loss the mission/business process can tolerate during recovery. Since the RTO must ensure compliance with the MTD, it is typically shorter than the MTD. For instance, if a system outage disrupts a process, additional time required to reprocess data must be included in the RTO to remain within the MTD's limits.

Foundation of BCP

The foundation of BCP is built on ensuring an organization can maintain essential operations and recover quickly from disruptions. It involves proactive strategies to safeguard against potential threats and minimize downtime. A strong BCP framework helps organizations stay resilient, minimize financial and reputational damage, and maintain stability even in times of crisis.

Prevention, preparedness, response, and recovery can serve as the foundation for BCP across an organization:

- **Prevention**: Integrated within risk management planning, this step focuses on identifying and addressing the likelihood and potential consequences of risks associated with an incident.

- **Preparedness**: Reflected in the BIA, this step emphasizes identifying and prioritizing crucial business activities that could be significantly affected by disruptions.

- **Response**: Embedded in incident response planning, this phase outlines immediate actions for incident containment, control, and impact minimization.

- **Recovery**: Central to recovery planning, this step defines strategies to restore operations after an incident, aiming to reduce disruption and accelerate recovery times.

The BCP framework provides organizations with a structured approach to ensuring resilience against disruptions. By integrating risk assessment, BIA, response strategies, and regular testing, businesses can minimize downtime and maintain critical operations.

Power backup is a critical component of BCP for IT systems, ensuring uninterrupted operations during outages. Organizations typically implement solutions such as **uninterruptible power supply (UPS)** for short-term backup, generators for extended power support, and redundant power sources to maintain system availability. A well-structured power backup strategy includes risk assessment, identifying potential power failure scenarios, and load balancing to distribute power efficiently across critical systems. Regular testing and maintenance of backup systems are essential to ensure reliability during emergencies.

Cloud data backup is a reliable and scalable solution for protecting critical information from loss or corruption. It involves storing copies of data on remote cloud servers, ensuring accessibility and security even in case of hardware failures or cyber threats. Cloud backup services offer automated backups, encryption for data protection, and disaster recovery options. These services allow businesses and individuals to securely store and retrieve their data from anywhere with an internet connection.

Network connectivity is yet another crucial aspect of BCP, ensuring uninterrupted communication and data access during disruptions. A resilient network minimizes downtime, protects business operations, and supports disaster recovery efforts. Key strategies for network connectivity in BCP include redundancy through multiple data paths, different service providers to ensure redundancy of localized risks, and proactive monitoring to detect potential issues before they escalate. Organizations should also implement failover mechanisms, scalable infrastructure, and cybersecurity measures to safeguard network integrity.

Succession planning is a vital component of BCP, ensuring that leadership transitions do not disrupt operations. It involves identifying key roles, assessing potential successors, and preparing individuals to step into critical positions when needed. A well-structured succession plan helps organizations maintain stability during unexpected events such as retirements, resignations, or emergencies. It ensures that essential functions continue without delays, reducing risks associated with leadership gaps.

Ensuring backup resources for critical support roles is essential for maintaining **service level agreements** (**SLAs**) and minimizing disruptions. Organizations can implement strategies such as cross-training employees, maintaining on-call support teams, and leveraging automated monitoring tools to ensure continuity in service delivery.

Key approaches include the following:

- **Redundant staffing**: Identifying secondary personnel who can step in when primary support staff are unavailable.

- **Knowledge management systems**: Documenting processes and solutions to enable seamless transitions.

- **Automated workflows**: Using AI-driven tools to handle routine tasks and escalate critical issues efficiently.

- **Third-party support**: Partnering with external vendors for additional expertise and emergency assistance.

A well-structured plan guarantees that essential roles can be filled promptly, mitigating risks associated with leadership vacancies or skill gaps. By integrating automated HR systems, documentation of key processes, and partnerships with external talent sources, organizations can sustain productivity and service quality even during unforeseen events.

A well-designed BCP enhances organizational preparedness, safeguards stakeholders, and ensures regulatory compliance. Ultimately, continuous improvement and adaptation to evolving threats are essential for maintaining an effective and resilient business continuity strategy.

Disaster recovery framework

Disaster recovery framework is a structured approach to restoring IT systems, data, and infrastructure after a disruption. It focuses on minimizing downtime, ensuring data integrity, and maintaining business operations. Key components include risk assessment, BIA, recovery objectives, RTO and RPO, backup strategies, redundancy planning, and regular testing. A well-defined DR framework enhances resilience, reduces financial losses, and ensures compliance with regulatory requirements, enabling organizations to recover swiftly from cyber incidents, natural disasters, or system failures.

Key components of a disaster recovery framework are as follows:

- **Risk assessment and BIA**: Identifies potential threats (cyberattacks, hardware failures, natural disasters), evaluates the impact of disruptions on business operations, and determines the criticality of various systems and data.

- **Disaster recovery objectives**: RTO, which is defined as the maximum acceptable downtime before critical operations must be restored, and RPO, defined as the maximum acceptable data loss in terms of time (e.g., last 1 hour of transactions).

- **Backup and data protection strategies**: Regular backups (full, incremental, differential) stored securely, onsite and offsite backup strategies (cloud, backup data centers, tape storage, etc.), and encryption and access controls for data protection.

- **Redundancy and failover mechanisms**: **High availability (HA)** where replicated systems are present to ensure continuous operations, failover systems with automatic switching to backup systems in case of failure, and load balancing whereby traffic gets distributed to prevent overload on a single system.

- **Disaster recovery plan (DRP) development**: Documented step-by-step recovery procedures, roles and responsibilities of DR team members, and communication protocols for internal teams, stakeholders, and customers.

- **Testing and validation**: Regular DR testing (tabletop exercises, failover tests, full-scale recovery tests), identifying gaps and continuously improving recovery strategies, and ensuring compliance with industry standards like ISO 22301.

- **Continuous monitoring and improvement**: Using automated monitoring tools to detect potential failures early, updating DR plans as business processes and IT infrastructure evolve, and conducting employee training on DR processes and security best practices.

The benefits of a strong DR framework can be summarized as follows:

- Minimizes downtime and reduces financial losses.
- Ensures data integrity and availability during disruptions.
- Enhances compliance with regulatory requirements.
- Improves customer trust by ensuring reliability.
- Supports business continuity with minimal service interruptions.

A well-structured disaster recovery framework ensures that an organization can respond swiftly and effectively to disruptions, maintaining operational resilience and safeguarding business-critical data.

DR actions and timeframes are dependent on the type of disaster event. Once an event is defined as a disaster, recovery actions start as soon as possible, but complications and delays may impede recovery so that full recovery may take some time.

DRPs and BCPs should be designed to handle the majority of disasters that can be anticipated, but as with any serious and unexpected interruption, there can be special situations that need to be dealt with. Actions, timeframes, and special circumstances associated with typical disaster types have to be captured as the first step in preparing a disaster recovery plan.

Disaster events can lead to confusion, panic, and the spread of misinformation. In such situations, it is crucial to provide clear and accurate information about the incident and the necessary response actions. Every staff member should be aware of their role beforehand to ensure a coordinated response. Establishing a well-defined communication channel is essential for reaching all affected parties, including both internal teams and external organizations. Additionally, maintaining an up-to-date list of key company contacts ensures that critical personnel can be reached immediately in the event of a disaster.

Network redundancy

Network redundancy is essential for ensuring BCP by minimizing downtime and maintaining seamless operations during failures. A redundant network architecture reduces the risk of disruptions caused by hardware failures, cyberattacks, or natural disasters.

Key redundancy requirements for BCP can be captured as follows:

- **Multiple Internet service providers (ISPs)**: Using multiple ISPs prevents connectivity failures in case one provider goes down, and implementing automatic failover to switch between ISPs seamlessly.

- **Redundant network** paths: Using multiple physical and logical paths for data transmission, deploying dual or multiple WAN links for critical locations, and implementing **multiprotocol label switching (MPLS)**, **software-defined wide area network (SD-WAN)**, or **virtual private network (VPN)** tunnels for resilient connectivity.

- **Backup data centers and cloud redundancy**: Hosting critical applications and services in geographically separated data centers, utilizing multi-cloud or hybrid cloud environments to ensure availability, and implementing real-time data replication between primary and backup locations.

- **HA and auto failover mechanisms**: Using load balancers to distribute traffic across multiple servers, deploying hot standby and active-passive configurations for mission-critical systems, and implementing automatic failover for servers, databases, and applications.

- **Redundant power and cooling systems**: Ensuring dual power supplies with UPS and backup generators and maintaining redundant cooling systems to prevent overheating and hardware failure.

- **Redundant network devices**: Deploying dual firewalls, routers, and switches for critical infrastructure, and using **Spanning Tree Protocol (STP)** to prevent network loops and ensure failover.

- **Regular network testing and DR drills**: Conducting failover tests to verify redundancy effectiveness, performing penetration testing and vulnerability assessments on redundant systems, and updating BCP strategies based on test results and emerging threats.

A redundant network infrastructure is critical for effective business continuity. By implementing multiple ISPs, backup data centers, redundant network paths, and failover mechanisms, organizations can reduce downtime, enhance reliability, and maintain seamless operations during disruptions.

Business continuity and disaster recovery drills

BCP and DRP drills are essential for testing preparedness and ensuring adequate response during disruptions. Conducting periodic drills strengthens an organization's resilience, minimizes downtime, and ensures employees are well-prepared to handle unexpected events.

BCP drills focus on simulating scenarios where critical business operations might be affected, such as supply chain disruptions, cyberattacks, or natural disasters. These drills help evaluate response strategies, communication protocols, and team coordination to ensure business functions remain operational.

DRP drills specifically target IT recovery, including testing data backup systems, infrastructure failover procedures, cybersecurity incident responses, and system restoration protocols. Regular DRP drills verify the effectiveness of recovery measures and identify gaps that need improvement.

Hot, warm, and cold backup locations are different types of disaster recovery sites that organizations use to ensure business continuity in case of disruptions. A hot backup site is a fully operational facility that mirrors the primary site, with real-time data replication and all necessary infrastructure ready for immediate use. It allows for minimal downtime and is ideal for businesses that require continuous operations. A warm backup site has essential infrastructure and some pre-configured systems but does not have real-time data synchronization. It requires some setup before becoming fully functional, making it a balance between cost and recovery speed. A cold backup site is the most cost-effective option, consisting of a basic facility without pre-installed systems or data replication. It requires significant time to set up and restore operations, making it suitable for businesses that can afford longer recovery times.

Mirrored systems in BCP refer to duplicate infrastructure that ensures seamless operations during disruptions. These systems continuously replicate data and applications in real time, allowing organizations to switch to an identical backup system without downtime. Mirrored sites function similarly to hot sites, providing an exact copy of critical systems that can take over instantly in case of failure. This approach enhances resilience, minimizes recovery time, and ensures business continuity.

To structure effective BCP and DRP drills, organizations should follow a systematic approach to testing their preparedness and response strategies.

Clear objectives for each drill have to be defined, specifying whether the focus is on business continuity or IT recovery. Critical processes, systems, and teams involved in executing the plan are to be identified. Realistic scenarios, such as cyberattacks, natural disasters, or infrastructure failures, to evaluate responses under different conditions, are to be identified. Tabletop exercises, where key stakeholders discuss the response strategies, followed by full-scale simulations to test actual procedures, are to be conducted. All use cases and roles are to be well understood, and communication channels are to be made functional. Recovery timelines are to be defined in alignment with predefined expectations.

After each drill, a post-evaluation review must be conducted to document findings, identify gaps, and refine the plan based on observed weaknesses. Continuous improvements through regular drills strengthen preparedness, ensuring the organization can withstand unexpected disruptions.

BCP drills often include crisis management simulations where employees practice responding to operational disruptions, emergency response exercises that test evacuation and safety measures, supply chain continuity drills to ensure alternative sourcing, and remote work capability tests that assess how effectively business functions can continue in unexpected scenarios. DRP drills focus more on IT recovery and may include data backup and restoration tests to verify recovery procedures, cyberattack simulations to evaluate security response plans, system failover testing to ensure infrastructure redundancy, and disaster recovery scenario exercises to practice restoring critical applications and network functions.

Conducting these drills regularly strengthens preparedness, helps refine response strategies, and ensures minimal downtime during real disruptions. Organizations often discover weaknesses in their backup systems, recovery timelines, or infrastructure failover processes, allowing them to make necessary improvements before a real incident occurs. Drills also help employees familiarize themselves with emergency procedures, making responses more efficient when faced with actual disruptions. Regular testing fosters adaptability, ensuring that contingency plans remain relevant to evolving threats and technological advancements. The results from these exercises contribute to strengthening resilience, reducing downtime, and enhancing overall organizational stability.

Comparison of BCP and DRP

BCP and DRP are essential frameworks for ensuring an organization's resilience against disruptions. While BCP focuses on maintaining critical business operations, DRP ensures the swift restoration of IT systems and data. Together, they minimize downtime, protect assets, and enable seamless recovery. A well-structured approach to both plans strengthens preparedness, mitigates risks, and safeguards business continuity.

BCP involves risk assessment, BIA, response strategies, and communication plans, ensuring operational continuity. DRP emphasizes IT recovery, including data backup, system restoration, infrastructure redundancy, and cybersecurity measures for quick recovery. Together, BCP and DRP minimize downtime, protect assets, mitigate risks, and strengthen preparedness. A well-developed plan enhances business stability and ensures a swift recovery from unforeseen events.

Choosing the right backup strategy depends on an organization's RTO and budget constraints. A well-balanced approach ensures business continuity while optimizing costs and efficiency. Hot, warm, and cold backup solutions each offer different levels of preparedness for disaster recovery. Hot backups provide real-time data replication and immediate failover, ensuring minimal downtime. Warm backups maintain pre-configured infrastructure but require some setup before full functionality. Cold backups are the most cost-effective but take the longest to restore, as they lack pre-installed systems.

The critical role of DRP in ensuring business continuity during unexpected events such as cyberattacks, system failures, or natural disasters has to be understood. The essential components of a DRP are risk assessment, recovery strategies, backup procedures, and definition of roles and responsibilities. DRP emphasizes that regular testing and updates to keep the DRP effective and aligned with evolving threats and technologies are very important for an organization.

BCP and DRP drills are essential for testing an organization's preparedness for disruptions. These exercises help evaluate response effectiveness, identify gaps, and improve coordination among teams. Regular drills ensure that employees are familiar with emergency protocols, recovery timelines are met, and critical systems can be restored efficiently.

Conclusion

We saw how BIA and BCMS are essential for ensuring organizational resilience. BIA helps identify critical functions, assess potential disruptions, and prioritize recovery efforts, while BCMS provides a structured framework for maintaining operations during crises. Together, they enable businesses to mitigate risks, minimize downtime, and enhance preparedness. A well-implemented BIA and BCMS strengthen an organization's ability to adapt to unforeseen challenges and maintain stability.

DRP emphasizes the importance of preparedness and resilience in safeguarding an organization's operations against disruptions. In essence, a well-structured DRP is not just a contingency plan; it is a strategic approach to minimizing downtime, protecting assets, and maintaining operational stability in the face of unforeseen disruptions. Organizations that invest in robust disaster recovery measures position themselves for long-term success and resilience in an ever-changing technological landscape.

In the next chapter, we will be looking at how the IT services can be defined, keeping the context of an organization. We will also look at the responsibilities of the IT team surrounding the application management.

CHAPTER 11
Organization Context and IT Services

Introduction

In this chapter, we are going to look at what are the typical **information technology** (**IT**) services an organization has to manage. In today's technology-centric world, IT services have become the foundation upon which most modern organizations operate. Regardless of size, industry, or mission, IT is no longer merely a support function; it involves strategic and tactical operations, that drive efficiency, enable growth, and enhance competitiveness.

At its essence, IT services involve the application of both business and technical expertise to support and optimize access to information, automate processes, and manage technology infrastructure. These services play a pivotal role in ensuring seamless business operations and facilitating innovation. IT services has to be looked at, as the digital ecosystem that powers an organization, supporting daily activities, enhancing employee productivity, enabling secure communication, and safeguarding data. Whether it is basic network connectivity, cloud-based collaboration tools, or complex enterprise applications, IT services are integral to day-to-day functionality.

IT services are not a singular function, but a network of interconnected capabilities managed internally, outsourced to providers, or delivered through hybrid models. Grasping the scope and purpose of these services is essential to understanding how deeply they influence modern organizations and why they are vital for long-term success.

Structure

The chapter covers the following topics:

- Key concepts
- Business and IT operation context
- IT strategy, service and support
- Regulatory requirement
- Responsibility in application management

Objectives

In this chapter, we will learn how understanding IT services in an organizational context serves a wide range of purposes for business leaders, IT professionals, and end-users. Each group benefits from this knowledge in different, but interconnected ways. Ultimately, the goal of learning about IT services is to enable all stakeholders to use technology more effectively, align IT with business priorities, and support smooth and secure operations in today's digital environment.

By covering these key concepts, this chapter helps us provide a comprehensive understanding of the vital role IT plays in modern business operations. ISO 20000 ensures that organizations collaborate effectively with stakeholders to implement high-quality IT services that are continuously monitored, evaluated, and improved. Regular review of these processes helps uncover areas for enhancement, leading to more efficient operations and improved service delivery to customers.

Key concepts

IT services can vary significantly across different organizations depending on factors such as industry, business size, operational needs, regulatory environment, and technological maturity. While the core principles of IT services, enabling business operations, ensuring security, and supporting users, are consistent, the implementation, scope, and focus of those services differ based on the organization's unique context. Customizing IT services to meet specific business needs ensures greater efficiency, compliance, and alignment with strategic goals.

IT service management (**ITSM**) provides a structured framework that helps organizations develop an IT service management plan with clearly defined objectives and targets. It also guides them in specifying service delivery requirements, clarifying roles and responsibilities, regularly assessing the performance of IT services, and identifying opportunities for ongoing improvement. The various stakeholders of IT services are as follows:

- **Business professionals**: Learning about IT services helps business leaders recognize how technology supports strategic objectives, drives operational efficiency, and creates competitive advantage. It enables them to make informed decisions about IT investments, outsourcing, and technology adoption. A clear understanding of IT services also fosters effective communication with technical teams, aligns IT initiatives with broader business goals, and strengthens risk management and compliance efforts. Furthermore, it supports process improvement and better vendor management through knowledge of service expectations and performance metrics.

- **IT specialists**: IT professionals benefit by adopting a service-oriented mindset, focusing not just on technology but also on the value delivered to users and the business. It encourages best practices in service delivery and management, helps in understanding user needs, and supports continuous improvement of services. It also enhances resource optimization, problem-solving capabilities, and the ability to introduce innovative technologies that improve service quality and efficiency.

- **End-users**: End-users gain awareness of the IT services available to them and how to use them effectively. They learn how to report issues, follow security best practices, and use technology responsibly. By understanding the role of IT in their daily work, users can increase their productivity and contribute valuable feedback to help improve services.

Organizations adopt IT services to fulfil several key objectives given as follows:

- Increase productivity through automation and smarter workflows.

- Enable effective communication and collaboration across teams and geographies.

- Maintain business continuity with robust backup, disaster recovery, and cybersecurity systems.

- Foster innovation through emerging technologies and digital solutions.

- Safeguard critical information and ensure compliance with data protection laws.

- Enhance customer experience by supporting digital platforms and engagement tools.

IT services in a typical organization can be explained through the following key concepts:

- **Foundational concepts**: Definition of IT services, detailing types of IT services, listing all stakeholders of IT services, defining the role of the IT department, capturing business alignment of IT services, etc.

- **Core service management principles**: Introducing service lifecycle, creation of service value, understanding customer-centricity, defining **service level agreements** (**SLAs**), capturing **key performance indicators** (**KPIs**) for IT services, etc.

- **Key service areas**: IT infrastructure services part of ITSM, application services like software development and maintenance, IT support services like help desk or service desk operations, IT security services, data management services, communication and collaboration services, etc.

- **Delivery and sourcing models**: Internal IT and outsourcing, managed service providers, hybrid IT environments involving a combination of internal and external IT resources.

- **Emerging trends and considerations**: Enabling digital transformation initiatives, automation and **artificial intelligence** (**AI**), leveraging data analytics, considering sustainability in IT, etc.

The scope of typical IT services is broad, covering infrastructure, applications, support, security, and data management. Their delivery can involve internal teams, external providers, or a hybrid model, each with its own considerations. Furthermore, the management of these services is guided by strategic frameworks and best practices, aiming for efficiency, reliability, and alignment with business goals.

Business and IT operation context

Understanding both the business context and the IT operation context is essential for grasping how an organization functions and how its technology infrastructure supports its strategic objectives. These contexts offer the foundational insight required for effective planning, decision-making, and alignment between business priorities and IT capabilities.

Business context outlines the broader environment in which an organization operates. It explains the reasons behind the organization's existence, its long-term vision, and the various factors that shape its strategies and activities. This includes its goals, industry dynamics, competitive landscape, regulatory requirements, customer base, and key business processes. It also involves internal elements such as organizational structure, culture, and financial standing, along with external influences like economic conditions, technological trends, and political or legal developments. In short, the business context answers critical questions such as what the organization aims to achieve, who its customers and competitors are, and what internal and external factors impact its success.

The IT operation context focuses on the internal functioning and capabilities of the IT function. It defines how IT supports the broader business environment. This includes the organization's IT infrastructure, applications, systems, and services, as well as the teams, roles, and processes that manage them. It also considers the technical skills of IT staff, budgetary resources, governance structures, and the security measures in place to protect digital assets. Essentially, the IT operation context answers questions about the current state of technology, available resources, and how IT operations are structured and managed to support business needs.

The relationship between these two contexts is deeply interconnected. Business goals and strategies should shape IT decisions, meaning that IT must align its services, resources, and development efforts with what the business aims to accomplish. This alignment ensures that technology investments deliver tangible value and support growth, innovation, and resilience. Defining both contexts is crucial for several reasons. It ensures alignment between business and IT, enabling smarter investments and better resource allocation. It lays the groundwork for strategic planning and risk management, supports more effective communication between technical and business teams, and facilitates smoother problem-solving and change management. By clearly understanding where the organization stands and where it aims to go, both in business and in IT, leaders can make more informed decisions and ensure that technology serves as a true enabler of organizational success.

ISO 20000 does not mandate a specific structure for an ITSM, nor does it prescribe the terminology used for its components. *Figure 11.1* illustrates the main components of its high-level structure, including the ITSM, and the associated clauses outlined in the standard. However, this representation should not be interpreted as a rigid hierarchy, fixed authority levels, or a strict naming system. Instead, it serves as a flexible framework that can be tailored to meet the operational needs of each organization. For instance, in some cases, it may be practical to merge SMS support and operational processes if they overlap within your environment. Regardless of how the structure is adapted, it is important to note that all requirements of the standard remain mandatory, and none of the clauses can be omitted for compliance.

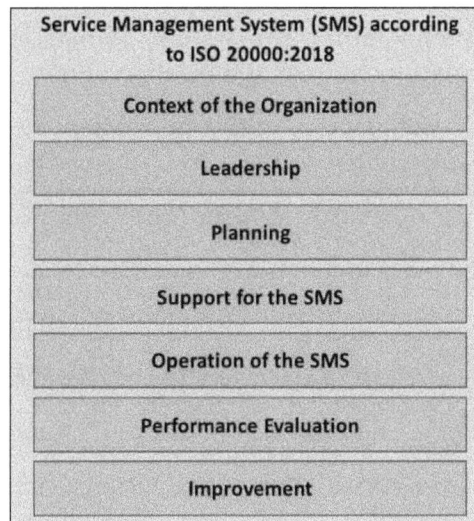

Service Management System (SMS) according to ISO 20000:2018
Context of the Organization
Leadership
Planning
Support for the SMS
Operation of the SMS
Performance Evaluation
Improvement

Figure 11.1: IT service management system

The *context of the organization* clause in ISO 20000 outlines the requirements for establishing, implementing, maintaining, and continually improving an ITSM. It emphasizes the need to understand both internal and external factors, as well as the influence and expectations of interested parties (such as stakeholders), which could affect the organization's ability to meet its objectives. Gaining a clear understanding of these elements is essential for successfully implementing an effective ITSM.

Defining the business context with a focus on IT services involves understanding the overarching organizational environment and, crucially, how IT services are perceived, utilized, and expected to contribute within that context. It is about seeing the business landscape through the lens of its technological dependencies and opportunities.

Here is a breakdown of key elements to consider when defining the business context with a specific focus on IT services:

- **Business goals and strategic objectives (and IT's role)**: Overall business strategy, IT's contribution to goals, key business initiatives, etc.

- **Industry and market dynamics (and IT's impact)**: Industry trends, market demands, regulatory environment, etc.

- **Business processes and IT dependencies**: Core business processes, IT enablement of business processes, opportunities for IT optimization, etc.

- **Organizational structure and culture and IT adoption strategy**: Interfaces in organizational structure, organizational culture, etc.

- **Key stakeholders and their IT needs**: End customers, employees, management, partners and suppliers, etc.

- **Financial considerations and IT investment**: IT budget and spending, **return on investment (ROI)** expectations, cost optimization opportunities, etc.

- **Risk and compliance and IT's role in risk mitigation**: Business risks, IT's role in risk mitigation, compliance requirements, etc.

In essence, defining the business context with a focus on IT services means understanding:

- Where the business is going and how IT is expected to reach the goals.

- Technological landscape of the industry and how IT can provide a competitive edge.

- Critical business processes and the level of their dependence on IT.

- Organizational dynamics and how they influence IT adoption and effectiveness.

- Needs of various stakeholders and how IT services can meet them.

- Financial implications of IT investments and the expected business value.

- Risks the business faces and how IT services contribute to their mitigation.

By thoroughly defining the business context with this IT-centric lens, organizations can make more informed decisions about their technology strategy, prioritize IT investments effectively, and ensure that IT services are truly aligned with and contribute to achieving overall business success.

Service management continues to evolve in response to these organizational shifts, ensuring that emerging technologies and modern work practices are effectively leveraged to maximize opportunities. As customer expectations rise, service management adapts to maintain relevance and drive innovation.

IT strategy, service and support

Service management can be defined as a set of specialized organizational capabilities for enabling value for customers in the form of services. A strategy for ITSM provides a structured approach for how an organization will manage its IT services to best support its business goals and meet the needs of its users. It is a high-level plan that outlines the guiding principles, objectives, and key initiatives for how IT services will be delivered, managed, and improved over time.

Here is a breakdown of the key elements involved in developing an effective ITSM strategy:

- **Understanding business context**:
  - o **Business goals and objectives**: ITSM strategy must be directly aligned with the overall business strategy, goals, and objectives. And the strategy should understand what the business aims to achieve and how IT can contribute to achieving the same.
  - o **Organizational culture**: Consider the organization's culture, values, and how it approaches technology advancements and service delivery.
  - o **Stakeholder needs**: Identify all key stakeholders (customers, employees, partners) and understand their expectations and requirements from IT services to support their business transactions.
  - o **Industry and market trends**: Be aware of relevant industry trends and how technology is being used by competitors.
  - o **Regulatory and compliance requirements**: Ensure the ITSM strategy addresses any relevant legal, regulatory, or compliance obligations.
- **Defining vision, mission, and objectives for IT services**:
  - o **Vision**: A concise statement outlining the desired future state of IT services within the organization.
  - o **Mission**: A statement that describes the purpose and role of IT services in supporting the business.
  - o **Objectives**: **Specific, Measurable, Achievable, Relevant, and Time-bound (SMART)** goals for IT service management. These should directly support the business objectives.
- **Assessing the current as-is state**:
  - o **Service portfolio**: Understand the current IT services offered, their capabilities, and their value to the business.
  - o **Processes and procedures**: Evaluate existing IT processes (e.g., incident management, change management, problem management) and identify areas for improvement.

- o **Technology and infrastructure**: Assess the current IT infrastructure, tools, and technologies in place.

- o **People and skills**: Analyze the skills and capabilities of the IT staff.

- o **Maturity level**: Determine the current maturity level of ITSM practices.

- **Defining the desired future to-be state**:

  - o **Target service portfolio**: Outline the future services that will be required to meet business needs and strategic goals.

  - o **Improved processes**: Define the optimized and standardized IT processes that will be implemented.

  - o **Technology roadmap**: Plan for the adoption of new technologies and the evolution of the existing infrastructure.

  - o **Required skills and organization**: Identify the necessary skills and organizational structure for the future ITSM model.

  - o **Target maturity level**: Set a target maturity level for ITSM practices based on business requirements and industry best practices.

- **Developing the ITSM roadmap**:

  - o **Prioritized initiatives**: Identify and prioritize the key initiatives required to move from the current state to the desired future state. This could include process implementation, tool deployments, training programs, and organizational changes.

  - o **Timeline and milestones**: Define a realistic timeline with key milestones for each initiative.

  - o **Resource allocation**: Plan for the necessary resources (budget, personnel, tools) to execute the roadmap.

- **Choosing an ITSM framework**:

  - o **Information Technology Infrastructure Library (ITIL)**: A widely adopted framework providing best-practice guidance for ITSM, especially at the initial implementation phase.

  - o **Control Objectives for Information and related Technology (COBIT)**: Focuses on IT governance and management, ensuring IT aligns with business goals.

  - o **ISO 20000**: An international standard for ITSM systems.

- **Defining key processes**: Establish and document the core ITSM processes based on the chosen framework and the organization's specific requirements. Examples include: incident management, problem management, change management, service request and service level management, asset management, configuration management, etc.

- **Establishing governance and measurement**:
  - o **Roles and responsibilities**: Clearly define the roles and responsibilities for ITSM activities.
  - o **Policies and procedures**: Develop and implement clear policies and procedures to guide ITSM practices.
  - o **KPIs**: Identify relevant KPIs to measure the effectiveness and efficiency of IT services and processes.
  - o **Reporting and monitoring**: Establish mechanisms for regular reporting and monitoring of KPIs to track progress and identify areas for improvement.
- **Communication and stakeholder engagement**:
  - o Develop a communication plan to keep stakeholders informed about the ITSM strategy and progress.
  - o Actively engage with stakeholders to gather feedback and ensure their needs are being met.
- **Continual service improvement (CSI)**:
  - o Embed a culture of continual improvement within the IT organization.
  - o Regularly review the ITSM strategy, processes, and performance against KPIs.
  - o Identify and implement opportunities for improvement based on data analysis, feedback, and evolving business needs.

By following an integrated strategic approach, organizations can establish well-defined and effective IT support processes that contribute significantly to user satisfaction, business productivity, and the overall success of the IT function. Remember that this is an iterative process, and the strategy should be reviewed and updated regularly to adapt to evolving needs and technologies. Key considerations for defining strategy should include the following:

- **User experience**: Focus on making the support experience as smooth and efficient as possible for the end-user.
- **Efficiency and effectiveness**: Aim to resolve issues quickly and accurately, minimizing downtime and maximizing productivity.
- **Scalability**: Design processes that can adapt to changes in the organization's size and IT environment.
- **Cost-effectiveness**: Optimize resource utilization and minimize the cost of providing support.
- **Automation**: Explore opportunities to automate repetitive tasks (e.g., password resets, initial diagnostics) to improve efficiency.
- **Self-service empowerment**: Encourage users to resolve simple issues themselves through a comprehensive and user-friendly self-service portal and knowledge base.

In summary, an effective ITSM strategy is aligned with the business, directly supporting organizational goals and objectives, customer-centric, focusing on meeting the needs and expectations of users, process-driven, utilizing well-defined and standardized processes, measurable, helping track progress and demonstrating value through KPIs, adaptive by adapting to changing business needs and technological advancements, and collaborative, involving all relevant stakeholders.

Service relationships

A service relationship can be defined as cooperation between a service provider and a service consumer. Service relationships include service provision, service consumption, and service relationship management as elaborated here:

- **Service provision**: Activities performed by an organization to provide services. Service provision includes management of the provider's resources, configured to deliver the service, ensuring access to these resources for users, fulfilment of the agreed service actions, service level management, and continual improvement. Service provision may also include the supply of goods.

- **Service consumption**: Activities performed by an organization to consume services. Service consumption includes management of the consumer's resources needed to use the service, service actions performed by users, including utilizing the provider's resources, and requesting service actions to be fulfilled. Service consumption may also include the receiving (acquiring) of goods.

- **Service relationship management**: Joint activities performed by a service provider and a service consumer to ensure continual value creation based on agreed and available service offerings.

Achieving desired outcomes involves the use of resources, which incur costs and are often linked to certain risks. Service providers support their consumers in reaching these outcomes by sharing some of the associated risks and expenses. However, engaging in service relationships can also bring about new risks and additional costs, and in some instances, may hinder certain intended results while enabling others. A service relationship is considered valuable only when its overall benefits outweigh its potential drawbacks.

By developing and implementing a comprehensive ITSM strategy, organizations can significantly improve the efficiency, effectiveness, and value of their IT services, ultimately contributing to greater business success.

To remain competitive and adaptable, many organizations are undergoing significant transformation initiatives to harness these technological advancements. While often labeled as *digital transformations*, these changes go beyond technology. They represent a shift in how organizations operate, enabling them to thrive amid continuous and rapid change. Businesses must strike a balance between stability and predictability while also enhancing agility and speed. The integration of information and technology with other business functions is deepening, silos are dissolving, and cross-functional collaboration is becoming more prevalent.

Regulatory requirement

Specific regulatory requirements for IT services can vary significantly based on the industry, the geographical location of the organization and its customers, and the nature of the data handled.

Key aspects of IT regulatory compliance are given as follows:

- **Data security**: Implementing measures to protect data from unauthorized access, use, disclosure, alteration, or destruction. This often includes encryption, access controls, and security monitoring.

- **Data privacy**: Adhering to regulations regarding the collection, use, and storage of personal information, including obtaining consent, providing individuals with rights over their data, and implementing data minimization principles.

- **Incident response**: Establishing procedures for detecting, reporting, and responding to security incidents and data breaches. Many regulations have specific timelines for breach notifications.

- **Business continuity and disaster recovery**: Implementing plans and procedures to ensure the availability of critical IT services in the event of disruptions. Some regulations mandate specific **recovery time objectives** (**RTOs**) and **recovery point objectives** (**RPOs**).

- **Audit trails and logging**: Maintaining records of system activities and access to data to facilitate monitoring, auditing, and forensic investigations.

- **Access controls**: Implementing mechanisms to ensure that only authorized individuals have access to IT systems and data, often based on the principle of least privilege.

- **Regular audits and assessments**: Conducting periodic reviews of IT systems and processes to ensure ongoing compliance with relevant regulations.

- **Employee training and awareness**: Educating employees about their responsibilities related to data security and compliance.

- **Vendor management**: Ensuring that third-party vendors who provide IT services or handle organizational data also comply with relevant regulations.

Organizations must identify the specific regulatory requirements that apply to their operations and implement appropriate policies, procedures, and technical controls to ensure compliance. Failure to comply can result in significant financial penalties, legal repercussions, and reputational damage. Consulting with legal and IT security professionals is often necessary to navigate the complex landscape of IT regulatory compliance. Key areas typically covered in an IT audit for regulatory compliance are as follows:

- **Access controls**: Reviewing user access management, authentication, and authorization mechanisms.

- **Data security**: Assessing data encryption, integrity controls, and data loss prevention measures.

- **Change management**: Evaluating processes for implementing and managing changes to IT systems.

- **Business continuity and disaster recovery**: Auditing plans and procedures for ensuring business resilience.

- **Incident response**: Reviewing the organization's ability to detect, respond to, and recover from security incidents.

- **IT governance and policies**: Assessing the framework of IT policies, procedures, and organizational structure.

- **Risk management**: Evaluating the processes for identifying, assessing, and mitigating IT-related risks.

- **Vendor management**: Ensuring third-party IT service providers comply with relevant regulations.

When formulating the internal audit plan, the audit team should take into account several key factors. IT audits to have mandatory audits required by legal or regulatory obligations, strategic and mission-critical audits that directly support the organization's core objectives, high-risk areas, activities, and functions that involve significant levels of risk, allocation of resources like the time and resources necessary for each engagement, etc. By carefully considering these elements, the audit plan can effectively support organizational stability and strategic success.

The IT audit process often involves:

1. **Planning**: Defining the scope, objectives, and methodology of the audit.

2. **Evaluation**: Assessing the effectiveness of IT controls and compliance with relevant requirements.

3. **Evidence collection**: Gathering and analyzing data through interviews, documentation review, and system testing.

4. **Reporting**: Documenting findings and recommendations for improvement.

5. **Follow-up**: Monitoring the implementation of audit recommendations.

Adhering to these regulatory requirements and relevant IT audit standards is essential for organizations to maintain the trust of their stakeholders, avoid legal and financial penalties, and ensure the security and integrity of their IT systems and data.

Responsibility in application management

The IT team plays a vital role in application management, encompassing the oversight and maintenance of software applications throughout their lifecycle. Their responsibilities are diverse and critical to ensuring that applications meet business needs, perform efficiently, and remain secure.

Here is a breakdown of the IT team's key responsibilities:

- **Application lifecycle management**:

  o **Planning and procurement**: Collaborating with business stakeholders to define application requirements, evaluate build-versus-buy options, and select appropriate software.

  o **Deployment**: Overseeing the installation, configuration, and rollout of new applications or updates to existing ones.

  o **Operation and maintenance**: Ensuring the continuous and reliable operation of applications, including monitoring performance, applying patches and updates, and troubleshooting issues.

  o **Optimization**: Identifying areas for improvement in application performance, efficiency, and functionality.

  o **Retirement (Sunsetting)**: Planning and executing the decommissioning of outdated or redundant applications, including data migration and user transition.

- **Application support**:

  o **Providing technical assistance**: Responding to user inquiries, troubleshooting problems, and guiding application usage.

  o **Incident management**: Managing and resolving application-related incidents to minimize disruption to users.

  o **Problem management**: Identifying the root causes of recurring application issues and implementing solutions to prevent future occurrences.

  o **User training and documentation**: Developing and delivering training programs and creating user manuals to enhance user proficiency.

- **Performance and security management**:

  o **Monitoring application performance**: Utilizing monitoring tools to track application performance, identify bottlenecks, and ensure optimal responsiveness.

  o **Security management**: Implementing and enforcing security measures to protect applications and their data from unauthorized access, cyber threats, and vulnerabilities. This includes regular security patching and vulnerability scanning.

  o **Data management**: Ensuring the integrity, security, and availability of data associated with applications.

- **Change management**:

  o **Coordinating changes and updates**: Planning, testing, and implementing changes and updates to software applications in a structured way to minimize disruptions.

  o **Managing releases**: Overseeing the release of new application versions and features to ensure a smooth transition for users.

- **Vendor management**:

  o **Liaising with vendors**: Communicating with software vendors for technical support, issue resolution, and software updates.

  o **Managing contracts and SLAs**: Ensuring that vendor agreements and service level agreements are met.

- **Strategic planning and alignment**:

  o **Developing application strategies**: Aligning application strategies with the overall business objectives and IT roadmap.

  o **Identifying business opportunities**: Analyzing business workflows and identifying opportunities for new applications to improve efficiency.

- **Communication and collaboration**:

  o **Communicating with stakeholders**: Keeping business users and other IT teams informed about application-related issues, changes, and plans.

  o **Collaborating with other IT teams**: Working closely with infrastructure, security, and other IT teams to ensure the smooth operation and integration of applications.

In essence, the IT team acts as the custodian of the organization's applications, ensuring they are available, reliable, secure, and aligned with business needs throughout their entire lifecycle. Their responsibilities require a blend of technical expertise, problem-solving skills, communication abilities, and a customer-centric approach.

Conducting application vulnerability scans is a crucial responsibility of the IT team, particularly within application management and cybersecurity functions. These scans are a proactive measure to identify security weaknesses within software applications before they can be exploited by malicious actors. In conclusion, application vulnerability scanning is a critical security practice and a key responsibility of the IT team. By proactively identifying and addressing weaknesses in applications, the IT team plays a vital role in protecting the organization's data, systems, and reputation. The specific methods and tools used may vary depending on the organization's size, industry, risk tolerance, and the complexity of its applications.

In today's dynamic technological and regulatory landscape, the importance of robust IT services cannot be overstated. Compliance with regulations, proactive security measures, and a focus on continuous improvement are integral to ensuring the ongoing success and resilience of any organization. Ultimately, well-defined and effectively managed IT services empower organizations to thrive in the digital age, enabling them to achieve their objectives, serve their customers better, and navigate the complexities of the modern business environment.

Conclusion

Services play a vital role in enabling organizations to generate value for both themselves and their customers. With most services now being IT-driven, businesses can significantly benefit from developing, expanding, and refining their IT service management capabilities. Technology is evolving at an unprecedented pace, with innovations such as cloud computing, **infrastructure as a service (IaaS)**, machine learning, and blockchain creating new avenues for value generation. As IT becomes a critical business enabler and a source of competitive advantage, IT service management is positioned as a key strategic function.

In conclusion, typical IT services form the indispensable digital foundation of modern organizations. They are no longer a mere support function but have evolved into a strategic enabler of business operations, innovation, and competitive advantage. From the fundamental infrastructure that keeps the lights on to the sophisticated applications that drive core business processes, IT services encompass a vast and interconnected ecosystem.

Understanding the definition, objectives, and key concepts surrounding IT services is crucial for everyone within an organization, not just the IT department. Business professionals need to appreciate the value IT brings and make informed decisions, while IT specialists must focus on delivering and managing these services effectively and with a customer-centric approach.

In the next chapter, we will look at the importance of functions, logging and monitoring the critical functions. This will help in identifying the deviations and their causes, and defining best practices to ensure these deviations are never repeated.

Join our Discord space

Join our Discord workspace for latest updates, offers, tech happenings around the world, new releases, and sessions with the authors:

https://discord.bpbonline.com

CHAPTER 12
Logging and Monitoring Services

Introduction

In this chapter, we will explore logging and monitoring services: essential functions for tracking policy compliance and system configuration. In the ever-evolving landscape of modern IT infrastructure and applications, these services serve as critical pillars for maintaining stability, performance, security, and overall operational health. They act as the vigilant observers of your digital environment, delivering invaluable real-time and historical insights into system activities.

Structure

The chapter covers the following topics:

- Key concepts
- Logging services
- Log management
- Monitoring services
- Monitoring metrics

Objectives

The learning objectives for logging and monitoring services span multiple roles within an organization, ultimately fostering a more stable, secure, and efficient IT environment.

Logging and monitoring systems offer real-time insights into system behavior, enabling organizations to swiftly identify suspicious activities, security threats, and policy violations as they arise. This proactive detection facilitates rapid incident response, reducing potential damage. In the aftermath of a security breach or cyber incident, detailed logs play a crucial role in forensic investigations. They help assess the scope of the attack, pinpoint its origin, analyze the attacker's tactics, and implement necessary corrective measures. By tracking user actions and system modifications, logs establish accountability, discouraging unauthorized behavior and fostering a culture of responsibility.

As we progress, we will examine the various components, methodologies, and best practices associated with effective logging and monitoring. A firm grasp of their principles and the value they offer is the key to building a resilient, high-performing, and secure IT infrastructure.

Key concepts

Logging and monitoring play a crucial role in **IT service management (ITSM)**, ensuring the efficiency, reliability, and security of IT services. Their impact spans multiple ITSM processes, reinforcing proactive management, issue resolution, and continuous improvement.

At their core, logging services involve the structured collection, storage, and management of logs generated by various IT components, including operating systems, applications, network devices, and security systems. These logs contain key information about events, transactions, errors, and activities, effectively chronicling the behavior of your IT ecosystem over time.

Complementing logging, monitoring services focus on continuously assessing the performance, availability, and health of IT resources in real-time. They track metrics such as CPU usage, memory consumption, network traffic, application response times, and error rates. When thresholds are exceeded or anomalies arise, monitoring systems generate alerts, enabling swift intervention before minor issues escalate into major disruptions.

Together, logging and monitoring services provide a holistic view of an IT environment's past, present, and future. They function as interconnected disciplines rather than isolated operations; logs offer detailed historical records crucial for troubleshooting, while monitoring delivers immediate visibility and alerting mechanisms for proactive issue detection and resolution.

Integrating comprehensive logging and monitoring allows organizations to continuously track compliance, enabling proactive identification and resolution of potential gaps in real time. This approach minimizes reliance on periodic audits, which may offer only a limited perspective of an organization's adherence to regulations.

Security information and event management (SIEM) is a cybersecurity solution designed to gather and analyze security-related data from across an organization's IT environment. By correlating log files, event data, threat intelligence, and security alerts, SIEM provides real-time visibility and helps identify, investigate, and respond to potential threats more effectively—ultimately strengthening an organization's threat detection and incident response capabilities.

Logging and monitoring and SIEM systems both deal with IT data, but they serve different purposes and operate at varying levels of depth and specialization. The purpose of logging and monitoring is to maintain the operational health, performance, and availability of IT systems and applications. This covers a wide array of data types like logs, metrics, traces, and works towards analyzing, creating alerts, and retaining the logs that are monitored.

On the other hand, SIEM tools are dedicated to security, for monitoring, detecting threats, managing incidents, and supporting compliance efforts with a scope of emphasizing security-specific sources for security logs, system logs, network data and threat feeds, along with analyzing, creating alerts, and retaining the logs that are monitored. SIEM is purpose-built for security visibility and response.

Ultimately, logging and monitoring go beyond technical necessities—they serve as essential pillars of a strong compliance framework. They enhance visibility, accountability, and documentation, ensuring regulatory adherence, risk mitigation, and effective security incident response. Organizations that emphasize robust logging and monitoring are better equipped to fulfill compliance requirements and sustain stakeholder trust. By mastering these objectives, organizations can strengthen their IT operations, bolster security measures, and drive smarter business decisions. Logging and monitoring are not just technical processes—they are essential tools for maintaining a resilient, high-performing infrastructure.

The implementation of robust logging and monitoring services is driven by several fundamental needs, given as follows:

- **Proactive issue detection and prevention**: Identifying potential problems before they affect users or operations.
- **Faster incident resolution**: Providing detailed data for diagnosing and resolving issues efficiently.
- **Performance optimization**: Gaining insights into system performance to address bottlenecks and enhance efficiency.
- **Security analysis and threat detection**: Identifying anomalies and potential security breaches through log analysis.
- **Compliance and auditing**: Maintaining audit trails to meet regulatory requirements and support security investigations.
- **Capacity planning**: Understanding resource utilization trends to predict future infrastructure needs.
- **Enhanced visibility and control**: Centralizing monitoring data for a comprehensive view of system health.

Significance of logging and monitoring

In incident management, logs provide a historical record of system behavior, helping support teams quickly pinpoint the root cause of problems. Monitoring tools offer real-time insights, often detecting issues before users are affected, leading to faster diagnosis and resolution. They also improve communication by providing concrete evidence of an incident's impact, and historical analysis can identify recurring patterns that need addressing.

Within problem management, logs serve as valuable tools for root cause analysis, enabling teams to correlate events across systems and uncover underlying issues. Monitoring solutions assist in detecting emerging problems, allowing for early intervention before they escalate. The data derived from logs contributes to a knowledge base that facilitates quicker resolutions in future occurrences.

Change management benefits from logging and monitoring by enabling pre- and post-implementation validation. Logs provide baseline data before a change and comparative insights afterward, ensuring its success or identifying unintended consequences. If a rollback is necessary, detailed logs help streamline the process and minimize disruptions.

In service level management, monitoring tools track **key performance indicators** (**KPIs**) against defined **service level agreements** (**SLAs**), offering insights into compliance and potential risks. By alerting teams to service performance issues early, monitoring helps prevent SLA breaches and ensures corrective actions are taken promptly.

Availability management relies on continuous monitoring to track uptime and downtime accurately, ensuring service reliability. Logs and monitoring data can highlight single points of failure, helping organizations strengthen their infrastructure and minimize risks.

Capacity management is enhanced through monitoring resource utilization and analyzing trends in CPU, memory, network, and storage consumption. These insights assist in forecasting future resource needs and identifying performance bottlenecks that could hinder service delivery as demand grows.

Security management benefits significantly from logging and monitoring, as security logs from firewalls, intrusion detection systems, and applications help identify potential threats. Real-time alerts support swift incident response, while detailed forensic analysis of logs enables organizations to understand the extent of security breaches and take corrective measures. Additionally, compliance auditing relies on comprehensive logging to demonstrate adherence to security policies and regulations.

Continual service improvement (**CSI**) is driven by the analysis of log data and monitoring trends, helping IT teams identify opportunities to enhance performance, reliability, and efficiency. Measuring KPIs before and after implementing improvements allows organizations to quantify their effectiveness and refine future strategies.

Objectives of logging and monitoring

Here is a refined breakdown of the key objectives:

- **For IT operations and system administrators**:

  o **Mastering fundamentals**: Developing a solid understanding of logs, key metrics, and monitoring methodologies.

  o **Strategizing logging implementation**: Learning how to design efficient logging strategies, including log levels, formats, and storage solutions.

  o **Deploying monitoring tools**: Gaining proficiency in configuring and managing monitoring platforms to track KPIs and system health.

  o **Setting up alerts**: Defining meaningful thresholds and notifications for proactive issue identification and response.

  o **Enhancing troubleshooting skills**: Utilizing logs and monitoring data to diagnose system and application failures efficiently.

  o **Optimizing performance**: Analyzing monitoring data to uncover bottlenecks and enhance system performance.

  o **Planning for capacity needs**: Using historical monitoring data to forecast resource demands and ensure scalability.

  o **Automating monitoring tasks**: Implementing automation techniques for routine monitoring and alert management.

- **For security professionals**:

  o **Interpreting security logs**: Identifying and analyzing logs from firewalls, authentication systems, and intrusion detection tools.

  o **Detecting security threats**: Using monitoring data to recognize suspicious activities and potential security breaches.

  o **Configuring security alerts**: Setting up security monitoring tools to provide early warnings and facilitate rapid incident response.

  o **Conducting forensic analysis**: Leveraging historical logs to assess the scope and impact of security incidents. Ensuring compliance: Utilizing logging and monitoring to meet security regulations and maintain audit trails.

  o **Integrating threat intelligence**: Enhancing monitoring capabilities by incorporating threat intelligence feeds for proactive defense.

- **For developers and application teams**:

  o **Implementing application logging**: Adopting best practices for structured logging to improve debugging and performance analysis.

  o **Monitoring application performance**: Tracking critical metrics like response times, error rates, and resource utilization.

  o **Tracing requests across applications**: Using logging and tracing tools to analyze distributed application workflows and identify errors.

  o **Resolving bugs efficiently**: Leveraging logs for diagnosing and fixing production issues.

  o **Assessing code changes**: Utilizing monitoring insights to evaluate the impact of new deployments on performance and stability.

- **For business and management professionals**:

  o **Understanding IT health**: Interpreting monitoring reports to assess the availability and stability of critical services.

  o **Quantifying IT issues**: Using logging and monitoring data to measure the business impact of outages and performance disruptions.

  o **Making data-informed decisions**: Leveraging insights to guide IT investments and resource allocation.

  o **Evaluating compliance status**: Understanding how monitoring supports regulatory requirements and security audits.

- **Universal objectives**:

  o **Recognizing the importance**: Understanding the vital role of logging and monitoring in IT stability and security.

  o **Grasping interdependencies**: Seeing how logging and monitoring complement each other for comprehensive system visibility.

  o **Adopting a proactive approach**: Transitioning from reactive troubleshooting to preventive issue resolution.

  o **Fostering collaboration**: Enhancing teamwork by sharing monitoring insights across IT departments.

Ultimately, logging and monitoring provide essential visibility, contextual understanding, and historical insights fundamental to effective ITSM. They empower IT teams to shift from reactive troubleshooting to proactive issue resolution, optimize service performance, ensure regulatory compliance, and enhance collaboration across teams. Without comprehensive logging and monitoring, ITSM processes would face significant challenges, resulting in decreased service quality, increased downtime, and higher operational costs.

Logging services

Logging services encompass the structured processes and infrastructure designed to collect, store, manage, analyze, and retain logs generated across various IT components, including operating systems, applications, servers, network devices, security systems, and cloud environments. The primary function of logging services is to provide a detailed and auditable record of events within an organization's IT ecosystem.

These logs serve crucial purposes such as:

- **Troubleshooting**: Enabling swift identification of errors and system failures.

- **Performance monitoring**: Offering insights into system and application efficiency to address bottlenecks.

- **Security analysis**: Facilitating the detection of suspicious activities, policy violations, and security breaches.

- **Compliance**: Ensuring adherence to regulatory requirements by maintaining structured audit trails.

- **Capacity planning**: Analyzing resource utilization trends to inform future infrastructure decisions.

- **Business intelligence**: Extracting valuable insights regarding user behavior and application usage.

A logging framework is an organized system that enables the systematic creation, collection, storage, and analysis of log data within an IT environment. It offers standardized approaches to capturing events, system activities, and errors, ensuring consistency and efficiency in managing logs. These frameworks typically support different log levels, such as debug, info, warning, error, and fatal, allowing logs to be classified based on their severity.

The choice of a logging framework often depends on the programming language and specific application needs. A robust logging framework significantly improves the ability to troubleshoot issues, monitor performance, conduct security assessments, and support compliance through well-organized and easily searchable log data.

A robust logging framework typically incorporates:

- **Log generation**: Ensuring systems and applications produce structured and meaningful logs.

- **Log collection**: Aggregating logs from diverse sources using agents or protocols like Syslog.

- **Log transportation**: Securely transmitting logs to centralized systems for processing.

- **Log storage**: Providing scalable solutions with defined retention policies to maintain historical records.

- **Log processing and enrichment**: Parsing and contextualizing raw log data for improved searchability and usability.

- **Log analysis and visualization**: Leveraging tools to filter, correlate, and visualize log insights effectively.

- **Alerting**: Setting up triggers based on log patterns or thresholds to promptly notify relevant teams.

Logging tools are built to simplify the lives of IT professionals by automating various aspects of the log management process. By using application logging tools, routine tasks can be streamlined, allowing teams to save time and achieve more effective outcomes from their logging efforts. Logging tools facilitate the implementation and management of logging services, varying in complexity from basic log viewers to advanced centralized platforms for in-depth analysis. Selecting the right logging tool depends on an organization's scale, complexity, technical expertise, and specific log management and analysis needs. Many enterprises adopt a hybrid approach, integrating multiple solutions to achieve comprehensive logging and monitoring objectives.

Log management

Key components of log management include log collection, where logs are gathered from various sources such as servers, applications, and network devices; log storage, ensuring logs are retained efficiently for future reference; log analysis, which involves processing data to identify patterns, trends, and potential security threats; real-time monitoring, enabling proactive detection of anomalies; and log retention policies, ensuring compliance with regulatory requirements.

By implementing a robust log management strategy, organizations can improve operational efficiency, enhance security, and gain valuable insights into system performance, ultimately strengthening IT governance and incident response capabilities.

Log management encompasses the end-to-end process of gathering, storing, organizing, and overseeing log data from various components within an organization's IT infrastructure. Whether the data originates from servers, applications, databases, or supply chain systems, log management consolidates it into a centralized platform or data lake, enabling more efficient access and future analysis.

Log management is the foundational practice of dealing with the massive volumes of computer-generated log data. It encompasses the entire lifecycle of log data, ensuring it is collected, stored, secured, and available for analysis when needed.

Key aspects of log management include:

- **Log collection**: Gathering log data from various sources (servers, applications, network devices, operating systems, etc.) into a centralized location.

- **Log aggregation**: Combining logs from different sources into a unified system.

- **Log parsing and normalization**: Converting logs from various formats into a consistent, structured format for easier analysis.

- **Log storage**: Securely storing log data, often with considerations for scalability, cost-effectiveness, and retention policies.

- **Log rotation and archiving**: Managing the size of log files and moving older logs to archives based on defined retention policies (often driven by compliance or business needs).

- **Log retention and disposal**: Defining how long logs are kept and securely disposing of them when they are no longer needed.

- **Log security and integrity**: Protecting logs from unauthorized access, modification, or deletion to maintain their trustworthiness for auditing and investigations.

In essence, log management sets the stage for understanding what is happening in your IT environment by making the raw data accessible and organized.

Log monitoring refers to the continuous real-time observation and review of log data in real-time or near real-time, with the primary objective of detecting specific events, patterns, or anomalies as they happen. This proactive approach allows organizations to quickly become aware of potential issues and respond before they escalate into major problems. It involves streaming incoming log data as it is generated, recognizing known errors, security incidents, or performance-related signals, and applying threshold-based rules that trigger alerts when certain conditions are met. Monitoring tools often include visual dashboards that display key data and alerts in an intuitive format, providing at-a-glance awareness of system health. In some cases, these tools also apply basic event correlation to link related log entries from different sources. It often includes configuring alerts or notifications based on specific conditions, such as system outages, connectivity issues, or performance bottlenecks. This proactive approach helps organizations maintain system uptime and quickly address operational disruptions. Ultimately, log monitoring helps teams maintain operational stability and security by enabling rapid detection and intervention.

Log analytics involves examining historical log data collected by log management systems for patterns, anomalies, and trends to extract actionable insights, uncover trends, and diagnose the root causes of issues. It moves beyond basic real-time monitoring by enabling deeper analysis and understanding of system behavior over time. This process includes searching and filtering logs to locate relevant entries based on keywords, timestamps, or sources. It also involves aggregating and summarizing large volumes of data to reveal recurring patterns or anomalies. Visual tools such as charts and dashboards help interpret these historical trends more clearly. Advanced correlation techniques connect events across multiple systems, offering a more complete picture of incidents or performance fluctuations. Machine learning and artificial intelligence further enhance analysis by detecting subtle anomalies, forecasting potential problems, and identifying security threats that may not be evident through manual review. Log analytics supports root cause analysis, allowing teams to trace issues back to their origin, and it also enables detailed reporting for audits, compliance, or performance assessments. In addition, it provides business intelligence by analyzing user activity and application behavior, helping organizations improve user experiences and make data-informed decisions. It plays a crucial role in diagnosing issues and enhancing system performance.

In conclusion, log management activities, which comprise log analytics and log monitoring, are integral components of modern IT and security operations. While log management provides the foundation by centralizing and organizing log data, log analytics extracts valuable insights by identifying trends and anomalies, and log monitoring ensures real-time visibility for immediate issue detection and response. Together, they form a comprehensive approach to maintaining system health, enhancing performance, and strengthening security posture. Adopting all three practices enables organizations to be more proactive, resilient, and data-driven in managing their IT environments.

Log management tools

Log management tools are software solutions that collect, process, and store log data generated by devices, applications, and systems within an organization's IT environment. They help monitor and analyze this data to detect issues, evaluate performance, and understand system behavior. These tools typically offer features such as advanced search and filtering capabilities, report and alert generation, and integration with other IT management and security platforms.

When assessing log management solutions, consider the following key aspects:

- **Data collection**: Ensure the solution can ingest log data from a broad range of sources, including applications, servers, network devices, and operational technology. It should support both structured and unstructured data formats to accommodate different logging needs.

- **Search functionality**: The platform should offer robust search capabilities that allow for quick and precise retrieval of log data. Effective filtering, aggregation, and query tools are essential for narrowing down search results and accessing relevant information efficiently.

- **Scalability**: Choose a solution that can handle your current log data volume and scale seamlessly with your organization's growth. It should accommodate increasing data loads and adapt to fluctuating demands without performance degradation.

- **Security**: The solution must align with your organization's security standards, ensuring log data is protected from unauthorized access. Look for features such as encryption at rest and in transit, fine-grained access controls, and role-based permissions or data masking where applicable.

- **Advanced analytics**: Select a log management tool that incorporates advanced analytics capabilities, including machine learning or artificial intelligence. These features can help detect patterns, identify anomalies, uncover trends, and provide actionable insights to enhance system performance and security.

It is recommended to evaluate your needs carefully and potentially test out a few different tools before making a final decision. Open-source tools offer flexibility and cost savings but may require more in-house management, while commercial tools often provide more features, support, and ease of use but come with licensing costs.

Best practices

Best practices for secure log management begin with clearly defining security use cases. Before implementing a logging system, organizations should identify the specific risks they aim to mitigate, including compliance requirements, internal misuse, and external threats. This planning phase should involve determining which dashboards, alerts, and metrics will provide the most actionable insights, with frameworks like MITRE ATT&CK serving as a guide for identifying relevant threat vectors and indicators of compromise.

Establishing appropriate data retention policies is equally important. Since security incidents can go unnoticed for long periods, organizations must decide which log data is essential and how long it should be preserved. Regulatory obligations often require logs to be kept for a year or more, with some extending up to six years. To meet these requirements cost-effectively, organizations should select log management solutions that support data compression and storage optimization.

Centralizing logs across the organization enhances both security and accessibility. A centralized system enables faster anomaly detection, supports streamlined incident response, and eliminates the inefficiencies of managing siloed log data. It helps IT and security teams maintain complete visibility over system activity and identify potential threats more quickly.

Logs should also be context-rich to maximize their value. Including metadata such as IP addresses, user identifiers, error codes, and the source of the event helps reduce noise and provides clarity during analysis. Logs that offer detailed information improve both troubleshooting and forensic capabilities, enabling quicker root-cause identification.

Access to logs must be tightly controlled. Since logs often contain sensitive data, it is critical to enforce role-based access controls and restrict log deletion to authorized personnel only. Logs should be logically grouped, for example, by system type, location, or business unit, to enable structured access and minimize the risk of unauthorized exposure. Regulatory compliance further emphasizes the need for secure log handling.

Lastly, cloud-based log management solutions offer scalability to support growing data volumes. These platforms allow organizations to scale storage and processing power based on current needs, providing the flexibility to manage peak loads and long-term retention efficiently. Cloud-native tools are particularly well-suited for modern IT environments where infrastructure must adapt rapidly to changing demands.

By following these best practices, organizations can strengthen their security posture, streamline log analysis, and maintain compliance while ensuring effective threat detection and response.

Monitoring services

Monitoring services play a crucial role in maintaining the health, performance, and security of IT systems. They provide real-time visibility into infrastructure, applications, networks, and databases, enabling organizations to detect and address issues before they impact operations. By continuously collecting and analyzing data, monitoring services help optimize system performance, ensure availability, and support compliance requirements.

At their core, monitoring services track key metrics such as CPU utilization, memory consumption, network traffic, application response times, and security events. Alerts and notifications are configured to warn teams when predefined thresholds are exceeded, allowing for swift intervention. Modern monitoring solutions also incorporate advanced analytics, automation, and integration capabilities to streamline operations and improve efficiency.

As technology landscapes grow more complex, the need for robust monitoring becomes increasingly critical. Whether deployed on-premises or in the cloud, monitoring services enhance proactive management, reduce downtime, and provide insights that drive strategic decision-making. In the following subsections, we will explore the different types of monitoring, best practices, and tools available to help organizations build a resilient IT infrastructure. IT team needs a comprehensive understanding of monitoring services to ensure the health, performance, and security of the organization's IT infrastructure and applications.

Types of monitoring

Monitoring plays a vital role in maintaining a stable and efficient IT environment by providing continuous insights into system health and performance. Understanding what to monitor is key to ensuring seamless operations, encompassing critical components such as servers, networks, applications, databases, cloud resources, and end-user experience. Each of these elements has specific key metrics that must be tracked, including CPU utilization, memory usage, network latency, application response times, and error rates. Defining thresholds and baselines is essential for setting acceptable performance ranges, allowing for alerts to be triggered when deviations occur. Establishing these baselines helps in detecting abnormal behaviors early.

Effective alerting and notification mechanisms ensure that the right personnel receive timely updates about potential issues while minimizing unnecessary alerts through intelligent filtering. Data visualization and dashboards play a crucial role in presenting monitoring data in an intuitive and actionable format, providing both real-time insights and historical trends for deeper analysis. Let us look at the types of monitoring:

- **Infrastructure monitoring**: Tracks the health of physical and virtual systems, including servers, network devices, and storage.

- **Network monitoring**: Assesses performance, bandwidth utilization, latency, and overall connectivity.

- **Application performance monitoring**: Ensures applications remain responsive and reliable by tracking response times, error rates, and resource consumption.

- **Security monitoring**: Detects and responds to threats, vulnerabilities, and suspicious activities.

- **Cloud monitoring**: Addresses challenges unique to cloud-based resources and services.

- **Database monitoring**: Ensures optimal performance, resource utilization, and availability of databases.

- **End-user experience monitoring**: Simulates user interactions to evaluate application performance from a real-world perspective.

Log monitoring provides valuable insights by analyzing logs for operational and security-related data.

Infrastructure monitoring

Infrastructure monitoring plays a vital role in enabling organizations to proactively address issues, preventing costly disruptions and inefficiencies. As a core component of mission-critical operations, it provides essential capabilities that enhance performance, scalability, and resilience. By optimizing business requirements and ensuring a seamless user experience, infrastructure monitoring helps maintain high service quality and reliability. Its flexibility and scalability allow organizations to ingest data from multiple sources, effectively managing both planned and unexpected traffic fluctuations. Detecting outages, tracking resource utilization, and identifying performance degradations ensure downtime is minimized, boosting overall operational efficiency. A key advantage of infrastructure monitoring is its ability to pinpoint the exact origin of problems within applications or infrastructure components. This precise root cause identification accelerates troubleshooting, reducing the time spent on manual investigations. Additionally, the ability to drill down into specific faulty components enables swift remediation, ensuring systems remain stable and performant in dynamic IT environments.

Merits of monitoring

The importance of monitoring extends beyond just tracking system performance. It enables proactive issue detection, helping to identify problems before they affect users or business operations. Faster incident resolution is facilitated by real-time data, allowing for quick diagnosis and troubleshooting. Performance optimization becomes possible through the identification of bottlenecks and inefficiencies. Capacity planning benefits from historical monitoring data, offering a clearer understanding of resource utilization to anticipate future needs. Monitoring also enhances security threat detection, helping to identify suspicious activities and potential breaches. Compliance and auditing are supported by detailed records of system performance and security events. Ultimately, improved uptime and reliability ensure that services remain available, minimizing disruptions and maintaining business continuity.

Monitoring responsibilities encompass several critical aspects, starting with planning and strategy, which involves defining monitoring objectives and selecting the most suitable tools. Implementation and configuration require setting up monitoring solutions, establishing relevant metrics, determining thresholds, and configuring alerts to track system health effectively. Maintenance and optimization ensure that monitoring configurations remain efficient and up to date by conducting regular reviews and necessary adjustments.

Alert handling and triage play a crucial role in responding to alerts, investigating issues, and escalating incidents as needed to minimize downtime and service disruptions. Analysis and reporting involve interpreting monitoring data to identify patterns and generate meaningful insights. Additionally, integrating monitoring with other ITSM processes, such as incident, problem, change, and capacity management, helps enhance overall IT operations and decision-making.

Selecting the right monitoring tools is essential to align with the organization's objectives, budget, and technical requirements. Automation streamlines monitoring tasks and alert management, improving efficiency and responsiveness. Addressing alert fatigue by filtering out unnecessary notifications ensures that only critical alerts are acted upon. Scalability is a key consideration to ensure monitoring solutions can expand alongside organizational growth. Integration with other ITSM and security systems enhances visibility and coordination. At the same time, ongoing training ensures that team members are equipped with the necessary skills to use and manage monitoring tools effectively.

By understanding these aspects of monitoring services, the IT team can proactively manage the IT environment, ensure service reliability, enhance security, and contribute to the overall success of the organization.

Monitoring metrics

Monitoring metrics are measurable data points that reflect the performance, health, and resource usage of IT systems, infrastructure, and applications over time. These metrics serve as the foundation for observability, enabling organizations to detect issues early, optimize operations, plan capacity, and monitor security posture effectively.

Metrics can be categorized across several layers of the IT environment. At the infrastructure level, key indicators include CPU and memory usage, disk **input/ output (I/O)**, and network performance. These metrics help identify system stress, resource shortages, or hardware-level issues. Server uptime, load average, and system-level error logs also contribute to understanding overall infrastructure stability.

Network metrics focus on traffic flow and quality, such as bandwidth utilization, packet loss, latency, throughput, and network errors. These metrics help pinpoint connectivity issues, bottlenecks, or potential failures within network components.

Application performance metrics provide visibility into how software systems behave and respond to user demands. Critical data includes response times, error rates, throughput, database performance, and resource consumption by applications. Additionally, transaction tracing and user satisfaction scores (like Apdex) offer deeper insight into end-user experience and system performance.

Security-related metrics, such as failed login attempts, alerts from IDS or IPS, firewall activity, and vulnerability scan results, are essential for identifying potential threats and assessing the effectiveness of security controls. Monitoring user activity and patch compliance helps maintain accountability and reduce the attack surface.

In cloud environments, specialized metrics track the performance of virtual instances, managed services, and APIs, alongside cost and billing trends. Monitoring cloud resources ensures scalability, cost-efficiency, and service reliability.

Guidelines for effective monitoring

Developing an effective monitoring strategy requires aligning the approach with the specific needs and functionalities of your applications. Since different types of monitoring prioritize different metrics, the monitoring strategy has to be defined by assessing the organization's objectives and user expectations to identify the most relevant performance indicators.

Setting up alerts and thresholds ensures that teams receive timely notifications of performance deviations, allowing for rapid intervention. Define clear thresholds for each key metric, triggering alerts when these limits are exceeded. Maintaining continuous monitoring keeps IT system behavior insights up-to-date, while ongoing analysis helps identify patterns, trends, and emerging issues over time. Using an application performance monitoring tool enhances real-time tracking and ensures that applications maintain optimal performance.

For monitoring to be effective, organizations must choose metrics that are relevant to their goals, actionable in case of deviation, and placed within context using baselines and thresholds. Visualization tools like dashboards and automated alerts enhance decision-making and responsiveness. Through smart metric selection and continuous monitoring, IT teams can maintain system health, improve user experience, and safeguard digital assets.

When conducting audits of monitoring metrics, it is essential to focus on key performance indicators that provide a comprehensive view of system health, security, and compliance. These metrics help assess whether IT infrastructure, applications, and networks are functioning optimally and adhering to regulatory requirements.

Critical metrics to evaluate include system performance indicators, such as CPU utilization, memory consumption, disk I/O, and network traffic, which provide insights into resource efficiency and potential bottlenecks. Application performance metrics, including response times, error rates, and transaction volumes, are crucial for identifying service disruptions and optimizing user experience. Security-related metrics, such as failed login attempts, firewall rule violations, intrusion detection alerts, and log anomalies, help uncover potential security threats and vulnerabilities. Additionally, availability metrics, including uptime percentages, downtime records, and failure response times, ensure that services meet operational expectations. Compliance metrics, such as audit trail completeness and adherence to industry regulations, validate whether monitoring processes align with legal requirements.

Monitoring metrics should also assess alerting effectiveness by reviewing false positives, missed alerts, and response times. Evaluating historical trends can highlight emerging issues and long-term performance patterns. Organizations should ensure that monitoring dashboards provide clear data visualization for easy interpretation and actionable insights.

Significance of monitoring tools

Monitoring tools play a vital role in ensuring the stability, performance, and security of IT environments. They provide insights into system health, detect anomalies, and facilitate proactive issue resolution. Choosing the right monitoring tools depends on an organization's infrastructure, applications, and operational needs. Best practices for effective monitoring include defining clear objectives, ensuring that monitoring aligns with business needs and technical requirements. Establishing meaningful metrics and baselines helps track system health and detect anomalies early. Setting up intelligent alerting mechanisms minimizes false positives and ensures that critical incidents receive timely attention. Centralizing monitoring data improves visibility across different systems, and integrating monitoring with other ITSM processes enhances efficiency. Automating monitoring tasks, such as log analysis and performance tracking, reduces manual effort and speeds up issue detection. Regularly reviewing and refining configurations ensures monitoring remains effective as systems evolve. Investing in training and documentation equips IT teams with the skills needed to interpret and act on monitoring insights effectively.

By leveraging the right tools and following best practices, organizations can build a resilient IT infrastructure, minimize downtime, enhance security, and optimize performance across their digital ecosystem. Well-structured monitoring metrics enable proactive issue detection, optimize resource allocation, strengthen security measures, and ensure regulatory compliance, contributing to a robust and efficient IT environment.

Logging and monitoring in ITSM

Logging and monitoring should always move together, like salt and pepper shakers. These offer broad visibility into IT operations and performance, whereas SIEM leverages selected security-relevant data from this pool and adds advanced analysis to protect against threats and ensure compliance. Most mature organizations deploy both solutions, using logging and monitoring for infrastructure health, and SIEM for proactive security management and incident response. Together, these practices contribute to more reliable systems, improved troubleshooting, and stronger operational visibility.

SIEM systems depend on a strong logging and monitoring foundation. They ingest data from various IT systems; without it, a SIEM cannot function effectively. Logging and monitoring supply the raw input. SIEM adds intelligence and security analytics. Together, they create a full-spectrum view. Operational monitoring ensures systems run smoothly, while SIEM helps detect and respond to threats.

Think of logging and monitoring as providing general visibility into the health and performance of your IT environment. SIEM takes a subset of that data (primarily security-related) and applies specialized intelligence and analytics to identify and respond to security threats and meet compliance mandates. Many organizations implement both robust logging and monitoring solutions alongside a SIEM to achieve comprehensive visibility across their IT operations and security landscape.

Conclusion

We saw in this chapter how the relationship between log management, log analytics, and log monitoring is a layered and interdependent framework within the broader context of IT operations and security. While log management, log analytics, and log monitoring are interconnected, each serves a unique function within IT and security operations.

In the context of ITSM, logging and monitoring are critical areas of scrutiny. Diligence has to be given to the organization's logging and monitoring practices to ensure they are adequate for security, compliance, operational stability, and forensic investigations. Review or audit of ITSM practice has to focus on comprehensiveness of logging, completeness of log details, adequacy of monitoring, security and integrity of logs, compliance requirements, operational efficiency and use of logs, governance and policies, etc. In summary, an IT audit in the context of logging and monitoring aims to ensure that the organization has implemented adequate controls to record, monitor, and analyze system activities effectively for security, compliance, and operational purposes. The auditor will look for evidence that these processes are in place, functioning correctly, and aligned with best practices and regulatory requirements.

In the next chapter, we will be learning about the importance of the governance process in ITSM, through defining proper KPI and meaningful metrics, and instilling the practice of reporting mechanisms. The roles and responsibilities that we learned in *Chapter 5, IT Policies, Processes and SOPs*, will have to depict the reporting structure and the periodicity of reporting clearly. The **standard operating procedures** (**SOPs**) that we saw in the same chapter will explain the procedures that need to be followed in each and every step of ITSM for status reporting and governance mechanisms.

Join our Discord space

Join our Discord workspace for latest updates, offers, tech happenings around the world, new releases, and sessions with the authors:

https://discord.bpbonline.com

CHAPTER 13
KPIs and Status Reports

Introduction

In this chapter, we will have a look at an overview of **key performance indicators** (**KPIs**) and status reports in IT auditing. In IT auditing, KPIs and status reports serve as critical tools for evaluating the effectiveness, efficiency, and compliance of an organization's IT systems and controls. They provide auditors with both quantitative data and qualitative insights, enabling informed assessments and strategic recommendations.

KPIs in IT auditing must be specific, measurable, and time-bound metrics, used to assess the performance of IT controls, processes, and resources. These indicators help identify strengths, weaknesses, and areas for improvement within an organization's IT environment. KPIs have to be looked at as the health indicators of IT systems, revealing how well security measures, operational processes, and governance frameworks are in operation.

A **service level agreement** (**SLA**) is a formal agreement between a service provider and a customer (internal or external). It clearly defines the services being provided and the expected level of performance. The SLA explicitly outlines the specific services covered, including what is in scope and what is not.

Status reports provide a summarized review of ongoing audit activities, highlighting progress, key findings, and potential risks. Unlike KPIs, which focus on specific metrics, status reports incorporate both quantitative and qualitative insights, offering a narrative overview of IT operation effectiveness. Serving as a communication bridge between audit teams, management, and stakeholders, these reports ensure transparency and allow organizations to take corrective action in response to identified risks or inefficiencies.

Structure

The chapter covers the following topics:

- Key concepts
- IT service SLAs
- Governance and definition of KPIs
- ITSM status reports
- Best practices for effective reporting and KPI tracking

Objectives

Understanding and applying IT operation KPIs and status reports are essential for effectively managing IT services and infrastructure. Upon completion of this chapter, you will be able to define KPIs in the context of IT operations, recognizing their role in measuring performance. This will provide the ability to identify, categorize, and review KPIs across various IT domains, including infrastructure, applications, service desks, and security. The importance of KPIs in monitoring performance, identifying areas for improvement, and aligning IT with business objectives will be understood by the readers. Additionally, one will get the ability to distinguish between leading and lagging KPIs, learning how proactive and reactive indicators shape IT management. Selecting and defining relevant KPIs for specific IT services and processes will be a key focus, ensuring that performance measurement aligns with operational goals. Learning about KPIs will help in establishing baselines and targets for performance, setting meaningful benchmarks to evaluate progress. Furthermore, KPIs work with logging and monitoring in facilitating the collection and analysis of data, using appropriate methods and tools for tracking performance. Interpreting and communicating KPI results will allow for actionable insights, enabling meaningful dialogue with stakeholders. KPIs will also be explored as tools for continuous improvement, helping organizations identify optimization opportunities. Finally, you will understand how IT operation KPIs relate to broader business outcomes, reinforcing their strategic value.

Regarding IT operation status reports, you will gain a clear understanding of their purpose and significance in IT operations, recognizing their role in communication and transparency. You will identify different types of status reports and their varying frequencies, including daily, weekly, and monthly reports, adapting the content to suit different audiences. You will explore the key elements and structure of effective status reports, ensuring clarity and relevance. Gathering and synthesizing information for these reports will be a crucial skill, helping summarize key activities, progress, and challenges efficiently. Communicating progress, issues, and risks clearly will be emphasized, ensuring both technical and non-technical audiences grasp important findings. You will learn to identify and escalate key risks appropriately, ensuring critical concerns are addressed on time. Tailoring status reports to different audiences will help optimize the impact of IT communication, ensuring decision-makers receive actionable insights. Utilizing status reports in decision-making and planning will reinforce their role in shaping IT strategies and improvements. You will also develop an understanding of the complementary relationship between KPIs and status reports, recognizing how they provide a holistic view of IT operations.

By mastering these learning objectives, individuals will be equipped to define, track, and analyze IT operation KPIs and status reports effectively, improving IT service management, enhancing communication, and driving operational excellence.

Key concepts

In today's data-centric organizations, KPIs and operational metrics are invaluable tools for decision-making. IT teams rely on these measures to assess system efficiency, resolve technical issues, and optimize workflows. When IT teams collaborate with external vendors, such as SaaS providers, cloud storage, or security platforms, KPIs and SLAs serve as benchmarks for performance evaluation.

KPIs, SLAs, and status reports are core tools for managing performance and expectations. KPIs measure progress toward strategic goals, turning subjective views into objective data and driving continuous improvement. SLAs define what good service looks like through clear, measurable standards, aligning providers and customers while reducing risks. Status reports keep stakeholders informed, track progress against KPIs and SLAs, and highlight issues early. Together, they ensure focus, accountability, and clear communication.

Tracking KPIs over time enables auditors to identify trends, evaluate the impact of changes, and detect areas requiring attention or intervention. KPIs offer an objective assessment by moving beyond subjective opinions and providing concrete data on control effectiveness. They facilitate risk identification, highlighting deviations from target metrics that may indicate vulnerabilities. By continuously monitoring IT controls, auditors can assess ongoing performance, compare results against industry benchmarks, and prioritize audit activities. Well-defined KPIs also enhance communication, allowing auditors to convey findings and recommendations effectively to management.

SLAs establish a clear understanding between the service provider and the customer about what services will be delivered. They explicitly define the expected levels of service quality, availability, and responsiveness through measurable metrics (often KPIs within the SLA). SLAs proactively manage customer expectations by clearly outlining what they can expect from the service. They hold the service provider accountable for meeting the agreed-upon performance standards. In cases where service levels are not met, the SLA often outlines the remedies or compensation the customer is entitled to. By clearly defining responsibilities and performance expectations, SLAs can help mitigate potential disputes and misunderstandings. SLAs should be reviewed and updated as services evolve and business needs change.

Status reports maintain accountability by keeping all stakeholders informed about audit developments. They facilitate early issue identification, helping teams address roadblocks before they escalate. As audits progress, reports track completion timelines, highlight critical risks, and provide management with the information needed for proactive decision-making. Additionally, these reports form part of the official audit documentation, ensuring consistency in audit procedures.

IT service SLAs

IT and **IT service management (ITSM)** are data-driven functions, where nearly every aspect of operations is measured and analyzed. KPIs and other metrics are fundamental to managing IT teams, providing IT operations managers with a clear way to demonstrate performance to senior business leaders. An IT SLA is a documented agreement between an IT service provider and a customer (which could be internal, like another department, or external). It clearly defines the services being provided and the expected level of performance for those services.

Performance-based success metrics are essential for IT leaders seeking to maintain or expand budgets, workforce, and investments in new technologies and transformation initiatives. Business leaders establish goals, and IT operations managers execute them using available talent and tools. KPIs help gauge how IT teams perform against these strategic objectives. Internally, KPIs, SLAs, and other operational metrics provide insights into IT teams' alignment with business goals, budgetary adherence, software performance, and the impact of IT transformation projects. With such an extensive range of available metrics, IT operations managers must focus on those that directly support organizational priorities.

KPIs differ from other IT metrics in that they measure an IT team's daily activities against predefined targets. While KPIs track specific objectives, broader metrics assess whether resources are effectively deployed, IT initiatives are successful, and overall operational goals are being met.

Importance

The importance of SLAs can be elaborated as follows:

- **Establish clear expectations**: SLAs define precisely what services will be delivered and the standards they must meet, ensuring alignment between provider and customer.

- **Clarify responsibilities**: They outline the roles and obligations of both the service provider and the customer, promoting smooth service delivery.

- **Enable performance measurement**: SLAs include specific, measurable metrics (often KPIs) to track and assess service performance against agreed standards.

- **Promote accountability**: They hold the service provider responsible for maintaining the defined service levels.

- **Provide a structure for issue resolutions**: SLAs outline procedures for reporting, escalating, and resolving service-related problems.

- **Foster trust**: By clearly defining services and expectations, SLAs help build a strong, trust-based relationship between provider and customer.

- **Drive continuous improvement**: Regularly monitoring SLA performance highlights areas for service enhancement and optimization.

Key components

The key components of an IT service SLA are as follows:

- **Agreement overview**: Introduces the SLA, identifies the involved parties, and provides a general description of the services covered.

- **Service description**: Details the specific IT services provided, including dependencies, deliverables, and exclusions.

- **Service level objectives**: Define clear, measurable targets for service performance, often using KPIs such as:

  o **Uptime or availability**: E.g., 99.9% system uptime.

  o **Response time**: E.g., response to critical incidents within 15 minutes.

  o **Resolution time**: E.g., resolve critical issues within 4 hours.

  o **Error rates**: Acceptable limits for service errors or failures.

  o **Throughput**: Service capacity to handle workloads.

  o **First-call resolution**: Percentage of issues resolved at initial contact.

- **Performance monitoring and reporting**: Explains how service performance will be measured, monitored, and reported, including frequency and reporting formats.

- **Responsibilities**: Specifies the duties of both the service provider (e.g., infrastructure maintenance) and the customer (e.g., providing necessary access).

- **Escalation procedures**: Describes the steps and contacts for escalating unresolved or critical issues.

- **Remedies and penalties**: Outlines compensation methods, such as service credits or discounts, if service levels are not met.

- **Security standards**: Details the security protocols the provider will follow to protect systems and data.

- **Disaster recovery and business continuity**: Defines procedures for service recovery during major disruptions.

- **Review and update processes**: Establishes how and when the SLA will be reviewed and revised as business needs change.

- **Termination clauses**: Specifies conditions under which either party may terminate the agreement.

As explained, IT SLAs are essential tools for managing expectations, ensuring accountability, and driving continuous improvement in the delivery of IT services. They provide a clear framework for both the service provider and the customer, leading to more effective partnerships and better service outcomes.

SLAs in ITSM

Popular types of IT SLAs used in a typical ITSM are as follows:

- **Customer-based SLA**: Tailored to a specific customer or group, covering all their services.

- **Service-based SLA**: A standardized agreement for a specific service offered to all customers (e.g., email services).

- **Multi-level SLA**: A layered approach addressing corporate-wide standards, specific customer needs, and individual service requirements.

The ISO 20000 standard defines the requirements for establishing, implementing, maintaining, and continuously improving an organization's **IT service management System (ITSMS)**. A crucial component of ITSMS is service level management, which encompasses the processes necessary to define, document, agree upon, evaluate, measure, report, and review the service levels provided to customers and stakeholders. The primary objectives of service level management include developing and defining SLAs that establish the expected quality standards for services delivered to customers, ensuring that services consistently meet the specified quality levels, monitoring and evaluating service performance in relation to agreed-upon standards, and identifying deviations to take corrective action as needed.

Service level management activities are typically carried out by a dedicated team or department within an organization. These processes are supported by specialized tools and technologies that facilitate monitoring, measurement, reporting, and analysis of service performance. The ISO 20000 standard provides guidance on best practices for service level management, detailing the necessary steps, roles, responsibilities, and tools that can enhance the effectiveness of service level processes. SLAs are established and provided by service vendors, allowing organizations to tailor them according to specific service and customer needs. In some cases, a single service may have multiple SLAs, each outlining different service levels at varying price points. SLAs are generally structured in a way that benefits the service provider more than the customer. To ensure fairness, customers are advised to carefully review SLAs before committing and, when necessary, seek legal counsel to verify that the terms are reasonable. This proactive approach helps prevent misunderstandings and ensures that customers receive the level of service they expect.

An SLA is a legally enforceable agreement, ensuring that specified service levels are met. If the provider fails to deliver the agreed-upon standards, consequences must follow. This section defines those repercussions and outlines the compensation or remedial actions the service recipient is entitled to. In the case of internal SLAs, remediation plans may be established to help the responsible party support dependent teams in meeting their objectives despite service shortcomings. We can see that an IT service SLA is a foundational agreement that promotes clarity, accountability, and mutual understanding between IT service providers and customers. It defines expectations, measures success, and supports a strong, collaborative relationship over time.

Governance and definition of KPIs

Every organization operates under the guidance of a governing body, which consists of an individual or group responsible for overseeing its performance and ensuring compliance. Governance activities are essential for organizations of all sizes and types, with leadership structures such as boards of directors or executive managers assuming governance responsibilities when required. The governing body holds ultimate accountability for adherence to internal policies and external regulations, playing a crucial role in maintaining organizational integrity and effectiveness. Organizational governance is the framework through which an organization is guided and regulated. It encompasses the evaluation, direction, and oversight of all organizational activities, including service management, ensuring alignment with strategic objectives and regulatory requirements.

IT governance ensures that stakeholder needs, requirements, and available options are thoroughly assessed to establish well-balanced and agreed-upon enterprise objectives. It also sets the strategic direction through prioritization and decision-making while continuously monitoring performance and compliance against established goals. Management is responsible for planning, implementing, overseeing, and evaluating operations in alignment with the governance body's directives to achieve organizational objectives. The IT governance framework operates through three core processes: evaluate, direct, and monitor. Metrics serve as a key monitoring tool, enabling management to track the progress of both business-related and IT-specific objectives. Well-defined metrics provide the governing body with actionable insights, helping to shape strategic direction based on performance data.

Evaluating the performance of IT services is essential to maintain their efficiency and effectiveness. Within the IT governance framework, KPIs and metrics are defined to measure service performance against established benchmarks and standards. Metrics such as service availability, response times, customer satisfaction, and other key indicators enable ongoing monitoring and drive continuous improvement in service quality.

Metrics allow enterprises to answer essential questions such as:

- Has IT performance improved compared to the previous year?

- What value is the organization deriving from IT investments?

- How can performance be benchmarked effectively?

In cases where measurable metrics are unavailable, alternative assessments can be made using risk management, loss expectancy models, attack vectors, or correlation analysis.

Metrics quantify specific aspects of IT operations and require an established measurement baseline—for instance, tracking the resolution rate of reported incidents (e.g., 87% resolved within two hours). These measurements illustrate workloads and operational activity. They play a crucial role in evaluating compliance, assessing process efficiency, and measuring success against predefined objectives. Organizations expect IT and its associated resources, including skilled personnel, to contribute positively to business outcomes. To effectively manage IT performance, leaders rely on metrics to provide the necessary insights for informed decision-making and continuous improvement.

Establishing effective performance metrics involves defining critical processes that align with customer requirements, ensuring that metrics remain relevant and actionable. Identifying quantifiable outputs from these processes enables organizations to set meaningful benchmarks against which performance can be measured. The development of metrics involves balancing performance objectives, measurable indicators, targets, and benchmarks. These metrics should encompass both lead and lag indicators and maintain a mix of financial and nonfinancial measures to ensure comprehensive evaluation. Regular reviews and agreements with IT and other business functions help refine and enhance the effectiveness of metrics.

When developing metrics, organizations should normalize data to a standard parameter, such as time intervals or cost per unit, to ensure accurate trend analysis. A well-structured metric should enable reliable comparisons, be quantitatively defined, and provide actionable insights. Rather than comparing performance with similar enterprises, given variations in goals and structures, organizations should focus on internal benchmarks that reflect operational effectiveness. Cost-related comparisons should be limited to value assessments, ensuring that IT investments translate into measurable benefits. Metrics should focus on work activities and outcomes. Keeping metrics manageable ensures that top management receives concise reports that emphasize the most critical aspects of performance.

Effective metrics are consistently measured, allowing for accurate trend analysis over time. They must be easy to collect through routine operational processes while remaining contextually relevant to IT objectives. Expressing metrics in numerical values or percentages enhances clarity and comparability, ensuring that the data accurately reflects business realities.

KPIs as per ITSM standards

Various frameworks, including ITIL and ISO standards, emphasize the importance of performance measurement, though specific indicators are typically defined by organizations based on their unique needs. ITIL categorizes metrics into technology metrics, process metrics, and service metrics:

- **Technology metrics**: Evaluate infrastructure performance, such as CPU utilization, storage capacity, and network responsiveness.

- **Process metrics**: Assess operational efficiency, tracking aspects like incident resolution times and the percentage of employees completing assigned tasks on schedule.

- **Service metrics**: Focus on end-to-end service delivery, incorporating factors such as customer satisfaction ratings and transactional efficiency.

Service metrics are particularly valuable for management, providing a holistic view of IT service performance and identifying areas for strategic improvement. However, due to the intangible nature of service levels, these metrics may require qualitative assessments and indicative measurements to provide actionable insights. By leveraging well-designed performance metrics, organizations can enhance operational efficiency, drive continuous improvement, and ensure alignment with business objectives.

The role and positioning of governance within the ITIL **service value system** (**SVS**) vary depending on how the SVS is implemented in an organization. The SVS serves as a flexible model that can be applied across the entire organization or targeted toward specific units or products. In cases where the SVS is applied at a unit or product level, organizations may delegate governance responsibilities accordingly. However, the organization's primary governing body must retain overall oversight to ensure consistency with broader organizational goals and priorities.

In ITIL, governance is influenced by the guiding principles and the practice of continual improvement, both of which apply across all SVS components. The governing body may choose to adopt and tailor ITIL's guiding principles or establish a unique set of principles, ensuring they are communicated clearly throughout the organization. It should also stay informed about the results of continual improvement initiatives and how value is measured for both the organization and its stakeholders.

Regardless of the scope or structure of the SVS, it is essential to ensure that:

- The service value chain and organizational practices align with the strategic direction set by the governing body.

- The governing body, either directly or through delegated authority, maintains oversight of the SVS.

- There is alignment between the governing body and all levels of management through shared principles and clearly defined objectives.

- Governance and management functions across the organization are continuously improved to meet stakeholder expectations.

Strategic IT operations KPIs evaluate the performance of IT teams and software, focusing on elements like application load times, system availability, production incidents, and service desk responsiveness. These KPIs help organizations understand the efficiency and reliability of their IT environments. Efficiency KPIs ensure IT teams function optimally. Key measures include service availability (often targeting 99.999% uptime), incident resolution speed, **mean time between failures** (**MTBF**), and customer satisfaction scores. Metrics such as ticket close rates, resolution times, and first-call resolution rates gauge IT service desk effectiveness, helping managers assess operational success.

IT operations managers can be overwhelmed with data, making it crucial to prioritize metrics that have a tangible impact. Essential KPIs include **platform as a service** (**PaaS**) and **infrastructure as a service** (**IaaS**) uptime, which reflect the stability of hybrid and multi-cloud environments. IT security metrics, such as attack rates and system vulnerabilities, help evaluate an organization's cybersecurity resilience. Managing IT KPIs effectively requires striking a balance between meaningful insights and data overload. New IT operations managers should start by tracking foundational metrics, uptime, ticket resolution times, customer satisfaction, and overall system performance, before gradually expanding their dashboards based on organizational needs. An efficient, streamlined approach ensures teams focus on actionable intelligence rather than drowning in unnecessary data. By strategically selecting and analyzing KPIs, IT leaders can optimize operations, ensure compliance, and drive business success. Thoughtful metric selection enables IT operations managers to maintain control over their teams while making informed decisions that enhance organizational performance.

KPIs for ITSM help organizations measure the efficiency, effectiveness, and overall success of their IT services. Some of the most commonly tracked ITSM KPIs include service availability, which ensures critical IT services remain operational; **mean time to resolve** (**MTTR**), which tracks the average time taken to resolve incidents; first-call resolution rate, which measures how often issues are resolved on the first interaction; SLA breach rate, which monitors compliance with SLAs; **customer satisfaction** (**CSAT**), which gauges user experience with IT services; and cost per contact, which evaluates the financial efficiency of IT support operations. In addition, there are KPIs like critical vulnerability remediation rate, unauthorized access attempts blocked, uptime percentage of critical systems, overdue audit findings, etc. These KPIs provide valuable insights into IT service performance, helping organizations optimize processes, improve user experience, and align IT operations with business goals.

ITSM status reports

Clear communication and structured reporting are fundamental to effective IT governance, ensuring that stakeholders remain informed about IT initiatives, performance, risks, and compliance matters. Well-defined communication channels and reporting frameworks facilitate transparency, enabling data-driven decision-making and fostering accountability within ITSM operations. A commitment to continual improvement is equally vital in IT governance, emphasizing the need for ongoing evaluation and refinement of governance processes. Through audits, reviews, and feedback mechanisms, organizations can proactively identify opportunities for enhancement, strengthening adaptability and resilience in response to evolving business and technological landscapes.

A status report is a concise, easy-to-read document that answers a simple question on how the IT operations are progressing. Delivery owners typically create these reports regularly, weekly, monthly, or quarterly, to update stakeholders on the team's progress toward goals and whether the project remains on schedule. Each status report begins with a brief recap of the IT operation's overall objectives and the key sub-projects supporting them. It then evaluates the status of these sub-projects, indicating whether they are on track, at risk, or overdue. Finally, the report highlights any emerging risks to the timeline and offers recommendations to address them. Creating well-structured status reports is essential for keeping stakeholders informed, tracking service progress, and maintaining alignment with ITSM goals.

Here is how to approach status report design:

- **Understand your audience and their information needs**:
    - Identify who will read the reports (e.g., IT leadership, service owners, end-users, business stakeholders).
    - Determine the information they need (e.g., service health, incident trends, project updates).
    - Clarify the decisions they will make based on the report (e.g., resource allocation, risk prioritization).
    - Gauge their technical background to adjust the report's complexity accordingly.
    - Decide the reporting frequency (daily, weekly, monthly, ad-hoc).
- **Define the purpose and objective for each report type**: Different audiences and situations may require different reports. Also, each report should include a purpose, defining what the report aims to achieve, key focus areas highlighting the topics or metrics that are covered, expected outcomes of the results from the decisions or actions, etc.
    - **Daily operational reports**: Focused on current service health, major incidents, and urgent priorities, for IT operations teams and service owners.
    - **Weekly service performance reports**: Overview of KPIs, incident trends, problem management, and upcoming changes, for IT leadership and service owners.
    - **Monthly management reports**: Summarizing service performance, strategic initiatives, challenges, and plans for IT leadership and business stakeholders.
    - **Project status reports**: Progress tracking for ITSM projects or initiatives, for project teams, and IT leadership.

- o **Incident or problem management reports**: Status updates on major incidents, root cause analysis, and problem resolution, for incident or problem managers and service owners.

- o **Change management reports**: Updates on planned, ongoing, and completed changes, with success rates and issues, for the change advisory board, and IT teams.

- **Structuring and formatting the content by clearly outlining the structure for each report**:

  - o **Key metrics and KPIs**: Indicators of service health, performance against SLAs.

  - o **Standard sections**: Executive summary, key highlights, challenges, KPIs, risks or issues, and next steps.

  - o **Level of detail**: Adjust based on the audience's needs.

  - o **Data visualizations**: Use charts, graphs, and tables for clarity.

  - o **Reporting frequency**: Define how often each report is delivered.

  - o **Distribution method**: Email, shared documents, dashboards, etc.

  - o **Template consistency**: Standardize templates for easy comparison and readability.

- **Set up a reporting schedule and governing process**:

  - o Define reporting timelines based on audience needs.

  - o Assign responsibilities for creating and distributing each report.

  - o Establish a process for accurate data collection and validation.

  - o Identify distribution lists for each type of report.

  - o Create a feedback loop to review and improve reports regularly.

- **Continuously improve the reporting process:**

  - o Regularly review the effectiveness of your reports by asking whether these reports are delivering the correct information, whether they are easy to understand, whether they drive informed decision-making, whether the reporting process is efficient, etc.

  - o Adapt reports based on feedback and evolving business needs to ensure they stay relevant and valuable.

By focusing on the audience, defining clear objectives, standardizing formats, and using automation tools, ITSM status reports can become powerful tools for transparency, accountability, and continuous service improvement.

Best practices for effective reporting and KPI tracking

In ITSM, establishing a strong IT governance framework is essential for organizations to optimize service delivery, manage risks effectively, and align IT initiatives with overall business objectives. By adopting the key principles and best practices discussed in this extended blog, organizations can enhance their IT governance within ITSM, driving greater efficiency, compliance, and long-term value creation.

This comprehensive overview offers a foundational insight into the critical role of IT governance in ITSM, underscoring its importance in today's technology-driven business environment. Successfully implementing and adapting these frameworks and practices is vital for organizations to navigate the complexities of IT governance, ensuring agility, resilience, and sustainable success in the digital age.

Effective KPI tracking and reporting demand a structured approach to deliver meaningful insights and drive action. It begins with setting clear objectives, ensuring KPIs are directly aligned with organizational goals, and focusing on key success factors. Defining precise, measurable metrics with specific targets promotes consistency and reliability in performance evaluation. KPIs should be quantifiable, relevant, and time-bound to allow for accurate and efficient tracking.

Consistent data collection is essential, and leveraging automation tools can streamline the process while minimizing human error. Establishing benchmarks, whether historical or industry-based, provides valuable context for assessing performance and identifying deviations. Using dashboards and visual reports enhances data accessibility, enabling stakeholders to spot trends and insights quickly.

Status reports and KPIs are crucial in ITSM audits as they provide measurable evidence of service performance, ensure compliance, and foster transparency. KPIs offer objective data on how well IT services meet predefined targets, such as uptime and resolution times. At the same time, status reports consolidate this information into a structured narrative, allowing auditors to assess service health effectively over time.

Compliance verification is a key aspect of ITSM audits, and consistent reporting backed by KPI data demonstrates that the organization actively monitors and manages its services in line with internal standards, contractual obligations, and external regulations. Transparency and accountability are reinforced through regular reporting, which shows that service performance is not only tracked but also analyzed and acted upon to support management accountability and continuous improvement.

Risk identification and management are strengthened by status reports highlighting recurring issues, outages, and vulnerabilities. Auditors examine whether risks to IT services are proactively identified and mitigated through KPI tracking. Additionally, audits evaluate how an organization evolves, making historical KPI trends and periodic reports valuable in demonstrating a commitment to continuous improvement, a principle aligned with ITSM frameworks such as ITIL and ISO 20000.

Decision-making justification is another critical function of KPIs and status reports, as auditors need to confirm that IT decisions regarding resources, priorities, and changes are based on data rather than assumptions. Furthermore, compliance with SLAs is assessed during audits, with KPIs serving as direct proof of adherence to agreed-upon service levels. Ultimately, KPIs provide measurable insights, while status reports effectively communicate findings, ensuring compliance, operational control, and a commitment to ongoing service enhancements.

To stay effective, KPIs must undergo regular review and adjustment to keep pace with shifting business priorities. Promoting stakeholder involvement builds a culture where data-driven decision-making is standard practice. Most importantly, KPIs should be closely linked to actionable strategies, ensuring they directly support continuous improvement rather than acting as static metrics.

Defining KPIs and status reports effectively is essential for tracking performance, ensuring accountability, and driving continuous improvement in ITSM. Best practices for KPI development start with aligning indicators with business objectives, ensuring they are measurable, relevant, and actionable. KPIs should be specific, quantifiable, and time-bound, offering clear insights into IT service performance. Establishing benchmarks and historical comparisons helps gauge success and highlight trends.

Status reports should be structured, concise, and data-driven, providing an accurate reflection of performance, compliance, and operational challenges. Reports should integrate KPI data with qualitative analysis to offer a holistic perspective on service health. Maintaining consistency in reporting frequency and format ensures stakeholders receive actionable insights without unnecessary complexity.

KPIs and status reports complement each other in IT auditing, providing valuable perspectives on control effectiveness and audit progression. KPIs deliver data-driven insights into IT security and compliance, while status reports offer a narrative summary of findings and risks. Leveraging both tools allows auditors to conduct well-informed evaluations, enhance communication, and contribute to a resilient IT environment within the organization. Together, governance, KPIs, and status reporting create a well-rounded ITSM framework that enhances service reliability, streamlines processes, and drives continuous improvements, ultimately strengthening the organization's IT capabilities and business alignment.

Both KPIs and status reports should emphasize transparency and continuous improvement by identifying key risks, tracking remediation efforts, and informing decision-making. Regular reviews ensure metrics remain relevant as business needs evolve. By following these principles, organizations can enhance ITSM effectiveness, strengthen governance, and support informed strategic planning.

Conclusion

We saw in this chapter that governance provides the overarching structure for managing IT services in alignment with business objectives, while status reporting acts as a critical feedback mechanism within this structure. By providing timely, relevant, and insightful information about IT service performance through KPIs, status reports enable effective governance, drive continuous improvement, and demonstrate the value of IT to the organization.

Governance, KPIs, and status reporting are fundamental components of ITSM, ensuring structured oversight, measurable performance, and transparent communication. Governance establishes accountability by defining strategic objectives, regulatory compliance, and decision-making frameworks, guiding IT teams in aligning operations with business goals. KPIs serve as measurable indicators of IT service effectiveness, allowing organizations to monitor performance, identify areas for improvement, and ensure service levels meet predefined standards. They provide actionable insights into critical metrics such as uptime, incident resolution times, and security compliance, helping IT leaders optimize workflows and resource allocation. Status reporting consolidates KPI data into structured narratives, offering stakeholders a clear view of service health, operational risks, and ongoing improvements. Regular reporting fosters transparency, strengthens management accountability, and supports informed decision-making by presenting real-time performance trends.

In the coming chapters, we will be looking at specific reports for BCP, configuration management and change management processes, which are the lifeline processes in ensuring successful IT operations.

Join our Discord space

Join our Discord workspace for latest updates, offers, tech happenings around the world, new releases, and sessions with the authors:

https://discord.bpbonline.com

CHAPTER 14

BCP Drills, Plans and Reports

Introduction

In this chapter, we will explore the **business continuity plan** (**BCP**), a strategic approach that outlines how an organization will sustain operations during and after disruptive events. These disruptions may include natural disasters, cyberattacks, power failures, or supply chain interruptions. The core objective of a BCP is to minimize downtime, safeguard critical functions, and ensure a timely restoration of normal operations.

This chapter on BCP and **disaster recovery plan** (**DRP**) drills and their associated metrics outlines essential principles for helping organizations effectively prepare for, respond to, and recover from disruptions. We begin with the purpose and goals of BCP and DRP drills, emphasizing their role in validating resilience, uncovering gaps, and enhancing recovery processes. Various types of drills, from tabletop scenarios to comprehensive simulations, should be discussed to address different levels of preparedness.

The use of performance metrics is crucial for evaluating drill effectiveness. These include response time, how quickly teams react, **recovery time objective** (**RTO**), the time required to restore operations, and **recovery point objective** (**RPO**), the acceptable limit for data loss. Additional indicators, such as communication effectiveness, success rate of failover operations, and accuracy in incident resolution, further enrich performance assessment.

This chapter will also outline best practices for executing drills, such as scheduling regular tests and involving all relevant stakeholders to drive ongoing improvement. By incorporating structured drill procedures and actionable metrics, organizations can enhance their crisis readiness, reduce operational disruption, and ensure sustained business continuity.

Structure

The chapter covers the following topics:

- Key concepts
- BCP drills
- Drill metrics
- Learnings from drills

Objectives

By the end of this chapter, we will learn that the drills conducted for BCP and DRP go far beyond simply *checking a box* for compliance; they provide invaluable insights and tangible benefits. Conducting BCP and DRP drills is an absolutely critical practice for any organization aiming for true resilience. BCP and DRP drills serve as essential tools for organizations to refine their preparedness and response strategies. Through these exercises, teams uncover potential gaps and weaknesses, identifying unforeseen issues such as outdated contact information, inefficiencies in recovery steps, or insufficient resources. By validating plans and procedures, organizations can test whether their documented strategies effectively achieve objectives like recovery time and data preservation.

Moreover, these drills enhance team readiness, familiarizing personnel with their roles, strengthening communication, and building confidence in crisis response. They also help optimize recovery times, ensuring that set objectives remain achievable and that recovery processes are streamlined. From a compliance standpoint, conducting drills demonstrates due diligence, supports audit readiness, and reveals areas requiring improvement to meet regulatory standards.

Beyond compliance, these exercises foster continuous improvement by creating feedback loops and adapting to emerging threats like ransomware or supply chain disruptions. Organizations that prioritize regular drills cultivate a culture of resilience, transforming preparedness into a practical, actionable capability rather than a theoretical plan. Through these evaluations, businesses are better equipped to navigate disruptions, minimize downtime, and safeguard their operations for long-term sustainability.

Key concepts

While designing and conducting drills, a high-level comparison of the difference between BCP and DRP has to be understood. BCP focuses on maintaining an organization's essential functions during major disruptions, ensuring operations continue despite challenges affecting IT systems, infrastructure, personnel, or facilities. DRP, on the other hand, specifically addresses IT and technology infrastructure, aiming to restore critical systems and services following an emergency that renders them inoperative. DR typically involves transitioning services from the primary site to an alternate location and reverting once normal conditions are restored. As a specialized aspect of business continuity, disaster recovery plays a crucial role in safeguarding technology-driven processes.

ISO 22301 is the globally recognized standard for **business continuity management systems** (**BCMS**). It offers a structured approach for organizations to develop, implement, operate, monitor, and continuously enhance a documented system that safeguards against disruptions, minimizes risks, and ensures effective recovery from unforeseen incidents.

BCP drills

A BCP drill is a crucial exercise that tests the effectiveness of an organization's continuity strategy. Developing a BCP is only the first step; without thorough testing, potential weaknesses may go unnoticed until an actual disaster occurs, leaving the organization vulnerable. Conducting regular drills ensures that the plan functions as intended, identifying gaps and refining response procedures before they are needed in a real crisis.

Drills are a vital component of both BCP and DRP, serving as the primary method for validating their effectiveness. They provide a real-world test to assess whether documented procedures are practical and can be executed under pressure, while also identifying weaknesses, inconsistencies, and gaps that may not be apparent during the planning phase. Additionally, drills verify assumptions regarding resource availability and staff preparedness, ensuring plans remain realistic and actionable.

Beyond validation, drills play a critical role in team readiness by familiarizing personnel with their roles and responsibilities during disruptions. They serve as a training tool that reinforces essential skills, boosts confidence, and improves response efficiency, ultimately minimizing downtime and mitigating potential damage. Communication and coordination also benefit from drills, as they test the effectiveness of communication protocols among teams, stakeholders, and external parties, fostering collaboration and resolving potential breakdowns.

Successful drills instill confidence among stakeholders, demonstrating an organization's preparedness and commitment to resilience. Employees become more aware of business continuity and disaster recovery procedures, strengthening the overall culture of readiness. Furthermore, regulatory compliance requirements often mandate testing of BCP and DRP plans, and conducting regular drills ensures adherence to these standards while reducing the risk of penalties.

Drill metrics

BCP and DRP drill metrics are vital for assessing the effectiveness of an organization's preparedness and identifying areas needing improvement. These metrics evaluate how well teams respond to disruptions, how quickly services are restored, and how closely actions align with defined recovery goals.

Key BCP metrics include response time, i.e., the speed at which teams react to an incident, RTO, which is the targeted duration for resuming operations, and RPO, the acceptable threshold for data loss. Other critical indicators, such as communication clarity, stakeholder involvement, and resource readiness, help measure overall resilience.

For DRP drills, essential metrics include system recovery time, success rate of failover processes, and post-recovery data integrity checks. Additional indicators like accuracy in incident handling, adherence to recovery protocols, and efficiency of escalation paths support the continuous improvement of recovery efforts. By regularly tracking and evaluating these metrics, organizations can strengthen their ability to withstand and recover from disruptions, ensuring greater operational continuity and resilience.

Reasons for conducting BCP drills

The best way to evaluate BCP preparedness is to conduct tests that address critical questions to enable continuous availability, such as:

- What are the backup plans for critical assets and services?
- Can we withstand a cyberattack?
- Does everyone know their role during and after an emergency?
- What happens if we lose access to our offices?

These tests, known as BCP drills, come in various forms and play a vital role in continuity planning. Without conducting these exercises, an organization remains uncertain about its readiness until faced with an actual disaster.

Risks associated with ensuring continuous operations

When planning BCP testing, it is important to assess key risks that could impact operations. Common risks include natural disasters such as fires, floods, and hurricanes, as well as property or network disruptions, like power outages, restricted facility access, transportation delays, and communication failures. Employee health concerns, including accidents, illness, injury, and extreme conditions like exhaustion or hypothermia, also pose significant threats. Additionally, cyberattacks such as phishing scams and ransomware breaches must be factored into continuity planning. Addressing these risks during BCP testing ensures a well-rounded strategy for maintaining business operations during unforeseen events.

While the specifics of a BCP drill vary across organizations, the core purpose remains the same—it is a structured test of the BCP. Conducting a single drill may provide insights, but running multiple drills, each focusing on different scenarios and methods, ensures a more robust assessment. The approach to designing and executing these drills is entirely customizable; however, adopting a thorough strategy increases the likelihood of sustaining business operations in any disruptive event.

How BCP drills help

Running BCP drills is essential to ensure organizational preparedness and resilience. These exercises enable the organization to ensure the following:

- Validate your ability to meet strategic continuity objectives.

- Minimize risks to personnel, infrastructure, and operations.

- Uncover gaps or weaknesses in your current BCP.

- Test your response across various disruption scenarios.

- Confirm that employees understand the BCP and their responsibilities.

- Continuously enhance BCPs and processes.

- Demonstrate compliance with internal policies and external audit requirements.

Core components

Drills vary in complexity, ranging from tabletop exercises that involve structured discussions of hypothetical scenarios to full-scale tests that simulate actual system disruptions and rely on recovery sites. Walkthrough and functional drills provide intermediate levels of engagement, allowing personnel to simulate responses and refine their coordination.

Ultimately, drills are more than just exercises; they are essential investments in organizational resilience. They provide valuable insights into the effectiveness of continuity and recovery plans, enhance preparedness, strengthen collaboration, and ensure that an organization is well-equipped to manage and recover from disruptive events.

The following are the core components for designing and assessing BCP and DRP drills to ensure organizational preparedness and resilience:

- **Define the purpose and objectives:**
  o Validate the organization's ability to respond to disruptions.
  o Identify gaps and weaknesses in current plans.
  o Improve recovery time and reduce data loss risks.
  o Align with business continuity and compliance goals.

- **Select the right drill type by choosing based on risk level, maturity, and objectives**:
  - o **Tabletop exercises**: Discussion-based, scenario walkthrough.
  - o **Walkthrough drills**: Step-by-step review of recovery procedures.
  - o **Simulation drills**: Hands-on testing in a controlled environment.
  - o **Full-scale exercises**: Realistic testing of all recovery elements.
- **Execute drills effectively**:
  - o Schedule drills regularly (e.g., semi-annually or quarterly).
  - o Involve cross-functional teams and the management team.
  - o Follow a clear drill plan with defined roles, objectives, and scenarios.
  - o Document everything, timelines, decisions, gaps, and outcomes.
- **Review drill reports and refine drills continuously**:
  - o Integrate feedback from drills into updated BCP / DRP documents.
  - o Conduct lessons-learned sessions with stakeholders.
  - o Track follow-up actions and assign ownership.
  - o Adjust strategies to address evolving risks and technologies.

By following this structured approach, organizations can systematically improve their resilience, reduce downtime, and maintain operational continuity during unexpected disruptions.

BCP standard

ISO 22301 standard plays a vital role in helping organizations strengthen their ability to withstand unexpected disruptions, ensuring the seamless continuation of operations and services. It aids in identifying potential risks, preparing for emergencies, and accelerating recovery efforts.

The key benefits of implementing BCMS as per ISO 22301 are as follows:

- Strengthens organizational resilience.
- Enhances risk management strategies.
- Establishes a structured approach to crisis response.
- Builds stakeholder confidence through improved preparedness.

To sustain long-term operational resilience, organizations should follow standards like ISO 22301, and also establish, uphold, implement, and record a business continuity **Testing, Training, and Exercise (TT&E)** program. The BCP must outline these training elements, procedures, and requirements to ensure the uninterrupted execution of critical business functions. Training records should capture key details such as event dates, event types, and participant names. Additionally, documentation should encompass test results, feedback forms, participant surveys, and other materials generated from the exercise.

Types of BCP drills

BCP drills come in various forms, ranging from simple desk-based evaluations of specific components to comprehensive real-world simulations that test multiple scenarios and involve the entire organization. Each type of BCP drill serves a distinct purpose, and organizations should tailor them to align with their specific continuity needs and operational circumstances.

The five primary types of BCP drills are as follows:

- **BCP walkthrough**: Offers a desk-based introduction to the plan, familiarizing staff with its structure and content through informal methods such as videos, presentations, or physical documentation. This type of drill helps identify early gaps in the plan that require refinement.

- **Facilitated discussion**: Takes a more structured approach, testing responses to a specific disruptive scenario, such as a fire evacuation. While still desk-based, this drill is more formal than a walkthrough, involving guided discussions where participants analyze activation and recovery procedures. The findings are recorded in a detailed BCP drill report, which is then used to update the continuity plan.

- **Single team simulation**: Shifts toward a more practical, real-world format, bringing together a single team to manage a fictional incident. Participants navigate communication challenges, decision-making, issue resolution, and coordination. This type of drill aims to be as immersive as possible, allowing teams to experience the pressures of crisis response firsthand. Ideally, every team in the organization should undergo this type of drill using a range of scenarios. As with facilitated discussions, a formal BCP drill report should be generated to document observations and required updates.

- **Multi-team simulation**: Introduces interactions between different teams, testing coordination and communication across departments. This approach helps identify inefficiencies in team collaboration, ensuring critical actions are neither missed nor duplicated. Findings from these simulations contribute to refining interdepartmental continuity strategies.

- **Full-scale exercise**: Engages the entire organization in a real-time crisis scenario. This drill should only be conducted after the previous exercises have established readiness and necessary improvements have been incorporated into the BCP. A prerequisite is that all teams are familiar with their responsibilities and confident in executing recovery procedures. As with other drills, a comprehensive report should be generated to analyze performance and inform future updates.

Types of DRP drills

The methodology used for BRP testing can be adapted for DRP assessments, applying similar drill formats while focusing on different infrastructure components rather than teams. Let us look at the types of DRP drills:

- **DRP walkthrough**: Provides a desk-based review of the DRP with IT teams, ensuring familiarity with recovery protocols.

- **Facilitated discussions**: Allow participants to explore responses to specific technical failures, such as a complete server outage, with key findings documented in a disaster recovery drill report.

- **Single-component simulation**: Presents a realistic test of the failure of a specific technical component, such as an Internet connection loss, assessing how teams manage recovery efforts.

- **Multi-component simulation**: Introduces simultaneous failures affecting multiple infrastructure elements, such as a power supply disruption impacting multiple servers.

- **Full-scale exercise**: Evaluates an organization's ability to recover from the total failure of a data center, testing all aspects of disaster recovery strategies.

Additionally, certain scenarios necessitate both BCP and DRP activation, where a critical technical failure triggers broader business continuity measures. These integrated drills are among the most challenging to plan, as they typically involve extensive organizational participation, yet they offer invaluable insights into the organization's ability to withstand major crises such as cyberattacks.

By progressively conducting these drills, organizations can strengthen their preparedness, enhance response coordination, and ensure their BCP remains robust in the face of disruptions.

Drill metrics

Once a BCP test is completed, several necessary steps must be taken to process the results effectively. Begin by reviewing the findings with all participants immediately after the test and again once all notes have been compiled. Assign responsibility for any outstanding action items to the appropriate individuals to ensure necessary improvements are implemented.

Update the written continuity plan based on the test outcomes and distribute the revised version to relevant stakeholders. Additionally, identify key insights that should be considered in future BCP tests to enhance preparedness.

Documenting test results and recording actionable findings is essential for refining business continuity strategies. This process helps employees and contractors recognize areas for improvement, providing a clear picture of the progress made toward strengthening organizational resilience.

Common BCP drill metrics are to be broken down and categorized for clarity:

- Execution metrics (how the drill was conducted).
- Recovery metrics (how well recovery objectives were met).
- Post-drill assessment metrics (lessons learned and improvement).

BCP drill metrics

Tracking and analyzing metrics during and after a BCP drill is essential for assessing its effectiveness and uncovering areas that need enhancement. The choice of metrics should align with the drill's specific goals and scope.

Identify key metrics for evaluation:

- **BCP metrics include:**
  o **Response time**: How fast teams respond after a disruption.
  o **RTO**: Time to resume operations.
  o **RPO**: Maximum acceptable data loss.
  o **Communication effectiveness**: Clarity and speed of information flow.
  o **Stakeholder engagement**: Participation and accountability.
  o **Resource availability**: Readiness of systems, tools, and personnel.
- **DRP metrics include:**
  o **System restoration time**: Time to bring systems back online.
  o **Failover success rate**: Frequency of successful switchovers.
  o **Data integrity verification**: Accuracy and completeness of recovered data.
  o **Incident resolution accuracy**: Effectiveness in resolving issues.
  o **Protocol compliance**: Adherence to documented recovery steps.

The drill results have to be analyzed based on comparison of outcomes against KPIs and objectives, and reported with details on actions taken, timeframes, observed issues and delays, lessons learned, recommendations for improvement, etc.

Use of BCP drill metrics

BCP drill metrics can be effectively used to:

- **Establish performance baselines**: Monitor metrics across multiple drills to identify patterns and track progress over time.

- **Set clear targets**: Align key metric goals with RTOs, RPOs, and business continuity needs.

- **Investigate variances**: Analyze significant gaps between actual results and targets to uncover root causes.

- **Prioritize improvements**: Address the most critical issues first—those that pose the most significant risk to the effectiveness of recovery.

- **Share outcomes**: Communicate findings and metrics with stakeholders to foster transparency and encourage commitment to enhancements.

By defining, tracking, and evaluating BCP drill metrics thoughtfully, an organization can strengthen its resilience and continuously refine its continuity planning. Always align the metrics with the drill's specific objectives and scope for maximum relevance.

Learnings from drills

Conducting BCP drills is only truly valuable if organizations actively extract insights from the exercise and apply them to strengthen their resilience. The goal is not just to run a simulation, but to use it as a learning opportunity that drives continuous improvement.

To make maximum learning out of BCP drills, the following measures have to be used during the different drill phases:

- **During the drill**:

  o **Thorough observation**: Assign observers to carefully document all aspects of the drill, including what went well, what did not, delays, workarounds, communication issues, resource challenges, and the time taken for each step. Focus equally on successes and setbacks.

  o **Real-time participant input**: If feasible without interrupting the drill, gather live feedback from participants on unclear instructions, inefficiencies, or obstacles. This adds context to the observations.

- **Immediately after the drill (debriefing)**:

  o **Facilitated debrief session**: Hold a structured debrief with all participants as soon as possible post-drill.

  o **Acknowledge successes**: Start by highlighting what worked to reinforce effective practices and boost morale.

  o **Focus on process**: Create a safe, constructive environment where the emphasis is on improving systems, not pointing fingers at the mistakes.

- o **Encourage open dialogue**: Ask open-ended questions about challenges faced, areas for improvement, or what did not go as planned to gather input from all participants.

- o **Document learnings**: Appoint someone to capture key observations, insights, and proposed improvements during the session.

- **Post-drill analysis and action planning**:

  - o **Comprehensive data review**: Analyze observations, feedback, and metrics to spot patterns, deviations from expectations (e.g., RTOs, RPOs), and performance gaps.

  - o **Identify root causes**: Go beyond surface issues to understand why something failed. For instance, if communication lagged, was the issue due to unclear procedures, outdated contact lists, or insufficient training?

  - o **Organize findings**: Group insights into relevant categories (e.g., communication, coordination, recovery processes, documentation) for structured analysis.

  - o **Prioritize improvements**: Focus on high-impact issues that significantly affect recovery performance.

  - o **Create a targeted action plan**: For each issue, define what needs to be fixed (specific action), who is responsible, timelines, required resources, etc.

  - o **Update the BCP**: Revise the BCP to incorporate the improvements and lessons learned.

  - o **Share results**: Communicate findings and next steps to leadership and BCP stakeholders to foster transparency and alignment.

- **Continuous improvement**:

  - o **Monitor progress**: Track completion of action items and ensure accountability.

  - o **Refine future drills**: Apply learnings to the design of future exercises, testing new scenarios and validating changes.

  - o **Keep the BCP current**: Even in the absence of a drill, regularly review and update your plan to reflect organizational changes, new risks, or past lessons learned.

Learning cycle

Organizations conduct BCP drills to ensure that the activities planned during any outages affecting operations can be addressed with the alternative plans that have been defined to ensure continuity in operations. The steps are as follows:

1. Conduct the drill.

2. Observe and collect feedback.

3.   Analyze and identify weaknesses.

4.   Implement corrective actions.

5.   Update the BCP.

6.   Feed improvements into future drills.

By treating BCP drills as learning tools, and not just compliance exercises, organizations can build a more resilient, agile response to disruptions and safeguard critical operations more effectively. By integrating these learnings into the business continuity strategies, organizations can enhance their ability to mitigate disruptions, minimize downtime, and maintain operational stability.

Conclusion

A BCP serves as the foundation of an organization's resilience, ensuring it can effectively withstand disruptions. It reduces risks in an unpredictable environment, safeguards essential operations, and strengthens stakeholder confidence. Through comprehensive risk assessment, strategic implementation, and ongoing testing and refinement, organizations can proactively manage disruptions and secure long-term stability.

Conducting drills to test BCPs is a crucial component of any effective continuity strategy. Without proper testing, plans hold little practical value and may create a false sense of security. Drills not only assess the strength of a BCP but also ensure that all staff are adequately prepared to respond to a disaster. Implementing a structured testing approach that incorporates various drill types is highly recommended for organizations seeking to enhance resilience and readiness.

In the following chapters, we will look at IT audit frameworks and the processes surrounding people, data, and technology in a typical organization. We will be able to link the BCP drill plans and learnings to many of the steps in the upcoming chapters.

Join our Discord space

Join our Discord workspace for latest updates, offers, tech happenings around the world, new releases, and sessions with the authors:

https://discord.bpbonline.com

CHAPTER 15

Configuration and Change Management

Introduction

In this chapter, we will look at how the configuration of an organization's network and assets can be managed, how new assets can be onboarded to production, how assets can be retired, etc. We will also see how the changes are documented, necessary approvals are obtained, and changes are implemented.

Configuration management (CM) is a foundational **IT service management (ITSM)** process dedicated to systematically identifying, tracking, and managing IT assets, referred to as **configuration items (CIs)**, and their interrelationships across their entire lifecycle. Its primary goal is to maintain accurate and up-to-date information about what assets exist, where they are located, how they are configured, and how they interact to support business services. CM and asset management are interconnected yet distinct disciplines within ITSM, each playing a vital role in maintaining visibility and control over an organization's IT ecosystem. While they share some data points and objectives, their core focus and purpose differ.

Change management within ITSM is the structured process that oversees the entire lifecycle of changes to IT systems and services. Its purpose is to facilitate beneficial changes while minimizing the risk of disruption to business operations and IT service delivery. This involves carefully evaluating, authorizing, planning, testing, implementing, documenting, and reviewing each change.

Structure

The chapter covers the following topics:

- Key concepts
- Configuration management process
- Change management process
- Configurable items and CMDB
- Problem management process
- Problem management database and known error database

Objectives

CM, change management, and problem management each play a crucial role in ITSM, helping organizations maintain stability, efficiency, and proactive issue resolution. This chapter talks about the way an organization sets up the infrastructure, manages the infrastructure, in terms of integrating configuration setup with asset management, managing changes to the configuration, and managing problems or incidents in ITSM processes.

By the end of this chapter, the learners will have obtained an understanding of how configuration management enables individuals to recognize the importance of managing IT assets and their configurations. A solid grasp of CM enhances service stability, facilitates seamless change implementation, and mitigates risks while ensuring integration with other ITSM processes like incident management and problem management.

We will also learn how change management focuses on maintaining control over IT modifications by minimizing disruptions and risks associated with system updates. By understanding change management, one can gain the ability to distinguish different types of changes, follow the structured lifecycle of a change from request submission to closure, and understand stakeholder roles involved in change management. Effective change management enhances service reliability, compliance, and operational efficiency while integrating seamlessly with related ITSM processes.

Key concepts

In essence, CM builds and maintains a detailed and reliable blueprint of the IT environment. This *blueprint* provides visibility into the complex ecosystem of hardware, software, network components, documentation, and personnel involved in delivering and supporting IT services. CM focuses on managing the setup and relationships of IT assets, known as CIs, to ensure seamless service delivery. It is concerned with how components interact, their dependencies, and how changes impact overall system stability. The primary objective is to provide accurate and reliable information that supports ITSM processes such as incident management, problem management, change management, and release management. The key deliverable is the **configuration management system** (**CMS**), which includes a **configuration management database** (**CMDB**) storing CI records and their relationships. This process prioritizes technical details, dependencies, and service mappings.

Change management has to be looked at as the orchestrator and gatekeeper for all modifications in the IT environment. It serves to strike a critical balance between the drive for innovation and the need for service stability. Without a disciplined approach to managing change, organizations face the risk of uncoordinated updates, service downtime, security flaws, and other disruptions that can adversely affect business performance.

Asset management, on the other hand, focuses on managing the lifecycle, value, and ownership of IT assets. It encompasses financial, contractual, and inventory aspects, ensuring optimal cost management, utilization, and compliance throughout an asset's lifespan—from procurement to disposal. The primary deliverable is an asset register or an **IT asset management (ITAM)** tool that tracks asset details, contracts, financial records, and lifecycle stages. Asset management emphasizes financial information, contractual obligations, ownership, location, and lifecycle status.

Also, problem management is designed to prevent incidents and reduce their impact by identifying root causes and implementing long-term solutions. Learning about problem management involves distinguishing between incidents and problems, understanding reactive and proactive approaches, and navigating the lifecycle from identification to resolution. It also includes mastering techniques such as **root cause analysis** (**RCA**) and documenting known errors in the **known error database** (**KEDB**). A well-executed problem management strategy strengthens IT service stability and efficiency, supporting continuous improvement across the organization.

By integrating these three processes, IT teams can achieve a more resilient and optimized IT environment, ensuring seamless service delivery and effective risk management.

Configuration management process

Effective CM plays a crucial role in maintaining IT service reliability, optimizing processes, and ensuring operational efficiency. Some of its key advantages include:

- **Enhanced service reliability and availability**: Understanding relationships between CIs enables quicker incident diagnosis and resolution, reducing downtime.

- **Efficient change management**: Assessing the impact of proposed changes on related CIs improves planning, risk assessment, and implementation, minimizing disruptions.

- **Optimized incident and problem management**: Accurate configuration data facilitates faster RCA and resolution of issues.

- **Improved asset management**: Maintaining a clear inventory of IT assets supports tracking, lifecycle management, and compliance.

- **Strengthened security**: Identifying system configurations helps mitigate vulnerabilities and enforce consistent security policies.

- **Compliance and audit readiness**: Ensuring adherence to regulatory requirements through structured documentation and auditing processes.

- **Cost efficiency**: Reducing unnecessary purchases while optimizing asset utilization.

- **Better planning and decision-making**: Accurate configuration records support strategic IT decisions, capacity planning, and disaster recovery.

- **Knowledge sharing and documentation**: A centralized repository enables seamless knowledge transfer and training within the organization.

CM establishes and maintains control over an organization's IT environment. By understanding how IT services function and interact, businesses can enhance reliability, efficiency, and security while supporting long-term strategic objectives.

Key concepts in CM are as follows:

- **Configuration item (CI)**: Any managed component critical to IT service delivery, including hardware, software, networks, documentation, and even personnel.

- **Configuration management system (CMS)**: A set of tools and databases used to collect, store, update, and manage information about CIs and their relationships.

- **Configuration management database (CMDB)**: The central repository that maintains detailed records of all CIs, their attributes, and dependencies.

- **Identification**: Assigning unique identifiers and attributes to CIs for consistency and tracking.

- **Control**: Managing authorized changes to CIs while maintaining data integrity, often integrated with change management.

- **Status accounting**: Tracking the lifecycle and current state of each CI, including updates and modifications.

- **Verification and audit**: Regularly reviewing the accuracy and completeness of configuration data and conducting audits for compliance.

The CMS comprises a combination of tools and processes designed to monitor and control the configuration of IT assets—spanning hardware, software, and network components. Its primary goal is to maintain consistency, reliability, and performance by ensuring systems remain desired and by managing changes to CIs throughout their lifecycle. CMS is tightly integrated with key ITSM functions such as change management, incident management, and problem management. CMS supplies the data and capabilities necessary to support these processes and help ensure the efficient delivery of IT services. In modern IT environments, a CMS is essential for managing configurations, particularly within hybrid and multi-cloud infrastructures.

At its core, CM is about gaining and maintaining control over the IT environment. By clearly identifying the components of your IT services and understanding their interdependencies, you can enhance operational reliability, efficiency, and security—ultimately aligning IT performance more closely with business objectives.

Configuration management

Experts in asset management and CM often operate within distinct domains, using different processes and terminology to manage their respective practices. However, the reality remains: CIs are a subset of assets, and every asset has a configuration.

While both asset management and CM deal with IT components, their scope differs significantly. CM has a narrower, more technical focus on how components function together. In contrast, asset management adopts a broader approach, including financial and contractual considerations that may not directly impact service configurations.

In terms of lifecycle management, asset management oversees the full asset lifecycle from acquisition to retirement. In contrast, CM is concerned with the operational lifecycle of CIs in relation to service delivery. Configuration data primarily supports operational and service management, while asset data is more relevant to financial oversight, procurement, and regulatory compliance. The questions that they address are:

- **Configuration management**: What IT components exist, how are they configured, and how do they function together to deliver services?
- **Asset management**: What IT assets do we own, what is their value, where are they located, and how are they financially and contractually managed?

By recognizing the distinct roles of CM and asset management, organizations can enhance IT service delivery, optimize costs, and mitigate risks, ensuring a well-structured and efficient IT environment.

Asset management

ITIL asset management focuses on overseeing the complete lifecycle of an asset—from acquisition or leasing, through deployment and utilization, to eventual retirement. It ensures accurate tracking of the asset's location and usage, while also managing appropriate depreciation for capital assets.

CM focuses on how service assets are used and configured, rather than on managing their financials, contracts, licensing, ownership, or disposal. CM addresses the specific segment related to asset configuration. It deals with the usage type, whether it is assigned to an individual or part of shared infrastructure, the connections to other assets, the IT service(s) it supports, the relationships with other assets (i.e., CIs), the detailed configuration state, etc.

CMDB is only useful for ITAM if it is well integrated with ITAM processes. Most CMDBs act as a central repository of configuration data, and can be easily integrated with other processes and their datastores. Some store information about the devices connected to a network and about software contracts and licenses associated with ITAM. Storing all this data within a CMDB allows information to be generated in a single process that can be seen easily by other similar processes. This strong integration enhances those similar and other associated processes. Strong integration between CMDB and ITAM reduces risk, as it has the capability to log a server's CPU, RAM, IP address, MAC address, etc., which provides the opportunity to identify any red flags if this information changes unexpectedly. If a scanning tool finds an application that did not go through the approved channels, it can be a rogue or harmful application that may introduce vulnerabilities.

Benefits of effective configuration management

A well-implemented CM process delivers a wide range of advantages, including:

- **Greater service reliability and uptime**: Understanding how CIs interconnect enables faster diagnosis and resolution of incidents and problems, minimizing service interruptions.

- **Streamlined change management**: With clear visibility into CI dependencies, teams can more accurately assess the impact of proposed changes, plan effectively, and reduce the risk of disruptions during implementation.

- **Enhanced incident and problem resolution**: Accurate configuration data helps IT teams quickly pinpoint root causes, improving the speed and effectiveness of incident and problem management.

- **Improved asset oversight**: Maintains an up-to-date inventory of IT assets, supporting better tracking, lifecycle management, and compliance.

- **Stronger security posture**: Insight into system configurations aids in identifying vulnerabilities and enforcing consistent security controls across the environment.

- **Support for compliance and auditing**: Provides detailed records needed for audits and helps demonstrate adherence to regulatory and internal standards.

- **Cost efficiency**: Helps avoid unnecessary asset purchases and maximizes the use of existing resources.

- **Informed planning and strategic decisions**: Reliable configuration data underpins better capacity management, disaster recovery planning, and long-term IT strategies.

- **Support for knowledge management**: Acts as a centralized source of IT environment information, useful for onboarding, documentation, and knowledge sharing across teams.

CM plays a foundational, though often behind-the-scenes, role in supporting robust **business continuity planning (BCP)**. While BCP outlines the strategic approach for maintaining and restoring business operations during disruptions, CM provides the essential data, structure, and control mechanisms necessary to execute recovery effectively. CM provides the factual foundation, the *what* and *how* of the IT landscape, that empowers the *how* and *when* of BCP. Without accurate, current configuration data, BCPs are prone to outdated assumptions, increasing the likelihood of failure during real incidents.

To effectively manage both configuration and asset management, organizations should:

- Establish clear policies defining scope, objectives, and workflows.
- Maintain a detailed inventory of IT assets and CIs.
- Implement robust lifecycle management processes.
- Utilize automated tools for discovery and tracking to ensure accuracy.
- Integrate ITAM tools with the CMDB for a unified data repository.
- Conduct regular audits to verify asset and configuration records.
- Train personnel to understand these processes and the importance of accurate data.

Although distinct, CMDB (for configuration management) and ITAM tools frequently integrate. Configuration data enriches asset records with technical details, while asset information provides context to CIs, resulting in a more comprehensive view of the IT environment.

Change management process

Change management in ITSM is a structured process designed to control all changes to the IT environment in a way that minimizes disruptions and risks while maximizing benefits. It is not about preventing change; it is about enabling changes to be introduced safely, efficiently, and with minimal negative impact.

Effective change management ensures stability, efficiency, and risk mitigation in IT operations. Key benefits include:

- **Minimized service disruptions**: Thoughtful planning and control prevent outages and incidents caused by poorly executed modifications.
- **Enhanced reliability and stability**: A structured approach to change results in a more predictable and resilient IT environment.
- **Reduced risk**: Comprehensive assessment and authorization help identify and mitigate security vulnerabilities and performance issues.
- **Improved communication and collaboration**: Facilitates better coordination among IT teams and stakeholders, ensuring smooth transitions.
- **Increased efficiency**: A standardized change process reduces rework, delays, and emergency interventions.

- **Stronger compliance and auditability**: Detailed documentation supports adherence to internal policies and external regulatory requirements.

- **Greater stakeholder satisfaction**: Reliable IT services and well-executed changes lead to improved user confidence and business trust.

- **Optimized cost control**: Preventing unplanned outages and emergency fixes helps maintain cost efficiency.

- **Support for innovation**: A structured framework allows for the seamless introduction of new technologies with minimal risk.

Typical steps in the change management process are:

1. **Request submission (RFC)**: A formal change request is submitted, outlining the proposed change, rationale, and benefits.

2. **Impact assessment**: The RFC is reviewed to determine potential impacts, risks, required resources, and business alignment.

3. **Authorization**: The change authority (often with CAB input) decides whether to approve, reject, or defer the request.

4. **Planning**: A comprehensive plan is created, covering implementation steps, testing, fallback procedures, communication, and timelines.

5. **Implementation**: The change is executed as planned, with appropriate monitoring and coordination.

6. **Validation**: Post-deployment testing confirms the change functions as intended and has not caused unintended issues.

7. **Documentation**: All relevant details, configuration updates, execution steps, and test results are recorded.

8. **Review**: The change is evaluated to determine success, identify lessons learned, and drive continuous improvement.

9. **Closure**: Once reviewed and confirmed, the change is formally closed in the system of record.

The change management process has different components. Key roles and responsibilities can be captured as shown in the following table:

Role	Responsibility
Change manager	Oversees the entire change process, ensuring policies are followed.
Change authority	Approves or rejects changes based on risk and impact.
Change advisory board (CAB)	Provides input and guidance on high-impact or complex changes.

Role	Responsibility
Change implementer	Executes the change per the approved plan.
Change requester	Submits and justifies the change proposal.

Table 15.1: Key roles in change management

Types of changes can be seen in the following table:

Type	Description
Standard change	Pre-approved, low-risk, routine changes (e.g., routine updates, password resets).
Normal change	Requires assessment, authorization, and planning due to potential risk.
Emergency change	Implemented urgently to resolve critical incidents or security vulnerabilities.

Table 15.2: Types of changes

Key metrics and KPIs are given in the following table:

KPI	Purpose
Number of changes implemented	Tracks overall change activity.
Percentage of successful changes	Assesses change effectiveness.
Number of failed changes	Highlights issues in planning or execution.
Number of emergency changes	Indicates potential gaps in proactive planning.
Average time to implement changes	Measures process efficiency.
Number of change-related incidents	Evaluates the risk level associated with changes.
Customer satisfaction with the change process	Gauges user perception and experience.

Table 15.3: Key metrics and KPI of the change management process

Change management is closely connected with other ITSM processes:

- **Incident management**: Changes can lead to incidents or be part of their resolution.

- **Problem management**: Helps prevent recurring issues by controlling potentially disruptive changes.

- **Configuration management**: Provides the data required to assess the impact and dependencies of changes.

- **Release management**: Oversees the actual rollout of changes into the live environment.

- **Service level management**: Ensures changes align with SLAs and service expectations.

Best practices for effective change management are given as follows:

- **Define clear policies**: Establish the scope, rules, and objectives of the change management process.

- **Standardize procedures**: Maintain consistency in handling all types of changes.

- **Leverage automation**: Use ITSM tools to automate submission, approvals, and reporting.

- **Ensure clear communication**: Keep stakeholders informed throughout the change lifecycle.

- **Test thoroughly**: Always test in a controlled environment before deploying to production.

- **Maintain comprehensive records**: Document all change-related activities for accountability and learning.

- **Continuously improve**: Use feedback and metrics to refine the process over time.

- **Train staff**: Ensure everyone involved understands their roles and responsibilities.

Implementing a structured and mature change management process enables organizations to adopt new technologies and business initiatives without compromising stability or performance. By aligning change efforts with broader business goals and embedding change controls across ITSM, organizations can drive innovation with confidence and control.

Configurable items and CMDB

A CMDB is a centralized repository that serves as a comprehensive data hub, systematically storing and organizing information about an organization's IT environment. It provides visibility into the relationships between hardware, software components, and networks, enabling efficient CM and improved operational oversight.

A CMDB provides a common place to store data associated with IT assets and CIs. The fundamental building block of a CMDB is the CI. A CI represents an item under CM, such as a router, a server, an application, a virtual machine, a container, or even a logical construct such as a portfolio. Data import tools are usually used to identify CIs in the environment and transfer them to the CMDB. Some IT teams may also use manual tools to keep their CMDB updated, but this is not a good practice as it cannot scale and introduces errors, duplicates, and unnecessary CIs. Once all the information is gathered and unified, it must be reviewed for accuracy and consistency, and any data gaps should be identified and resolved. For a CMDB to function optimally, it must remain highly accurate, necessitating constant updating and ideally automated updates.

The diverse features of a CMDB translate into a range of capabilities that enhance operational efficiency and facilitate informed decision-making. Some of the most critical functions include:

- **Scanning**: A core function of a CMDB is scanning, which systematically examines an organization's IT environment to identify and document CIs. Using automated discovery tools and manual audits, the CMDB maps networks, servers, and devices to create a comprehensive inventory of hardware and software assets. Continuous scanning ensures an up-to-date representation of the IT landscape, preserving configuration data integrity and swiftly detecting changes.

- **Visualization**: Advanced visualization tools enable IT teams to understand the relationships between CIs at a glance. Graphical interfaces, such as dashboards and dependency maps, facilitate troubleshooting and incident resolution while providing a clearer view of the IT ecosystem. These visual aids improve decision-making and encourage a more proactive approach to managing configurations.

- **Relationship mapping**: Beyond identifying individual components, relationship mapping establishes the dependencies between various elements. This capability helps organizations anticipate the impact of changes to any CI, whether in servers, applications, or network infrastructure. By offering a holistic view of the IT environment, CMDB relationship mapping supports smarter decision-making and minimizes the risk of disruptions.

- **Metrics and analytics**: By collecting and analyzing data related to CIs, incidents, change history, and system performance, the CMDB delivers valuable insights into IT infrastructure health. Key metrics such as uptime, downtime, and incident frequency provide a quantitative assessment of service reliability. Leveraging analytics, organizations can proactively identify vulnerabilities, optimize resource management, and refine configuration strategies. This data-driven approach enhances IT operations while informing long-term planning and system improvements.

By integrating these capabilities, a CMDB becomes a powerful tool for managing IT assets, maintaining service stability, and fostering business resilience.

Configuration management database

CM, as we saw earlier in this chapter, ensures comprehensive visibility into the IT environment by identifying, controlling, and documenting CIs and their interdependencies. The strength of a CMDB lies in its ability to map and understand the intricate relationships between different CIs. Relationships define how CIs interact with one another, creating a complete picture of the business's IT landscape. This includes dependencies and associations between various components. Version control is crucial for maintaining a historical record of changes made to CIs over time. This component ensures that organizations can track modifications, updates, and alterations to CIs, allowing for better traceability and compliance with regulatory requirements. A well-integrated CMDB can optimize incident and problem management. By linking configuration data with incident and problem records, organizations can expedite issue resolution, identify root causes, and enhance overall service quality.

Key characteristics of a CMDB are given as follows:

- **Intuitive dashboards**: CMDB dashboards integrate seamlessly with CI metrics and analytics, allowing teams to monitor the health of data, analyze the impact of changes, detect patterns that could lead to incidents or problems, and evaluate the overall state of CIs. These real-time insights into past incidents, concerns, and changes related to a CI significantly accelerate issue resolution.

- **Granular access controls**: Access control mechanisms ensure that individuals and teams have appropriate levels of access to CMDB data. These controls also enable complete traceability of any changes, making it easier to investigate incidents or audit data changes.

- **Audit-ready compliance support**: CMDB maintains detailed, traceable records that support regulatory compliance and audit requirements. These records provide visibility into the current state of CIs, their change history, and related checks, incidents, and balances.

- **CI creation and data population**: Data can be populated into the CMDB through three main methods: automated integrations, discovery tools, and manual input. These approaches scan IP ranges within the organization's infrastructure to detect hardware, software, and cloud resources, creating a comprehensive asset inventory.

- **Federated data set support**: CMDBs support federated data models, enabling the reconciliation and normalization of CIs across multiple data sources. This ensures consistency and accuracy across all CI records.

- **Automation capabilities**: Automation plays a vital role in the CMDB by streamlining data collection, updates, reconciliation, and custom workflows. These automated functions reduce manual errors, improve data accuracy, and allow organizations to tailor the CMDB to their specific needs. Alerts and notifications tied to key CIs help proactively monitor events that could impact business operations.

Best practices

Effectively managing a CMDB is essential for maintaining accurate configuration information and maximizing its value as a strategic ITSM asset. To ensure optimal performance, consider the following best practices:

- **Understand organizational needs**: Before building and managing a CMDB, clearly define the specific requirements and objectives it must support. Align the CMDB with business processes and IT services to ensure relevance and effectiveness.

- **Ensure accessibility**: Make the CMDB easily accessible to relevant stakeholders, including IT teams, engineers, and users. Implement intuitive interfaces and navigation to encourage adoption. A well-designed CMDB fosters collaboration, transparency, and efficient use of configuration data.

- **Integrate with other systems**: A CMDB functions best when seamlessly integrated with other IT systems and workflows. Connecting it with incident management, change management, and other IT processes enhances data accuracy, reduces redundancy, and ensures consistency across the IT environment.

- **Assign ownership**: Define clear ownership responsibilities for CIs. CI owners must understand their role in maintaining accurate data and keeping the CMDB up to date. Establishing accountability ensures reliable and effective management of IT assets.

- **Leverage automation**: Automation enhances CMDB efficiency while minimizing manual errors. Utilize automated discovery tools to update records, track changes, and maintain data integrity. As automation technology evolves, incorporating it into CMDB processes can further streamline operations and improve accuracy.

By following these best practices, organizations can optimize their CMDB to support ITSM, improve decision-making, and enhance overall operational stability.

With organizations increasingly adopting off-premises solutions, CMDBs are evolving to accommodate the dynamic nature of the cloud-based infrastructure. Cloud-based CMDBs offer scalability, flexibility, and accessibility, allowing organizations to centralize configuration data across on-premises and cloud environments seamlessly. This trend aligns with the broader shift towards cloud-centric IT strategies, enabling efficient management of hybrid and multi-cloud configurations.

As businesses continue to grow and diversify their IT assets, the need to maximize the potential of CMDBs has never been more critical. A well-implemented CMDB not only streamlines asset management but also serves as a foundational tool for enhancing service delivery and operational resilience. By leveraging the full capabilities of CMDBs, businesses can unlock significant advantages, fostering a more proactive, efficient, and agile IT environment.

At its core, one of the most significant benefits of CMDB is that it takes all the siloed data across the enterprise required to run IT, and it brings it all together in a single place, giving IT Operations visibility into all the IT resources in the enterprise. It prevents data from being scattered across multiple locations. A CMDB helps IT teams in several ways. Here are just a few: it helps eliminate outages, significantly reduces the time it takes to remediate an outage, remains in compliance, avoids security and audit fines, understands important service contexts when making decisions, which benefits risk assessment and reporting, and tracks software license and cloud costs.

Problem management process

Problem management plays a crucial role in ITSM by identifying, analyzing, and resolving the root causes of incidents to prevent recurrence. Unlike incident management, which focuses on restoring services quickly, problem management seeks long-term solutions that enhance system stability and minimize future disruptions.

Incident management and problem management are tightly interconnected, with incidents frequently catalyzing the problem management process, particularly when they occur repeatedly or have a significant impact. The data collected during incident resolution plays a vital role in diagnosing underlying issues, helping teams uncover root causes more efficiently. At the same time, problem management supports incident management by providing known errors and workarounds, enabling faster service restoration and minimizing disruption. Essentially, incident management ensures immediate operational stability by addressing service interruptions as they arise. In contrast, problem management works to maintain long-term reliability by resolving the fundamental causes of those incidents. Together, they form the foundation of a resilient and efficient IT service framework.

Problem management focuses on preventing incidents or minimizing their impact, while incident management is dedicated to addressing incidents as they occur. The ITIL framework ensures that both practices maintain their distinct yet equally critical roles, helping IT teams balance immediate resolution with long-term stability. By keeping them separate, ITIL aims to prevent organizations from constantly reacting to incidents without addressing their underlying causes. If incident managers prioritize rapid resolution and problem managers focus on prevention, merging these roles could lead to an imbalance where one goal takes precedence over the other, potentially compromising service reliability and efficiency.

The incident management process and problem management process can be compared by keeping the goal, focus, and outcome of both these processes. Both these processes support in ensuring disruptions in IT services are captured, analyzed for causes, and known errors from the incidents are captured for future management. The following table shows the comparison between incident and problem management:

Feature	Incident management	Problem management
Goal	Restore service quickly	Prevent recurrence of incidents
Focus	Reactive (addressing current disruptions)	Proactive (preventing) and Reactive (analyzing)
Timeline	Short-term	Long-term
Objective	Service restoration	Identify root cause and prevent future issues
Trigger	Service disruption occurs	Incident(s) occur or potential issues are identified
Outcome	Restored service	Root cause identified, solutions implemented
Key question	What is broken? How to fix it now?	Why did it break? How to prevent it?
Value proposition	Minimizes downtime, maintains SLAs	Improves stability, reduces future incidents

Table 15.4: Comparison of incident and problem management

The primary objective of problem management is to proactively prevent incidents by identifying potential causes and addressing them before they occur. It also works to eliminate recurring issues by investigating underlying factors and implementing permanent fixes. When certain incidents are unavoidable, problem management helps reduce their impact through documented workarounds and known error records, ensuring faster resolution and minimized service disruption. By tackling these challenges, problem management strengthens service reliability and enhances IT operational efficiency, freeing up resources for strategic initiatives.

Within this process, key concepts include problems, which refer to the root cause of one or more incidents, even when the exact source is not initially known. Incidents, on the other hand, are unplanned interruptions or degradations in service quality. Known errors are problems for which the root cause and a workaround or permanent solution have been identified and documented. These errors are stored in the KEDB, which helps incident management teams quickly address recurring issues. A workaround serves as a temporary resolution that mitigates an incident's impact until a complete solution is implemented. Meanwhile, RCA is a structured process that identifies the fundamental causes of a problem, ensuring long-term stability by addressing systemic weaknesses.

Problem management is closely integrated with several key ITSM processes to enhance service reliability and efficiency. In relation to incident management, it focuses on preventing incidents by analyzing underlying causes and providing known errors and workarounds, which accelerate incident resolution. Often, data gathered from incident records serves as a trigger for problem management activities. When it comes to change management, permanent solutions to identified problems are implemented through controlled changes. Additionally, problem management plays a crucial role in assessing risks associated with planned modifications, ensuring changes do not introduce new issues.

Within CM, the accuracy of CI data stored in the CMDB is essential for diagnosing problems and identifying affected components. A well-maintained CMDB allows IT teams to pinpoint relationships between infrastructure elements, which aids in effective RCA. Knowledge management benefits from problem management by documenting root causes, workarounds, and solutions, making valuable insights accessible to IT teams and reducing resolution time for recurring issues. Through these interconnected processes, problem management helps maintain a stable and efficient IT environment.

By integrating problem management effectively, organizations can move from a reactive approach to a more proactive strategy, improving IT service stability, reducing incident frequency, and optimizing efficiency across the IT landscape.

Problem management database and known error database

Problem management and change management are interconnected yet distinct IT processes. Problem management aims to identify, analyze, and eliminate the underlying causes of recurring issues, ensuring long-term stability. In contrast, change management is responsible for the structured planning, execution, and oversight of modifications to the IT infrastructure, minimizing risks and disruptions. Together, these processes help maintain system stability, enhance performance, and minimize operational risk through seamless execution of necessary changes; thus, they contribute to maintaining reliable and efficient IT services.

Problem management benefits from CMDB in that it helps with root-cause analysis, which allows teams to get to the source of a problem more quickly. It also supports proactive management by assisting teams in identifying assets that need an upgrade to reduce service costs and downtime.

The **problem management database (PMDB)** plays a vital role in ITSM, serving as a centralized repository for tracking, analyzing, and resolving problems, known errors, and potential solutions within an organization's IT environment. PMDB contributes to IT service stability by documenting identified problems, their root causes, often determined through RCA, and any corresponding workarounds or permanent solutions. This database supports incident management by expediting the resolution of recurring issues and change management by facilitating targeted fixes that prevent future disruptions. A key output of problem management is the KEDB, a curated subset of the PMDB, containing documented known errors, along with their resolutions or workarounds. KEDB enables incident management teams to swiftly address recurring problems while informing change management of areas requiring systematic improvements. By linking KEDB entries to CIs in the CMDB, organizations streamline issue resolution and enhance service reliability.

The purpose of the PMDB can be captured as follows:

- **Centralized tracking**: Provides a structured system to log, track, and manage the lifecycle of problems, from identification to resolution.

- **Historical record**: Maintains documentation of problems, their root causes, workarounds, and permanent solutions, supporting trend analysis and prevention.

- **Knowledge sharing**: Acts as an essential resource for problem management teams and feeds into the KEDB.

- **Trend analysis**: Identifies recurring issues and weaknesses within IT infrastructure, enabling proactive intervention.

- **Operational efficiency**: Reduces diagnostic time for recurring incidents by providing insights into known errors and solutions.

- **Proactive problem management**: Helps predict and address potential issues before they escalate into service disruptions.

- **Collaboration and communication**: Enhances coordination between IT teams by providing a structured approach to issue resolution.

- **Reporting and metrics**: Supplies valuable data for assessing KPIs and overall system health.

PMDB typically consists of records containing key attributes:

- **Problem ID and description**: A unique identifier for each problem entry and detailed information on symptoms, impact, and affected systems.

- **Related incidents**: Links to incidents associated with the problem.

- **Affected CIs**: Identification of impacted hardware, software, or services, linked to the CMDB.

- **Category**: Classification of the problem for easier reporting and assignment.

- **Priority and urgency**: Assessment of business impact and response requirements.

- **Status**: Current lifecycle stage (e.g., open, under investigation, known error, resolved, closed, etc.).

- **Assigned to**: Team or individual responsible for resolving the issue.

- **Root cause analysis**: Findings from investigations into underlying causes.

- **Workaround or permanent solution**: Temporary solutions to minimize the problem's impact until a permanent resolution is deployed. The corrective actions taken to eliminate the root cause.

- **Known error record ID**: Links to corresponding entries in the KEDB, if applicable.

- **Resolution details**: Information on how and when the problem was resolved.

- **Date and time stamps**: Tracking of significant events in the problem's lifecycle.

- **User information**: Details of affected users or business services.

An RCA within ITSM and problem management is a structured approach aimed at identifying the underlying factors responsible for incidents or recurring issues. Rather than simply addressing the immediate problem, RCA seeks to understand its origins to prevent future occurrences.

Key steps in RCA are as follows:

1. **Identify the root cause(s)**: Move beyond surface-level symptoms to uncover the fundamental reasons behind the problem. Some issues may have multiple root causes that contribute to the failure.

2. **Understand the causal chain**: Analyze the sequence of events and contributing factors that led to the problem. Mapping out the cause-and-effect relationship helps pinpoint critical areas for intervention.

3. **Implement preventive solutions**: Address weaknesses in existing processes or systems that enabled the problem to occur. Introduce improvements that minimize the likelihood of recurrence.

4. **Document and share findings**: Compile RCA results in a structured knowledge base. Sharing insights across the IT organization ensures that lessons learned can be applied to similar issues elsewhere.

5. **Eliminate the root cause**: Introduce permanent fixes by updating procedures, modifying configurations, or implementing new controls.

6. **Take proactive measures**: Prevent similar incidents by implementing recommended corrective actions. This may involve changes to systems, operational workflows, or staff training programs.

7. **Monitor and evaluate**: After applying solutions, track the IT environment to confirm the problem does not reappear and that the corrective measures are effective.

8. **Update documentation and knowledge base**: Ensure that findings, recommendations, and actions taken are recorded within the KEDB for future reference.

By conducting thorough RCA, organizations can transition from reactive problem-solving to a proactive approach, improving service reliability, reducing incidents, and increasing operational efficiency. A well-executed RCA strengthens IT stability and helps teams anticipate potential issues before they escalate into major disruptions.

PMDB is closely tied to the KEDB. When a root cause is identified and either a workaround or a permanent solution is established, the relevant details are recorded in the KEDB. The KEDB serves as a subset of the PMDB, offering documented references for recurring issues and their resolutions. Incident management teams leverage this resource to expedite troubleshooting and reduce downtime.

A structured PMDB and KEDB strengthen IT stability by improving service reliability through comprehensive issue tracking, reducing downtime by providing quick access to known errors and solutions, supporting continuous improvement through data-driven problem analysis, and enhancing incident resolution by linking problems to their root causes and resolutions. By implementing a robust PMDB, organizations can improve overall IT service quality, enhance operational efficiency, and build resilience against recurring issues.

Conclusion

CM and change management are closely interconnected disciplines within ITSM, each playing a crucial role in maintaining stability and efficiency within an organization's IT infrastructure.

At the core of this process is the CMDB, a centralized repository that provides valuable insights into system relationships, impact assessments, and decision-making support across various ITSM processes.

Together, CM, change management, and problem management create a highly interdependent ITSM framework. The CMDB delivers essential configuration data that enables strategic change management decisions, while problem management insights, captured in the PMDB and distilled into the KEDB, drive proactive improvements and incident prevention. A fragmented or poorly executed approach to any of these elements increases risks, service instability, and overall business impact. A holistic, integrated ITSM strategy, featuring robust CM, structured change management, and proactive problem management, ensures operational stability, optimized service delivery, and long-term value creation for the business.

In summary, the CMDB, PMDB, and KEDB are essential internal knowledge repositories that play a crucial role in strengthening BCP. These resources provide structured, actionable insights that make BCP more informed, responsive, and effective in managing disruptions. When properly maintained and integrated, they go beyond ITSM best practices; they become foundational elements of a resilient and reliable business continuity framework. Organizations should treat CM as a strategic pillar of resilience. Investing in a mature CM process and maintaining an accurate CMDB are critical to building, executing, and sustaining an effective and agile BCP.

We have completed all the essential ITSM processes in all the chapters till now. We will now be focusing on the audit process, people process, and processes surrounding databases. We will also look at processes defining supplier/partner engagements in the upcoming chapters.

Join our Discord space

Join our Discord workspace for latest updates, offers, tech happenings around the world, new releases, and sessions with the authors:

https://discord.bpbonline.com

CHAPTER 16
IT Audit Frameworks ISO 20000 and ITIL

Introduction

In this chapter, we will look at the IT audit framework, which provides guidelines and checklists for conducting the infrastructure audit. An IT audit framework provides a structured set of guidelines, best practices, and standards that ensure consistency, thoroughness, and objectivity in evaluating an organization's IT processes, controls, and overall environment. Two key elements frequently considered within **IT service management (ITSM)** audits are ISO 20000 and the **Information Technology Infrastructure Library (ITIL)**. While distinct in purpose, both contribute to a comprehensive IT auditing strategy.

ISO 20000 is an internationally recognized certifiable standard that outlines requirements for establishing, implementing, maintaining, and continuously improving an organization's **service management system (SMS)**. Certification is granted after an accredited audit verifies compliance with the standard's defined criteria. ISO 20000 emphasizes a structured approach to ITSM by ensuring processes are properly documented, monitored, and improved over time.

From an audit standpoint, ISO 20000 serves as a concrete benchmark against which ITSM processes are evaluated. Auditors assess whether the organization has formalized and effectively implemented essential service management components, including **service level management (SLM)**, incident management, change management, release and deployment management, capacity management, IT service continuity management, and problem management. They also examine whether ongoing monitoring and continual improvement practices align with ISO 20000's requirements.

ITIL is a widely used ITSM framework offering guidance on best practices for managing IT services. Unlike ISO 20000, ITIL does not establish certifiable compliance standards for organizations, though individuals can obtain ITIL certification, which helps in implementing the ITIL framework. It provides flexible recommendations that organizations can adapt based on their specific operational needs. In audits, ITIL serves as a benchmark for evaluating ITSM maturity and efficiency rather than a strict compliance requirement. Auditors assess whether organizations follow ITIL best practices in service management, identifying areas for improvement and ensuring service delivery aligns with industry standards. ITIL's four principles, including focus on value, collaborate and promote visibility, and optimize and automate, inform audit evaluations of operational effectiveness and risk management strategies.

Structure

The chapter covers the following topics:

- Key concepts
- ISO 20000 and ITIL standards
- IT audit framework based on ISO 20000
- IT audit framework based on ITIL

Objectives

Upon completing the study of an IT audit framework incorporating ISO 20000 and ITIL, individuals will be equipped with a comprehensive understanding of its purpose, benefits, and implementation. They should be able to define an IT audit framework, explain its key components, and describe why organizations conduct IT audits. Additionally, they should recognize the difference between mandatory standards and best practice frameworks, understand the connection between IT governance and IT audits, and navigate the various stages of an audit lifecycle, including planning, fieldwork, reporting, and follow-up.

The ability to integrate ISO 20000 and ITIL within an IT audit should allow individuals to leverage both frameworks effectively, identifying points of alignment and divergence between them. They should be capable of developing audit objectives and scopes that incorporate both perspectives, reporting findings in a manner that reflects both compliance and best practice adherence, and understanding how a combined approach enhances audit outcomes.

Finally, practical skills in IT auditing should include determining relevant audit objectives based on scenarios, selecting appropriate audit procedures for assessing ISO 20000 compliance and ITIL alignment, analyzing audit evidence to form conclusions, documenting audit findings and recommendations, and understanding the roles and responsibilities of IT auditors in these frameworks. By achieving these competencies, individuals will be well-equipped to conduct audits that provide a thorough evaluation of an organization's IT service management capabilities, ensuring operational efficiency, regulatory compliance, and continuous improvement.

Key concepts

As seen in the previous section, both ISO 20000 and ITIL play crucial roles in IT auditing, but in distinct ways. ISO 20000 is an established standard for ITSM that sets auditable requirements for an organization's SMS, whereas ITIL is a widely accepted framework offering best practices for implementing effective ITSM processes.

ISO 20000 outlines the necessary criteria for organizations to develop, implement, maintain, and enhance an SMS. This provides IT auditors with a defined benchmark to evaluate ITSM maturity and compliance. This comprises auditors assessing the SMS's policies, processes, and resources to ensure efficient service delivery, and a structured service management across key areas such as SLM, continuity and availability, change and configuration management, incident and problem management, continual improvement, compliance and documentation, etc.

ITIL serves as a framework rather than a certification standard. It provides guidance for ITSM implementation, helping IT auditors assess maturity and effectiveness, such as **service value system** (**SVS**), **service value chain** (**SVC**), etc. Key ITIL practices guide auditors in assessing areas of incident and problem management, change enablement, continual improvement, and providing a holistic approach emphasizing the four dimensions across people and organizations, information and technology, partners and suppliers, and value streams and processes.

ISO 20000 defines what must be done, while ITIL outlines how best practices can be implemented. ISO 20000 enables compliance auditing, whereas ITIL supports effectiveness evaluations. Using ITIL principles, auditors can assess an organization's readiness for ISO 20000 certification. Both emphasize risk mitigation and continual service improvement, ensuring operational excellence.

For IT auditors, combining ISO 20000's structured compliance framework with ITIL's practical insights enables a thorough assessment of ITSM maturity and efficiency.

ISO 20000 and ITIL complement each other in IT audits. ISO 20000 establishes compliance-driven requirements, while ITIL offers adaptable best practices for optimizing ITSM maturity. Organizations undergoing IT audits may be assessed against ISO 20000 standards for certification or ITIL principles for service management effectiveness. Employing both frameworks reinforces a commitment to well-managed, resilient IT services. Ultimately, an audit approach that incorporates ISO 20000 for compliance assessments and ITIL for process evaluation ensures a well-rounded audit strategy, enhancing IT service management while demonstrating accountability to stakeholders.

ISO 20000 and ITIL standards

ISO 20000 is an IT service management standard with the latest version as ISO/IEC 20000-1:2018. This is a global standard that sets requirements for managing IT services. organizations can get certified to prove they meet these requirements, ensuring IT services are well-organized, efficient, and continuously improving.

The key features of this standard are given as follows:

- **Certification**: Organizations can get third-party validation.

- **Structured processes**: Covers service planning, design, delivery, problem resolution, and change management.

- **SMS**: Helps businesses coordinate IT service policies and objectives.

- **Continual improvement**: Requires organizations to keep refining their processes.

- **Integration with other standards**: Aligns with ISO 9001 (quality management) and ISO 27001 (information security).

- **Documentation**: Requires detailed records of service management policies and procedures.

The interfaces between the service management processes and the relationships between different components of the SMS may be implemented differently by different service providers. The nature of the relationship between the service provider and the customer can also influence how the SMS is implemented to fulfil the requirements of ISO 20000. For these reasons, the interfaces between processes are not represented in the following figure:

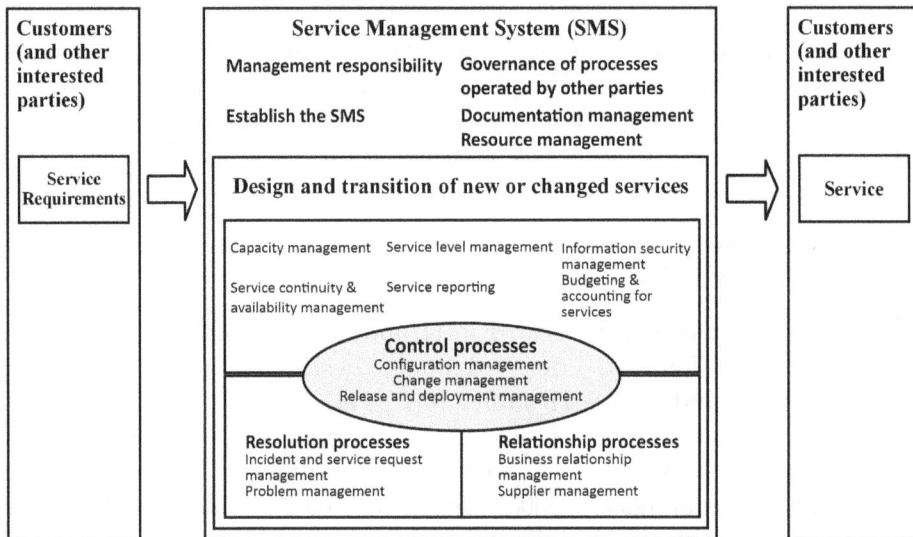

Figure 16.1: Service management system

The service provider holds full responsibility for the SMS and cannot delegate compliance with ISO 20000 to another party. However, certain tasks can be carried out by external entities under the service provider's supervision. For instance, a service provider may hire an external party to conduct internal audits or to develop the initial service management plan. Once finalized and approved, the plan remains under the direct ownership and ongoing management of the service provider. In these cases, external parties assist with specific short-term activities, but overall accountability, authority, and responsibility for the SMS remain with the service provider. This ensures that the service provider can provide evidence of meeting all ISO 20000 requirements. A strong grasp of ISO 20000 should allow individuals to explain its purpose and principles, identify its key clauses, and understand how its requirements serve as audit criteria. They should be able to conduct audits against ISO 20000, recognize areas of non-conformity, and comprehend the certification process. Furthermore, ISO 20000 should be seen as a tool for demonstrating effective IT governance and service management.

ITIL provides a best-practice framework for ITSM and the latest version ITIL 4 (2019). ITIL is a flexible framework guiding organizations in managing IT services effectively. Unlike ISO 20000, ITIL does not provide formal certification for organizations. The ITIL standard helps in improving IT service quality and efficiency through best practices.

The key features are given as follows:

- **SVS**: Helps organizations structure IT services for better business value.

- **Guiding principles**: Practical advice for decision-making, like focusing on value and collaboration.

- **Service value chain**: Defines steps to plan, design, build, deliver, and improve services.

- **Management practices**: 34 structured ways to manage IT service operations, including handling incidents, problems, and changes.

- **Continual improvement**: Encourages ongoing refinement of IT service processes.

- **Adaptability**: Can be customized for different industries and integrates with agile, DevOps, and lean methodologies.

Understanding ITIL in the context of IT audits should enable individuals to articulate its guiding principles, recognize how it can be used to benchmark ITSM process maturity, and differentiate between auditing for compliance with ISO 20000 versus evaluating ITSM effectiveness using ITIL best practices. They should be able to assess ITIL implementations, identify areas for process improvement, and understand how ITIL contributes to IT service governance and due diligence.

The IT service management landscape is complex, with organizations striving to provide reliable, high-quality, and cost-effective IT services that genuinely support business objectives. IT auditors play a crucial role in ensuring compliance and guiding improvement, and frameworks such as ISO 20000 and ITIL are essential tools in achieving this goal.

ISO 20000 serves as a formal, certifiable standard that defines precise, auditable requirements for establishing, implementing, maintaining, and continuously improving an SMS. For IT auditors, it provides a structured benchmark against which to assess an organization's adherence to industry best practices. Auditing against ISO 20000 focuses on verifying whether an organization's policies, processes, and documentation meet globally recognized standards, minimizing risk and demonstrating a solid foundation for ITSM maturity.

IT audit framework based on ISO 20000

The **International Organization for Standardization (ISO)** and **International Electrotechnical Commission** (**IEC**) are specialized bodies dedicated to global standardization. Member nations contribute to the creation of international standards through technical committees that focus on specific areas of technical activity. These committees collaborate on topics of mutual interest, alongside other international, governmental, and non-governmental organizations associated with ISO and IEC.

ISO/IEC 20000 can be utilized by:

- Organizations that seek services from providers and need assurance that their requirements will be met.

- Organizations that demand a standardized approach across all service providers, including those within a supply chain.

- Service providers aiming to showcase their capability in designing, transitioning, delivering, and enhancing services to meet specified requirements.

- Service providers looking to track, evaluate, and review their service management processes and overall service performance.

- Service providers focused on improving the design, transition, delivery, and continuous enhancement of services through the effective implementation of the SMS.

- Assessors use it as a benchmark for evaluating a service provider's SMS compliance with ISO 20000 standards.

ISO 20000 audit framework

The ISO 20000 audit framework systematically evaluates an organization's compliance with ISO/IEC 20000-1, ensuring effective service management and readiness for certification. Let us look at the framework in detail:

1. **Audit principles**: ISO 20000 audits follow essential principles:

   - **Integrity**: Auditors must act ethically and responsibly.

   - **Fair presentation**: Findings must be truthful and accurate.

   - **Confidentiality**: Audit information should be protected.

- **Independence**: Auditors must remain unbiased.
- **Evidence-based approach**: Conclusions rely on objective proof.

2. **Types of audits**:
   - **Internal audits:** Conducted by the organization to assess its own compliance.
   - **Second-party audits**: Performed by customers to evaluate their suppliers.
   - **Third-party certification audits**: Conducted by accredited external bodies to determine ISO 20000 compliance.

3. **Phases of a certification audit**:
   - **Stage 1- Documentation review**: Assesses SMS documentation, policies, and preparedness for the formal audit.
   - **Stage 2- Implementation verification**: Evaluates service management processes, conducts staff interviews, and reviews compliance evidence.
   - **Post-audit activities**: Address nonconformities with corrective actions, and certification is granted after compliance is reconfirmed. Surveillance audits are conducted annually, and re-certification audits occur every three years.

4. **Audit scope definition**: Defines which services, locations, technologies, and third-party providers fall within the audit's focus.

5. **Audit checklist and key focus areas**: Follows ISO 20000 structure for the focus areas.
   - **Leadership and planning**: Management commitment, risk assessment, service objectives.
   - **Operational processes**: Incident management, change control, service level agreements, supplier management.
   - **Performance monitoring**: Internal audits, evaluations, and continual improvement measures.

6. **Audit report requirements**: Includes audit scope, findings, nonconformities, opportunities for improvement, and recommendations.

7. **Nonconformity management:**
   - **Identification**: Document issues based on audit evidence.
   - **Root cause analysis**: Investigate underlying reasons for noncompliance.
   - **Corrective actions**: Implement fixes and prevent recurrence.
   - **Verification**: Ensure improvements are effective before certification.

By following this structured approach, organizations can streamline IT service management, improve efficiency, and achieve ISO 20000 certification.

Structure of the ISO 20000 audit framework

Here are some examples of how an ISO 20000 audit framework can be structured:

1. **Basic internal audit framework (self-assessment model)**: Used by organizations before external audits to assess their IT service management system. The example structure consists of:

    a. **Audit planning**: Define audit scope, objectives, and schedule.

    b. **Document review**: Assess policies, service management plans, and process documentation.

    c. **Process verification**: Evaluate incident management, change management, and SLM.

    d. **Interviews**: Engage process owners and IT staff for compliance insights.

    e. **Findings and corrective actions**: Identify gaps, implement improvements, and prepare for certification audits.

2. **External certification audit framework (third-party assessment)**: Used by accredited certification bodies to evaluate compliance with ISO 20000. Example structure comprises stage 1 audit to assess SMS documentation and policies, check readiness for the formal audit, and identify preliminary nonconformities. Stage 1 audit is followed by stage 2 audit, which happens through on-site verification of ITSM processes, analyzing service performance records (SLA reports, change logs), interviewing stakeholders, and assessing SMS effectiveness. Audit report and certification decision are the next steps, where findings and required corrective actions will be outlined. Certification is granted if compliance is confirmed.

3. **Comprehensive ITSM audit framework (governance and risk-based approach)**: Ideal for large organizations integrating ISO 20000 with other standards (ISO 9001, ISO 27001). This structure comprises governance review ensuring alignment between IT services and business objectives, risk-based assessment ensuring identification of potential service risks (security breaches, operational failures, etc.), performance evaluation for measuring service effectiveness using KPIs (incident response times, system availability), and a continuous improvement cycle by implementing findings into an ongoing **Plan-Do-Check-Act** (**PDCA**) improvement strategy.

Service management system

SMS, as outlined in ISO 20000, provides the structured backbone for an organization to design, implement, manage, and continuously refine its IT services. It represents a globally recognized standard that outlines certifiable requirements to ensure IT services are aligned with both business objectives and customer expectations.

Rather than simply having individual IT processes in place, an ISO 20000-based SMS establishes a cohesive, controlled, and measurable management system. This elevates service delivery from ad hoc efforts to a consistent and auditable discipline, anchored in internationally accepted best practices. The result is a reliable and efficient IT service environment capable of supporting high-quality outcomes and continuous improvement over time. Let us look at it in detail:

- **Context of the organization (Clause 4):**
  - o Organization and its context
  - o Interested parties
  - o Scope of the SMS
  - o Establish the SMS

- **Leadership (Clause 5):**
  - o Leadership and commitment
  - o Policy
  - o Roles, responsibilities, and authorities

- **Planning (Clause 6):**
  - o Risks and opportunities
  - o Objectives
  - o Plan the SMS

- **Support of the SMS (Clause 7):**
  - o Resources
  - o Competence
  - o Awareness
  - o Communication
  - o Documented Information
  - o Knowledge

- **Operation of the SMS (Clause 8):**
  - o **Operational planning and control:**
    - ▪ Relationship and agreement
    - ▪ Business relationship management
    - ▪ Service level management
    - ▪ Supplier management

- o **Service design, build, and transition**:
  - Change management
  - Service design and transition
  - Release and deployment management

- o **Service portfolio**:
  - Service delivery
  - Plan the service
  - Control the parties involved in the service lifecycle
  - Service catalog management
  - Asset management
  - Configuration management

- o **Supply and demand**:
  - Budgeting and accounting for services
  - Demand management
  - Capacity management

- o **Service assurance**:
  - Service availability management
  - Service continuity management
  - Information security management

- **Performance evaluation (Clause 9)**:
  - o Monitoring, measurement, analysis, and evaluation
  - o Internal audit
  - o Service reporting
  - o Management review

- **Improvement (Clause 10)**:
  - o Nonconformity and corrective action
  - o Continual improvement

ISO 20000 follows the PDCA methodology and structure for effective implementation, like all ISO management systems. The ISO 20000 clauses can be matched to the PDCA cycle, as shown in the following figure:

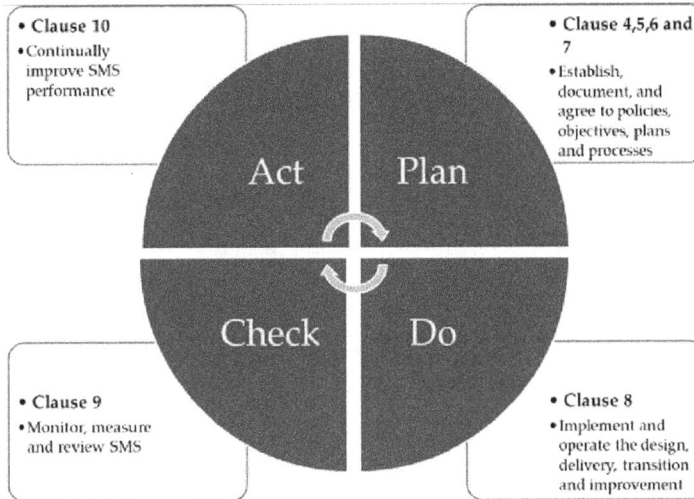

Figure 16. 2: PDCA and ISO clauses

The PDCA cycle should remain active throughout the lifespan of the SMS. Once the system is established, the focus shifts to the Do, Check, and Act phases. However, whenever significant changes occur, such as scope expansion, leadership transitions, process modifications, or shifts in the risk landscape, it becomes necessary to reassess and update the Plan (covering clauses 4, 5, 6, and 7). After revising the Plan, the organization should then apply the Do, Check, and Act steps to ensure those changes are effectively implemented and managed.

ISO 20000 audit checklist

An ISO 20000 audit checklist is fundamentally structured around the clauses of the ISO 20000-1:2018 standard. This standard, like other modern ISO management system standards, follows the high-level structure, also known as annex SL. This means there are 10 main clauses, each representing a key area of focus for an IT audit.

The first three clauses of any of the ISO standards are scope, normative references, and terms and definitions. Clause 1 (Scope) outlines what the standard covers, clause 2 (Normative references) lists other standards that are referenced within, and clause 3 (Terms and definitions) clarifies key terms used in the standard.

Here are the primary focus areas (clauses 4 to 10) in an ISO 20000 audit checklist for IT auditing, broken down by clause:

1. **Context of the organization (Clause 4):**

    - **Understanding the organization and its context (4.1):**

        o Has the organization determined relevant internal and external issues that affect its ability to achieve the intended outcomes of its SMS?

        o Is there documented evidence of this understanding?

- **Understanding the needs and expectations of interested parties (4.2):**
  - o Has the organization identified all relevant interested parties (e.g., customers, users, regulators, suppliers, employees, shareholders)?
  - o Are their needs and expectations (requirements) understood and documented?
  - o How are these requirements addressed within the SMS?
- **Determining the scope of the service management system (4.3):**
  - o Is the scope of the SMS clearly defined and documented (which services, locations, organizational units, and parties involved in the service lifecycle are included)?
  - o Does the defined scope accurately reflect the services managed by the SMS?
- **Service management system (4.4):** Has the organization established, implemented, maintained, and continually improved the SMS in accordance with the standard's requirements?

2. **Leadership (Clause 5):**

- **Leadership and commitment (5.1):**
  - o Is top management actively involved in the SMS?
  - o Does top management ensure that value for the organization and its customers is determined and delivered?
  - o Is there clear control over other parties involved in the service lifecycle?
  - o Is the SMS integrated into the organization's business processes?
- **Policy (5.2):**
  - o Is there a documented service management policy that is appropriate to the purpose of the organization and provides a framework for setting objectives?
  - o Is the policy communicated, understood, and applied throughout the organization?
- **Organizational roles, responsibilities, and authorities (5.3):** Are roles, responsibilities, and authorities for the SMS clearly defined, communicated, and understood?

3. **Planning (Clause 6):**

- **Actions to address risks and opportunities (6.1):**

- o Has the organization identified risks and opportunities related to the SMS and its services (considering internal/external issues and interested party requirements)?

- o Are plans in place to address these risks and opportunities (e.g., risk assessment, mitigation strategies)?

- o Is the effectiveness of these actions evaluated?

- **Service management objectives and planning to achieve them** (**6.2**):

  - o Are measurable service management objectives established at relevant functions and levels?

  - o Are plans developed to achieve these objectives, including resources, responsibilities, timelines, and evaluation methods?

- **Plan the service management system** (**6.3**): Is there a comprehensive service management plan, including a list of services within scope and how they are managed?

4. **Support (Clause 7)**:

   - **Resources** (**7.1**): Are adequate resources (people, infrastructure, environment) provided for the SMS?

   - **Competence** (**7.2**):

     - o Is there a process to determine the necessary competence for personnel working on the SMS?

     - o Is training provided to ensure competence, and are records maintained?

   - **Awareness** (**7.3**): Are personnel aware of the service management policy, objectives, and their contribution to the SMS's effectiveness?

   - **Communication** (**7.4**): Are there defined processes for internal and external communication related to the SMS (what, when, with whom, how, who is responsible)?

   - **Documented information** (**7.5**): Is all required documented information (policies, procedures, records) maintained, controlled, and accessible? (This is a cross-cutting clause, as most processes require documentation.)

   - **Knowledge** (**7.6**): Is there a process for capturing, maintaining, and sharing knowledge relevant to the SMS?

5. **Operation (Clause 8)**: The core service management processes. This is where the detailed audit of individual service management processes takes place. Auditors will look for evidence that these processes are planned, implemented, controlled, and effective.

- **Operational planning and control (8.1)**: General controls over SMS operations.

- **Service portfolio (8.2)**:

  o **Service delivery (8.2.1)**: Planning and controlling service delivery.

  o **Plan the services (8.2.2)**: Requirements for planning individual services.

  o **Control of parties involved in the service lifecycle (8.2.3)**: Managing internal and external suppliers providing components of the service.

  o **Service catalogue management (8.2.4)**: Is there an accurate, up-to-date service catalogue?

  o **Asset management (8.2.5)**: Are IT assets identified and managed to support services?

  o **Configuration management (8.2.6)**: Is there an effective **configuration management system (CMS)** that accurately reflects **configuration items (CIs)** and their relationships?

- **Relationship and agreement (8.3)**:

  o General (8.3.1)

  o **Business relationship management (8.3.2)**: How IT interfaces with the business and customers.

  o **Service level management (8.3.3)**: Are service level agreements (SLAs) defined, monitored, reported on, and reviewed? Are targets being met?

  o **Supplier management (8.3.4)**: How external and internal suppliers are managed to ensure they meet their commitments.

- **Supply and demand (8.4)**:

  o **Budgeting and accounting for services (8.4.1)**: Is there transparency and control over IT service costs?

  o **Demand management (8.4.2)**: How customer demand for services is managed and influenced.

  o **Capacity management (8.4.3)**: Is IT capacity sufficient to meet agreed service requirements and future demand?

- **Service design, build, and transition (8.5)**:

  o **Change management (8.5.1)**: How changes to services and CIs are planned, assessed, approved, implemented, and reviewed to minimize risk.

  o **Service design and transition (8.5.2)**: How new or changed services are designed, developed, and prepared for operation.

     o **Release and deployment management (8.5.3)**: How new or changed services are packaged, built, tested, and deployed into the live environment.

- **Resolution and fulfilment (8.6)**:

     o **Incident management (8.6.1)**: How incidents are recorded, categorized, prioritized, diagnosed, and resolved to restore regular service.

     o **Service request management (8.6.2)**: How routine service requests are managed and fulfilled.

     o **Problem management (8.6.3)**: How root causes of recurring incidents are identified, analyzed, and removed to prevent future incidents.

- **Service assurance (8.7)**:

     o **Service availability management (8.7.1)**: Ensuring services meet agreed-upon availability targets.

     o **Service continuity management (8.7.2)**: Planning and preparing for service recovery in the event of major disruption or disaster.

     o **Information security management (8.7.3)**: Protecting the confidentiality, integrity, and availability of information and information assets.

6. **Performance evaluation (Clause 9)**:

- **Monitoring, measurement, analysis, and evaluation (9.1)**: Are the SMS and services being monitored and measured? Is the performance data analyzed and evaluated to assess effectiveness?

- **Internal audit (9.2)**: Is there a planned and implemented internal audit program for the SMS? Are internal audits conducted by independent and competent auditors? Are audit results reported and corrective actions taken?

- **Management review (9.3)**: Does top management regularly review the SMS to ensure its continuing suitability, adequacy, and effectiveness? Are the inputs (e.g., audit results, performance data, feedback) and outputs (e.g., decisions, actions) of these reviews documented?

- **Service reporting (9.4)**: Are service reports generated and communicated to relevant stakeholders, providing insights into service performance?

7. **Improvement (Clause 10)**:

- **Nonconformity and corrective action (10.1)**: Is there a process for identifying nonconformities (deviations from requirements)? Are corrective actions taken to address nonconformities and prevent recurrence, including root cause analysis?

- **Continual improvement (10.2)**: Is there an ongoing commitment to continually improve the suitability, adequacy, and effectiveness of the SMS and the services? Are opportunities for improvement identified and acted upon?

An IT auditor conducting an ISO 20000 audit will typically use a detailed checklist derived from these clauses, often with specific questions for each requirement, to gather objective evidence through documentation review, interviews, and observation.

IT audit framework based on ITIL

ITIL is a widely recognized framework that provides best practices for ITSM. It establishes a structured approach for efficiently managing and delivering IT services to align with business objectives and customer expectations. ITIL focuses on a service-oriented methodology rather than being tied to specific hardware or software. It defines key processes and functions essential for maintaining high-quality IT service delivery, such as incident management, change management, and service design. Rather than serving as a rigid, one-size-fits-all model, ITIL is designed to be adaptable, allowing organizations to tailor its principles to their unique needs and challenges. By adopting ITIL best practices, businesses can foster continuous improvement while enhancing the value provided to customers and stakeholders.

The advantages of the ITIL framework go beyond enhancing service delivery. By applying ITIL best practices, organizations can:

- Streamline IT operations while minimizing costs.

- Ensure IT alignment with business objectives and strategic goals.

- Enhance customer satisfaction and improve the overall user experience.

- Increase the return on IT investments, maximizing their impact.

- Foster a culture of continuous improvement to drive ongoing service excellence.

The ITIL framework includes several processes and functions that can be broken down into key areas, as shown in *Figure 16.3*. These are the basic blocks of ITIL, new processes around SVS, focusing on creating value through effects for the business stakeholder, and consumers have been introduced in ITIL v4. ITIL v4 also introduces the concept of the SVC to replace the service lifecycle. Let us look at the basic ITIL processes in the following figure:

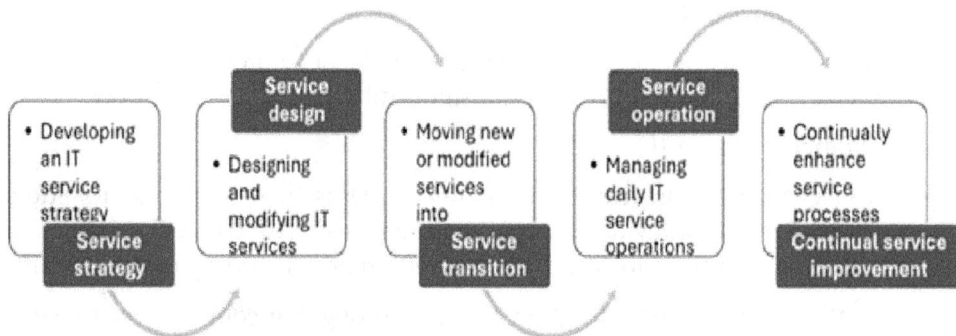

Figure 16.3: Basic ITIL processes

In ITIL, service management is the cornerstone of delivering effective IT services, ensuring they align with business needs. Service design focuses on developing new IT services and enhancing existing ones by defining the requirements, resources, and capabilities to meet organizational goals. Change management oversees modifications to IT services to prevent disruptions, while incident management identifies, tracks, and resolves IT issues to minimize operational impact. The ITIL service lifecycle provides a structured framework for managing IT services from inception to ongoing refinement, covering service strategy, service design, service transition, service operation, and continual service improvement.

The core components of the ITIL SVS are ITIL SVC, ITIL practices, ITIL guiding principles, governance and continual improvement. Governance was introduced in ITIL 4 to strengthen the SVS, addressing a key gap in previous versions. As IT organizations gain more influence, governance plays a crucial role in ensuring accountability and strategic alignment. Its structure varies across organizations, adapting to their specific needs. Governance can apply to an entire enterprise or focus on a particular product, service, program, or process. It must be aligned with corporate goals and have the authority to direct, monitor, and evaluate performance. Strong governance relies on leadership support to be effective.

ITIL v4's SVS encompasses essential concepts for creating business value through products and services. It encourages internal and external service providers to consider how various components contribute to co-creating value. At the core of the SVS is the SVC, which is transformed by four key elements:

- **Practices (Processes)**: Structured methods for managing IT services.

- **Guiding principles**: Foundational recommendations for decision-making.

- **Governance**: Ensuring oversight and accountability.

- **Continual improvement**: Driving ongoing enhancements to service delivery.

SVS is a core concept in ITIL 4, offering a comprehensive framework that guides how organizations can collaboratively generate value through IT-enabled services. Unlike previous ITIL versions, which centered around processes and service lifecycle stages, the SVS focuses on organizational alignment, adaptability, and seamless integration of various practices to support value creation.

The following figure shows an overview of the key elements that make up the ITIL 4 service value system:

ITIL service value chain	ITIL practices	ITIL guiding principles	Governance	Continual Improvement
• Plan • Engage • Design and Transition • Obtain/Build • Deliver and Support Improve	• General management practices • Service management practices • Technology management practices	• Focus on value • Start where you are • Progress iteratively with feedback • Collaborate and promote • Think and work holistically • Keep it simple and practical • Optimize and automate	• Directs and controls the organization	• Seven step improvement

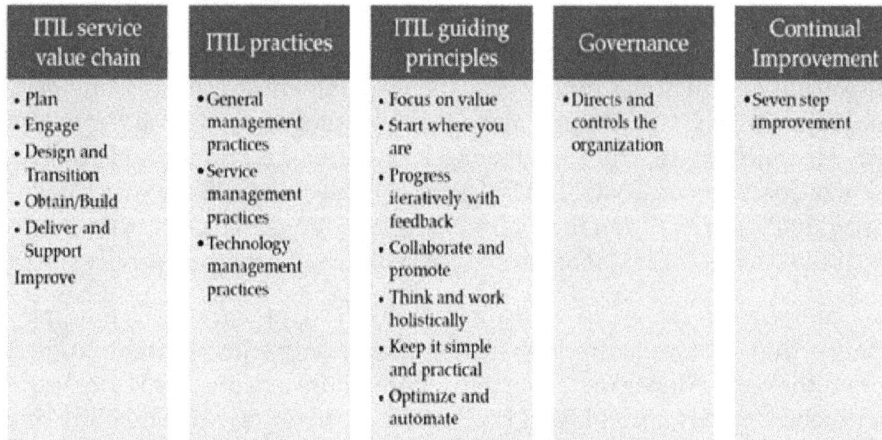

Figure 16.4: ITIL V4 service value system

ITIL4 introduced four dimensions to the framework to ensure the ITSM processes are defined in alignment with the business goals. These are given as follows:

- Organization and people
- Information and technology
- Partners and suppliers
- Value streams and processes

Together, these elements enhance, control, and improve the SVC, making ITSM a more efficient and value-driven exercise.

Implementing an ITSM program based on ITIL processes offers significant benefits, but it also comes with challenges that can hinder success. While standardization and governance help transform the chaos into structured operations, organizations often struggle with two primary issues:

- **Lack of leadership support**: Without strong backing from leadership, ITSM initiatives fail to gain traction. Change management and incident resolution depend on executive commitment. If some teams fail to report incidents, the organization cannot fully grasp the impact of service disruptions. Similarly, if changes are not assessed consistently, businesses risk repeated outages due to poor implementation.

- **Overloading the system too quickly**: Trying to implement too many processes at once overwhelms the organization, leading to confusion and resistance. Change needs to be gradual, aligning with the company's capacity for adaptation.

A significant barrier arises when organizations attempt to establish policies before processes. Policy adherence is often tied to performance goals and job security, making it a contentious issue. Leadership might verbally support the initiative, but hesitate if enforcing compliance risks losing a top-performing employee. Without consistency and leadership solidarity, ITSM initiatives fail to create real value, regardless of their potential benefits. Addressing these challenges head-on is essential for success.

With the introduction of ITIL 4, the industry is shifting toward a more holistic and integrated approach to managing IT services. Focus on outcomes, not just outputs, is one of the strategies for successful transition. Instead of simply increasing workloads, streamline tasks to eliminate inefficiencies. The goal is to shift from doing things right to doing the right things. Another strategy is prioritizing culture and practices over tools and processes. Fostering an open and collaborative environment and enabling your organization to adapt to change quickly help an organization shift towards an integrated approach. Instead of rigid workflows, establish flexible practices that encourage the right behaviors and accelerate value creation. The third strategy is adopting modern methodologies like agile and DevOps. Depending on the team's needs, the best practices have to be integrated into existing workflows, such as promoting open team communication, continual improvement, and value stream management. Alternatively, ITSM processes can be designed by incorporating peer reviews in change management or applying continuous delivery. Now is the time for IT teams to embrace more agile ITSM approaches, emphasizing collaboration, simplicity, and value-driven services.

Focus areas in ITIL compliance assessment

When creating an ITIL audit checklist for IT auditing, the emphasis moves away from strict compliance, such as ISO 20000. Instead, it focuses on evaluating the adoption, effectiveness, and ongoing improvement of IT service management practices. ITIL 4, the latest iteration, centers around the SVS, which defines the core areas for assessment.

As part of assessing guiding principles, auditors will examine if the organization's culture and practices reflect ITIL's guiding principles. This is not about specific processes, but the underlying philosophy.

While assessing governance practices, strategic direction by top management, definition of roles and responsibilities, and whether there are clear policies and decision-making structures for IT services are evaluated. For understanding compliance and control, checks on whether IT governance frameworks are aligned with overall organizational governance and whether IT service management activities are subject to appropriate oversight and audits are conducted.

SVC activities get assessed when auditors trace how value flows through the organization's service management activities. This involves examining the inputs, activities, and outputs of each activity.

Assessment of ITIL practices covers the detailed evaluation of specific ITSM areas. This is where the bulk of the ITIL audit checklist typically resides. Auditors will select relevant practices based on the audit scope and organizational priorities.

Four dimensions of service management will be assessed by looking at the SMS with a holistic perspective. Auditors will determine if the organization considers these four dimensions holistically when managing services. The audit framework considers key elements of IT service management, starting with organizations and people, to ensure roles and responsibilities are clearly defined and understood. It also examines whether staff possess the necessary skills and training and whether the organizational culture fosters effective service management. Information and technology play a crucial role in service delivery, requiring an appropriate technology stack that is both efficiently utilized and aligned with service goals. Information management, including service data and performance metrics, must be structured and effectively used to support decision-making. Partners and suppliers must be assessed to determine if relationships with external entities are well-managed and whether contracts are clear and regularly monitored to maintain service quality. Value streams and processes should be mapped and thoroughly understood, ensuring that workflows are well-defined, documented, and consistently followed. Optimization is key, ensuring processes are efficient and contribute to meaningful value creation within the organization.

An ITIL audit checklist is less about pass or fail and more about assessing maturity, identifying strengths, and uncovering opportunities for enhancement to drive greater value from IT services. It is a tool for driving continuous improvement rather than just proving compliance.

IT auditors should recognize ISO 20000 and ITIL as complementary frameworks to each other, rather than separate frameworks. ISO 20000 establishes the necessary rigor for compliance and risk management, while ITIL offers the flexibility and depth required to assess real-world service management effectiveness. By integrating both, auditors can provide more comprehensive and actionable assessments, ultimately strengthening an organization's IT service capabilities and enhancing its resilience in an ever-evolving digital landscape.

Conclusion

In summary, ISO 20000 establishes the formal, auditable requirements for a strong SMS, ensuring organizations meet standardized criteria. ITIL complements this by offering practical guidance and best practices to implement these requirements effectively, with a focus on value creation.

A well-rounded IT audit typically incorporates both frameworks, using ISO 20000 to confirm compliance with essential standards and ITIL to evaluate the maturity, efficiency, and effectiveness of service management processes. This combined approach ensures organizations achieve regulatory compliance while also driving operational excellence in IT service delivery.

While ISO 20000 defines the *what* of service management compliance, ITIL provides the *how* by offering best practices that enable operational excellence. ITIL's emphasis on the service value system, guiding principles, and management practices allows auditors to go beyond mere compliance and assess how effectively IT services align with business objectives. ITIL helps auditors evaluate whether IT operations are not only functioning but actively contributing to resource optimization, service efficiency, and a culture of continual improvement.

Upon learning the critical ITSM audit frameworks, next, we will cover the essential processes that we need to focus on while conducting IT audits. In the upcoming chapters, we will learn about organizations, people, data and technology processes, and the partner frameworks, value streams, and processes that need to be focused on for getting a holistic picture of the ITSM operations in an organization.

CHAPTER 17

Organizations, People, Data and Technology Processes

Introduction

In the contemporary business landscape, where information technology forms the backbone of business operations, strategic decision-making, and competitive advantage, the role of IT audit has become crucial. Beyond merely ensuring compliance, modern IT audits delve into the effectiveness, efficiency, and resilience of an organization's technological ecosystem. This holistic assessment warrants a focus that extends beyond technical infrastructure to encompass the critical interplay of organizations, people, data, and technology processes. These four interconnected pillars represent the fundamental dimensions of any IT environment and are the key areas where an auditor must scrutinize to provide comprehensive assurance. A deficiency in any one of these can significantly undermine the integrity, security, and value delivery of an organization's IT services.

The first element, organizations, refers to the governance structures, strategic alignment, and the overall framework within which IT functions. Then comes the next element, people, which encompasses the human element, their skills, roles, responsibilities, culture, and adherence to established procedures. The third, data, represents the lifeblood of modern enterprise, requiring meticulous attention to its integrity, security, availability, and how it flows through the systems. Finally, technology processes are the methodologies and systematic approaches by which IT services are managed, delivered, and supported.

This chapter will introduce the critical audit considerations within each of these intertwined domains, highlighting how a robust IT audit strategy must meticulously evaluate their interactions to provide a truly insightful and value-adding assessment of an organization's technological health and its contribution to business objectives.

Structure

The chapter covers the following topics:

- Key concepts
- Processes, the integrated framework
- Strategic and operational processes
- Governance and compliance processes
- People processes
- Innovation
- Data life cycle
- Continuous improvement

Objectives

The learning objectives for this chapter focus on the importance of organizations, people, data, and technology processes in IT audits, ensuring auditors gain a comprehensive understanding of these key areas.

Upon completion, participants will be able to explain the role of organizational structure and IT governance in maintaining effective IT systems, identify essential IT governance frameworks such as COBIT, ITIL governance principles, and ISO 20000 leadership clauses, and assess how IT strategy aligns with broader business objectives. They will also be equipped to evaluate IT risk management processes, analyze the influence of organizational culture and communication on IT control effectiveness, and assess the management of third-party relationships, including vendors and cloud providers.

In terms of people, participants will learn to evaluate roles, responsibilities, and segregation of duties within IT to prevent errors and fraud, assess IT personnel competencies and training programs, and examine the effectiveness of HR processes related to onboarding, offboarding, performance management, and security awareness.

For data, we will cover fundamental principles such as confidentiality, integrity, and availability within the CIA triad. As part of the audit, we will have to evaluate controls for data accuracy, completeness, and validity across its lifecycle, assess security measures including encryption and access controls, examine backup and recovery strategies for business continuity, and ensure compliance with relevant data privacy regulations. Additionally, auditors have to focus on how to analyze data flows across systems to identify vulnerabilities and control gaps.

Technology processes will be another key area, enabling participants to evaluate the maturity and effectiveness of core IT service management processes such as incident management, change management, configuration management, etc., using frameworks like ITIL and ISO 20000. Lastly, the assessment will include evaluation of an organization's continuous improvement approach within IT processes, considering performance measurement and corrective action mechanisms.

Key concepts

As seen in the previous section, key concepts for organizations, people, data, and technology processes in ITSM follow the principles of ITIL 4 and its four dimensions of service management. These dimensions form the foundation of a successful ITSM strategy.

Organizations and value streams center on an organization's structure, culture, and governance. They define how services are delivered effectively, emphasizing organizational hierarchy, team collaboration, and communication. Governance establishes policies, roles, and responsibilities to align IT activities with business objectives, while value streams guide how services are designed and optimized to create customer value.

People play a crucial role in ITSM by influencing service delivery through roles, competencies, and leadership. Clearly defined responsibilities ensure operational efficiency, while staff training and skill development maintain expertise in emerging technologies and ITSM methodologies. Leadership fosters accountability and motivation, ensuring IT teams remain engaged in delivering high-quality services. This will help in identifying compliance levels with security training programs, analyzing the impact of staff turnover on IT operations, and assessing audit risks associated with resource constraints.

Data encompasses the information that drives service management. Effective information management ensures data integrity, accuracy, security, and availability. Knowledge management structures this information into valuable resources, such as a knowledge base, **known error database (KEDB)**, and **configuration management database (CMDB)** to support ITSM processes. Reporting and analytics further enhance decision-making, identifying trends and driving continuous improvement.

Technology and processes integrate ITSM tools and operational workflows. Service management platforms facilitate tracking and resolution of incidents, changes, and service requests. Infrastructure, automation, and emerging technologies such as **artificial intelligence (AI)**, **Internet of Things (IoT)**, and **machine learning (ML)** enhance efficiency. Critical ITSM processes, including incident management, change enablement, service level management, and service continuity management, help organizations maintain stability and resilience. Assessment focus will also include **software development lifecycle (SDLC)** controls, examine infrastructure management processes related to network security and cloud infrastructure, audit IT operations controls such as monitoring and patch management, and identify automation risks and benefits.

Each of these dimensions is interconnected. A weakness in one will inevitably affect the others, making a balanced ITSM approach essential for optimizing IT services and achieving operational excellence.

Processes, the integrated framework

In the domain of **IT service management** (**ITSM**), processes serve as the integrative framework that binds together the various elements of an organization to deliver services effectively. They are the conduits through which the strategic intent of the organization, the capabilities of people, the insights from data, and the power of technology are transformed into tangible value for customers.

Here is how processes act as the integrated framework:

- **Connecting the what to the how**: Processes translate strategic objectives (from the organization dimension) into actionable steps. For example, a strategic decision to improve customer satisfaction (organizational goal) is achieved by refining the incident management process (technology process) to ensure faster resolution times, which relies on the competence of the service desk people and accurate incident data.

- **Orchestrating people and teams**: Processes define the roles, responsibilities, and handoffs between different individuals and teams within an organization. They ensure that work flows smoothly across departments, reducing silos and promoting collaboration. For instance, the change management process integrates the efforts of various people, namely, requesters, assessors, approvers, and implementers, guiding them through standardized steps, irrespective of their specific organizational unit.

- **Leveraging data for action and improvement**: Processes are the mechanisms through which data is captured, analyzed, and utilized. Incident management processes capture incident data, problem management processes analyze this data to identify root causes, and continuous improvement processes use performance data to drive enhancements. Without well-defined processes, data remains raw information; it is the process that transforms data into actionable insights, feeding back into the organization's ability to make better decisions.

- **Harnessing technology for efficiency**: Technology provides the tools and platforms (e.g., ITSM software, automation scripts) that enable processes to be executed efficiently and consistently. Processes dictate how these technologies are used, ensuring that system capabilities are leveraged to automate tasks, track progress, and provide real-time information. For example, a well-designed service request management process automates request routing and approval workflows within an ITSM tool, maximizing the efficiency of technology.

- **Ensuring consistency and predictability**: By providing repeatable steps and clear guidelines, processes standardize service delivery. This consistency is crucial for maintaining quality, meeting **service level agreements** (**SLAs**), and ensuring that outcomes are predictable. This predictability benefits the organization through reliable service offerings and enables people to perform their tasks more effectively.

- **Facilitating continuous improvement**: Processes are not static; they are living frameworks that should be continuously reviewed and improved. Performance metrics, often generated through process execution, provide the data necessary to identify bottlenecks, inefficiencies, and opportunities for optimization. This feedback loop allows the organization to adapt its technology processes and invest in its people to enhance overall service value.

In essence, processes act as the nervous system of ITSM, connecting the strategic brain (organization) with the operational limbs (people and technology) and ensuring that the lifeblood (data) flows effectively throughout the entire service value system. They are the glue that integrates the diverse elements into a cohesive, value-delivering whole, making them a critical focus area for both effective ITSM implementation and comprehensive IT auditing.

Strategic and operational processes

In ITSM, processes can be broadly classified based on their scope and timeframe, often falling into two primary categories: strategic processes and operational processes. While ITIL 4 has moved away from the rigid lifecycle phases of previous versions, the concepts of strategic and operational activities remain fundamental within its **service value system** (**SVS**) and practices.

Strategic processes in ITSM focus on long-term planning, direction, and alignment of IT services with business objectives. They define what services should be provided, why they are necessary, and how they contribute to the organization's broader goals. Typically, these processes involve senior decision-makers and extend over months or years.

The key traits of strategic processes are shown as follows:

- **Long-term orientation**: Address future needs, risks, and opportunities.

- **High-level perspective**: Establish policies, principles, and overarching direction.

- **Business alignment**: Direct IT capabilities toward business value creation.

- **Resource allocation**: Involve significant investments in IT infrastructure and services.

- **Proactive approach**: Shape IT services rather than react to current issues.

Examples of strategic ITSM processes (based on ITIL 4 framework) are:

- **Strategy management for IT services**: Defines the organization's service management vision, market positioning, and capabilities.

- **Service portfolio management**: Determines which services to offer, invest in, or retire, ensuring alignment with business strategy.

- **Financial management**: Manages budgeting, accounting, and charging to enable cost transparency and strategic decision-making.

- **Demand management**: Anticipates, influences, and aligns IT capacity with business needs to prevent inefficiencies.

- **Business relationship management**: Establishes strong customer relationships, ensuring services deliver value.

- **Risk management**: Identifies and addresses IT-related risks to support organizational resilience.

Operational processes in ITSM center on the day-to-day management, delivery, and support of IT services. They focus on how services are executed efficiently to meet expected performance standards and user needs. These processes are transactional and emphasize immediate or short-term actions.

The key traits of operational processes can be depicted as follows:

- **Short-term focus**: Handle present service requests and issues.

- **Detailed execution**: Follow step-by-step workflows and procedures.

- **Performance-driven**: Ensure effective service delivery and support.

- **Reactive and proactive**: Can address unexpected issues (incident management) or prevent problems (proactive maintenance).

- **Standardization and efficiency**: Streamline processes for consistency and reliability.

Examples of operational ITSM processes (based on ITIL 4):

- **Incident management**: Quickly restores service following interruptions or performance degradation.

- **Service request management**: Efficiently handles routine user requests (password resets, software installations).

- **Problem management**: Identifies and resolves recurring issues to prevent future incidents.

- **Change enablement**: Manages IT service changes to minimize disruptions.

- **Release and deployment management**: Plans, tests, and implements new or modified services in the live environment.

- **Configuration management**: Maintains accurate records of IT components and their relationships to support operational processes.

- **Event management**: Monitors IT infrastructure to detect and address service-affecting conditions.

- **Access management**: Controls authorized user access while preventing security breaches.

- **IT asset management**: Oversees the lifecycle of IT assets, including hardware, software, and licenses.

Integration of strategic and operational processes

Integrating strategic and operational processes within ITSM is crucial for ensuring that everyday service delivery supports the organization's broader business goals. Instead of treating strategy and operations as separate functions, effective ITSM approaches foster a unified framework where strategic planning guides operational activities, and feedback from daily operations continuously shapes and improves strategic decisions. Strategic and operational processes are deeply interconnected, complementing one another to achieve effective ITSM. Let us look at their features:

- Strategic decisions guide operational activities, for instance, introducing a new cloud service (service portfolio management) drives design, implementation, and support processes.

- Operational feedback fuels strategic planning, and data from incidents, problems, and service performance informs future investments and service improvements.

ITIL's SVS and **service value chain** (**SVC**) emphasize seamless integration, where strategic and operational elements work together to create, deliver, and enhance service value.

By understanding these two categories, organizations can ensure their IT services remain efficient in daily operations while continuously aligning with long-term business goals.

Governance and compliance processes

In ITSM, governance and compliance are fundamental components that ensure the effective delivery of IT services, alignment with organizational objectives, risk mitigation, and adherence to legal and regulatory requirements. While governance establishes strategic direction and control mechanisms, compliance ensures conformity with predefined policies, standards, and external mandates.

Governance in ITSM refers to the structured framework through which an organization exercises oversight, control, and strategic direction over its IT service-related activities. This framework delineates accountability, decision-making authority, and policy enforcement, ensuring IT services effectively support business objectives.

The key characteristics of ITSM governance are:

- **Strategic oversight**: Establishes policies, principles, and guidelines that govern IT service delivery.

- **Accountability framework**: Defines roles and responsibilities to ensure operational clarity.

- **Risk management protocols**: Identifies, assesses, and mitigates IT-related risks proactively.

- **Value optimization**: Ensures that IT investments contribute meaningfully to business value.

- **Performance evaluation mechanisms**: Monitors service effectiveness and adherence to strategic objectives.

- **Enterprise alignment**: Integrates IT governance within the broader corporate governance framework.

ITSM governance provides the structure and discipline to ensure IT delivers consistent, high-quality services that meet business needs and contribute to organizational success. The objective and significance of each of the practices are given in the following table:

Practice	Objective	Governance significance
Strategy management	Defines ITSM vision, objectives, and service strategy.	Ensures alignment with organizational goals and strategic direction.
Service portfolio management	Manages the lifecycle of IT services, including initiation, modification, and retirement.	Facilitates informed decision-making regarding IT investments and risk exposure.
Financial management	Oversees IT budgeting, cost accounting, and financial transparency.	Ensures responsible allocation of financial resources and budgetary oversight.
Business relationship management	Strengthens collaboration between IT and business units.	Aligns IT service offerings with enterprise needs and stakeholder expectations.
Risk management	Identifies and mitigates potential threats to IT services.	Maintains service continuity and operational resilience.
Continuous improvement	Implements strategic enhancements across ITSM capabilities.	Ensures ongoing evolution to meet emerging business and technological demands.

Table 17.1: Core governance practices in ITSM

By embedding these core governance practices, organizations can foster a disciplined yet agile IT environment, enabling sustainable service delivery, effective risk management, and continuous improvement that underpins overall business success.

Compliance in ITSM

Compliance within ITSM encompasses the adherence to legal, regulatory, contractual, and internal policies governing IT operations, service delivery, and data management. Compliance efforts serve to mitigate risks associated with regulatory violations and ensure IT services operate within prescribed guidelines.

The key characteristics of ITSM compliance are given as follows:

- **Regulatory adherence**: Maintains conformity with legal requirements and industry standards.

- **Risk prevention**: Reduces exposure to financial, operational, and reputational risks.

- **Audit preparedness**: Ensures readiness for internal and external compliance assessments.

- **Control enforcement**: Establishes mechanisms to uphold IT governance mandates.

Compliance is crucial not only for avoiding severe legal and financial penalties but also for building trust with customers and stakeholders, enhancing reputation, and ultimately contributing to the organization's overall success and resilience. The following table gives the purpose and relation to compliance for each of the ITSM practices:

Practice	Purpose	Compliance link
Information security management	Protects **confidentiality, integrity, and availability (CIA)** of data.	Supports adherence to regulatory requirements and internal security policies.
Audit management	Verifies IT process conformity through periodic reviews.	Ensures compliance with ISO 20000, ISO 27001, and regulatory requirements.
Service level management (SLM)	Defines and monitors IT service performance.	Guarantees services meet contractual and regulatory commitments.
Change enablement	Controls IT service modifications to minimize disruption.	Ensures compliance with governance mandates for regulated environments.
IT asset management (ITAM)	Manages IT assets throughout their lifecycle.	Ensures adherence to licensing agreements and hardware disposal regulations.

Practice	Purpose	Compliance link
Supplier management	Oversees third-party service providers.	Ensures vendor compliance with regulatory and contractual obligations.
Continuous improvement	Implements operational enhancements based on audit findings.	Supports compliance by evolving IT processes to meet standards.

Table 17.2: Core compliance practices in ITSM

In summary, these core compliance practices are indispensable for safeguarding the organization, maintaining legal standing, and ensuring the ethical and secure delivery of all IT services.

Governance and compliance

In today's fast-evolving business and regulatory landscape, governance and compliance are no longer separate functions; they operate as interwoven disciplines that, when effectively aligned, strengthen organizational resilience, reinforce accountability, and support sustainable success. As we have seen earlier in this chapter, governance provides the structural foundation through which policies, authority, and performance oversight are defined, ensuring that the organization's strategic direction remains consistent with ethical principles and stakeholder expectations. Compliance serves as the mechanism to ensure that actions, operations, and behaviors adhere to applicable laws, regulations, standards, and internal controls.

When governance and compliance operate in concert, organizations shift from a reactive, compliance-only mindset to a proactive and integrated risk management approach. This alignment promotes a culture rooted in transparency, informed decision-making, and disciplined execution. It empowers organizations not just to meet regulatory expectations, but to build trust, optimize internal controls, and enhance operational performance. Let us look at some of their features:

- **Governance establishes the framework for compliance**: IT governance bodies define policies, strategic objectives, and regulatory mandates that compliance practices must uphold.

- **Compliance provides actionable feedback to governance:** Audit findings, regulatory assessments, and compliance reports inform governance decision-making and policy adjustments.

- **Integrated approach to ITSM**: Best practices such as ITIL 4 and ISO 20000 advocate for embedding compliance requirements within ITSM processes, ensuring adherence is sustained as an integral component rather than treated as a separate function.

By integrating robust governance and compliance measures, organizations ensure that their IT services are strategically aligned, operationally efficient, risk-mitigated, and regulatory-compliant, thereby fostering trust, reliability, and sustainable value delivery. Ultimately, integrating governance and compliance is about more than meeting external demands; it becomes a strategic asset that enables agility, fuels innovation, and drives long-term organizational value.

Governance and compliance are intrinsically interconnected, functioning as complementary mechanisms within ITSM.

People processes

In ITSM, people-centric processes encompass structured activities and procedures designed to optimize human interactions within the IT organization, ensuring effective service delivery. Regardless of technological sophistication or well-defined technical processes, human expertise, collaboration, and communication remain pivotal to ITSM success.

The ITIL 4 framework underscores the importance of organizations and people as one of the four key dimensions of service management, emphasizing the essential role of personnel in sustaining operational excellence.

The key people-centric processes in ITSM can be captured as follows:

- **Workforce planning and management**: Ensuring that the IT organization has the right personnel with the required competencies available at the appropriate time to support service delivery.

  Key components in workforce planning are skills gap analysis, resource allocation and scheduling, capacity planning for human resources, succession planning, etc.

  o **Relevance of workforce planning to ITSM**:

    ▪ Determines service delivery capacity and response efficiency.

    ▪ Helps mitigate workload fluctuations through proactive resource planning.

- **Competence, training, and development**: Fostering and maintaining the requisite knowledge, skills, and experience across the IT workforce to facilitate operational effectiveness and adaptability.

  Key components of this phase are skills assessments and gap analysis, training programs covering ITSM frameworks like ITIL, certification programs, on-the-job training and mentoring, etc.

  o **Relevance of competence management to ITSM**:

    ▪ Enhances incident resolution rates and minimizes errors.

    ▪ Encourages continual learning and professional development.

- **Roles, responsibilities, and authority**: Establishing clear definitions for individual and team responsibilities, accountabilities, and communication flows within ITSM processes.

Key components of this phase are role delineation and job descriptions, the **Responsible, Accountable, Consulted, Informed (RACI)** model, defined escalation pathways, etc.

    o   **Relevance of this phase to ITSM:**

        ▪   Prevents process ambiguity and duplication of efforts.

        ▪   Streamlines workflows and enhances accountability.

- **Communication and collaboration**: Facilitating effective information exchange and cross-functional collaboration between IT teams, business units, customers, and suppliers.

Key components of this phase are defined communication protocols for incidents and service changes, regular team meetings and stakeholder interactions, utilization of collaboration tools (e.g., Microsoft Teams, Slack), transparent service announcements and knowledge sharing, etc.

    o   **Relevance of this phase to ITSM:**

        ▪   Enhances coordination and speeds up issue resolution.

        ▪   Strengthens customer satisfaction through improved service transparency.

- **Performance management and feedback**: Monitoring and evaluating individual and team performance to ensure alignment with ITSM objectives and service delivery expectations.

Key components for this phase include performance metrics and KPI tracking (e.g., incident resolution times), structured performance reviews and feedback mechanisms, employee recognition and incentive programs, etc.

    o   **Relevance of this phase to ITSM:**

        ▪   Motivates personnel and strengthens accountability.

        ▪   Identifies areas for improvement to optimize service execution.

- **Organizational culture and employee engagement**: Cultivating an organizational culture that promotes ITSM best practices, collaborative teamwork, proactive service improvement, and employee empowerment.

Key components for this phase are leadership-driven engagement strategies, recognition and rewards for ITSM contributions, employee satisfaction surveys and open-door communication policies, promotion of a service-first mindset, etc.

    o   **Relevance of this phase to ITSM:**

        ▪   Enhances employee morale and retention.

        ▪   Encourages adaptability and innovation within IT service practices.

- **Knowledge management (people aspect)**: While knowledge management is a distinct ITSM practice, its people-centric dimension involves fostering an environment where personnel actively contribute to, share, and utilize institutional knowledge.

  Key components to be looked at for this phase are incentives for knowledge documentation and sharing, training on knowledge base utilization, establishment of knowledge communities and peer coaching systems, etc.

  o **Relevance of this phase to ITSM**:

    ▪ Reduces dependency on individual expertise.

    ▪ Accelerates incident resolution and self-service capabilities.

- **Onboarding and offboarding**: Developing structured onboarding processes to integrate new IT personnel and offboarding protocols to ensure seamless transitions when employees depart.

  Key components here are comprehensive induction programs covering ITSM principles, access provisioning for new staff and secure access revocation upon departure, knowledge transfer initiatives to maintain service continuity, etc.

  o **Relevance of this phase to ITSM**:

    ▪ Reduces disruptions associated with personnel transitions.

    ▪ Strengthens security and compliance measures.

People-centric processes are integral to ITSM maturity, ensuring that IT professionals are equipped with the necessary skills, support systems, and collaborative frameworks to deliver high-quality services. By prioritizing workforce management, communication, competence development, and engagement, organizations can cultivate a highly skilled, motivated, and efficient IT workforce, driving superior service delivery and business alignment.

Innovation

Innovation in ITSM is a dynamic and ongoing process, continuously evolving to meet growing demands for efficiency, agility, and superior user experiences. As technological advancements reshape business environments, ITSM must adapt to remain relevant, value-driven, and strategically aligned with enterprise objectives. The latest innovations in ITSM are characterized by the integration of advanced technologies, a heightened focus on user-centric service delivery, and the extension of ITSM principles across organizational functions.

The key areas of innovation in ITSM are as follows:

- **AI and ML**: AI and ML are transforming ITSM by automating complex workflows, improving predictive capabilities, and enhancing service management efficiencies.

- o **Intelligent automation**: AI and ML advances beyond rule-based automation to enable sophisticated functions such as automated ticket classification, intelligent triaging of incidents, and autonomous resolution of low-level incidents.

- o **Predictive analytics**: AI-driven algorithms analyze historical data to forecast system failures, anticipate demand fluctuations, and proactively address potential service disruptions, shifting ITSM from a reactive to a proactive and prescriptive model.

- o **Generative AI (GenAI)**: A rapidly evolving field with significant applications:

  - ▪ **Enhanced knowledge management**: Auto-generates and summarizes knowledge articles, refines chatbot responses, and maintains up-to-date documentation by extracting insights from resolved tickets.

  - ▪ **Improved virtual agents and chatbots**: Enables conversational AI to comprehend natural language, facilitate complex interactions, and provide personalized responses, significantly improving self-service capabilities.

  - ▪ **Agent assistance**: Provides real-time recommendations, automated form completions, and drafted communications, increasing agent efficiency and accelerating resolution times.

  - ▪ **AI for IT operations**: Automates and optimizes IT operations by leveraging AI and ML for anomaly detection, event correlation, root cause analysis, and capacity planning, facilitating faster issue identification and resolution.

- **Enterprise service management (ESM)**: ESM extends ITSM principles and tools beyond IT to other business units such as human resources, facility management, finance department, and legal department, promoting streamlined workflows and cohesive enterprise-wide service delivery. ESM improves organizational efficiency, enhances employee experience, and reduces departmental silos by facilitating a unified service approach across multiple functions.

  - o **Enhanced user and employee experience**: The modern ITSM landscape prioritizes intuitive, seamless, and user-friendly service interactions, akin to consumer-driven digital experiences.

    - ▪ **Omnichannel support**: Enables seamless service accessibility across multiple channels (chat, email, phone, self-service portals) for a consistent user experience.

    - ▪ **Self-service and shift left approach**: Empowers users with comprehensive knowledge bases and AI-driven chatbots, reducing reliance on service desks and facilitating faster resolutions.

- **Integration and ecosystem thinking**: Modern ITSM fosters greater interoperability and collaboration across organizational processes.

o **DevOps integration**: ITSM aligns with DevOps methodologies to support continuous delivery, iterative development, and enhanced service reliability.

o **Service integration and management (SIAM)**: Establishes a framework to coordinate multi-provider service ecosystems, ensuring consistent service delivery and operational efficiency.

o **Unified service management platforms**: Consolidates service management functions into a single, integrated platform, minimizing fragmentation and improving data visibility.

- **Emphasis on value and business outcomes**: The ITSM paradigm is shifting from technology-centric service delivery to outcome-driven, value-based management.

o **ITIL 4's service value system**: Reinforces co-creation of value between ITSM and customers, focusing on delivering tangible business benefits rather than just technical capabilities.

o **Product-centric approach**: Reframes IT services as managed products with dedicated lifecycle teams, continuously improving services based on user feedback and business impact.

- **Cloud-based ITSM**: Adoption of cloud native ITSM platforms facilitates scalability, operational agility, and enhanced accessibility, particularly for remote workforces.

o Supports hybrid cloud environments, optimizing resource management and operational cost efficiencies.

These advancements in ITSM are transforming traditional service management practices, shifting ITSM from a reactive, operational cost center to a proactive, strategic business enabler. By embracing these innovations, organizations ensure IT services remain resilient, adaptable, and aligned with the evolving digital landscape.

Data life cycle

Data plays a fundamental role in ITSM, serving as the cornerstone for decision-making, process execution, and continuous improvement. Effective management of data throughout its lifecycle is essential for operational efficiency, regulatory compliance, and strategic insights. The ITSM data lifecycle encompasses a sequence of stages from initial creation or acquisition to its eventual archival or deletion.

While terminologies may differ across organizations, the general phases of the data lifecycle in ITSM include:

- **Creation or acquisition**: This phase involves the generation or collection of data through various sources, including manual input, automated systems, and external integrations.

- o Logging an incident via a self-service portal or a service desk agent.
- o Submitting a change request through an ITSM system.
- o Discovering **configuration item** (**CI**) data via inventory management tools.
- o Collecting performance metrics from servers and applications.
- o Creating knowledge articles authored by subject matter experts.

The key considerations for the creation of data in ITSM can be called out as follows:

- o Data accuracy, completeness, and classification.
- o Unique identification mechanisms to maintain data integrity.

- **Storage**: Once created, data must be securely stored and managed across appropriate repositories.

  - o Incident, problem, change, and request records are maintained in the ITSM tool's database.
  - o CI data stored within the CMDB.
  - o Knowledge articles are managed within a centralized knowledge repository.
  - o Performance logs and monitoring metrics are retained in data warehouses.
  - o Service catalogs storing SLA details, contact information, and service definitions.

  The key considerations can be captured as follows:

  - o Data security (access controls, encryption).
  - o Integrity (ensuring prevention of unauthorized modifications).
  - o Availability (reliable access and retrieval efficiency).
  - o Scalability for long-term storage optimization.

- **Use or processing**: In this stage, data is actively utilized, analyzed, and processed to support service management operations, automation, and reporting.

  - o Incident data used by service desk agents for issue resolution.
  - o CI data referenced by change managers for impact assessment.
  - o Historical incident records analyzed for trend identification and problem management.
  - o Performance metrics leveraged to monitor SLA adherence.
  - o Automated workflows processing service requests based on predefined policies.
  - o Reports and dashboards generated for executive decision-making and service performance tracking.

The key considerations can be called out as follows:

o   Data access control and role-based permissions.

o   Transformation of raw data into actionable insights.

o   Real-time vs. batch processing for reporting efficiency.

- **Retention**: Data is retained for a predefined duration based on legal, regulatory, contractual, or business requirements.

    o   Retaining incident logs for audits and long-term analysis.

    o   Maintaining change records for compliance and historical reference.

    o   Archiving performance data for trend assessments and capacity planning.

The key considerations in this stage can be captured as follows:

o   Compliance with data regulations.

o   Internal policy-driven data retention requirements.

o   Cost-effective storage solutions for long-term retention.

- **Archival**: Archived data is no longer actively used but must remain accessible for compliance or historical reference.

    o   Moving closed incident records to an archive database.

    o   Storing historical CMDB snapshots for audit purposes.

The key considerations can be captured as follows:

o   Data integrity during archival processes.

o   Efficient retrieval mechanisms for audit inquiries.

o   Cost-effective archival storage solutions.

- **Purge or deletion**: Once data exceeds its retention period or is no longer required, it must be securely removed from all storage locations.

    o   Secure deletion of **personally identifiable information (PII)** in compliance with privacy laws.

    o   Removing outdated knowledge articles from service portals.

    o   Eliminating obsolete CI records with no historical value.

The key considerations for data deletion can be captured as follows:

o   Irreversibility of deletion to prevent unauthorized recovery.

o   Compliance with data protection mandates (e.g., right to be forgotten regulations).

o   Implementation of secure data sanitization methods.

We can see that a well-defined data lifecycle strategy enhances ITSM operations by ensuring:

- **Data quality**: Improves accuracy, consistency, and reliability.

- **Operational efficiency**: Ensures the right data is accessible at the right time.

- **Cost optimization**: Reduces unnecessary storage expenses.

- **Risk mitigation**: Minimizes exposure to security threats and non-compliance penalties.

- **Regulatory compliance**: Adheres to legal, contractual, and industry standards.

- **Informed decision-making**: Provides actionable insights for service optimization.

- **Audit and accountability**: Facilitates traceability for governance and reporting.

By systematically managing the data lifecycle, organizations can maximize ITSM value, enhance operational excellence, and maintain compliance with governance obligations.

Continuous improvement

Continuous improvement is a fundamental principle of effective ITSM, spreading through all aspects of ITIL 4 and mandated by standards such as ISO 20000. It is an ongoing, iterative process designed to enhance the efficiency, effectiveness, and quality of an organization's services, service management practices, and overall SVS. The primary objective of continuous improvement is to ensure continuous enhancement, fostering greater operational excellence, adaptability, and value creation.

The importance of continuous improvement in ITSM can be captured as follows:

- **Adapting to evolving business needs**: Business environments are dynamic, necessitating IT services that align with new strategies, technological advancements, and market fluctuations.

- **Enhancing user experience and employee** experience: Continuous feedback collection and improvement initiatives result in more intuitive, reliable, and efficient IT services.

- **Driving operational efficiency and cost optimization**: Process refinement, automation, and elimination of inefficiencies contribute to reduced operational costs and increased service effectiveness.

- **Improving service quality and reliability**: Addressing root causes, optimizing workflows, and implementing technological advancements lead to more stable and higher-performing services.

- **Proactive risk mitigation**: Regular process evaluations facilitate early identification and resolution of risks, strengthening organizational resilience.

- **Fostering a culture of excellence**: Encouraging learning, innovation, and proactive engagement establishes a continuous improvement mindset across IT operations.

- **Ensuring compliance**: Frameworks such as ISO 20000 mandate continuous improvement as a key component of maintaining an effective **service management system** (**SMS**).

ITIL 4 introduces a structured seven-step model for continuous improvement, derived from the **Plan-Do-Check-Act** (**PDCA**) cycle. This model is applicable across services, practices, processes, and relationships, facilitating incremental and sustainable enhancements. Refer to the following table:

Steps	Purpose	Key questions
1. Define the vision	Establishes strategic alignment by defining improvement objectives.	What are we aiming to achieve? How does this support business objectives? What is the ideal future state?
2. Assess the current state	Evaluates the existing performance of services or processes.	What are the current KPIs? What challenges or inefficiencies exist? What resources are available?
3. Set target objectives	Establishes SMART (Specific, Measurable, Achievable, Relevant, Time-bound) improvement goals.	What measurable outcomes define success? What performance levels are required? What is the timeline?
4. Develop an improvement plan	Outlines the necessary steps, actions, and resource allocation.	What actions will be taken? Who is responsible? What risks exist, and how will they be mitigated? What technologies or methodologies will be employed?
5. Implement changes	Executes the improvement plan.	Is the plan being implemented as designed? Are there unforeseen challenges?
6. Evaluate performance	Monitors results to determine the effectiveness of the improvements.	Have the changes produced the expected outcomes? Are performance metrics aligned with targets? What value has been realized?
7. Sustain and expand improvements	Embeds improvements into daily operations and identifies further enhancement opportunities.	How do we institutionalize new processes? How can success be communicated? What additional improvements can be pursued?

Table 17.3: Seven steps of the ITIL continuous improvement model

These seven steps collectively provide a powerful, systematic roadmap for transforming IT service delivery, moving beyond mere problem-solving to proactively optimize performance, enhance efficiency, and drive strategic advantage.

Continuous improvements

Achieving sustainable continuous improvement requires a structured approach, strong leadership, and effective resource utilization. The following factors are critical enablers:

- **Organizational culture**: Establishing an environment that promotes innovation, learning, and proactive enhancement.

- **Metrics and measurement**: Defining **key performance indicators** (**KPIs**) to track effectiveness and impact.

- **Continuous improvement register** (**CIR**): A structured database for recording, prioritizing, and tracking improvement initiatives.

- **Feedback mechanisms**: Integrating user and stakeholder feedback to refine services dynamically.

- **Knowledge management**: Capturing and disseminating insights gained from improvement projects.

- **Automation technologies**: Leveraging AI and process automation to facilitate data-driven improvements and workflow efficiency.

Continuous improvement is not a singular project but an ongoing strategic imperative within ITSM. By embracing structured improvement methodologies, organizations can achieve higher levels of service excellence, optimize resource utilization, enhance user satisfaction, and foster long-term resilience, directly contributing to overarching business success and ITSM maturity.

Conclusion

In summary, effective ITSM is more than just a collection of technical processes or software tools; it is a dynamic balance of four essential dimensions: organizations, people, data, and technology processes. A strong ITSM strategy requires a comprehensive approach, as weaknesses in one area can significantly impact overall service delivery.

The organization sets the strategic direction, cultural foundation, and governance framework that define how services are managed and delivered. Without strong leadership, clear structures, and a culture of collaboration and continuous improvement, even the most advanced technology and skilled personnel may fail to function cohesively. People are the driving force behind ITSM, including service architects, engineers, desk agents, and users. Their expertise, engagement, and commitment to defined roles ensure that processes are executed effectively and value is delivered to customers.

Data or information serves as the backbone of ITSM, providing essential insights for informed decision-making, problem resolution, and ongoing improvement. The accuracy of a CMDB, the security of sensitive data, and the accessibility of a well-maintained knowledge base all contribute to the reliability and efficiency of service management. Technology processes transform strategy into action. Whether resolving incidents, deploying changes, or proactively identifying potential risks, well-structured processes supported by the right technology turn organizational intent into measurable results.

Successful ITSM depends on balancing these four dimensions. Organizations that invest in their workforce, implement strong governance frameworks, manage data effectively, and refine technology-driven processes can create IT services that are not only functional but also optimized for efficiency, innovation, and business alignment. By continuously improving these interconnected elements, businesses can deliver lasting value to their stakeholders and adapt to the ever-evolving demands of the digital landscape.

In the next chapter, we will be looking at the partner system, the value streams, and processes around these in ITSM.

Join our Discord space

Join our Discord workspace for latest updates, offers, tech happenings around the world, new releases, and sessions with the authors:

https://discord.bpbonline.com

CHAPTER 18
Partners, Value Streams and Processes

Introduction

In this chapter, we will explore the vital role played by IT audit in the evolving landscape of IT, where technology is deeply embedded in business operations. Effective IT audits go beyond technical assessments, requiring a holistic approach that examines the interconnected relationships between partners, value streams, and processes within an organization's IT ecosystem.

Partners in IT audits include both internal and external stakeholders who influence or rely on IT services, such as business units, third-party vendors, suppliers, and regulatory bodies. Understanding their roles, responsibilities, and contractual agreements is essential for assessing risks, evaluating controls, and ensuring compliance.

Value streams represent the complete sequence of activities that deliver value, from initial request to final implementation. Auditing value streams shifts focus from isolated IT components to the broader flow of work, uncovering inefficiencies, bottlenecks, and gaps in controls that may span multiple systems and teams.

Processes provide the structural foundation for IT operations, encompassing IT service management, security, governance, and software development workflows. Evaluating processes involves assessing both their design effectiveness, whether they are properly defined to achieve control objectives, and their operational effectiveness, ensuring they are consistently followed and delivering intended outcomes.

Structure

The chapter covers the following topics:

- Key concepts
- Supplier and partner management process
- Role of IT in delivering value
- IT process life cycle

Objectives

The study of IT audit requires a comprehensive understanding of how partners, value streams, and processes contribute to its effectiveness and business relevance. At its core, IT auditing should provide a holistic assessment of an organization's IT environment, ensuring it aligns with and supports broader business objectives.

Once we finish this chapter, we will learn how to audit the complete landscape by looking at the complete asset inventory and the ownership cum custodianship of the assets. Along with capturing the ownership, there will be a responsibility and accountability matrix defined for each of the activities where these assets are involved. The section on value stream will help us to understand how values are created and maintained during the ITSM processes. A strong understanding of these processes enables auditors to pinpoint potential control failures and their impact on confidentiality, integrity, and availability.

Integrating these three elements allows auditors to conduct more comprehensive, risk-aware IT audits. Weaknesses in one area, such as partner management, can directly impact the effectiveness of value stream delivery or create inefficiencies within IT processes. By examining these relationships holistically, auditors can communicate their findings in a way that highlights broader business implications and supports continuous improvement in IT governance and security.

Key concepts

Partners and third-party relationships play a vital role in IT service delivery and operations, encompassing vendors, service providers, and consultants. Auditing these relationships involves assessing **third-party risk management** (**TPRM**), contractual compliance, and adherence to **service level agreements** (**SLAs**) while ensuring data protection and security obligations align with frameworks like ISO 27036 and **service organization control 2** (**SOC 2**).

Value streams represent the complete sequence of activities that create and deliver value to stakeholders. These workflows rely on inputs, outputs, supporting systems, and enabling roles, with dependencies influencing their efficiency. Auditors focus on identifying critical value streams, mapping their delivery paths to uncover control gaps, and ensuring they align with business objectives.

Processes form the structural backbone of IT operations, consisting of structured activities designed to achieve specific outcomes. Their effectiveness depends on proper documentation, clear roles and responsibilities, and well-implemented control mechanisms. Auditing processes involve evaluating their maturity, assessing compliance with regulatory policies, and examining integration with frameworks like ITIL.

By integrating these elements—partners, value streams, and processes—IT auditors can move beyond surface-level examinations to provide a comprehensive evaluation of an organization's IT risk management, control framework, and overall ability to maintain and safeguard critical business functions.

Process and value stream mapping serve as essential tools for visualizing workflows, highlighting inefficiencies, and pinpointing redundant steps. These audits enhance traceability, improve accountability, and strengthen visibility across audit trails.

Governance and oversight ensure that partners, processes, and value streams remain aligned with enterprise goals. Steering committees, governance boards, and audit functions play key roles in maintaining regulatory adherence and operational effectiveness.

Risk and control integration embeds risk identification and mitigation strategies within processes and partner interactions. Areas such as segregation of duties, change management, and access control are closely examined to minimize vulnerabilities and ensure system integrity.

Performance and compliance monitoring relies on **key performance indicators** (**KPIs**) and **key risk indicators** (**KRIs**) to track partner effectiveness, process efficiency, and potential bottlenecks in value streams. Dashboards and monitoring tools help organizations ensure consistent adherence to internal policies and external regulations, reinforcing a secure and well-governed IT environment.

Supplier and partner management process

In **IT service management** (**ITSM**), supplier and partner management processes are essential for ensuring that external providers contribute effectively to IT service delivery while aligning with business objectives. This process involves selecting, managing, and optimizing supplier relationships throughout their lifecycle, from initial engagement to contract termination.

The primary objectives include maximizing value for investment, ensuring high-quality service delivery, mitigating risks, and maintaining regulatory compliance. Given the complexity of IT ecosystems, managing supplier relationships effectively is critical for service reliability and organizational success. Let us look at the process in detail:

1. **Strategy and policy definition**:

   - **Supplier strategy**: Establishes criteria for sourcing, partnership types (e.g., strategic, tactical, commodity), and risk management approaches.

   - **Policies and procedures**: Define standardized guidelines for supplier engagement, ensuring consistency and compliance.

   - **Categorization and segmentation**: Prioritizes suppliers based on their strategic importance, service impact, and risk level.

2. **Supplier evaluation and selection**:

   - **Requirements definition**: Specifies business and technical needs, including performance metrics, security measures, and compliance expectations.

   - **Market research and sourcing**: Identifies potential suppliers using **request for proposals (RFPs)** to assess market offerings.

   - **Due diligence**: Conducts background checks, financial assessments, security audits, and reference verifications.

   - **Selection and evaluation**: Reviews supplier proposals systematically, conducts interviews, and selects the most suitable partner.

3. **Contract negotiation and establishment**:

   - **Contract negotiation**: Defines pricing, SLAs, KPIs, **intellectual property rights (IPR)**, and dispute resolution processes.

   - **Underpinning contracts**: Ensures that external service agreements align with internal SLAs to maintain operational integrity.

   - **Legal review**: Confirms compliance with regulatory and contractual obligations before finalizing agreements.

   - **Formal agreement signing**: Concludes negotiations with legally binding contracts.

4. **Performance monitoring and relationship management**:

   - **Performance tracking**: Monitors supplier adherence to SLAs and KPIs using reporting tools and dashboards.

   - **Regular reviews**: Conducts periodic evaluations to assess performance, identify improvements, and address concerns.

   - **Collaborative relationship building**: Fosters transparency, trust, and open communication for mutual success.

   - **Issue and dispute resolution**: Establishes structured escalation procedures for resolving conflicts efficiently.

- **Risk mitigation**: Continuously assesses supplier-related risks, including financial, security, operational, and reputational threats.

5. **Contract management and renewal or termination**:

   - **Contract repository management**: Maintains centralized records of all agreements, including modifications and amendments.

   - **Change control**: Implements formal processes for updating contract terms and scope adjustments.

   - **Invoice and cost oversight**: Verifies financial transactions to ensure accuracy and prevent discrepancies.

   - **Contract renewal**: Evaluates supplier performance before extending agreements, renegotiating terms if necessary.

   - **Exit strategy and transition planning**: Ensures seamless service handover during contract termination or supplier disengagement.

Through a well-defined supplier and partner management framework, organizations can strengthen IT service delivery, optimize costs, enhance vendor collaboration, and maintain compliance, ensuring operational resilience and business continuity.

Supplier evaluation and selection in ITSM

Supplier evaluation and selection within ITSM is a critical phase that establishes the foundation for successful external partnerships. It involves a structured approach to identifying, assessing, and selecting the most suitable providers for IT-related goods, services, or resources. Making the wrong choice can lead to financial losses, service disruptions, security vulnerabilities, and reputational damage, making this process essential for maintaining operational stability.

The supplier selection process is a critical stage and contains the following steps:

1. **Defining requirements**: A well-defined set of requirements forms the foundation of supplier selection. Organizations must clearly specify functional needs such as software features, network capacity, and support availability, alongside non-functional considerations like performance expectations, security protocols, and regulatory compliance. SLAs outline measurable targets for service delivery, while integration expectations ensure seamless compatibility with existing IT systems. Budget constraints and cultural alignment also play a role in shaping supplier decisions.

2. **Market research and supplier identification**: Scanning the industry landscape helps organizations identify potential suppliers capable of meeting their requirements. This involves consulting analyst reports, networking at industry events, researching online forums, and seeking recommendations. Organizations may issue **requests for information** (**RFIs**) to gather preliminary insights from suppliers before shortlisting candidates.

3. **Formal procurement requests**: Once potential suppliers are identified, organizations issue RFPs, **requests for quotation (RFQs)**, or **invitations to tender (ITTs)**, depending on the nature of the engagement. An RFP seeks solutions to specific business challenges, an RFQ focuses on predefined specifications and pricing, while an ITT invites formal bids, often within the public sector. These documents detail evaluation criteria, submission deadlines, and required response formats.

4. **Supplier evaluation and assessment**: The selection process involves a systematic assessment of proposals based on predefined criteria, ensuring an objective comparison. Key factors include technical expertise, service quality, financial stability, total cost of ownership, security and compliance standards, risk management strategies, reputation, customer support capabilities, and cultural fit. Organizations often use evaluation matrices to score suppliers against weighted criteria, making selection more transparent.

5. **Due diligence and final selection**: Before finalizing a decision, organizations conduct thorough due diligence, which may involve on-site visits, **proof of concept (PoC)** tests, interviews with key personnel, and detailed policy reviews. The final selection is made through a collaborative decision-making process involving IT, procurement, legal, and business stakeholders. The chosen supplier is justified based on overall value and alignment with strategic objectives.

A well-executed supplier evaluation and selection process mitigates risks and enhances the likelihood of a successful, long-term partnership that supports IT service delivery and organizational goals. By following a structured approach, organizations ensure that external collaborations contribute to efficiency, security, and sustained performance.

Supplier due diligence

One of the main processes in supplier management is the due diligence process. Supplier due diligence in ITSM is a structured and thorough process used to assess and evaluate prospective or current third-party IT suppliers. It forms a key element of the broader supplier and partner management discipline within ITSM, aimed at ensuring that suppliers are credible, competent, and aligned with the organization's needs and expectations, while also managing potential risks effectively.

The term due diligence reflects the obligation to take reasonable, informed steps before entering or continuing a supplier relationship, especially given the critical nature of IT services, infrastructure, and data management often entrusted to external providers.

The importance of supplier due diligence in ITSM can be seen as follows:

- **Risk mitigation**: Identifies potential risks in financial, operational, cybersecurity, compliance-related, or reputational processes that the supplier may pose.

- **Assurance of service quality**: Ensures the supplier can consistently deliver services that meet predefined performance and quality standards.

- **Cost effectiveness**: Validates pricing transparency and helps avoid hidden costs or future financial instability.

- **Regulatory and policy compliance**: Confirms alignment with applicable laws and standards as well as internal security and governance requirements.

- **Reputation safeguarding**: Avoids partnerships with vendors that have poor ethical standards, service failures, or security breaches.

- **Informed decision-making**: Equips IT and procurement teams with the information necessary to make strategic supplier selections.

Key focus areas in ITSM supplier due diligence are as follows:

- **Financial health and stability**:
    - o Review audited financial reports and credit ratings.
    - o Analyze past financial performance and future forecasts.
    - o Assess pricing models, payment terms, and financial sustainability.
    - o Identify indicators of financial distress that may disrupt services.

- **Technical capability and delivery readiness**:
    - o Evaluate infrastructure, tools, platforms, and technology stacks.
    - o Verify certifications, technical expertise, and delivery track record.
    - o Understand methodologies (e.g., Agile, DevOps) used for solution delivery.
    - o Test feasibility via demos, PoCs, or pilot engagements.
    - o Check scalability and adaptability to future business needs.

- **Information security and data protection**:
    - o Assess security governance policies, technical controls, and frameworks in place.
    - o Review cybersecurity practices: encryption, access control, intrusion detection, etc.
    - o Validate incident management and breach response preparedness.
    - o Examine certifications such as ISO 27001, SOC 2, or CSA STAR.
    - o Ensure ongoing vulnerability assessments and employee awareness programs are conducted.

- **Operational maturity and service delivery**:
    - o Evaluate ITSM processes like incident, change, and problem management.
    - o Check historical SLA adherence and service performance metrics.
    - o Review organizational roles, staffing capabilities, and escalation models.

- o   Assess quality assurance practices and continuous improvement mechanisms.
- o   Examine business continuity and disaster recovery preparedness.
- **Legal and regulatory compliance**:
    - o   Validate compliance with relevant regulations.
    - o   Check for licenses, legal disputes, and regulatory penalties.
    - o   Review adherence to intellectual property laws and anti-corruption policies.
    - o   Understand legal liabilities and indemnity clauses in contracts.
- **Reputation and client feedback**:
    - o   Gather client references and testimonials.
    - o   Search public databases, press releases, and online forums for past issues.
    - o   Assess market reputation, leadership standing, and industry credibility.
    - o   Verify affiliations, awards, and professional recognition.
- **Methods for conducting due diligence**:
    - o   **Supplier questionnaires**: Customized assessments covering operational, security, and compliance areas.
    - o   **Document review**: Analysis of internal policies, certifications, audit reports, financial data, and service agreements.
    - o   **Interviews and meetings**: Direct discussions with key supplier stakeholders (management, tech leads, compliance officers).
    - o   **On-site assessments**: Physical verification of facilities, processes, and security controls (especially for critical suppliers).
    - o   **Third-party risk tools**: Use of external platforms that provide supplier risk ratings, cyber risk scores, and financial health indicators.
    - o   **Reference validation**: Engaging with existing clients to gather feedback on reliability, responsiveness, and issue resolution.
- **Ongoing monitoring and reassessments**: Supplier due diligence should be seen as a continuous process, not a one-time check. Critical suppliers must be reviewed periodically, typically on an annual or semi-annual basis, to ensure sustained compliance, service quality, and alignment with evolving business and regulatory needs.

Third-party risk management

TPRM in ITSM is a continuous process of identifying, assessing, mitigating, and managing risks associated with external vendors, suppliers, and partners interacting with an organization's

IT services, systems, or data. IT organizations rely on a vast network of third parties for cloud infrastructure, **software as a service (SaaS)** applications, managed services, data analytics, and hardware procurement. The goal is to prevent third-party relationships from introducing security vulnerabilities, regulatory non-compliance, financial losses, or reputational damage. A breach or operational failure at a vendor can have a severe impact, similar to an internal incident.

Key components of TPRM in ITSM are as follows:

1. **Vendor identification and inventory**:

   - **Comprehensive listing**: Maintain an up-to-date inventory of all third parties categorized by service type, data access, and criticality.

   - **Fourth party awareness**: Understand vendors' subcontractors (fourth parties) and assess their risks within the extended supply chain.

2. **Risk tiering and categorization**:

   - **Risk-based approach**: Classify vendors based on their impact on IT services, data sensitivity, operational dependency, and financial risks.

   - **Prioritization**: Focus due diligence and monitoring on high-risk suppliers handling critical services or sensitive data.

3. **Due diligence (Pre-engagement assessment)**:

   - **Thorough vetting**: Assess a vendor's financial stability, security posture, compliance history, and reputation before engagement.

   - **Evaluation methods**: Utilize security questionnaires, audit reports, reference checks, and on-site assessments.

4. **Contractual agreements and SLAs**:

   - **Defined expectations**: Ensure contracts outline security requirements, data protection clauses, compliance obligations, audit rights, and business continuity plans.

   - **Risk allocation**: Establish clear accountability for incidents, breaches, and performance failures.

5. **Ongoing monitoring and performance management**:

   - **Continuous oversight**: Regularly review third-party performance, security posture, and regulatory adherence through:
     - SLA or KPI assessments.
     - Security audits and penetration tests.
     - Monitoring financial health and regulatory changes.
     - Reviewing SOC 2 reports for cloud vendors.

- **Incident management processes**: Define structured processes for reporting security incidents and service failures.

6. **Risk treatment and mitigation**:

   - **Proactive adjustments**: Identify risks and implement strategies such as enhanced controls, contractual amendments, or alternative solutions.

7. **Offboarding and termination**:

   - **Secure transition**: Ensure access is revoked, data is securely returned or destroyed, and services are smoothly transitioned upon disengagement.

TPRM in ITSM is essential for maintaining security, compliance, and operational stability. Cybersecurity protection plays a crucial role in mitigating threats arising from third-party breaches and attacks, helping organizations safeguard sensitive data and IT infrastructure. Regulatory compliance ensures adherence to frameworks, reducing legal and financial exposure. Operational resilience strengthens an organization's ability to withstand disruptions caused by vendor failures, ensuring continuity in service delivery. Reputation management helps prevent damage stemming from third-party security incidents, protecting customer trust and brand integrity. Cost efficiency is achieved by proactively managing risks, avoiding penalties, and minimizing expensive remediation efforts. Strategic alignment ensures that third-party engagements contribute positively to business objectives, reinforcing service excellence and long-term success. By integrating TPRM into ITSM, organizations can proactively manage external risks, secure their IT environments, and optimize vendor relationships to support operational success.

Role of IT in delivering value

In ITSM, IT has evolved from simply maintaining technology to becoming a strategic enabler of business success. Value is no longer just about system uptime or technical performance; it is about how IT services align with business objectives, enhance customer satisfaction, and strengthen competitive advantage.

Here is a breakdown of how IT delivers value in ITSM:

- **Enabling business operations and outcomes**: IT serves as the backbone of modern business functions, ensuring operations run smoothly. Through ITSM practices, IT aligns services with strategic business goals such as improving efficiency, enhancing customer experience, and reducing costs. By automating processes and integrating systems, IT boosts productivity, minimizes errors, and accelerates workflows.

- **Enhancing customer and user experience**: A seamless, user-centric IT service approach improves both employee and customer interactions. ITSM focuses on streamlined service portals, rapid issue resolution, and proactive communication. Incident and problem management help reduce downtime, while self-service tools empower users to resolve issues independently, improving satisfaction and optimizing IT support resources.

- **Risk management and security**: IT safeguards organizational assets through cybersecurity measures, data protection strategies, and access controls. Compliance with regulatory frameworks helps avoid legal and financial risks. Business continuity and disaster recovery planning ensure resilience, allowing IT services to recover swiftly from disruptions and maintain operational stability.

- **Innovation and competitive advantage**: Digital transformation initiatives, such as **artificial intelligence** (**AI**), cloud computing, and **Internet of Things** (**IoT**), enhance business models and improve customer engagement. IT enables data-driven decision-making through analytics and reporting, helping organizations anticipate trends and optimize performance. Agile methodologies and DevOps practices accelerate service delivery, making businesses more adaptable to evolving market conditions.

- **Cost optimization and resource efficiency**: Effective ITSM facilitates strategic resource allocation, prioritizing investments that drive business value. Process streamlining and automation help reduce waste and optimize costs. Predictable IT spending models provide transparency, ensuring financial planning aligns with corporate objectives and supports sustainable growth.

IT's role in ITSM goes beyond system maintenance; it is about proactive partnership in achieving business success. By continuously improving service delivery, security, innovation, and cost efficiency, IT strengthens the organization's ability to adapt, compete, and thrive in a dynamic business environment.

IT process life cycle

In ITSM, the concept of the IT process lifecycle is most comprehensively represented through the ITIL service lifecycle. While individual processes like incident management or change management have their process flows, the ITIL lifecycle provides a broader, strategic framework for managing IT services from their initial concept to eventual retirement. It ensures IT services are aligned with business objectives and continue to deliver value throughout their lifespan.

The foundation of successful ITSM lies in the seamless integration of partners, value streams, and processes. ITSM organizations must strategically collaborate with partners to leverage their capabilities and expand service delivery. These partnerships must align with well-defined value streams, mapping the complete journey of how IT contributes to business objectives and customer satisfaction. Supporting these value streams are efficient, adaptable processes that ensure consistency and facilitate continuous improvement.

Overlooking any of these elements weakens the ITSM framework, creating inefficiencies and risks that disrupt service delivery. A narrow focus on processes without considering the broader value stream can lead to isolated optimizations that fail to deliver meaningful business impact. Similarly, neglecting partner management can introduce vulnerabilities that threaten operational stability. A comprehensive approach that harmonizes these three components enables ITSM to function as a strategic business enabler, delivering high-quality, cost-effective IT services that drive sustainable success.

IT process lifecycle as per ITIL

The ITIL service lifecycle consists of five core stages. Each stage has a specific purpose and set of processes that work together to enable effective service management. These five stages are as follows:

1. **Service strategy**: To define the strategic approach for service management by determining what services to offer, to whom, and why. It positions IT as a strategic partner that contributes to business value.

    *   **Key processes**: The key processes here are strategy management for IT services, service portfolio management, financial management for IT services, demand management, business relationship management, etc.

    *   **Value contribution**: Aligns IT investments with business goals, transforming IT from a cost center into a value-creating function.

2. **Service design**: To design new or changed services and the supporting processes, architectures, technologies, and measurements required to meet business needs effectively.

    *   **Key processes**: The key processes here are design coordination, service catalog management, service level management, capacity and availability management, IT service continuity management, information security management, supplier management, architecture management, etc.

    *   **Value contribution**: Produces reliable, secure, and efficient service designs that reduce rework and ensure smooth future operations.

3. **Service transition**: To manage the planning and coordination of resources to deploy new or modified services into the live environment with minimal risk and disruption.

    *   **Key processes**: Transition planning and support, change management, **service asset and configuration management** (**SACM**), release and deployment management, service validation and testing, change evaluation, knowledge management, etc.

    *   **Value contribution**: Enables controlled, predictable service deployment, protecting the stability and integrity of live operations.

4. **Service operation**: To deliver and support IT services in a live environment, ensuring stable, effective, and efficient day-to-day operations.

- **Key processes**: Event management, incident management, problem management, request fulfillment, access management, IT operations control and facilities management, application and technical management, etc.

- **Value contribution**: Maximizes service uptime and user satisfaction through responsive and proactive operations.

5. **Continual service improvement (CSI)**: To continually enhance the effectiveness, efficiency, and alignment of IT services and processes with evolving business needs.

   - **Key processes**: Key activities in the CSI process are service and process reviews, CSI Initiative planning and monitoring, performance analysis and reporting, use of the Deming cycle (PDCA) for iterative improvement, etc.

   - **Value contribution**: Promotes ongoing optimization of services, leading to increased quality, agility, and cost-efficiency.

These five stages are interdependent and iterative; insights gained in one stage feed into others, creating a feedback loop that supports continuous service improvement. This comprehensive lifecycle model ensures that IT services are not only operationally effective but strategically aligned and responsive to changing organizational goals.

IT process life cycle as per ISO 20000

ISO 20000 is the internationally recognized standard for ITSM, and it provides a structured and comprehensive framework that helps organizations deliver high-quality, efficient, and continually improving IT services. Although ISO 20000 does not explicitly use the term value stream as defined in ITIL, its principles strongly promote a value-driven, process-focused, and partner-aware approach to service management.

ISO 20000 is fundamentally a process-based standard and it requires organizations to establish, implement, operate, monitor, review, and continually improve a **service management system** (**SMS**). The standard defines a set of interrelated service management processes to ensure consistent, reliable, and value-focused service delivery.

The core process domains include:

- **Service portfolio processes**: Service catalog, asset, and configuration management.

- **Relationship and agreement processes**: SLAs, business relationships, and supplier management.

- **Supply and demand processes**: Budgeting, accounting, and capacity management.

- **Design, build, and transition processes**: Change, release, and deployment management.

- **Resolution and fulfillment processes**: Incident, request, and problem management.

- **Assurance processes**: Availability, continuity, and information security management.

- **Improvement processes**: Continual improvement and performance evaluation.

Partners in ISO 20000 emphasize the effective management of internal and external suppliers and partners who contribute to IT service delivery. The supplier management process is central here, ensuring alignment and accountability across all third-party engagements.

Key requirements include:

- Identifying and categorizing all service providers (internal/external).

- Establishing formal agreements (contracts, SLAs, etc.) that define roles, expectations, and performance metrics.

- Regularly reviewing supplier performance and compliance.

- Maintaining governance over outsourced processes to ensure conformance with the SMS.

- Establishing structured communication channels with all partners.

The standard recognizes that modern IT services depend on a network of collaborators. ISO 20000 requires organizations to maintain visibility and control over supplier relationships, ensuring that partnerships enhance—not compromise—service quality, security, and compliance.

While ISO 20000 does not explicitly define or use the term value stream, its principles support the concept indirectly through its structured focus on:

- **Customer orientation**: All service processes aim to deliver outcomes that meet customer needs and expectations.

- **End-to-end integration**: Processes are designed to work together seamlessly, supporting the complete service lifecycle from strategy through design, transition, operation, and improvement.

- **Continual improvement** (**PDCA cycle**): Promotes ongoing optimization of services and workflows, essential for refining value delivery.

- **Context and stakeholders**: ISO's high-level structure emphasizing alignment with organizational objectives and stakeholder value.

Though implicit, the value stream perspective is woven into the fabric of ISO 20000. By emphasizing integrated service delivery, continual improvement, and customer value, the standard naturally supports the identification, optimization, and management of value streams across the service lifecycle.

ISO 20000 enforces a disciplined, integrated, and outcome-oriented process approach. It does not prescribe implementation methods but ensures that every required process is defined, documented, and effectively controlled to support consistent and aligned service delivery across the organization. This international standard offers a robust, certifiable framework that tightly integrates defined processes, structured partner management, and a consistent focus on value delivery. It enables organizations to transform IT services into strategic business assets by ensuring that each element of service management, from design and sourcing to delivery and improvement, is governed by clear requirements and measurable outcomes.

Certification to ISO 20000 demonstrates not only ITSM maturity but also a deep organizational commitment to delivering dependable, value-driven services through disciplined practices and collaborative partnerships.

From an IT audit standpoint, evaluating these elements provides valuable insights into an organization's maturity, operational efficiency, and adherence to industry frameworks such as COBIT, ITIL, and ISO 27001. Ultimately, maintaining a clear understanding of partner relationships, value delivery mechanisms, and operational processes—while continuously refining them—reinforces the organization's control environment and enhances its ability to manage emerging risks effectively.

Conclusion

Effective governance and management of partners, value streams, and processes are essential for building a resilient, audit-ready IT environment. Establishing strong partnerships ensures third-party risks are properly managed while maintaining security, compliance, and performance standards. A well-structured approach to value streams allows organizations to trace how value is created and delivered, helping auditors pinpoint inefficiencies, control gaps, and areas for improvement throughout the service lifecycle. Standardized and well-defined processes enhance consistency, accountability, and traceability, which are crucial for maintaining compliance and meeting audit requirements.

In ITSM, the integration of partners, value streams, and processes forms the backbone of delivering effective, efficient, and customer-centric services. Trusted partners and suppliers expand the organization's capabilities, providing critical expertise, technologies, and support functions that enable scalable and reliable service delivery. Effective value streams ensure that service activities are aligned with business outcomes, streamlining workflows from demand to value realization. Meanwhile, well-defined ITSM processes bring structure, consistency, and control, helping organizations manage complexity, ensure compliance, and drive continual improvement.

Together, these elements enable IT to move beyond operational support and become a strategic enabler of business value. A mature ITSM environment leverages these components cohesively—ensuring that services are not only delivered efficiently but are also adaptive, secure, and aligned with organizational goals.

In the upcoming chapters, we will see the *audit steps*, namely defining the scope of the audit, planning the audit, and conducting audits by review of policy and controls, interviews, site visits, technical testing, etc. We will see how, during the evaluation phase, the collected evidence is analyzed against the audit criteria to identify strengths, weaknesses, and potential risks. Through these steps, the IT audit delivers assurance that systems are secure, reliable, and aligned with organizational and regulatory expectations.

Join our Discord space

Join our Discord workspace for latest updates, offers, tech happenings around the world, new releases, and sessions with the authors:

https://discord.bpbonline.com

CHAPTER 19
Scope of Audit and Audit Plan

Introduction

An IT audit is a systematic examination of an organization's information technology infrastructure, policies, and operations. Its primary goal is to evaluate the adequacy and effectiveness of IT controls, assess risks, and ensure that IT assets are protected and aligned with business objectives. The success of an IT audit heavily relies on clearly defining its scope and developing a meticulous audit plan.

The scope of an IT audit defines the boundaries and focus areas of the audit engagement. It specifies what will be covered, what will be excluded, and the specific objectives to be achieved. A well-defined scope is crucial for managing stakeholder expectations, allocating resources effectively, and ensuring the audit remains focused and relevant. The scope clearly articulates the various standards or regulations that are addressed in the audit. E.g.: ISO 20000, ISO 27001, **National Institute Of Standards And Technology Cybersecurity Framework (NIST CSF)**, **Control Objectives for Information and Related Technologies (COBIT)**, **Sarbanes-Oxley Act (SOX)**, **General Data Protection Regulation (GDPR)**, **Health Insurance Portability And Accountability Act (HIPAA)**, and **Payment Card Industry Data Security Standard (PCI DSS)**, etc. The audit plan is a detailed roadmap that outlines how the audit will be conducted to achieve its defined scope and objectives. It ensures that the audit is systematic, efficient, and thorough.

By meticulously defining the scope and crafting a detailed audit plan, IT auditors can ensure that their work is purposeful, effective, and delivers valuable insights to the organization, helping to strengthen its IT controls and achieve its strategic objectives.

Structure

The chapter covers the following topics:

- Key concepts
- Audit scope
- Audit plan
- IT process and the apex processes
- Audit of data management

Objectives

By the end of this chapter, the readers will gain the knowledge and skills necessary to define, scope, and plan an effective IT audit. This can be started by developing a clear conceptual understanding of what an IT audit scope entails, why it is critical to success, and how it differs from yet complements audit objectives. Learners will be able to identify the typical components of an audit scope, such as the relevant systems, processes, locations, and time frames, as well as understand how specific audit objectives like compliance or operational efficiency influence the scope. Once the scope is defined, the audit plan has to be drafted, keeping the auditee in mind. We need to include the different teams in ITSM, the detailed schedule and the expected deliverables in the audit plan. To reinforce application, learners will practice selecting appropriate audit methodologies for specific scenarios, building a high-level audit timeline, estimating necessary resources, and designing audit deliverables for each audit phase. They will also develop basic communication strategies to engage stakeholders effectively throughout the audit lifecycle, identify and manage risks to audit execution, and learn how to ensure the audit plan aligns with recognized professional standards, such as those from the **Information Systems Audit and Control Association (ISACA)**.

In total, this chapter equips participants to scope and plan IT audits that are purposeful, risk-aware, and aligned with both organizational goals and professional best practices.

Key concepts

In an IT audit, clearly defining the scope establishes the boundaries and focus areas that determine what will be examined and what will be excluded. This clarity is essential for ensuring alignment among all stakeholders—from auditors to auditees—avoiding ambiguity, resource misallocation, and unexpected changes during the audit. The audit scope must be precise, serving as a common reference point that helps avoid misunderstandings and scope creep.

The scope is not defined in isolation; it is shaped directly by the audit's overarching objectives, whether that involves evaluating security controls, verifying compliance, or assessing system efficiency. These objectives drive the selection of systems, infrastructure, and processes to be included in the audit, along with key exclusions. It is equally important to specify time periods, organizational units, and locations under review to manage expectations and keep the audit focused.

Prioritizing areas with the highest IT risk, such as critical applications or sensitive data, ensures the audit delivers maximum value by addressing the most impactful concerns. Additionally, the scope may need to accommodate specific regulatory obligations like GDPR or industry frameworks such as ISO 27001 or COBIT, thereby ensuring legal and policy compliance. To solidify alignment, the finalized scope should be reviewed and formally approved by key stakeholders, reinforcing shared accountability and cooperation throughout the audit.

Once the scope is set, the audit plan takes shape as the operational blueprint that guides how those boundaries and objectives will be addressed. This plan defines the audit methodology, be it risk-based, compliance-driven, or hybrid, and outlines the overall approach, ensuring consistency and discipline in execution. The plan drills into detailed procedures and audit techniques, including the use of interviews, technical tests, and data analysis, enabling the team to gather thorough, reliable evidence.

Effective planning also involves allocating the right resources, including skilled personnel, proper tools, and access permissions, to ensure the team is empowered to perform effectively. A well-constructed timeline assigns milestones for every audit phase, including planning, fieldwork, reporting, and follow-up, providing a schedule for key deliverables and stakeholder interactions. Deliverables themselves are clearly defined in terms of format, content, audience, and timing, from kickoff presentations to final reports and follow-ups.

Communication strategies embedded in the plan outline how and when information will flow between the audit team and the auditees, promoting transparency and collaboration. The plan should also document any assumptions and constraints, such as limited access to personnel or time restrictions, alongside execution risks, like data unavailability, and plans for mitigating them.

Together, a clearly articulated scope and a robust, practical audit plan lay the foundation for an IT audit that is targeted, efficient, and meaningful. They ensure the audit stays on course, remains aligned with strategic business needs, and provides actionable insights that enhance IT governance and strengthen risk management practices.

Audit scope

Auditing plays a vital role in empowering an organization to generate, safeguard, and maintain value. It does so by offering the board and senior management independent, risk-oriented, and objective evaluations, along with informed advice and strategic foresight. This function contributes significantly to the organization's ability to meet its goals, reinforce governance and internal controls, elevate decision-making and oversight capabilities, build stakeholder trust, and uphold its responsibility to the public.

Its impact is most profound when the audit work is conducted by qualified professionals adhering to the global internal audit standards, which are designed with the public interest in mind. Effectiveness is further ensured when the audit function maintains independence through direct accountability to the board and when auditors operate free from undue influence, upholding their commitment to objective and unbiased assessments. This structure allows the internal audit to serve as a cornerstone of organizational integrity and resilience.

The IT audit scope is the precisely defined set of boundaries and focus areas for an IT audit engagement. It explicitly outlines what will be included in the audit, what will be excluded, and the specific objectives the audit aims to achieve. It acts as the initial contract or agreement between the auditors and the auditee regarding the parameters of the examination. The audit scope should clearly articulate the subject of the audit and establish its boundaries. It may encompass an entire organization, a specific division, a business process, an application, or an underlying technology such as a network or platform. The scope statement should also specify the timeframe being reviewed, as well as the period during which the audit was conducted. For someone familiar with the subject, the scope should provide a clear understanding of the anticipated extent of the audit activities and the topics addressed.

A clear and well-defined IT audit scope is more than a procedural necessity—it is a foundational element that determines the overall success and relevance of the audit. It creates transparency and shared understanding among all parties involved. For auditors, it serves as a directional guide, outlining focus areas, required resources, and investigative paths. For auditees, it clarifies which systems, teams, and processes will be under review, enabling them to prepare and cooperate effectively. For management and stakeholders, it ensures consensus on the audit's purpose and deliverables, reducing the risk of misalignment or misinterpretation.

When the scope is precisely articulated, resource planning becomes far more efficient. The audit team can identify the skills and time required, minimizing waste and enabling a well-targeted approach. It also ensures that attention is directed where it matters most—toward areas of high risk within the IT environment—thus maximizing the audit's impact. In addition, a clear scope acts as a critical control against scope creep. It keeps the engagement focused, avoids unnecessary detours, and protects both timelines and budgets. When scope and objectives are clearly connected, assessing audit effectiveness becomes straightforward, as outcomes can be measured against defined intentions.

Defining audit scope

A precise audit scope ensures that legal and regulatory obligations are fully addressed. In audits where compliance is a key concern, this level of clarity guarantees that relevant standards and frameworks are neither overlooked nor inadequately covered. In sum, the scope sets the stage for a purposeful, controlled, and high-value IT audit.

Key considerations for defining the audit scope are:

- **Audit objectives**: What are the primary goals of this audit?

  o **Compliance**: Are IT systems and processes adhering to relevant laws, regulations, industry standards, and internal policies?

  o **Effectiveness**: Are IT controls working as intended and effectively mitigating risks?

  o **Efficiency**: Are IT resources being used optimally? Can processes be streamlined?

  o **Reliability**: Is the IT infrastructure stable and available? Is the data accurate and reliable?

  o **Security**: Are information assets protected from unauthorized access, use, disclosure, disruption, modification, or destruction?

  o **Value for money**: Is the IT investment providing expected returns and supporting business goals?

- **Specific systems, applications, and infrastructure**: Which IT components will be examined?

  o **Core business applications**: ERP, CRM, financial systems, custom-built applications.

  o **Infrastructure components**: Servers (physical, virtual, cloud), networks, databases, storage, and operating systems.

  o **Cloud services**: **Software as a service (SaaS)**, **platform as a service (PaaS)**, **infrastructure as a service (IaaS)** providers and their security and control frameworks.

  o **End-user devices**: Desktops, laptops, mobile devices, and also **Internet of Things (IoT)** devices if applicable.

- **Processes and controls**: Which IT processes and related controls will be reviewed?

  o **IT governance**: IT strategy, organizational structure, roles and responsibilities.

  o **Risk management**: Identification, assessment, and mitigation of IT risks.

  o **Information security management**: Access control, incident response, vulnerability management, patch management, security awareness.

  o **Business continuity management (BCM) and disaster recovery (DR)**: Backup and restoration, recovery procedures.

  o **Change management**: Procedures for managing changes to IT systems.

  o **Problem management**: Identification and resolution of root causes of IT issues.

  o **IT service management (ITSM)**: Incident management, service level management.

- o **Software development life cycle (SDLC)**: Security throughout the development process.

- o **Data management**: Data privacy, data retention, data quality.

- o **Physical security**: Controls over IT facilities.

- **Organizational units and departments**: Which parts of the organization will be involved?

  - o Specific IT departments (e.g., network operations, development, IT security).

  - o Business units that rely heavily on specific IT systems.

  - o Third-party vendors or outsourced service providers.

- **Time period**: What period will the audit cover?

  - o Historical data review (e.g., last 12 months of logs, incidents).

  - o Current state assessment.

  - o Projected plans or future initiatives.

- **Exclusions**: Clearly state what is not included in the audit to avoid misunderstandings. For example, *This audit will not cover the physical security controls of the off-site data center operated by Vendor X.*

- **Regulatory and compliance frameworks**: Which specific regulations or standards will be referenced?

  e.g., ISO 27001, NIST CSF, COBIT, SOX, GDPR, HIPAA, PCI DSS.

Example scope statement

Let us look at an (illustrative) example of a scope statement:

The scope of this IT audit is to assess the effectiveness of information security controls pertaining to the financial reporting systems (ERP and associated databases) and the underlying network infrastructure supporting these systems within the company's head office in Thiruvananthapuram, Kerala, India. The audit will cover the period from April 1, 2024, to March 31, 2025. Key areas of focus include access management, patch management, incident response procedures, and data backup and recovery for these specific systems. Third-party cloud service providers for non-financial applications are excluded from this audit scope.

IT audit professionals rightfully devote considerable time and attention to selecting and refining audit programs, given the significant influence these have on the quality of audit execution and the assurance ultimately provided to the enterprise. Yet, the content of audit reports, the very output that drives follow-up actions and can lead to tangible costs for the organization, is often overlooked in comparison. To address this gap, there is a range of resources, including standards, guidelines, a white paper, and a report template, that should be consulted to ensure that audit reports consistently meet high professional standards. Following these frameworks is not only key to producing clear and credible reports but also serves as a crucial defense when audit findings come under scrutiny.

Audit plan

An IT audit plan serves as a structured blueprint that outlines the execution of an IT audit, providing clarity and direction for the audit team and stakeholders involved. It begins with an introduction that establishes the audit's overarching intent, covering its purpose, scope, and key objectives. These objectives are typically formulated using the SMART framework, ensuring they are Specific, Measurable, Achievable, Relevant, and Time-Bound.

The scope is then detailed, specifying the systems, processes, departments, and time periods that will be covered in the audit. This is followed by a delineation of the audit team structure, highlighting individual roles and responsibilities to ensure accountability and efficiency. The methodology section outlines the strategic approach—whether risk-focused, compliance-driven, or a hybrid—and describes the techniques to be used, such as interviews, document reviews, data analysis, and technical assessments. Clearly defined deliverables such as reports and follow-up actions are outlined alongside a project timeline that maps out milestones for each phase of the audit.

Resource planning identifies the people, tools, and access required to carry out the audit effectively. A communication plan ensures stakeholders stay informed through structured reporting timelines and feedback loops. The audit plan also acknowledges any assumptions made during preparation, constraints that may impact execution, and known risks to the audit process itself, along with strategies to mitigate those risks.

Together, these components form a comprehensive roadmap that ensures the audit is both well-coordinated and aligned with organizational priorities.

While the specifics may vary based on the organization's size, industry, and the audit's focus (e.g., compliance, cybersecurity, efficiency), a typical IT audit plan follows a structured, phased approach:

1. **Audit planning phase (Pre-fieldwork)**: This foundational phase defines the audit's direction and framework. The plan will also include applicable frameworks and standards.

2. **Audit fieldwork and execution phase**: This phase involves the execution of audit procedures and evidence collection.

3. **Audit reporting phase**: This phase involves compiling, reviewing, and presenting the audit results.

4. **Audit follow-up phase**: Post-audit activities ensure that issues identified are addressed and resolved.

An IT audit plan is a comprehensive, methodical roadmap that outlines the full lifecycle of an audit engagement—from initiation to completion. It ensures the audit is conducted systematically, efficiently, and in alignment with its defined objectives and scope.

Key components of an IT audit plan are:

- **Introduction and executive summary**: Brief overview of the audit purpose, scope, and objectives.

- **Audit objectives (refined)**: **Specific, Measurable, Achievable, Relevant, And Time-bound (SMART)** objectives derived from the scope.

- **Audit scope (detailed)**: As defined previously, listing specific systems, processes, departments, and timeframes.

- **Audit team and responsibilities**:
    o Identify the audit lead, team members, their roles, and specific areas of responsibility.
    o Identify key stakeholders within the auditee organization who will be involved.

- **Audit methodology and approach**:
    o **Risk-based approach**: Prioritizing audit efforts based on identified risks to the organization's IT environment.
    o **Compliance based**: Focusing on adherence to specific regulations or standards.
    o **Hybrid**: A combination of approaches.
    o **Phased approach**: Breaking the audit into logical stages (e.g., planning, fieldwork, reporting).
    o **Techniques**: Interviews with IT staff, management, and key users, review of documents like policies, procedures, standards, architecture diagrams, previous audit reports, observation during audit by witnessing processes in action (e.g., data center access, backup operations), technical testing like vulnerability scans, penetration testing (if within scope and expertise), configuration reviews, log analysis, analysis of data by reviewing logs, access lists, system configurations, and sampling or selecting a representative subset of data or transactions for review.

- **Audit deliverables**:
    o **Opening meeting presentation**: To kick off the audit.
    o **Interim findings and management letters**: For urgent issues or progress updates.
    o **Draft audit report**: For review and feedback.
    o **Final audit report**: Containing findings, recommendations, and management responses.

- o **Follow-up plan**: For tracking corrective actions.
- **Timeline and milestones**:
  - o Detailed schedule for each phase of the audit (e.g., planning, fieldwork, reporting, follow-up).
  - o Key dates for meetings, data requests, and report submission.
- **Resource requirements**:
  - o **Personnel**: Number of auditors, specialized skills needed (e.g., network security, database administration).
  - o **Tools**: Audit software, vulnerability scanners, penetration testing tools.
  - o **Access**: Required system access, physical access to facilities.
- **Reporting structure and communication plan**:
  - o Who will receive audit reports?
  - o How will progress be communicated (e.g., weekly status meetings)?
  - o Process for escalating issues.
  - o Format of reports.
- **Assumptions and constraints**:
  - o Any assumptions made during planning (e.g., availability of personnel, access to systems).
  - o Any limitations or constraints (e.g., budget, time, scope limitations).
- **Risk assessment for the audit itself**: Potential risks to the audit process (e.g., lack of cooperation from auditee, data unavailability, scope creep) and mitigation strategies.

A well-designed IT audit plan ensures professionalism, thoroughness, and alignment with business goals. By detailing each phase—planning, fieldwork, reporting, and follow-up—organizations can conduct audits that not only ensure compliance and risk mitigation but also drive continuous improvement in their IT control environment. Particularly in areas like governance or data management, the audit plan ensures that the chosen approach is rigorous, appropriate, and capable of producing reliable evidence to support meaningful conclusions.

IT process and the apex processes

Evaluating how IT processes align with and contribute to an organization's overarching management systems, referred to here as enterprise management systems or governance frameworks, is essential for understanding their impact on overall performance, risk posture, and regulatory compliance. These high-level systems serve as the structural backbone for achieving strategic objectives and managing organizational accountability.

When an IT audit concentrates on these governance frameworks, the focus shifts to how technology supports, integrates with, and helps operationalize the processes dictated by systems like the **Information Security Management System (ISMS)**, **quality management system (QMS)**, and **environmental, social and governance (ESG)** management structures. The audit seeks to identify whether IT functions are enabling the intended controls, data flows, reporting mechanisms, and risk mitigation strategies embedded in each of these domains. When an IT audit focuses on enterprise management systems, it evaluates the IT components that enable, support, or are integral to the processes defined within those systems.

IT processes are structured activities carried out by IT functions, such as incident management, access control, change management, etc., that directly or indirectly contribute to the organization's ability to meet its strategic and operational goals.

Each apex management system sets a governance framework. IT audits assess how well IT processes align with and support the objectives of these systems. Let us look at the systems in detail:

- **ISMS**: An ISMS is a structured framework for managing and safeguarding information assets. It incorporates people, processes, and technology to ensure the **confidentiality, integrity, and availability (CIA)** of information. ISO 27001 is the leading standard.

  IT audit scope for ISMS can be defined focusing on the evaluation of the effectiveness of IT controls supporting the CIA of assets within the ISMS scope. This will include access management, incident response, patch management, backup and recovery, secure development, IT asset lifecycle, supplier IT security, and physical security of IT assets, etc. Non-IT systems' physical security, HR policies not related to IT, and non-technical legal compliance will not be part of the scope of this ISMS audit for IT systems.

- **QMS**: A QMS ensures that products or services consistently meet quality standards. ISO 9001 is the most widely adopted standard. IT audit scope for QMS focuses on evaluating IT's role in supporting quality data, documentation, and performance monitoring. Systems for document control, **corrective action and preventive action (CAPA)**, customer feedback, KPIs, and infrastructure supporting production are included as part of the audit scope here. Exclusions will be manual product manufacturing processes or non-IT HR training. Key IT processes audited will be data integrity, document control and version control, system reliability, IT security, backup and recovery process, change management, application support, etc.

- **ESG management system**: An ESG management system focuses on tracking and improving performance in environmental, social, and governance areas. IT audit scope for ESG includes assessment of IT controls over ESG data collection, processing, reporting, and integrity. Inclusions are systems capturing environmental metrics (e.g., energy use, emissions), social metrics (e.g., workforce diversity, safety incidents), and governance indicators (e.g., board diversity, ethics compliance), etc. Exclusions are strategic ESG goals and qualitative social initiatives outside IT's influence. Key

IT processes audited will be data governance and integrity, data collection and integration, reporting controls, etc.

Here, the focus shifts from routine operational checks to evaluating how well IT is integrated into the organization's overall direction, examining alignment with business goals, oversight mechanisms, risk governance, and investment prioritization. This top-down scrutiny ensures that IT is not only functional but also purpose-driven and accountable.

Cross-cutting role of IT audit in management systems

Across ISMS, QMS, and ESG management systems, IT audits play a pivotal assurance role by ensuring data integrity through verifying that data used in decision-making is reliable and accurate, assessing system reliability by confirming that IT infrastructure and applications are stable, secure, and available when needed, evaluating control effectiveness through determining whether IT controls are appropriately designed and functioning to meet security, quality, or ESG objectives, and checking for compliance by ensuring IT practices align with relevant internal policies, standards, and external regulations.

An effective IT audit validates that the organization's reliance on technology is not a blind spot. Instead, it demonstrates that IT systems and processes are well-governed, securely managed, and directly aligned with enterprise-wide frameworks for security, quality, and sustainability. This provides leadership, regulators, and stakeholders with confidence that the organization's strategic management systems are not only documented, but operational, effective, and resilient.

Audit of data management

Conducting an IT audit focused on data at rest and data in transit is essential in today's interconnected and data-centric environment. This audit aims to assess the robustness of security controls in place to safeguard sensitive information—both while it is stored and as it moves across networks. The primary objective is to determine how effectively these controls prevent unauthorized access, tampering, or exposure of critical data, thereby reducing the risk of compromise throughout the data lifecycle.

Auditing data at rest and data in transit is essential because any compromise of this information—whether stored or in motion—can have serious consequences for an organization. Unauthorized access to sensitive data can result in breaches that expose customer, employee, or proprietary information. Regulatory non-compliance may lead to significant fines and penalties, especially under frameworks like GDPR, HIPAA, or India's **Digital Personal Data Protection (DPDP)** act. Beyond financial repercussions, such incidents can erode public trust and tarnish the organization's reputation through negative publicity and diminished brand credibility. There is also the potential for substantial financial damage stemming from legal costs, notification efforts, incident response, and operational downtime. If **intellectual property (IP)** is compromised, it could lead to a loss of competitive advantage. Moreover, attacks that alter or corrupt critical system configurations or data could severely disrupt business operations and continuity. These risks underscore the importance of robust auditing to proactively identify and mitigate vulnerabilities in how data is stored and transmitted.

Data management audit, as part of an IT audit, assesses how effectively an organization governs, secures, processes, and utilizes its data throughout its entire lifecycle. Given the importance of data to business operations, compliance, and strategic insight, maintaining its integrity, availability, and confidentiality is vital to IT assurance.

Objectives of the audit can be captured as follows:

- Evaluate controls related to data governance, ownership, and classification.

- Confirm the accuracy, consistency, and reliability of key business data.

- Assess security and privacy measures like access management, encryption, and backups.

- Review lifecycle practices for data creation, storage, archival, and disposal.

- Ensure adherence to data protection laws and standards such as GDPR, HIPAA, ISO 27001, or SOX.

The scope of the audit will include the following areas:

- **Data governance**: Presence of clear ownership roles, stewardship responsibilities, policy enforcement, and escalation mechanisms.

- **Classification and handling**: Implementation of sensitivity-based labeling and handling procedures aligned with classification levels.

- **Storage and retention**: Assessment of storage models (on-premise, cloud, hybrid), legal retention schedules, and secure disposal protocols.

- **Integrity controls**: Use of input validation, reconciliation tools, audit trails, and mechanisms to prevent unauthorized data changes.

- **Security and access management**: Role-based access, monitoring, anomaly detection, and end-to-end encryption practices.

- **Backup and recovery**: Evaluation of backup frequency, restoration accuracy, and alignment with defined RTOs and RPOs.

- **Compliance and privacy**: Measures for consent management, data subject rights, international data transfers, and breach response readiness.

When defining the scope of an IT audit, it is essential to articulate the parameters of sensitive data protection with precision. This includes clearly identifying what constitutes sensitive data, such as **personally identifiable information** (**PII**), financial records, or IP, and specifying where this data is stored, be it in databases, cloud repositories, file servers, or backup systems. It is also important to map how this data flows across the environment, including applications involved in transmission, network paths, and remote access channels.

The scope should reflect applicable regulatory obligations like GDPR, HIPAA, and region-specific laws, such as the DPDP act, if it applies to the organization's operations, along with any relevant internal compliance policies. Additionally, the scope should account for the technology stack in use, highlighting the encryption tools, network infrastructure, and cloud platforms that support or secure the data ecosystem. Establishing these elements up front ensures the audit is focused, comprehensive, and aligned with legal and organizational expectations.

Key audit activities are reviewing internal policies and standards, inspecting systems for security and access controls, engaging data owners and custodians in interviews, mapping data flows and conducting tracing exercises, verifying data quality, accuracy, and protective controls, analyzing audit logs and historical incidents, etc.

Common audit findings are undefined or poorly enforced data ownership roles, gaps in classification consistency and labeling practices, overly permissive or poorly controlled data access, weaknesses in backup or recovery validation procedures, lack of structured data quality controls or documentation, failure to comply with regulatory requirements on data retention or privacy, etc.

Audit of data at rest and data in transit

An IT audit with a targeted emphasis on data at rest and data in transit plays a pivotal role in protecting sensitive information in a hyper-connected, data-centric environment. This specialized audit evaluates how effectively an organization safeguards data while it is stored and during transmission, aiming to reduce the risk of unauthorized access, alteration, or disclosure.

Data at rest includes stored data in any digital format, on hard drives, databases, cloud repositories, mobile devices, or backup media. Although not actively moving, this data remains susceptible to breaches if storage mediums are stolen, compromised, or poorly managed. Controls here aim to make the data unreadable or tamper-proof without proper authorization.

Data in transit encompasses data actively moving across networks, internet connections, or between applications. Since it traverses internal or external networks, it can be intercepted or manipulated during transfer. The goal is to maintain data confidentiality and integrity until it safely reaches its destination.

The compromise of either static or in-motion data can lead to serious consequences. These include breaches involving customer or employee records, regulatory penalties for non-compliance with laws like GDPR or HIPAA, erosion of public trust, financial and reputational loss, theft of IP, and operational disruptions caused by corrupted or inaccessible data. Auditing controls around data at rest and data in transit helps mitigate these risks and strengthens the organization's data resilience.

Key processes and controls under review here are a broad spectrum of technical and procedural safeguards, including:

- **Encryption practices**: Validation of full disk, file-level, or database encryption for stored data, and secure protocols, or **virtual private networks (VPNs)** for data in transit. The audit assesses algorithm strength, key management (including rotation and revocation), and consistency of implementation.

- **Access controls**: Assessment of authentication and authorization measures protecting storage systems, databases, and cloud environments. It also reviews access controls for network devices and enforcement of principles such as least privilege, role-based access control mechanisms, and **multifactor authentication (MFA)**.

- **Network security**: Inspection of firewall rules, configurations of intrusion detection and prevention systems, network segmentation, and secure remote access channels (e.g., VPNs) to ensure controlled and monitored data flow.

- **Data loss prevention (DLP)**: Evaluation of DLP tools and policies that detect and prevent the unauthorized movement of sensitive data, both in storage and in transit.

- **Backup and recovery**: Examination of encryption and secure storage practices for backup data, along with validation of backup integrity and restoration capabilities.

- **Data retention and disposal**: Verification of policies and procedures for securely erasing or destroying storage media when no longer needed.

- **Cloud security**: Analysis of cloud-specific protections, including access settings, storage encryption, and alignment with the provider's shared responsibility model.

To ensure relevance and accuracy, the audit scope should clearly outline which categories of sensitive data are being evaluated (e.g., PII, financial records, IP), where the data resides (specific servers, databases, cloud buckets, backup repositories), how the data flows through the environment (internal applications, external endpoints, remote access), applicable regulatory frameworks and internal policies, the technical environment, including encryption tools and network devices, etc.

By concentrating on the protection of data at both rest and in transit, this audit equips organizations with critical insight into how well they are defending their most valuable digital assets. It reinforces compliance, enhances trust, and ultimately ensures that data is managed safely and responsibly across its entire lifecycle.

Conducting a data management audit helps ensure that data is governed responsibly, protected effectively, and leveraged efficiently. By spotlighting control gaps and inefficiencies, these audits drive actionable improvements, strengthening an organization's information governance and reducing operational, legal, and reputational exposure.

Conclusion

The success and value of an IT audit depend on the cohesive interplay of several foundational elements: a clearly articulated audit scope, a comprehensive audit plan, a strategic assessment of enterprise governance processes like ISMS, QMS, etc., and a focused examination of data management practices. Together, these components elevate the audit beyond a procedural task, turning it into a forward-looking instrument that strengthens organizational resilience and delivers tangible business value.

The audit scope acts as the directional framework, establishing what the audit will cover and why. It defines specific boundaries, detailing which systems, processes, departments, and timeframes are involved, and aligns these with broader audit objectives shaped by risk, regulatory needs, or strategic goals. Building on that foundation, the audit plan translates scope into action. It lays out the execution strategy, specifying methodologies, procedures, timelines, required expertise, and communication protocols.

Assessing enterprise governance processes brings a critical strategic lens to IT auditing. Equally vital is the targeted audit of data management, given data's central role in today's digital enterprises. This encompasses a comprehensive review of how data is created, classified, stored, transmitted, secured, retained, and ultimately disposed of. By examining protections around data at rest and in transit, the audit affirms that the organization's most critical asset is reliable, compliant, and safeguarded against internal and external threats.

Taken together, these pillars transform an IT audit into a strategic asset. A well-scoped effort, supported by a thoughtfully executed plan, informed by governance insights, and anchored in strong data stewardship, enables organizations to anticipate and address risks, meet evolving regulatory demands, sharpen IT investments, and reinforce long-term operational strength in an ever-changing technological landscape.

In the next chapter, we will discuss the review of policy and controls.

Join our Discord space

Join our Discord workspace for latest updates, offers, tech happenings around the world, new releases, and sessions with the authors:

https://discord.bpbonline.com

CHAPTER 20
Review of Policy and Controls

Introduction

In this chapter, we will see how in today's fast-moving and often intricate IT environment, strong governance and sound risk management are essential. Central to achieving these goals is a well-established framework built on IT policies and IT controls. A review of policies and controls is a foundational and often the most extensive part of any IT audit. It forms the core of assessing an organization's information security posture, operational efficiency, and regulatory compliance.

This phase goes deep into the organization's operational framework. IT policies express management's intent by outlining the standards and expectations for how technology should be used, secured, and governed. They convey the overarching *what* and *why*, setting the tone for security, accountability, and regulatory alignment. Paired with these are IT controls, which represent the *how*, the procedures, technical tools, and operational safeguards that put policy into practice and tangibly manage risk.

The purpose of this review of operational processes and controls is twofold. It first evaluates whether the organization's policies are complete and appropriately tailored to address its specific risks, obligations, and operating context, whether for a single location or globally. Equally important, it assesses how effectively the controls are operating day to day, ensuring they fulfill their role in implementing policy and reducing risk.

This structured review confirms whether the organization's security and governance efforts are not just formally documented but are also actively working and dependable. By comparing policy with practice, the audit helps pinpoint deficiencies, highlight gaps in risk mitigation, and identify opportunities for improvement, building confidence that the organization's information assets are well protected in a continuously shifting threat landscape. It also lays a strong foundation for deeper analysis of how these practices are sustained and improved over time.

Structure

The chapter covers the following topics:

- Key concepts
- Understanding control frameworks in ITSM
- Design of IT process and controls
- Implementation of processes around IT systems

Objectives

This chapter equips the readers with both the theoretical grounding and practical capabilities necessary for reviewing policies and controls within the scope of an IT audit.

Readers will develop a solid understanding of foundational concepts, including the ability to define IT policies and differentiate them from related governance artifacts, such as procedures and standards. They will explore why IT policies are critical for managing risk, enforcing compliance, and steering IT operations. Similarly, they will learn to articulate what IT controls are, categorize them into preventive, detective, or corrective types, and recognize their role in safeguarding the confidentiality, integrity, and availability of systems and data. The chapter clarifies how policies serve as the guiding structure for controls and introduces commonly encountered examples of both, helping readers connect policy and implementation in a real-world context.

Next, we focus on how IT policies are audited. The readers will learn to state the objectives behind reviewing policies, such as verifying whether they exist, are approved, current, and sufficiently disseminated across the organization. They will understand the procedures for validating documentation, version control, and staff awareness, and gain insight into common policy deficiencies, like outdated or incomplete documents. Through guided scenarios, learners will evaluate whether policy content adequately addresses risks and aligns with compliance requirements.

In auditing IT controls, the readers will learn how to assess not only if controls are designed effectively but also whether they function consistently in practice. This includes mastering audit techniques like walkthroughs, inspections, observation, data analysis, and re-performance.

They will learn how to select the right method based on the nature of the control and how to analyze evidence to identify operational gaps or weaknesses. Additionally, learners will explore how policy inadequacies often underpin control failures, linking these audit findings back to their governance root causes.

The chapter concludes with a focus on reporting and communicating audit value. Readers will craft clear and actionable audit findings, integrating cause-and-effect analysis and well-structured recommendations. They will examine how to tailor messages to stakeholders, emphasizing clarity and strategic value. Finally, the chapter reinforces how policy and control reviews contribute directly to risk mitigation, operational excellence, and regulatory alignment, reinforcing the importance of this audit function within an organization's broader assurance landscape.

Key concepts

A deep understanding of certain core concepts is essential when learning how to review policies and controls in the context of an IT audit. These foundational principles guide both the evaluation process and the meaningful interpretation of findings.

At the center of this domain is the recognition that IT policies express management's strategic intent. They provide the formal, documented guidance that defines what should be done and why, establishing the expectations for responsible and secure technology use across the organization. IT controls, on the other hand, represent the *how*, the actual mechanisms, procedures, and safeguards implemented to enforce those policies and reduce IT-related risks. These controls may be preventive, detective, or corrective in nature, and their purpose is to ensure the confidentiality, integrity, and availability of systems and data.

The relationship between policies and controls is tightly woven. Policies without supporting controls are ineffective, while controls lacking policy backing may lack legitimacy or direction. Auditors explore this alignment to ensure that every key control supports a stated policy and that policies are backed by tangible enforcement mechanisms. Each control is tied to a specific objective, such as preventing unauthorized access or ensuring change approvals, and the audit evaluates whether the control, both in design and in daily operation, reliably achieves that objective.

Assessing control design focuses on whether a control, if properly implemented, would meet its purpose. Operational effectiveness is about whether the control is actually being performed as intended and on a consistent basis. This requires evidence: approved policy documents, communication records, logs, observations, test results, or interviews with staff. Evidence-based auditing ensures that all conclusions are grounded in verifiable facts.

Auditors also leverage established frameworks such as COSO and COBIT to benchmark an organization's practices against industry standards. These references help assess not just compliance, whether policies and procedures are being followed, but also effectiveness, whether the controls actually work as intended. It is not uncommon to find a situation where a control is technically compliant but fails to reduce risk due to poor implementation or weak design.

Finally, communicating findings with clarity is as important as identifying them. An auditor must clearly document observations, articulate the root cause and potential impact of any weakness, and offer practical, risk-aligned recommendations. This communication supports the organization's efforts to strengthen its control environment, improve compliance, and manage operational risk more effectively.

Altogether, mastering these concepts equips auditors to deliver insights that go far beyond checklists, guiding organizations toward more secure, efficient, and well-governed IT ecosystems.

Understanding control frameworks in ITSM

A controls framework in ITSM is a structured approach comprising guidelines, principles, and practices that help organizations deliver IT services securely, efficiently, and in compliance with business goals and regulations. ITIL is the most widely adopted best practice framework for ITSM, though it is typically paired with more formal control frameworks (like ISO 20000, NIST CSF) to reinforce governance and assurance.

The following points elaborate on what each of the previously mentioned frameworks focuses on in strengthening the ITSM processes:

- **ITIL as a foundational control framework**:
  - ITIL implicitly embeds control mechanisms within its service management practices rather than prescribing them in isolation.
  - ITIL calls for process-based control integration on change management, access management, etc.
  - ITIL guiding principles, such as focus on value and optimize and automate, support the creation of effective controls.
  - Specific ITIL practices like information security, availability, and capacity management incorporate controls such as encryption, redundancy, and monitoring.
  - **Continual service improvement** (**CSI**) facilitates regular evaluation of controls for relevance and performance.

- **ISO/20000 based controls**:
  - An international standard for **service management systems** (**SMS**) focused on auditable control requirements.
  - Requires structured documentation, measurable effectiveness, and evidence-based assurance mechanisms.

    o   Applies the **Plan-Do-Check-Act** (**PDCA**) model to ITSM for continual control improvement.

    o   Achieving certification confirms control maturity and alignment with global standards.

- **NIST Cybersecurity Framework (CSF) based controls:**

    o   A cybersecurity-centric framework with controls relevant to ITSM in areas like incident, security, and asset management.

    o   Organizes control practices into six functions, as follows:

        ▪   **Identify**: Includes asset inventory and risk assessment (e.g., CMDB, ITAM).

        ▪   **Protect**: Access controls, awareness programs, and data security.

        ▪   **Detect**: System monitoring, log analysis.

        ▪   **Respond**: Incident response planning.

        ▪   **Recover**: Backup, restoration, and continuity measures.

        ▪   **Govern**: Build a holistic view on the five practices to ensure these are not working in silos.

Characteristics of a strong ITSM control framework are risk-based design, comprehensiveness, balance, clarity, ownership, **segregation of duties** (**SoD**), auditability, performance tracking, flexibility, etc. Blending ITIL's best practices with structured governance models like ISO 20000, or NIST CSF creates a comprehensive, auditable, and risk-aware ITSM ecosystem. This integrated approach enhances service reliability, compliance, and continual improvement, which are hallmarks of a resilient IT organization.

Design of IT process and controls

Evaluating the design of IT controls is a critical first step in IT auditing. This phase, commonly known as the **Test of Design** (**ToD**), assesses whether controls are appropriately structured to address identified risks, serving as a prerequisite to testing operational effectiveness.

Here is a breakdown of how to approach this review:

- **Understand the IT process and its objectives**:

    o   Comprehend the process's purpose and the business objectives it supports.

    o   Identify key inputs, outputs, activities, and stakeholders through documentation review, process walkthroughs, and stakeholder interviews.

o   Assess related risks that may hinder the achievement of process goals and categorize risks by type (e.g., financial, operational, compliance, reputational, cybersecurity, data integrity).

- **Identify key IT controls**:

    o   Map controls to the identified risks to determine if they are preventive (e.g., access restrictions) or detective (e.g., monitoring logs).

    o   Classify controls as manual or automated by evaluating the reliability of automated controls by assessing the supporting **general IT controls** (**GITCs**).

    o   Account for entity-level controls (e.g., IT governance, risk frameworks), which influence the effectiveness of process-level controls.

- **Evaluate control design**: ToD assesses if a control, as designed, is capable of effectively preventing or detecting errors or irregularities.

    o   Review control design through documentation analysis, policies, procedures, system configurations, access matrices, and evidence of review and approval.

    o   Walkthroughs of designs by tracing data flows and transactions across the process.

    o   Interview control owners and observe the control in operation when possible.

- **Document the assessment**: Provide a structured summary including process description, associated risks, key controls and their purposes, evaluation of each control's design adequacy (e.g., adequate, minor deficiencies, deficient).

    o   Supporting evidence can be collected, which includes noted deficiencies and potential impacts.

- **Communicate design deficiencies**:

    o   Clearly present identified design flaws to management.

    o   Explain the potential risk exposure and implications.

    o   Offer actionable recommendations to improve control design.

By thoroughly assessing the design of IT controls, auditors help ensure the IT environment is robust, risk-aligned, and capable of supporting the organization's strategic and operational objectives.

Review of policies as part of the IT audit

While reviewing the design of control, we need to use well-established frameworks like ISO 20000 and ITIL, which we used throughout this book for defining and implementing ITSM processes.

Reviewing IT policies and controls in an IT audit is not just about ticking boxes; it is about assuring that the organization's IT environment is secure, reliable, and compliant.

Key principles for the review can be defined as follows:

- **Risk-based focus**: Prioritize controls that mitigate high-impact risks.

- **Professional validation**: Validate claims with evidence; do not rely solely on documentation.

- **Independence**: Maintain objectivity throughout the review.

- **Continuous improvement**: Feed findings into ongoing enhancement through the PDCA cycle of IT controls and processes.

By adhering to the previously mentioned principles, IT auditors can conduct thorough, reliable, and valuable reviews of IT policies and controls, ultimately contributing to the security, efficiency, and compliance of the organization's information systems.

When reviewing policies and controls in an IT audit, the goal is to assess their adequacy, effectiveness, and compliance with organizational objectives, regulatory requirements, and industry best practices.

Key evaluation questions while conducting a review of policy and controls can be captured as follows:

- Is the control clearly documented and well-understood?

- Is it executed by appropriately skilled and authorized personnel?

- Does it directly mitigate the intended risk?

- Is its scope adequate (i.e., applied consistently across relevant data/transactions)?

- Are there weaknesses (e.g., potential for override, poor SoD)?

- Is sufficient evidence of control execution retained (e.g., logs, approvals)?

- Are supporting IT general controls (access, change, operations) sound?

- Does the control rely on other controls, and are those also well-designed?

By asking these comprehensive questions, IT auditors can systematically evaluate the design effectiveness of an organization's IT policies and controls, identifying weaknesses and providing actionable recommendations for improvement.

A review of IT policies and controls as part of an IT audit yields far more than a checklist of deficiencies, as it results in a comprehensive, strategic assessment that delivers meaningful insights to both management and stakeholders. This outcome acts as a catalyst for enhancing an organization's overall IT governance and security posture.

The central deliverable of the review is a formal audit report that provides a detailed yet accessible summary of the audit's scope, objectives, and methodology. It opens with an executive summary outlining key findings and an overall opinion on the effectiveness of the organization's IT policies and controls. The report situates these findings within the broader IT environment, offering essential context on the systems and processes under review.

Perhaps most valuable are the audit's recommendations. These are practical, prioritized, and tailored to the organization's unique operating context. They might call for the development or revision of policies, implementation of new technical safeguards, enhanced monitoring, or targeted staff training. The report concludes with the auditor's professional judgment regarding the overall effectiveness of the organization's policies and controls, both in supporting business objectives and in reducing IT risk to acceptable levels.

Beyond the document itself, the audit enables a clearer understanding of the IT control environment. Through hands-on methods like interviews, document analysis, and control testing, auditors uncover insights into how IT is governed and operated on a day-to-day basis. This deeper knowledge is invaluable to both IT and non-IT leaders. Moreover, the process helps identify key IT risks and vulnerabilities, offering a current snapshot of the organization's risk landscape. It strengthens compliance by surfacing regulatory gaps and providing a roadmap to correct them. It also brings to light opportunities for optimizing processes—suggesting more efficient control mechanisms or automation that could reduce operational overhead.

Ultimately, the audit supports informed strategic decision-making. It provides board-level assurance on IT performance and control effectiveness, helps shape investment priorities, and defines the organization's tolerance for risk. It signals to customers, partners, and regulators a strong commitment to data protection and responsible IT management, enhancing overall credibility and trust. Perhaps most importantly, the audit establishes a benchmark. It lays the groundwork for future assessments, creating a feedback loop that promotes continuous improvement in the IT control environment over time. Rather than being a one-time event, it becomes an integral part of the organization's journey toward more resilient, compliant, and value-driven IT operations.

Overview of the ITIL framework

Designing IT processes and controls is not a one-time activity; it is an ongoing, integrated function that spans the service lifecycle, with its foundation rooted in the service design phase. ITIL stresses that each IT process should be purpose-driven, with well-defined inputs, outputs, ownership, and built-in controls to ensure effectiveness and risk mitigation.

ITIL defines the processes and controls as follows:

- **Core principles of process and control design (ITIL):**
    - **Focus on value**: Ensure every process and control delivers a measurable benefit to the business or end-user.

- o **Start where you are**: Utilize existing capabilities and build improvements from current strengths.

- o **Progress iteratively with feedback**: Implement and refine processes incrementally based on real feedback.

- o **Collaborate and promote visibility**: Engage stakeholders and maintain transparency throughout design.

- o **Think and work holistically**: Align processes and controls with the broader service value system.

- o **Keep it simple and practical**: Avoid excessive complexity—favor usability and clarity.

- o **Optimize and automate**: Streamline tasks and embed automation where beneficial.

- • **Designing processes and controls during service design**:

  - o **Service and architecture design**: Convert business needs into detailed service specifications, including infrastructure and security requirements.

  - o **Security, availability, and capacity planning**: Incorporate redundancy, disaster recovery, and protection mechanisms based on business needs.

  - o **Process structure**: Define goals, inputs/outputs, sequential tasks, and interdependencies with other ITIL practices (e.g., incident management connecting to problem management).

  - o **Role and accountability mapping**: Use **Responsible, Accountable, Controlled, Informed (RACI)** matrices to assign responsibilities and enforce SoD.

  - o **Control integration**: Design preventive, detective, and corrective controls based on identified risks.

  - o **Automation vs manual execution**: Determine where automated controls (like access restrictions) or manual interventions (like reviews) are most effective.

  - o **Documentation**: Clearly describe each control's function, execution method, ownership, and associated risk.

- • **Examples of processes with embedded control design**:

  - o **Incident management**: Includes logging, auto-alerts, escalation paths, and audit trails.

  - o **Problem management**: Applies root cause analysis, error tracking, and structured reporting.

  - o **Change management**: Enforces change authorization, testing protocols, SoD, and reviews.

o **Configuration and asset management**: Maintains an accurate **configuration management database (CMDB)** through reconciliations, scans, and change controls.

o **Security management**: Uses access control lists, **intrusion detection system (IDS)**, **intrusion prevention system (IPS)**, awareness training, and vulnerability scans.

o **Access management**: Enforces least privilege, periodic reviews, **multifactor authentication (MFA)**, and access provisioning controls.

- **Documentation and stakeholder review**:

o **Process design records**: Flowcharts, **standard operating procedures (SOPs)**, and RACI charts ensure clarity and traceability.

o **Control records**: Define objectives, operating procedures, frequency, responsible roles, and evidence requirements.

o **Review mechanism**: Stakeholders, including security, audit, and business leads, validate that controls and processes meet risk, compliance, and operational standards before implementation.

ITIL promotes a comprehensive and embedded approach to process and control design. Rather than retrofitting controls after services are built, ITIL ensures they are engineered into every layer of the service structure. This design discipline enhances consistency, security, accountability, and service quality across the IT landscape.

Implementation of processes around IT systems

Establishing structured processes around IT systems within an **IT service management (ITSM)** framework, typically guided by ITIL, is essential for delivering reliable, secure, and efficient IT services. It marks a shift from reactive issue resolution to proactive, disciplined IT service delivery.

Implementation of processes comprising policy and controls can be achieved through the following focused steps:

1. **Laying the foundation**: Understanding IT systems and services.

- **Service definition**: Clearly define the IT services being offered. Identify the supporting systems, components, interdependencies, and business impact of each service.

- **Service catalog**: Develop a detailed service catalog listing all IT services, including descriptions, availability, support hours, and associated costs. This becomes the reference point for user requests and service expectations.

- **Configuration management database (CMDB)**: Maintain a centralized repository of **configuration items (CIs)**, hardware, software, network devices, and documentation, along with their interrelationships. A reliable CMDB supports many ITSM functions and enables accurate impact analysis.

2. **Core ITSM processes aligned with IT systems**: The following are key ITIL-aligned processes and how they are implemented around IT systems:

   - Incident management for restoring normal service operations quickly to minimize business disruption.

   - Problem management for identifying root causes to prevent recurring incidents and minimize unresolved issues.

   - Change management by introducing changes to IT systems in a controlled manner with minimal disruption.

   - Service request management to manage routine service requests efficiently.

   - Monitoring and event management where systems are continuously observed and critical events are addressed on time.

   - CSI by driving ongoing improvements based on performance data and feedback.

3. **Enabling technologies**: ITSM platforms like ServiceNow, Jira service management, Freshservice, ManageEngine, etc., facilitate process implementations.

   - Workflow automation through streamlined ticket routing, approvals, task execution, etc.

   - Centralized data management by unified views of incidents, changes, assets, and requests.

   - Self-service portals empower users to request services or find solutions independently.

   - Integrations through seamless connections with monitoring systems, identity management, and deployment tools.

   - Reporting and dashboards delivering actionable insights into performance, bottlenecks, and trends.

Implementing ITSM processes around IT systems enables organizations to deliver IT services that are stable, secure, and aligned with business goals. Through structured processes, effective tools, and a culture of continuous improvement, IT can evolve from a support function to a strategic enabler.

Implementing IT processes and controls in ITIL

Implementing IT processes and controls under the ITIL framework involves turning process designs into practical operations that deliver value. It bridges the gap between theoretical best practices and real-world execution, aligning people, processes, and technology around your IT systems.

The general implementation steps for ITIL processes are as follows:

1. **Set clear objectives and define scope**: Determine specific outcomes, identify which services or systems are in scope, typically starting with critical areas, and define success criteria through KPIs and measurable metrics.

2. **Assess current state and identify gaps**: Review existing processes, tools, and roles, identify inefficiencies and missing controls compared to the intended design.

3. **Design or refine processes and controls**: Align workflows, responsibilities (RACI), and safeguards with ITIL practices, and translate conceptual designs into step-by-step procedures.

4. **Select and configure the ITSM tool**: Choose a platform (e.g., ServiceNow, Jira service management) to support ITIL-aligned workflows, set up forms, automation, notifications, and reporting within the tool.

5. **Integrate with IT infrastructure**: CMDB integration by populating and maintaining a dynamic CMDB, monitoring tools connecting tools to trigger incidents automatically, automation tools using platforms to carry out tasks like deployments or resets, and **identity and access management (IAM)** integration by linking with directory services for access provisioning.

6. **Training**: Train people and drive organizational change by delivering role-specific training to users and technical staff, communicating purpose, process changes, and expected benefits, and securing engagement and support from leadership.

7. **Iterative deployment and refinement**: Pilot and roll out gradually by starting with a limited group or process scope, gathering feedback, fine-tuning, and expanding implementation incrementally.

8. **Monitoring**: Monitor, evaluate, and improve by tracking KPIs and gathering user feedback, identifying improvement opportunities, and refining processes continuously.

The practical implementation of core ITIL processes is as follows:

- **Incident management**: Deploy monitoring tools on systems to detect issues, automatically create incidents from alerts, use a self-service portal for reporting and status updates, route tickets based on CMDB data, integrate knowledge articles, and enforce SLA tracking.

- **Problem management**: Analyze incident data to identify patterns, use root cause analysis tools, and maintain a **known error database (KEDB)**, trigger formal change requests for long-term fixes.

- **Change management**: Implement structured change workflows within the ITSM tool, link requests to relevant CIs for impact analysis, set up automated approvals for low-risk changes, and integrate with other tools, document rollback plans, and conduct post-implementation reviews.

- **IT asset and configuration management**: Use discovery tools to populate and update the CMDB, track assets through their lifecycle, and enforce standard configurations.

- **Service request management**: Create a service catalog for user requests, automate fulfillment where possible (e.g., password resets), use workflow automation for approvals, and offer knowledge resources via self-service.

ITSM platform essentials are:

- **Centralized ticketing and workflow engine**: Manages all types of requests and incidents.

- **CMDB and asset management**: Provides visibility into IT components and their relationships.

- **Knowledge base**: Offers users and technicians accessible information and workarounds.

- **Dashboards and analytics**: Support decision-making through insights and trends.

- **Integrations**: Connects to systems across monitoring, HR, and finance.

- **Self-service portal**: A central interface for end-user interaction.

Critical success factors are as follows:

- **Phased implementation**: Start with core processes and scale gradually.

- **Change management**: Address cultural and behavioral aspects alongside tools and processes.

- **Data accuracy**: Ensure the CMDB and process inputs remain clean and reliable.

- **Metrics and monitoring**: Use KPIs to track effectiveness and drive ongoing adjustments.

- **Continuous service improvement** (CSI): Create feedback loops to refine processes and adapt to evolving needs.

By anchoring implementation in clear goals, process integration, user engagement, and iterative refinement, organizations can unlock the full value of ITIL, strengthening service quality, agility, and risk control across the IT landscape.

Conclusion

Understanding control frameworks in ITSM reveals how vital structured governance is to achieve secure, efficient, and compliant service delivery. While ITIL forms the operational backbone with its best practices for managing IT services, it does not exist in isolation. When paired with compliance-driven standards like ISO 20000 and governance-oriented and risk-focused models like the NIST CSF, organizations can move beyond process maturity and toward true resilience. This integrated approach ensures that ITSM processes are not only well-designed and executed but are also measurable, auditable, and adaptable. Controls become more than just checkboxes; they function as embedded mechanisms of accountability, assurance, and continuous improvement. By aligning control design and implementation with business goals, regulatory obligations, and evolving threats, ITSM transforms into a dynamic capability that safeguards value and strengthens trust across the enterprise.

A thorough review of policies and controls lies at the heart of any meaningful IT audit, offering essential assurance that the organization's risk management framework is not only well-documented but also actively functioning as intended. The process begins by confirming the existence, formal approval, and proper dissemination of IT policies, ensuring that management's expectations and guiding principles are clearly communicated. The next step involves a meticulous evaluation of IT controls to determine whether these policies are effectively operationalized. Whether the controls are technical, procedural, or administrative, the audit assesses their real-world application and reliability.

This combined approach enables auditors to pinpoint misalignments between what is prescribed and what is practiced. It sheds light on deficiencies in control design or execution and provides a foundation for recommending targeted improvements. Such a review is indispensable, not only for organizations in Thiruvananthapuram, Kerala, India, but for any institution navigating the global landscape to uphold strong cybersecurity, meet regulatory expectations, improve IT performance, and safeguard digital assets in a constantly shifting threat environment.

In the next chapters, we will look at how all these processes are to be combined in conducting audit interviews, site visits to the infrastructure hosted areas like server rooms, and completing the technical testing to get the required evidence for compliance with policies and frameworks, as we saw in this chapter. We will also see how to analyze audit findings and come out with an audit report that has actions and recommendations with owners and timelines.

Join our Discord space

Join our Discord workspace for latest updates, offers, tech happenings around the world, new releases, and sessions with the authors:

https://discord.bpbonline.com

Chapter 21

Interviews, Site Visits and Technical Testing

Introduction

An IT audit digs beneath the surface of your digital ecosystem to uncover hidden risks that do not show up in financial statements. It examines the operational health of your systems, spotlighting issues like aging firewalls, weak access management practices, or unaddressed security gaps in your cloud platforms that could quietly undermine your organization's resilience.

In this chapter, we will see the steps that are part of the IT audit process, where the auditors will be working on evaluating the ITSM process and controls. In IT auditing, the collection of sufficient and reliable evidence is essential for forming an accurate assessment of an organization's IT processes, control mechanisms, and governance framework. While reviewing documentation is a key initial step, it must be complemented with a range of techniques that bring deeper insight into day-to-day operations and surface risks not evident on paper. Among the most critical of these are interviews, site visits, and technical testing.

Structure

The chapter covers the following topics:

- Key concepts
- Implementation effectiveness of processes

- Audit interviews with all stakeholders
- Site visits for IT control areas
- Technical practices

Objectives

This chapter equips the readers with the tasks that happen during the IT audits. By the end of this chapter, readers will gain a comprehensive understanding of evidence-gathering techniques essential to conducting effective IT audits. They will be able to explain the value of using multiple approaches, including inquiry, observation, inspection, and re-performance, and choose the most appropriate techniques depending on audit objectives, risk levels, and the type of control being assessed. Readers will develop the capacity to gather audit evidence that is both sufficient and reliable, apply professional skepticism during evidence collection, and document procedures and findings in a clear, complete, and retrievable manner.

When it comes to interviews, readers will understand their purpose in clarifying IT processes, exploring undocumented practices, and verifying control operations. They will know how to prepare thoroughly by identifying objectives, relevant personnel, and interview questions. They will be equipped to conduct interviews professionally and objectively, corroborate responses with other audit evidence, and clearly document the outcomes, including any divergent views and necessary follow-up.

For site visits and observation, readers will grasp their significance in evaluating physical and environmental security and understanding IT operations as they unfold. During visits, they will be able to conduct structured observations, noting real-time practices and any deviations from documented procedures. These observations will be recorded thoroughly, with visual evidence where permitted, and assessed for their impact on system availability and logical security.

On the technical testing front, readers will differentiate among various testing approaches such as configuration reviews, vulnerability scans, and access rights assessments. They will learn how to leverage relevant tools and techniques effectively and document their work with sufficient detail to ensure clarity, traceability, and reproducibility.

Altogether, this learning equips auditors with a well-rounded toolkit to substantiate audit conclusions, enhance the credibility of their findings, and contribute meaningfully to organizational assurance and risk management.

Key concepts

In the context of IT audits, interviews, site visits, and technical testing form a foundational triad for gathering comprehensive, credible evidence. Each method brings a different lens through which auditors can assess the effectiveness of controls and the integrity of IT processes in both design and operation.

Interviews, as a key inquiry technique, allow auditors to engage directly with personnel involved in IT operations. These conversations uncover how processes are performed, who is responsible, and why particular approaches are taken. They also help evaluate the awareness and competence of individuals in fulfilling their control responsibilities. However, interviews are not conclusive on their own—they must be corroborated with objective evidence to support audit conclusions.

Site visits complement interviews by enabling auditors to observe IT operations and environmental controls directly. By physically examining facilities such as data centers or server rooms, auditors can verify that physical safeguards—like access controls, environmental monitoring, or backup protocols—are present and functioning. Observations provide tangible insight into how procedures are actually carried out, as opposed to how they are described in policy documents. Site visits are also valuable in detecting informal practices that deviate from formal procedures, which could suggest control weaknesses or operational risks.

Technical testing, often the most objective and conclusive form of audit evidence, involves the direct evaluation of system configurations, access rights, vulnerability exposures, and security mechanisms. This technique allows auditors to validate the operational effectiveness of controls by simulating or re-performing processes, analyzing logs, or using automated scanning tools. It often requires specialized expertise and the use of dedicated tools.

Controls assessments evaluate the strength and reliability of your internal defenses against real-world threats. They are designed to test whether safeguards, like strong password protocols, properly enforced access controls, and timely patch management, are not just in place but also effective in practice. When these defenses are tight enough to keep attackers out or limit damage, that is precisely the kind of success these evaluations aim to showcase.

These techniques enable auditors to move beyond stated procedures and policies, offering firsthand perspectives into how controls are actually applied and maintained in real-world settings. Interviews reveal practical insights from personnel, site visits allow observation of the IT environment, and technical testing provides empirical validation of control functionality. Together, these methods present a well-rounded, evidence-based picture of control design and effectiveness, strengthening the credibility and depth of audit findings.

Together, these techniques provide a multidimensional view of an organization's IT control environment. They reinforce one another—interviews lay the groundwork for what to observe or test, observations provide context for what is tested, and technical testing delivers hard evidence that validates or challenges what was heard or seen. A well-executed IT audit weaves these strands into a cohesive assessment, ensuring that conclusions are grounded in both narrative insight and empirical validation.

Implementation effectiveness of processes

In IT audits, the goal is not merely to verify the existence of processes around IT systems; it is to assess how effectively those processes are implemented. Auditors evaluate whether processes are actively followed, aligned with organizational goals, and operating efficiently.

In IT audits, a comprehensive review of an organization's security posture involves a blend of process assessment and technical validation. Console monitoring, scan reports, technical testing, and remediation practices are crucial components of this technical validation, offering objective evidence of control effectiveness and identifying vulnerabilities.

Review techniques involve non-intrusive evaluation of systems, applications, networks, policies, and procedures to identify potential security weaknesses. These methods also help collect background information that enhances the effectiveness of other assessment approaches. Since they do not directly interact with or alter the target environment, review techniques carry minimal risk of disrupting system operations.

The following table gives the different review techniques and the outcome of those reviews:

Technique	Capabilities
Documentation review	Evaluates policies and procedures for technical accuracy and completeness
Log review	Provides historical information on system use, configuration, and modification
	Could reveal potential problems and policy deviations
Ruleset review	Reveals holes in ruleset-based security controls
System configuration review	Evaluates the strength of the system configuration
	Validates that systems are configured in accordance with the hardening policy
Network sniffing	Monitors network traffic on the local segment to capture information such as active systems, operating systems, communication protocols, services, and applications
	Verifies encryption of communications
File integrity checking	Identifies changes to important files; can also identify certain forms of unwanted files, such as well-known attacker tools

Table 21.1: Review techniques

The following are steps on how IT auditors review the implementation effectiveness of processes around IT systems:

1. **Understanding the process landscape**: By identifying relevant processes interacting with IT systems, such as ITSM processes, information security processes, data management processes, SDLC processes, IT operations processes, vendor management, review documentation, etc.

2. **Techniques to assess implementation effectiveness**: Interviews where staff insights are gathered on how processes operate in practice, walkthroughs and observation, data analysis, metrics and reporting review, etc.

3. **Evaluation criteria for effectiveness**: Policy adherence, control operation, efficiency, maturity, strategic alignment, etc.

4. **Audit reporting and recommendations**: Highlight strengths, identify gaps and weaknesses, analyze root causes, and recommend improvements like updating procedures, strengthening oversight, etc.

A well-executed audit of process implementation effectiveness provides valuable assurance that IT systems are managed in line with both policy and practice. It helps organizations reduce operational risk, improve process maturity, and ensure that IT functions are actively contributing to security, efficiency, and strategic success.

Audit techniques

Assessing the security posture of systems and networks involves a wide array of technical testing and examination methods. This guide focuses on the most commonly employed techniques, which fall into three primary categories:

- **Review techniques**: These are primarily manual evaluations used to uncover vulnerabilities in systems, networks, applications, policies, and procedures. They include reviewing documentation, logs, system configurations, rulesets, and conducting file integrity checks or network sniffing.

- **Target identification and analysis techniques**: These methods are used to detect systems, services, ports, and potential vulnerabilities. While some may be performed manually, they typically rely on automated tools. Common approaches include network discovery, port and service scans, vulnerability assessments, wireless network scanning, and examining application security.

- **Target vulnerability validation techniques**: These techniques are used to confirm the presence of identified vulnerabilities. Depending on the skill level of the test team and the tools available, they can be manual or automated. Examples include password cracking, penetration testing, social engineering, and application-level security validation.

No single method provides a complete view of a system's security posture. Comprehensive assessments often combine multiple techniques. For instance, penetration tests typically build upon prior discovery and scanning activities to identify viable targets. Furthermore, there may be several technical ways to validate a given control, for example, confirming whether patch management processes are functioning properly.

There are many non-technical assessment methods, which can complement or even substitute technical techniques when appropriate. Physical security testing, such as attempting to bypass locks or badge readers, is used to expose vulnerabilities in access controls. Manual asset identification, carried out through physical inspections, asset inventories, or facility walkthroughs, is an alternative to network-based discovery. Non-technical methods are critical tools in certain contexts and should be considered alongside technical assessments to ensure a more holistic security evaluation.

Audit interviews with all stakeholders

Interviews play a pivotal role in ITSM audits. While documentation reviews and system data provide structural insights, interviews deliver qualitative depth, offering a clearer view of how ITSM processes function in reality. Interviews are instrumental in understanding the reasoning behind control design and in identifying potential gaps, inconsistencies, or undocumented practices. They offer a vital channel for obtaining qualitative insights that extend beyond formal documentation such as policies, procedures, or system records. Interviews enable auditors to gain a practical understanding of how ITSM processes are actually performed, assess the clarity of roles and responsibilities, evaluate staff awareness and competence, and uncover discrepancies between documented procedures and real-world execution.

Unlike static documentation reviews or system-based testing, interviews are dynamic and interpersonal. Their success depends not only on asking the right questions but also on the auditor's ability to build a neutral, respectful, and professional atmosphere that encourages openness. When conducted skillfully, interviews can reveal informal workarounds, unreported risks, or control deficiencies that might otherwise go unnoticed.

The reasons why interviews are indispensable:

- **Bridging the gap between documented and actual practices**: Policies, procedures, and runbooks describe how processes should operate. However, interviews reveal how they are actually executed. Variations often exist due to informal practices, outdated documentation, or workarounds. This distinction is especially important for dynamic processes like incident, problem, change management, and service request handling, where human behavior and communication significantly influence execution.

- **Providing context and organizational insight**: Unlike static documentation, interviews uncover the context and rationale behind operational choices. Auditors gain insights into why certain steps are followed, challenges teams face, how communication flows across teams (formal and informal), etc. This context helps identify the gaps as well as their root causes.

- **Understanding gaps and inconsistencies**: By engaging different roles, support staff, managers, service desk agents, and business users, auditors can spot misaligned expectations, inconsistent process execution, training gaps, or unclear responsibilities, etc. Such discrepancies often highlight areas needing improvement in policy clarity, control design, or communication.

- **Assessing culture and human factors**: ITSM is fundamentally driven by people. Interviews help auditors evaluate staff awareness of policies and responsibilities, organizational commitment toward ITSM practices, commitment to continual improvement and service quality, etc. These human elements are difficult to measure, but they are very important for assessing process maturity and effectiveness.

- **Discovering unwritten controls and hidden risks**: Not all controls are formally documented; some will be managed as operating processes, many times unwritten. Through interviews, auditors may uncover informal practices that effectively mitigate risk, undocumented vulnerabilities that staff are aware of but have not formally reported, etc. This can reveal unseen strengths or overlooked weaknesses in the control environment.

- **Validating and corroborating evidence**: Interview responses can either reinforce or challenge findings from document reviews and system analysis. Consistent alignment across sources boosts confidence in control effectiveness. Contradictions signal the need for deeper investigation. This way of collaborative review will ensure accuracy and completeness in audit conclusions.

- **Building rapport and encouraging collaboration**: Well-conducted interviews foster trust and openness, promoting a collaborative tone for the audit. This encourages staff to share the challenges faced while managing the operations, and increases the likelihood that audit recommendations will be accepted and implemented.

- **Directing further investigation**: Interview findings often guide auditors to areas that require deeper technical testing or targeted document review, sharpening the audit focus and improving efficiency.

The following steps outline best practices for preparing, conducting, and documenting ITSM audit interviews. They cover key considerations such as selecting appropriate stakeholders, designing effective interview questions, navigating conflicting accounts, and validating responses with supporting evidence. When applied thoughtfully, these practices ensure that interviews produce reliable, insightful, and actionable findings that enhance the overall quality and impact of the audit. Let us look at the steps:

1. **Prepare thoroughly**: Understand the interviewee's role and tailor questions accordingly.

2. **Use open-ended questions**: Encourage detailed, thoughtful responses.

3. **Practice active listening**: Pay attention to both verbal and non-verbal cues; ask follow-ups.

4. **Stay objective**: Avoid assumptions or leading questions.

5. **Document clearly**: Record key responses, observations, and insights.

6. **Cross-verify statements with policy statements**: Confirm findings through supporting documentation and evidence.

Interviews in ITSM audits go beyond uncovering what is documented or what systems show; they reveal the how and why behind service delivery. This human-centric approach provides a comprehensive understanding of process effectiveness, operational challenges, and cultural factors, making interviews a vital tool in delivering meaningful, actionable audit outcomes.

Auditors should note, however, that individuals may modify their behavior when observed, making triangulation with other evidence sources essential. Auditors are expected to maintain professional skepticism, use a balance of open and closed questions, and be alert to potential biases in verbal responses.

Site visits for IT control areas

Site visits are a vital aspect of IT audits, especially when evaluating the effectiveness of physical and environmental controls and observing operational processes in real-time. While documentation reviews and technical data analysis form the foundation of most audits, being physically present on-site offers critical insights and validation that cannot be achieved remotely.

Key areas where site visits add value are as follows:

- **Physical and environmental security**: The most direct and essential area where on-site observation is mandatory to review the effectiveness of controls.

    o **Data centers and server rooms**: To confirm the presence and functionality of physical access mechanisms such as card readers, biometric scanners, and mantraps. To assess whether access logs are maintained and reviewed regularly, and verify that only authorized personnel have access. And to check for proper systems managing temperature, humidity, fire suppression, and water leakage. To observe the arrangement of cabling, grounding, and the presence of redundant power sources like **uninterruptible power supply (UPS)** or generators.

    o **Security infrastructure**: To evaluate physical security, including sturdy enclosures, surveillance systems, alarm coverage, and protection against tampering.

    o **Fire safety**: To ensure the availability and maintenance of fire extinguishers, clearly marked exits, and safety signage.

    o **Network racks and communication rooms**: To assess similar controls as those in data centers, ensuring consistent application across locations.

    o **Off-site backup locations**: To verify the physical security and environmental protections at remote storage facilities.

- **IT operations and monitoring**: Site visits offer direct observation of how operational controls function.

    o **Service desk operations**: To observe how incidents and service requests are handled, recorded, and escalated. To evaluate the service desk environment, communication practices, and tool usage.

- o **Network operation centre (NOC) and security operation centre (SOC) environments**: To review live dashboards, real-time alerts, and staff response protocols to understand how effectively issues are monitored and addressed.

- o **Backup activities**: To validate that backup media are handled securely and rotated as per policy. To observe off-site transfer procedures where applicable.

- **IT asset management**: Helps the auditor verify asset management practices, live assets, and retired assets.

  - o **Inventory validation**: To physically inspect a sample of IT assets (servers, laptops, network devices) and match them against inventory records to confirm accuracy.

  - o **Secure disposal**: To observe data destruction practices to ensure compliance with security policies.

- **Review of physical documentation**:

  - o **Paper records**: To examine physical logs, visitor registers, access request forms, and other relevant hardcopy documentation.

  - o **Network and system diagrams**: To ensure that physical infrastructure diagrams match the actual layout and reflect current configurations.

- **Environmental awareness and housekeeping**:

  - o **General maintenance**: To evaluate the tidiness and organization of IT-controlled spaces, which may indicate the broader control culture of the organization.

  - o **Disposal of confidential material**: To observe how sensitive physical waste (e.g., printed data, access badges) is handled and disposed of.

Site visits are indispensable as they help in the validation of controls, understanding deviations, contextual understanding, identification of unreported risks, compliance requirements, evidence corroboration, etc. They provide tangible verification that physical and procedural controls are in place and functioning as described in documentation. On-site observation often reveals informal workarounds, outdated practices, or security lapses not documented or reported, such as tailgating into secure areas or unauthorized access. Seeing the physical layout and interactions between systems gives auditors a more comprehensive view of the environment, interdependencies, and potential points of failure. Some risks, like exposed wiring, overloaded power outlets, or insufficient environmental monitoring, are only evident through physical inspection. Many standards explicitly require physical validation of control areas as part of audit assurance activities. Site visits strengthen the audit process by verifying whether the stated policies and procedures are practically enforced.

Best practices for conducting site visits can be captured as follows:

- **Plan ahead**: Define objectives, areas of focus, and coordinate with stakeholders in advance.

- **Obtain necessary access**: Ensure security clearances, escort arrangements, and facility permissions are in place.

- **Use structured checklists**: Ensure thoroughness by using standardized checklists tailored to each environment.

- **Document rigorously**: Take notes, and, where permitted, capture photographs or videos to support observations.

- **Maintain professionalism**: Be respectful of operational constraints, staff, and business continuity.

- **Cross-verify findings**: Validate observations against other audit evidence, such as interviews, logs, or system reports.

Site visits elevate IT audits from theoretical evaluations to practical, verifiable assessments. They provide critical insights into physical controls, operational discipline, and real-world risks, adding a layer of assurance that cannot be achieved through documentation alone. For auditors, they are an essential tool for forming a complete, accurate, and actionable picture of the IT control environment.

Technical practices

Technical testing (e.g., penetration testing, vulnerability scanning, configuration reviews) is considered proactive because its main goal is to identify weaknesses and potential vulnerabilities before they are exploited by an attacker. It is about finding problems before they cause harm. Console monitoring (reviewing logs, alerts, dashboards from **security information and event management systems (SIEM)**, firewalls, **intrusion detection system (IDS)** or **intrusion prevention systems (IPS)**, etc.) is primarily considered reactive because its main function is to detect security events, anomalies, or incidents as they are happening or after they have occurred. It is about responding to situations once they manifest.

Proactive technical testing and reactive console monitoring are not mutually exclusive; they are complementary and essential for a robust ITSM strategy. Technical testing identifies and fixes vulnerabilities before they are exploited, reducing the attack surface. Console monitoring acts as the sensors, detecting when proactive measures might have failed or when new, unknown threats emerge, allowing for a rapid response.

A mature security program integrates both. Proactive testing minimizes the likelihood of successful attacks, and robust reactive monitoring ensures that if an attack does occur, it is detected and responded to swiftly, minimizing damage. Ignoring one in favor of the other leaves significant gaps in an organization's defense.

When selecting techniques for a given assessment, organizations must weigh several key considerations. These include clearly defining the objectives of the assessment, identifying which categories of techniques are best suited to achieve those goals, and choosing the most appropriate methods within each category. Additionally, certain techniques may depend on the perspective from which the assessment is conducted, such as whether it is performed internally or by an external party, which can influence the selection of tools and methodologies used.

This section outlines the specific types of technical assessments to be performed, such as network scanning, asset discovery, and penetration testing. It should clearly state whether the creation, modification, execution, or installation of test files is permitted as part of the testing process, and specify what must be done with those files after testing concludes (e.g., removal, archival, or restoration). Any other relevant details concerning the testing of the organization's systems and infrastructure should also be documented here. It is essential to describe the planned activities in sufficient detail to ensure that all stakeholders understand what has been approved and what outcomes should be anticipated during the engagement.

Technical testing in IT audits

Testing involves direct interaction with IT systems and networks to uncover security weaknesses. It can be performed enterprise-wide or focused on specific systems, using techniques such as vulnerability scanning and penetration testing to identify exploitable flaws. These methods not only highlight where systems may be vulnerable, but also help assess how well controls are being enforced in areas like patching, password enforcement, and system configurations. While testing offers a clearer and often more precise view of technical security risk than standard reviews or documentation assessments, it comes with a higher potential for disruption. Depending on the method used, tests can range from benign network scans to more invasive activities, like sending custom packets designed to trigger weaknesses. Since these tests involve interacting with live environments, there is always a risk of unintended side effects, including system crashes or service outages. Organizations must therefore weigh the trade-off between depth of insight and acceptable operational impact, typically avoiding known disruptive techniques unless explicitly approved.

Technical testing involves actively probing systems and networks to find vulnerabilities, confirm the effectiveness of controls, and simulate attack scenarios. It goes beyond automated scans by often requiring human expertise and a nuanced understanding. **Penetration testing (Pen test)** is a simulated cyberattack against an organization's IT systems to find exploitable vulnerabilities and assess the effectiveness of its security controls. This can be internal, external, web application, or wireless pen-testing. Configuration review is a manual or automated verification of security configurations on servers, network devices, databases, and applications against security hardening guides and best practices. Access control testing verifies that user access rights align with the principle of least privilege, tests segregation of duties, and attempts to bypass access controls. **Wireless (Wi-Fi)** network testing assesses the security of Wi-Fi networks, including encryption, authentication, and rogue access point detection.

The role of technical testing in identifying vulnerabilities can be captured as follows:

- **Beyond known vulnerabilities**: Unlike automated scans that primarily look for known vulnerabilities, penetration testing can uncover complex, chained vulnerabilities, business logic flaws, and zero-day exploits that automated tools might miss.

- **Exploitability confirmation**: Technical testing confirms whether identified vulnerabilities are actually exploitable in the real-world context, providing a more accurate assessment of risk.

- **Control bypass testing**: Auditors attempt to bypass existing security controls on firewalls and ports to determine their true effectiveness.

- **Real-world attack simulation:** Simulating actual attack scenarios provides insights into an organization's detection and response capabilities.

- **Assessing impact**: By successfully exploiting vulnerabilities, auditors can demonstrate the potential impact of a breach (e.g., data exfiltration, system compromise).

- **Comprehensive coverage**: Combining various technical testing methods provides a holistic view of the attack surface, from network perimeter to individual applications.

It is also important to recognize the limitations of testing. Time constraints and scope boundaries often mean that not all systems or attack paths can be evaluated. Whereas real-world attackers operate without such constraints, testers must work within predefined limits. Moreover, some risks, particularly those tied to misaligned policies or poor configuration governance, may not surface through technical testing alone. For this reason, combining technical tests with broader audit methods, such as documentation reviews and interviews, provides a more holistic and realistic picture of an organization's overall security posture.

Scan reports in IT audits

Securing IT infrastructure is more critical than ever in today's business environment. Weaknesses across systems, networks, and applications can serve as entry points for cyber threats. One of the most effective defenses against such risks is vulnerability scanning of your IT infrastructure. This proactive method helps detect and address potential security flaws before malicious actors can exploit them. This guide outlines the essentials of IT infrastructure vulnerability scanning, why it matters, and how organizations can effectively implement it to strengthen their cybersecurity posture.

Scan reports are outputs from automated security scanning tools that identify potential vulnerabilities, misconfigurations, and non-compliance issues across an organization's IT environment. Common types of scans include vulnerability scans, web application scans, configuration scans, port scans, etc.

The scanning process in IT audits provides the following verifications:

- **Vulnerability identification**: Scan reports are a primary source for identifying technical vulnerabilities. Auditors review these reports to understand the organization's exposure to known threats.

- **Risk prioritization**: Reports typically classify vulnerabilities by severity (e.g., critical, high, medium, low) using scores like **Common Vulnerability Scoring System** (**CVSS**). Auditors use this to prioritize remediation efforts and assess the overall risk profile.

- **Evidence of weaknesses**: Scan reports provide concrete, technical evidence of security weaknesses that might not be apparent through policy review or interviews alone.

- **Tracking remediation progress**: Auditors can compare historical scan reports to current ones to assess the effectiveness of vulnerability management programs and track remediation efforts over time.

- **Compliance validation**: Many regulations mandate regular vulnerability scanning. Auditors verify that scans are performed as required and that findings are addressed.

- **Input for penetration testing**: Scan reports often serve as a starting point for more in-depth manual penetration testing, guiding testers to areas with known weaknesses.

IT infrastructure vulnerability scanning done by automated tools helps to detect security weaknesses across an organization's systems, networks, and applications. These vulnerabilities may include unpatched software, misconfigured firewalls, outdated components, weak credentials, or other exploitable gaps that could be targeted by cyber attackers. The core objective of vulnerability scanning is to proactively uncover and remediate these issues before they can be exploited, helping to ensure a secure and resilient IT environment.

Console monitoring in IT audits

Console monitoring refers to the continuous or periodic review of logs, alerts, and activity dashboards generated by various IT systems and security tools. This includes operating system logs, application logs, network device logs, SIEM systems, management consoles, etc.

Auditors review logs to identify evidence of unauthorized access attempts, malware activity, policy violations, failed logins, and other security anomalies. Logs provide objective evidence of whether security controls are operating as intended. For example, firewall logs can confirm that only authorized traffic is allowed, and access logs can show if access attempts from unauthorized users were blocked. Many compliance frameworks require logging and monitoring of critical systems. Auditors check if logging is enabled, logs are retained for the required period, and regular reviews are performed. Logs create an immutable audit trail of activities, which is vital for forensic investigations in case of a breach. Auditors assess the integrity and completeness of these audit trails. Console monitoring helps auditors understand normal system behavior and identify deviations, contributing to a more robust risk assessment.

Special attention is paid to logs related to privileged user accounts (e.g., administrators, root users) to detect potential abuse or unauthorized actions.

Monitoring and alerting play a vital role in the IT audit process by equipping organizations with real-time visibility into their systems. These mechanisms help identify emerging security threats as they occur, allowing for swift response and containment. By proactively detecting issues, they significantly reduce the chances of prolonged outages, data compromise, and the potential fallout to the organization's reputation.

There are several types of monitoring that organizations can implement as part of their IT audit process. These include:

- **Network monitoring**: This type of monitoring involves tracking network traffic to detect potential security threats, such as unauthorized access or malware.

- **System monitoring**: This type of monitoring involves tracking system performance to detect potential issues, such as system crashes or hardware failures.

- **Application monitoring**: This type of monitoring involves tracking application performance to detect potential issues, such as errors or slow response times.

- **Database monitoring**: This type of monitoring involves tracking database performance to detect potential issues, such as data breaches or corruption.

Monitoring and alerting play an essential role in the IT audit process, serving as frontline defenses against emerging security threats. These mechanisms allow organizations to detect issues as they occur, enabling prompt action to minimize the impact of potential breaches, system outages, or operational disruptions. When implemented effectively, monitoring and alerting not only bolster incident response capabilities but also support regulatory compliance, strengthen risk mitigation efforts, and contribute to better overall system stability and performance.

Remediation practices in IT audits

Remediation refers to the process of addressing and fixing the vulnerabilities, control deficiencies, and non-compliance issues identified during an IT audit or security assessment. It is the phase of fixing issues. During an IT audit, experts apply a combination of manual evaluations and automated tools to assess the strength and resilience of an organization's digital infrastructure. This involves examining critical areas such as access controls, encryption standards, firewall configurations, intrusion detection mechanisms, staff awareness initiatives, and incident response strategies. The objective is to uncover vulnerabilities, assess control effectiveness, and deliver actionable recommendations to enhance the organization's security posture.

The best practices for remediation can be captured as follows:

- **Prioritization based on risk**: Not all findings have equal importance. Remediation efforts should be prioritized based on the risk level of the vulnerability (severity, likelihood of exploitation, business impact) and regulatory requirements. Critical and high-risk findings should be addressed first.

- **Clear ownership and accountability**: Assign clear owners (individuals or teams) for each remediation task with defined responsibilities and deadlines.

- **Detailed action plans**: Develop specific, actionable remediation plans for each finding, outlining the steps to be taken, resources required, and estimated completion time.

- **Root cause analysis**: For significant findings, investigate the underlying cause (e.g., lack of policy, insufficient training, systemic misconfiguration) to prevent recurrence, rather than just applying a band-aid fix.

- **Verification and retesting**: After remediation, the auditor (or an independent party) must verify that the vulnerability has been successfully addressed. This often involves re-running scans or performing targeted re-tests to confirm the fix.

- **Change management integration**: Ensure that remediation activities follow established change management processes to prevent unintended negative impacts on IT systems or services.

- **Documentation**: Document all remediation efforts, including the actions taken, dates, personnel involved, and verification results. This is crucial for audit trails and demonstrating due diligence.

- **Continuous improvement**: Incorporate lessons learned from remediation into the **Information Security Management System** (**ISMS**) and ongoing security practices to continuously improve the organization's security posture.

- **Communication**: Maintain open communication with stakeholders, providing regular updates on remediation progress and any challenges encountered.

- **Management reporting**: Provide regular reports to management on the status of remediation, highlighting overdue items and residual risks.

Whether conducting configuration reviews or penetration testing, the goal is to determine whether the technical safeguards in place are functioning as intended and sufficiently mitigating risk. Given its invasive nature and potential to impact system performance, technical testing must be carefully scoped, authorized, and coordinated with IT operations.

Once audit findings have been communicated, taking timely and effective remediation action is essential to strengthening the organization's security posture and addressing identified weaknesses. The remediation process begins by evaluating and ranking the vulnerabilities based on their potential business impact and the likelihood of exploitation. Priority should be given to high-risk issues to quickly reduce the exposure to cyber threats.

Following prioritization, the necessary security enhancements must be implemented. This might include applying patches, refining access controls, updating security policies, or introducing new technical safeguards as outlined in the audit's recommendations. After implementation, it is important to maintain ongoing oversight by actively monitoring the newly established controls and assessing their effectiveness. Regular reviews and periodic reassessments help ensure that remediation measures are functioning as intended and continue to protect the organization as threats evolve and systems change.

Remediation practice gives one of several ways to respond to risks assessed during scanning, technical tests, or console monitoring. There are four types of risk responses, captured as follows:

- **Accept**: Accept the risk as is, such as by relying on existing security controls to prevent risk or vulnerability exploitation or by determining that the potential impact is low enough that no additional action is needed.

- **Mitigate**: Reduce the risk by eliminating the vulnerabilities (e.g., patching the vulnerable software, disabling a vulnerable feature, or upgrading to a newer software version without the vulnerabilities) or deploying additional security controls to reduce vulnerability exploitation.

- **Transfer**: Reduce the risk by sharing some of the consequences with another party, such as by purchasing insurance or by replacing conventional software installations with **software as a service (SaaS)** usage, where the SaaS vendor or managed service provider takes care of patching.

- **Avoid**: Ensure that the risk does not occur by eliminating the attack surface, such as by uninstalling the vulnerable software, decommissioning assets with the vulnerabilities, or disabling computing capabilities in assets that can function without them.

By default, an organization accepts the risk posed by using its software. Software could have vulnerabilities in it at any time that the organization does not know about, and sometimes, previously unknown vulnerabilities are exploited in a zero-day attack. Once a new vulnerability becomes publicly known, risk usually increases because attackers are more likely to develop exploits that target the vulnerable software.

Patching as a remediation process

Applying a patch, performing an update, or upgrading to a newer version of an operating system or software that no longer contains known vulnerabilities is the only risk remediation strategy that can fully eliminate the vulnerability while maintaining the software's functionality. However, implementing these changes immediately is not always feasible.

Several factors may delay patching or upgrading, including:

- **Patch unavailability**: A vulnerability may be disclosed before a patch is ready. It could take days, weeks, or even months before the vendor releases an appropriate fix.

- **End-of-life software**: If the software is no longer supported by the vendor, no patch will be issued, leaving the vulnerability unaddressed by default.

- **Operational constraints**: Organizations may need to wait for a scheduled maintenance window, conduct compatibility testing, coordinate updates across integrated systems, or provide user training on new features or interfaces.

- **Patching priority**: The challenge of having only limited resources may require prioritizing critical patches over others.

- **Vendor-imposed update delays**: In highly regulated industries, especially where human safety is involved, manufacturers may mandate delayed updates to allow time for thorough testing and certification. Bypassing this process could void warranties or prevent future support.

- **Compliance considerations**: Regulatory or contractual obligations may restrict immediate adoption of updated software.

Even when patching or upgrading is technically possible, organizations can also opt for alternative risk responses depending on their risk appetite, business priorities, and compliance obligations. These alternatives could include compensating controls, risk acceptance, or temporary mitigation measures, as outlined earlier.

Patch management plays a vital role in maintaining the security, stability, and functionality of an organization's IT environment. Regularly applying updates helps protect systems from vulnerabilities, ensures consistent performance, and enables access to new features that align with organizational priorities. It is also a key component in demonstrating and maintaining compliance with various security and privacy standards. Beyond improving security, patch management can enhance system efficiency and compatibility, particularly when adapting software to support newer hardware platforms.

Patch management varies based on whether the system is standalone or part of a broader enterprise network. For standalone machines, operating systems and applications typically perform routine automated checks for available updates. When new patches are detected, they are often downloaded and installed with minimal user intervention. In contrast, enterprise network environments prioritize uniformity and control, opting for centralized patch management solutions. These systems leverage dedicated server software to scan network-connected devices for missing patches, download necessary updates, and systematically deploy them across endpoints. This centralized approach ensures consistency, simplifies oversight, and reduces the risk of individual systems being left unpatched or misconfigured.

Maintenance plans

Proactive upkeep is a fundamental principle in IT, aiming to address potential issues before they lead to costly breakdowns. In organizations managing hundreds or even thousands of devices, adopting a preventive maintenance strategy is not just beneficial; it is essential. For IT teams overseeing hardware like laptops, desktops, and peripheral systems, a structured maintenance approach helps ensure smooth and reliable performance.

By implementing preventive maintenance across the infrastructure, organizations can significantly reduce unexpected outages and major system failures that may hinder business continuity. Moreover, for businesses that depend on effective IT asset management, such a strategy plays a crucial role in maximizing asset lifespan and performance efficiency.

IT preventive maintenance involves proactively servicing your technology assets before problems arise. By anticipating and addressing potential issues in advance, organizations can avoid costly disruptions and system failures. A preventive maintenance checklist serves as a reference guide during this process. It typically includes tasks such as updating hardware, operating systems, and software, cleaning physical components like cables and devices, removing inactive user profiles, and refining the checklist itself based on previous outcomes.

To ensure effectiveness, it is important to clearly define which IT assets need maintenance, set specific thresholds or conditions for their upkeep, and determine how often each task should be performed. Assigned personnel follow documented procedures and adjust the checklist after each maintenance cycle to capture lessons learned and evolving needs. This approach can be scheduled based on time, such as monthly updates, or triggered by usage intensity, for example, when a high-demand device reaches a certain workload threshold. Whether time-driven or condition-based, preventive maintenance helps extend the lifespan of IT equipment, improve system reliability, and support seamless business operations. The following figure gives the steps that are to be taken in the planned maintenance activity:

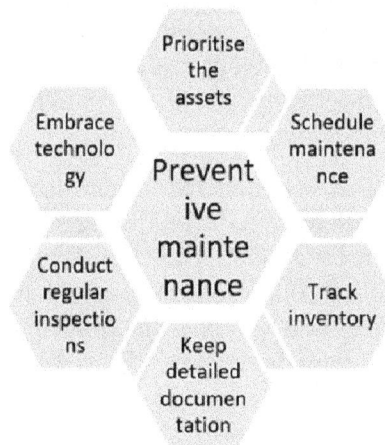

Figure 21.1: Steps in preventive maintenance

An effective preventive maintenance program consists of a range of proactive activities tailored to an organization's budget, technical capabilities, equipment requirements, compliance needs, and operational objectives.

Five key components of preventive maintenance can be elaborated as follows:

- **Proper asset installation**: The foundation of preventive maintenance lies in the correct installation of hardware and components. Improper setup can compromise asset performance and lead to unplanned outages. Adhering to manufacturer guidelines ensures reliable operation from day one, reducing the likelihood of early-stage failures.

- **Routine inspections**: Regular visual and technical inspections help detect early signs of wear, damage, or potential failures. The depth of inspection varies based on asset criticality, ranging from basic visual checks to detailed assessments using diagnostic tools. Establishing **standard operating procedures (SOPs)** empowers teams to identify and report issues systematically, enabling timely intervention.

- **Systematic testing**: Preventive testing goes beyond surface-level checks to assess performance under simulated or real workloads. Accurately interpreting this test data is crucial for identifying underlying issues early.

- **Scheduled servicing**: Regular servicing activities include firmware and software updates for devices like routers, switches, and controllers. Antivirus scans, patching of known vulnerabilities, and general system optimization are essential to maintaining performance and cybersecurity readiness.

- **Calibration**: Calibration ensures that devices deliver accurate readings and outputs. This is particularly important for certification and compliance. Devices such as displays, printers, scanners, and environmental sensors (e.g., for temperature or humidity) are calibrated against reference standards. Consistent calibration reduces data errors and enhances system reliability.

Preventive maintenance is critical for all businesses, but it is especially vital for organizations with remote or distributed teams. Since remote operations rely heavily on networked IT infrastructure, ensuring asset reliability and uptime is key.

Before starting any maintenance activity, it is important to have a pre-maintenance configuration checklist in place. This includes:

- Defining maintenance objectives.

- Identifying critical systems and assets.

- Scheduling downtime or access windows.

- Backing up configurations and data.

- Notifying stakeholders and end users.

- Preparing necessary tools and software.

- Ensuring compliance with internal SOPs and external standards.

By following a structured approach, preventive maintenance becomes a powerful tool for minimizing downtime, extending asset life, and ensuring optimal performance across your IT environment.

As we have seen, this chapter will help auditors develop an awareness of potential limitations or biases in interview-based evidence, along with strategies to address them. They may have learned to prepare strategically by identifying sensitive or critical infrastructure locations and access requirements. The readers now understand when these methods are warranted and how to plan and execute them without disrupting operations, securing the proper approvals and coordination. Interpreting test results to uncover vulnerabilities or misconfigurations, readers will be able to develop actionable recommendations.

In summary, console monitoring, scan reports, technical testing, and robust remediation practices form a continuous cycle of identification, assessment, and improvement within IT audits. They transform audit findings from theoretical observations into practical, actionable insights that strengthen an organization's information security posture.

Interviews bring forward the human dimension of IT operations, offering qualitative insight into how responsibilities are carried out, how controls are perceived, and where practical challenges may arise. Their value lies in the auditor's ability to foster open dialogue, ask purposeful questions, and interpret responses with a healthy degree of professional skepticism.

Site visits add crucial context by allowing auditors to directly observe the physical and environmental conditions surrounding IT operations. From validating security measures to witnessing operational procedures in action, site observations help bridge the often-present gap between documented controls and daily practice, while also surfacing potential risks that are not evident on paper.

Technical testing rounds out the triad by delivering objective, verifiable data about the design and operating effectiveness of IT controls. Whether through scanning for vulnerabilities, reviewing configurations, analyzing logs, or executing re-performance procedures, these activities provide solid, evidence-based confirmation (or refutation) of control functionality.

When used collectively, these techniques deliver a well-rounded understanding of the IT control environment. Interviews explain intent and accountability, site visits validate implementation, and technical tests measure actual effectiveness. A modern IT audit must do more than review documentation; it must actively engage with people, processes, and technology to assess risk and reliability in practice. As organizations continue to face increasingly complex technology landscapes, the skillful and coordinated use of these techniques remains fundamental to delivering meaningful, actionable audit outcomes.

Conclusion

In this chapter, we learnt about the different activities and techniques that have to become part of the audit activity. Audit has three phases, which can be classified as *before audit*, *during audit*, and *after audit*. We saw the different processes in ITSM in *Chapters 5 to 18*, which help us understand the activities the various teams in IT operations have to manage during their day-to-day operations. These help us understand the scope of the audit and the applicable processes that need to be reviewed during the audit. *Chapters 19, 20 and 21* talked about what has to be focused on during the audit. This chapter showcased the different processes that have to be part of the audit plan and audit schedule.

The effectiveness of an IT audit is greatly enhanced by the thoughtful integration of interviews, site visits, and technical testing. Together, these core techniques form a dynamic framework for examining the real-world implementation, consistency, and reliability of IT controls and processes. We saw the importance of technical testing, console monitoring, patching process, and maintenance process that are mandatory in an ITSM process. The review of policy should give inputs to remediation timelines, patching timelines, and the maintenance process. The maintenance process may also be part of the **business continuity plan** (**BCP**) drills. This helps us proactively address the outages that may impact the operations.

In the upcoming chapter, we will see how the audit report has to be structured and how the audit findings and follow-up actions can be articulated. The follow-up actions have to be practical and should have owners and expected completion timelines. The next chapter will address the after-audit phase, and this has to be done with a focus on the creation of value to the auditee and the auditee organization. We will be able to see how ITSM is the backbone operation of any organization; the ITSM processes may be managed in-house or managed by partner organizations, but each process plays an important role in ensuring successful business operation.

Join our Discord space

Join our Discord workspace for latest updates, offers, tech happenings around the world, new releases, and sessions with the authors:

https://discord.bpbonline.com

CHAPTER 22

Audit Findings and Actionable Audit Report

Introduction

This chapter delves into how IT audits have become vital tools for delivering assurance, managing risk, and refining IT governance frameworks in today's complex business environment. We will see how the true impact of an IT audit emerges through the thoughtful interpretation of the findings based on data and evidence gathered during the audit, and the creation of a meaningful, action-focused audit report.

A fundamental characteristic of any audit is its structured and methodical nature, encompassing activities such as defining the scope, developing control mechanisms, collecting and recording evidence, and reporting the outcomes. The process also highlights the importance of thorough documentation, which ensures transparency, traceability, and accountability throughout the audit lifecycle.

Here, we focus on those two essential phases: deep analysis and strategic reporting. It emphasizes that even the most thorough audit data lacks value until it is presented contextually and communicated in a way that helps in decision-making. We will explore how auditors convert technical observations, control evaluations, and procedural insights into clear, structured statements in the report.

Additionally, we will examine the principles behind crafting an audit report that does more than list issues. A truly effective report serves as a roadmap, translating findings into feasible recommendations that promote risk mitigation, enhance organizational resilience, and support regulatory alignment. The goal is to equip stakeholders with the understanding and confidence needed to take meaningful corrective action, ultimately advancing the organization's cybersecurity maturity, efficiency, and adaptability in an ever-changing digital landscape.

Structure

The chapter covers the following topics:

- Key concepts
- Audit findings
- Root cause analysis
- Actionable audit report with timelines
- Plans for re-audit as required

Objectives

By the end of this chapter, readers will be able to clearly understand the purpose and importance of audit findings, recognizing their role within the broader audit lifecycle and their influence on risk management, compliance, and operational improvement. They will be able to differentiate between observations, findings, and recommendations, and accurately categorize audit insights while transforming raw data into meaningful conclusions. The focus here is on the after-audit phase and the actions that need to be taken once the audit is concluded. Audits have to be conducted keeping the principle, *audit is not about fault finding, but it is about fact finding*, in mind. Equally important is the principle of independence; the audit function must operate autonomously within the organization, without influence from other departments or business units. Positioned as the third line of defense, it follows the operational and risk management layers, offering impartial evaluations of internal controls and practices.

Readers will gain the ability to apply analytical techniques to interpret audit evidence, synthesizing information from technical observations, testing outcomes, and interview feedback to uncover root causes, identify control weaknesses, and detect areas of non-compliance. They will also learn to assess the materiality and impact of findings by evaluating their risk level, business significance, frequency, and potential for exploitation.

This chapter will equip readers to prioritize issues for reporting and remediation using risk-based criteria to identify which findings require urgent attention or escalation. In addition, they will develop the skills to craft audit reports that are clear, concise, and actionable, presenting technical details in a way that is accessible to both technical and non-technical audiences within the auditee organization. Readers will also be trained to formulate practical and targeted recommendations that are realistic, effective, and aligned with the organization's resources and strategic goals. Through guided practice, they will enhance their ability to communicate audit results collaboratively, fostering constructive dialogue with stakeholders during remediation planning and post-audit follow-up.

Finally, the chapter will help readers appreciate the strategic role of audit reports as catalysts for change, enabling improved governance, strengthened compliance, and informed decision-making across the organization.

Key concepts

A strong foundation in IT auditing requires a thorough understanding of what constitutes an audit finding. Findings may include observations, nonconformities, or control gaps, and recognizing their validity depends on clear, consistent criteria. Auditors should be able to distinguish isolated incidents and recurring or systemic issues to accurately represent the organization's risk landscape.

Analyzing audit findings involves more than reviewing raw data; it requires correlating various sources of evidence, such as technical test results, interview insights, and observed practices. The objective is to interpret these elements collectively to uncover the root causes behind control failures and to distinguish whether shortcomings lie in the design of controls or their actual operation. Evaluating the significance of audit findings involves assessing their severity, the likelihood of exploitation, and their potential impact on the organization's strategic goals and regulatory obligations. This analysis should align with the organization's risk appetite and support prioritization efforts based on a risk-driven and business-aligned approach.

To ensure clarity and usability, findings should be systematically structured and categorized. Organizing them by domains such as access control, data security, or IT governance, and mapping them to relevant standards or frameworks like ISO 27001, NIST, or COBIT, can enhance traceability and aid in addressing them efficiently. Grouping related issues helps stakeholders understand the broader context and reduces duplication in remediation efforts. Recommendations based on audit findings should be practical and tailored to business realities. Translating technical risks into terms meaningful to business leaders ensures buy-in, while recommendations should ideally be Specific, Measurable, Achievable, Relevant, and Time-Bound. Balancing technical depth with feasibility and available resources is key to ensuring that recommendations are actionable and effective.

The audit report itself serves as the formal output of the audit process and must be thoughtfully developed. It typically includes an executive summary, details on scope and methodology, clear documentation of findings and recommendations, and a concluding overview. The language and structure should be adapted to suit both technical stakeholders and senior management, ensuring that the content is objective, clear, and logically organized. Once the report is finalized, effective communication of results becomes critical. During debriefs or post-audit discussions, auditors must convey findings constructively, engage stakeholders in open dialogue, and address any resistance or disagreement with professionalism and clarity. These conversations often play a vital role in fostering ownership and commitment to remediation.

Follow-up is an equally important phase. Audit teams should ensure that management responses are documented, remediation timelines are tracked, and escalation protocols are followed for unresolved high-risk findings. Depending on the audit framework, follow-up audits or continuous monitoring mechanisms may also be initiated to verify the closure of issues. Finally, audit findings should not merely conclude the audit—they should catalyze continuous improvement. Lessons learned can inform updates to internal policies, drive security awareness and training efforts, and enhance the design of IT controls. Over time, this process strengthens overall governance and supports more risk-informed strategic decisions.

Audit findings

An independent and objective auditor remains free from bias, personal or professional influence, and conflicts of interest. This means the auditor is not part of the organization's regular operations, has no personal or financial stake in the audit results, and maintains impartiality throughout the audit process. In addition to independence and objectivity, **International Standards Organization (ISO)** standards emphasize the importance of auditor competence. Auditors must possess the appropriate knowledge, skills, and experience necessary to carry out the audit effectively.

In the context of IT audits, audit findings represent the primary outcomes of the evaluation process. These findings highlight discrepancies, control weaknesses, non-compliance issues, or inefficiencies identified during the assessment of an organization's IT systems, processes, and controls. In essence, they capture what is not working as intended, or what could be improved, based on the evidence gathered.

As we have seen, before starting an audit, it is essential for the audit team to clearly define the scope of their work. This is where the concept of the audit universe becomes indispensable. The audit universe represents the full range of components within an organization that are subject to examination, such as business processes, IT systems, applications, servers, databases, personnel, operations, and research activities. It serves as a comprehensive inventory of areas relevant to the organization's functioning, helping auditors determine which processes should be prioritized for assessment.

Without a well-defined audit universe, both auditors and management may struggle to organize, structure, or rank audit priorities effectively. It also acts as a roadmap for identifying critical business processes that directly support organizational goals. For entities aiming to adopt a risk-based audit approach, the presence of an audit universe is non-negotiable. Without a clear picture of what processes and activities fall under the organization's umbrella, conducting a meaningful and targeted audit becomes nearly impossible.

When developing criteria specifically for an audit engagement, practitioners must ensure that these criteria are appropriate, particularly that they are objective, comprehensive, and measurable. Custom criteria are often presented as assertions tailored to the requirements of a particular user. While established frameworks may serve as standardized benchmarks for assessing internal controls, a user might instead create criteria to address a unique need, such as defining levels of authorized approval.

An audit report should clearly present all relevant observations, findings, conclusions, and recommendations, along with estimated remediation costs, where possible. Recommendations and conclusions should be accompanied by management's response, outlining how each issue will be addressed. Practitioners are expected to gather details on the proposed remedial actions and the timeline for their implementation.

To ensure clarity, completeness, and actionability, audit findings are typically structured using a standardized framework, commonly known as the 5 C's model:

- **Condition (what is)**: This element outlines the factual issue or observed deficiency. It describes the existing situation as discovered during the audit. An example of this is that the quarterly user access reviews for critical financial systems are not being conducted as required.

- **Criteria (what should be)**: This refers to the benchmark or standard, such as a policy, procedure, regulation, or best practice, against which the condition is assessed. An example here is the internal policy mandates quarterly access reviews for critical applications, aligned with ISO 27001:2022 control A.5.18.

- **Cause (why this occurred)**: This identifies the underlying reason for the deviation. It might relate to gaps in process design, lack of ownership, inadequate tools, or human error. An example of this is the absence of a centralized tracking system and a lack of accountability for access review tasks, which has led to irregular execution.

- **Consequence (outcome)**: This describes the potential or actual impact of the issue if left unaddressed, such as increased risk, regulatory non-compliance, or operational inefficiency. An example is failure to conduct access reviews, which increases the risk of unauthorized access, which may result in data breaches or regulatory penalties.

- **Corrective action or recommendation (going forward)**: This provides a specific, actionable response to resolve the issue or mitigate its associated risk. An example is introducing an automated tool to schedule and monitor access reviews, assigning a responsible owner, and providing training for all reviewers as a *follow-up* action.

Ultimately, audit findings are the tangible, evidence-based results of an IT audit. When documented clearly and prioritized appropriately, they serve as the foundation for actionable recommendations that guide organizations toward strengthened controls, reduced risk, and improved IT governance.

If disagreements arise between practitioners and the auditee regarding any recommendation or comment, the audit documentation may reflect both viewpoints, including the rationale behind each perspective. The auditee's formal response may be included within the body of the report, attached as an appendix, or referenced in a cover letter. Ultimately, executive leadership or governing bodies responsible for the audit function will determine which position to endorse.

Functional areas of audit findings

Each point should be framed for maximum visibility, drawing attention to critical insights with minimal ambiguity. Careful formatting, using consistent structure, headings, and emphasis, helps ensure that key messages stand out and that the report supports informed decision-making at all levels of the organization.

Audit findings typically fall into one or more of the following functional areas:

- **Information security controls**: This category includes issues related to access control (e.g., weak passwords, excessive user privileges), vulnerability management (e.g., missing patches, unaddressed critical findings), network security (e.g., exposed ports, poor segmentation), encryption (e.g., use of outdated algorithms), monitoring (e.g., missing **security information and event management** (**SIEM**) capabilities), and incident response (e.g., inadequate planning or testing).

- **IT operations and service management**: Findings here involve deficiencies in change management (e.g., unauthorized or undocumented changes), backup and recovery (e.g., lack of restoration testing, weak definitions for recovery time objective), problem management (e.g., unresolved recurring incidents), performance and availability (e.g., systems near capacity without alerts), and configuration management (e.g., inconsistent baselines, undocumented changes).

- **IT governance and compliance**: Common issues include outdated or missing policies and procedures, absence of formal risk assessments, non-compliance with regulatory standards, unclear roles and responsibilities, and inadequate oversight of third-party service providers.

- **Application development and maintenance**: This category captures weaknesses such as the lack of secure development practices, poor input validation leading to vulnerabilities, and insufficient testing (especially security testing) prior to application deployment.

It is important that the audit report clearly indicates when criteria have been uniquely developed for the engagement. Practitioners should evaluate whether these criteria could mislead the intended audience and, if necessary, provide additional context or clarification. Furthermore, if the criteria originate from management, external validation should be obtained and explicitly referenced in the report to support their legitimacy and transparency.

Framing the audit report

As we have seen, an IT audit is a detailed evaluation of an organization's information technology environment, encompassing its systems, policies, and operational processes. The main goals of this audit are to evaluate the effectiveness of IT controls, verify adherence to applicable regulatory standards, uncover potential risks, and provide actionable recommendations for improvement. In doing so, IT audits typically cover areas such as vulnerability management, data protection strategies, and governance practices within the IT domain.

Audit practitioners must ensure that all documentation related to the work performed is completed promptly, with sufficient detail and accuracy. Any information or evidence needed to support audit conclusions or opinions must be gathered before the audit report is finalized. Work papers from the engagement should clearly reflect preparation and review dates to establish a transparent timeline of activities.

Oversight of these work papers rests with IT audit management, which is responsible for regulating access to authorized individuals. If any external auditors request access, approval must be granted by executive management along with those responsible for governance. For any other external parties seeking access, authorization should also involve executive management and governance representatives, supported by legal counsel to ensure compliance with confidentiality and regulatory standards.

Assessment results play a critical role in shaping the implementation of **IT service management** (**ITSM**) controls, as well as in guiding the development of associated plans, including strategies, frameworks, and action milestones. Following an assessment, system owners and shared control providers, together with organizational decision-makers such as authorizing officials, senior information security officers, and system or application owners, review the findings detailed in security and privacy assessment reports, alongside updated risk documentation. These stakeholders collaboratively determine the appropriate course of action for addressing any weaknesses or deficiencies identified.

Assessment findings are typically categorized as either *satisfied* or *other than satisfied*, a structure that offers transparency and helps prioritize remediation efforts. This classification allows organizations to methodically assess risk levels and respond according to their strategic priorities. Findings marked as *other than satisfied* will fall under major NCs or minor NCs and will be taken further to corrective measures. Each such finding undergoes careful evaluation to determine its significance and whether further action is required.

Senior leadership may need to intervene to ensure that organizational resources are allocated effectively, focusing efforts on systems that support essential operations or those posing the highest level of risk. Ultimately, these findings and the corresponding responses, grounded in the updated risk assessment, prompt revisions to foundational documentation used for authorization decisions. These key artifacts include updated operational controls, assessment reports, and actionable milestones that ensure the system's continued alignment with organizational security and privacy standards.

Key categories of IT audit findings

The purpose of presenting audit findings is to deliver a clear and purposeful message to the audited organization. When initiating the audit report, the auditor must ensure that contributors are aligned on the intended outcomes of the report. If the audit impacts the business, its recommendations should inspire leadership to take meaningful action. Findings should be communicated with clarity and precision, free from unnecessary detail or jargon. The language and tone must be accessible to readers with varying degrees of technical knowledge and experience.

During an audit, auditors assess both compliance with regulations and non-conformance with specified requirements. It is normal for audits to uncover some level of issues, and classifications help determine the severity and response. Multiple findings may emerge, typically falling into one of the following three categories:

- **Major non-conformance** (**NC**): A systematic failure or significant deficiency, either as a single incident or a combination of several similar incidents in part of the quality system, or the lack of implementation of such a part, governed by applicable standards. Several NCs identified against one requirement of the relevant standards can represent a total breakdown of the system and thus be considered a major NC.

  o Significantly impacts the organization's ability to meet its intended objectives.

  o Indicates possible systemic failure when multiple minor issues point to the same root cause.

  o Suggests weak process control or potential product/service non-compliance.

  o Includes violations of legal or regulatory requirements (e.g., ISO standards).

- **Minor NC**: An isolated or sporadic lapse in the content or implementation of procedures or records that could reasonably lead to a systematic failure or significant deficiency of the system if not corrected. If a pattern of minor NCs occurs over successive assessments, it may represent a systematic failure or significant deficiency of the system, and a major NC shall be issued.

  o Has limited or no impact on the achievement of management system goals.

  o Typically, does not affect product or service quality directly.

  o Represents isolated or low-risk deviations from requirements.

- **Observations also called opportunity for improvement** (**OFI**): An area of concern, a process, document, or activity that is currently conforming but may, if not improved, result in a non-conforming system, product, or service. An OFI is simply an opportunity to improve your business system. It is not necessarily an item that will lead to future non-conformance if not addressed.

- o   Advisory remarks are meant to strengthen the management system.

- o   May signal potential risks or early-stage deficiencies.

- o   Based on the auditor's industry experience and benchmarking insights.

- o   Useful for preventive action and long-term improvement.

- **Noteworthy efforts (EF)**: Positive findings related to defined processes that perform better than expected.

The primary purpose of documenting audit findings is to communicate a clear, targeted message to the audited organization. While preparing the audit report, auditors must ensure that contributors grasp the intended impact of the information being presented. If the report influences business strategy or operations, it should be compelling enough to encourage leadership to act on the recommendations. Addressing audit findings depends on the internal policies of the organization; there will be timelines defined to address the different types of findings. These timelines will be arrived at based on the risks that arise from the deviation impacting the IT operations.

Tailoring the message to the audience is essential, particularly in light of the organization's culture. Whether the recipients are collaborative, compliance-driven, or part of a cross-functional team, the report must resonate with them. Findings should be expressed with clarity and precision, free from unnecessary elaboration or technical clutter. The report should be accessible and easy to understand across varying levels of expertise. Every finding must be articulated in straightforward language and formatted to emphasize key insights, ensuring that attention is drawn to the most critical points with minimal distraction. The goal is to make the report not just informative but also actionable and engaging.

Root cause analysis

In IT audits, identifying an audit finding is only the first step. To effectively address a problem and prevent its recurrence, it is crucial to perform **root cause analysis (RCA)**. RCA is a systematic process for identifying the underlying reasons for a problem or an audit finding, rather than just treating the symptoms. Without RCA, organizations risk repeatedly addressing the same issues, leading to wasted resources, continued exposure to risk, and a failure to achieve true improvement in their IT control environment.

Understanding the importance of RCA in the context of IT audit findings is critical for any organization aiming for lasting improvement and strong IT governance. While audit findings highlight issues, it is RCA that uncovers the deeper, systemic causes behind them. Without RCA, remediation efforts are likely to be surface-level, temporary fixes that address symptoms rather than the true problem. This approach increases the risk of repeated failures.

We can see why RCA is essential while addressing audit findings:

- **Prevents recurrence**: Addressing the root cause ensures the problem does not simply reappear later. If a symptom is fixed as a one-off action (e.g., patch one server), but does not address *why* it was unpatched (e.g., no patch management process), corrective action will not be completed and will not be effective.

- **Efficient resource allocation**: By understanding the fundamental cause, resources can be directed to the most effective solutions, rather than working in a continuous firefighting mode.

- **Drives systemic improvement**: RCA helps identify systemic weaknesses in processes, policies, tools, or training that contribute to findings, leading to more sustainable improvements across the organization.

- **Enhances learning**: It provides valuable lessons learned that can be incorporated into future planning, development, and operational activities.

- **Strengthens controls**: By identifying control deficiencies at their core, RCA enables the implementation of more robust and effective preventative or detective controls.

- **Better decision-making**: Understanding the *why* behind a finding allows management to make more informed decisions about risk acceptance, resource investment, and strategic direction.

By systematically applying RCA, organizations can achieve several key outcomes. They shift from reactive problem-solving to a proactive stance, where recurring issues are prevented by addressing their root causes. This strategic focus helps avoid repeated disruptions and enhances operational stability. RCA also ensures that resources are allocated efficiently. Instead of repeatedly spending time and effort fixing recurring problems, teams can implement long-term solutions that deliver lasting impact. Through RCA, organizations can identify weaknesses across processes, policies, technologies, and personnel, enabling targeted improvements that support continuous growth and maturity in IT practices. Moreover, RCA contributes to building a more resilient IT environment, one that can withstand threats, adapt to change, and maintain consistent performance. In essence, to derive real value from IT audits, RCA must be treated as a critical, integral step. It is the foundation for effective remediation, strategic improvements, and long-term risk mitigation across the IT landscape.

While various RCA techniques exist, some are particularly suited for IT audit findings. Common methodologies for RCA in audits are given as follows:

- **The 5 Whys method**: This is one of the simplest yet most effective techniques. You repeatedly ask *why?* until you get to the core reason. It helps peel back layers of symptoms to reveal the underlying cause.

  o **Problem statement**: Critical security patches are not consistently applied to all production servers.

  o **Why 1**: Because the patch management team does not have a complete inventory of all production servers.

  o **Why 2**: Because the asset management database is not regularly updated with new server deployments.

o **Why 3**: Because there is no mandatory process for development/operations teams to register new servers in the asset database.

o **Why 4**: Because the organization lacks a clear, enforced policy for asset lifecycle management.

o **Why 5**: Because there is insufficient management oversight and accountability for maintaining an accurate asset inventory.

These five questions boil down to the root cause—lack of an enforced asset lifecycle management policy and insufficient management oversight.

- **Fishbone diagram**: This visual tool helps categorize potential causes of a problem. It branches out from the main problem (the head of the fish) into main categories of causes (the bones), and then further sub-causes. Common categories in IT might include people, process, technology, environment, management, data, etc.

  o **Problem statement**: Frequent unauthorized changes are occurring in the production environment.

  o **Bones**: Lack of training on the change process, low awareness of policy, and insufficient staff. Undocumented change process, no clear approval workflow, emergency changes bypass controls, and no post-implementation review. No automated change management system, lack of audit trails, and weak access controls. Lack of clear policies, poor oversight, and no accountability for unauthorized changes. High pressure to deploy quickly, complex system interdependencies. By brainstorming specific causes under each bone, the team can identify the most probable root cause(s).

A typical fishbone diagram can be seen as follows, which shows the steps and flow for doing a causal analysis:

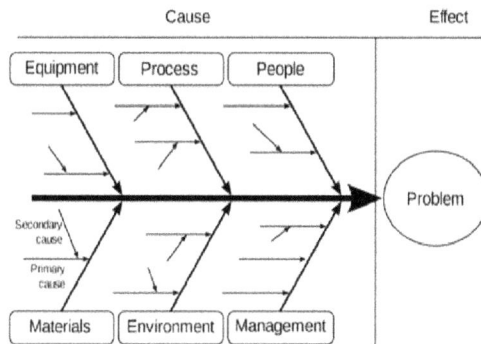

Figure 22.1: Sample fishbone diagram

- **Fault tree analysis (FTA)**: A top-down, deductive approach that graphically represents the logical relationship between a top-level undesired event (the audit finding) and the various combinations of failures or circumstances that can lead to that event. More complex findings where multiple factors must combine to cause the issue. For instance, analyzing why a critical system experienced an outage despite having backups.

- **Barrier analysis**: Focuses on identifying and analyzing the breakdown of *barriers* (controls) that were supposed to prevent the finding. Useful for security-related findings where a control failed. For example, if a data breach occurred, barrier analysis would examine which layers of defense (firewall, access control, encryption) failed to prevent or detect it.

Root cause analysis

RCA offers a wide array of methodologies that enable organizations to tackle problems and operational inefficiencies with precision and clarity. Tools such as the fishbone diagram provide visual insights into contributing factors, while more hands-on techniques like the 5 Whys and FTA help teams proactively dig into underlying causes. When applied thoughtfully, these strategies empower teams to diagnose problems accurately, make evidence-based decisions, and foster a culture of ongoing improvement.

The following are the major steps in performing RCA for IT audit findings:

1. **Define the problem (audit finding)**: Clearly state the finding as observed.

2. **Gather data**: Collect all relevant information related to the findings, like system logs, policies, procedures, interview transcripts, previous audit reports, and incident records.

3. **Identify immediate causes and symptoms**: What happened just before the finding became apparent?

4. **Ask why (repeatedly)**: Apply the chosen RCA methodology (e.g., 5 Whys, Fishbone Diagram) to drill down to the fundamental reasons.

5. **Identify root cause(s)**: Determine the deepest underlying factors that, if addressed, would prevent recurrence. There may be more than one root cause.

6. **Develop corrective actions**: Based on the root cause(s), propose specific, actionable recommendations that address the fundamental issues, not just the symptoms.

7. **Implement and monitor**: Implement the corrective actions and then monitor their effectiveness to ensure the problem is truly resolved and new issues are not introduced.

8. **Introduce preventive actions**: Include actions to address the root cause so that the problems do not occur again in the landscape.

By consistently applying RCA to IT audit findings, organizations can move from a reactive *fix-it* mentality to a proactive *prevent-it* approach, significantly enhancing their overall IT control environment and resilience.

Actionable audit report with timelines

Assessing the effectiveness of existing controls and pinpointing potential vulnerabilities allows your organization to take a proactive approach to risk management and minimize exposure. Although absolute compliance cannot be guaranteed, conducting thorough reviews and implementing appropriate security measures, including those discussed previously and others as needed, will significantly strengthen your organization's ability to defend against major threats.

The fundamental principles and requirements for internal auditing in ISO standards are defined across several key documents, including ISO 19011, which provides guidelines for auditing management systems, as well as within the specific clauses of the relevant ISO standards, such as ISO 9001 for quality management, ISO 27001 for information security management, ISO 14001 for environmental management, etc.

Certain organizations establish an internal audit function to support the achievement of their objectives by delivering independent and objective evaluations of operations and highlighting opportunities for improvement. This function systematically reviews and assesses the organization's activities, controls, and processes to pinpoint weaknesses and offer actionable recommendations to enhance overall performance. Internal audits play a vital role in helping organizations maintain compliance, strengthen operational efficiency, and proactively identify and manage risks.

Some of the key principles and requirements for conducting audits as per ISO standards are elaborated in the following figure:

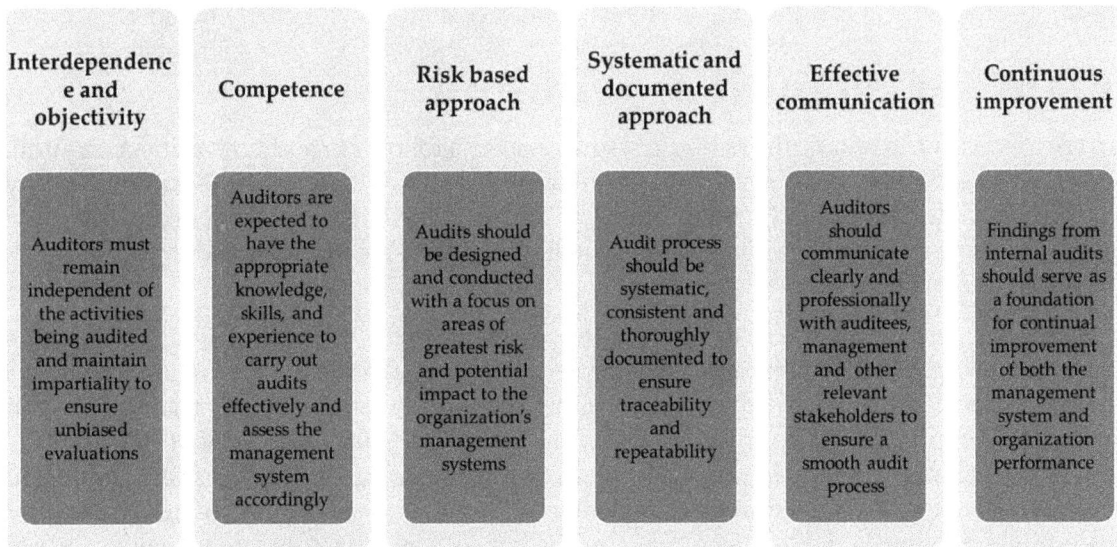

Interdependence and objectivity	Competence	Risk based approach	Systematic and documented approach	Effective communication	Continuous improvement
Auditors must remain independent of the activities being audited and maintain impartiality to ensure unbiased evaluations	Auditors are expected to have the appropriate knowledge, skills, and experience to carry out audits effectively and assess the management system accordingly	Audits should be designed and conducted with a focus on areas of greatest risk and potential impact to the organization's management systems	Audit process should be systematic, consistent and thoroughly documented to ensure traceability and repeatability	Auditors should communicate clearly and professionally with auditees, management and other relevant stakeholders to ensure a smooth audit process	Findings from internal audits should serve as a foundation for continual improvement of both the management system and organization performance

Figure 22.2: Core principles for audit in ISO standards

An organization can adopt many ways to respond to audit findings. They can choose not to respond, react positively to the results, make amendments immediately, or disagree with the conclusions. The key is to make the response clear and concise in a formal manner. Corrective actions refer to measures taken to resolve or lessen the impact of identified control weaknesses or non-conformities within an organization. A corrective action plan outlines a structured approach, detailing specific steps intended to achieve the resolution of these issues. To ensure these actions are effective, the auditee must conduct a RCA to determine the underlying factors contributing to the non-conformity or control failure, thereby enabling a targeted and thorough remediation.

The responsibility for carrying out corrective actions lies with the auditee. Upon completion, a compliance report or certificate is typically issued to confirm that some or all of the deficiencies have been addressed, either fully or in part. This report should include updated audit evidence that validates the remediation, which is then reviewed by the audit team during follow-up. If the corrective measures are deemed sufficient and fully resolve the noted issues, the audit team will mark the findings as closed in the follow-up documentation or issue tracker, confirming the effectiveness of the remediation.

After identifying audit findings, the next step is to formulate a structured action plan to resolve the issues effectively. This plan should clearly outline the necessary remediation steps, assign responsibilities to appropriate individuals or teams, establish realistic yet time-sensitive deadlines, and specify the resources required to carry out each task. To streamline efforts, the issues should be prioritized based on their severity and potential impact on the organization, with critical risks addressed first. Delegating tasks to team members with clear accountability ensures a smooth implementation process, while defined completion timelines promote urgency and maintain focus on resolving each concern in a timely manner.

Plans for re-audit as required

In the lifecycle of IT audits, the re-audit, also known as a follow-up audit or verification audit, is a vital phase that confirms whether previous audit recommendations have been successfully implemented and associated risks properly mitigated. This step goes far beyond checking boxes; it provides tangible evidence that remediation efforts are working and that IT controls have been strengthened.

The effectiveness of audit activity is ultimately judged by the tangible impact it has on the organization, particularly through the implementation of audit recommendations. It is therefore essential to regularly review and validate how these recommendations influence and enhance the control environment. Auditors typically use two main approaches to monitor the status of recommendations. The first is through formal follow-up audits. These are conducted to confirm whether the agreed-upon remediation actions have been fully executed. The auditor reexamines previously deficient controls, conducting both adequacy and effectiveness tests to determine if corrective measures have been sustained over time. As a result, follow-up audits are not immediate and are usually scheduled after sufficient time has passed to allow proper implementation.

The second, and more commonly applied, method focuses on control adequacy checks. Here, management provides the audit team with selected examples to verify that corrective actions have taken place. Known as an audit follow-up, this method is widely practiced by internal audit functions and facilitated by most modern audit management software. It allows for ongoing reviews and consistent tracking of implementation progress, giving clear visibility into how the control environment is evolving. External auditors often rely more heavily on traditional follow-up audits. Based on personal experience in external audit, annual audits typically include a thorough review of previous findings, especially if the scope has changed. The audit report may feature a summary table that shows the current status of earlier issues. Although less common, some internal audit teams adopt a similar format during re-audit cycles. Even if a dedicated follow-up audit is not listed in the audit plan, the expectation remains that audit teams will still track the implementation of key recommendations.

To be effective, a re-audit must follow a well-defined, objective, and disciplined approach.

The purpose of a re-audit is to:

- Verify that earlier findings have been addressed thoroughly.
- Confirm the improved effectiveness of revised controls.
- Ensure risks flagged in the original audit are now acceptable.
- Promote accountability by following up on agreed corrective actions.
- Foster continuous improvement across the organization's IT environment.
- Demonstrate due diligence to stakeholders and regulators.

In short, the re-audit helps in verifying that the corrective actions are taken to mitigate the findings that arose from the audit. All action owners, as marked in the audit report, should be present to share the details of the remediation efforts taken and how this will ensure that these findings will not occur again.

A well-crafted re-audit plan should:

- Define its scope by concentrating on unresolved or high-risk items from the original audit.
- Prioritize findings by risk rating, including a review of related or modified controls.
- Confirm that remediation efforts tackle the root cause, not just the symptoms.

Timing and frequency of re-audits are often driven by remediation deadlines, the severity of findings, scheduled audit cycles, or specific events (such as a major system upgrade).

To verify remediation, auditors use a mix of methods, including:

- Reviewing documentation such as change records, patching reports, updated procedures, and training logs.
- Conducting technical re-testing, including vulnerability scans, configuration checks, log reviews, and penetration tests where needed.

- Interviewing stakeholders involved in remediation to understand what changed and how.

- Observing operational processes directly to confirm implementation of procedural fixes.

- Analyzing data to validate long-term control effectiveness.

Roles and responsibilities in the re-audit process include:

- The audit team is responsible for planning and execution.

- The auditee or management is tasked with providing documentation and access.

- Executive sponsors, who oversee and endorse action on remaining issues.

The re-audit process is critical in verifying the remediation actions taken to address the audit findings. This works as the feedback in the **Plan–Do–Check–Act (PDCA)** loop, the act step once the check step is completed.

Re-audit report

The re-audit report classifies each prior finding as closed, partially closed, or still open. It also includes supporting evidence, notes residual risks, and offers updated recommendations. Occasionally, new related findings may emerge and should be documented separately.

The process is generally broken down into four phases:

1. **Planning**: Review original findings, define scope, and align resources.

2. **Execution**: Collect evidence, test controls, and assess outcomes.

3. **Reporting**: Draft the report, confirm factual accuracy, and gather responses.

4. **Follow-up**: Monitor unresolved findings and prepare for future reassessments.

Throughout, best practices like maintaining independence, basing conclusions on solid evidence, fostering collaboration, documenting verification activities, and weighing costs against risk help ensure the re-audit delivers meaningful value. Ultimately, the re-audit ensures that issues flagged in previous assessments are not just acknowledged—they are resolved. It is a key driver of improved resilience, control maturity, and trust across the organization's digital landscape.

ISACA's IT audit framework

The standards in ITAF contain key aspects designed to assist the IT audit and assurance practitioner. ITAF standards are periodically reviewed for continual improvement and amended as necessary to keep pace with the evolution of the IT audit and assurance profession.

Reporting as per ISACA's **IT audit framework (ITAF)** contains the following standards:

- **1401.1**: IT audit and assurance practitioners shall provide a report to communicate the results of each engagement.

- **1401.2**: IT audit and assurance practitioners shall ensure findings in the audit report are supported by sufficient and appropriate evidence.

- **1402.1**: IT audit and assurance practitioners shall monitor and periodically report to those charged with governance and oversight of the audit function (e.g., the board of directors and/or the audit committee) management's progress on findings and recommendations. The reporting should include a conclusion on whether management has planned and taken appropriate, timely action to address reported audit findings and recommendations.

- **1402.2**: Progress on the overall status of the implementation of audit findings should be regularly reported to the audit committee, if one is in place.

- **1402.3**: Where it is determined that the risk related to a finding has been accepted and is greater than the enterprise's risk appetite, this risk acceptance should be discussed with senior management. The acceptance of the risk (particularly failure to resolve the risk) should be brought to the attention of the audit committee (if one is in place) and/or the board of directors.

Audit follow-up process

The audit follow-up process can be understood through three key dimensions: structure, evaluation criteria, and reporting. Let us look at them in detail:

- **Structure**: Establishing a clear framework for the follow-up process is essential to ensure that auditors can effectively track the implementation of audit findings. As emphasized in various frameworks, while sound governance does not guarantee success, having a structured, evidence-based approach significantly enhances the likelihood of meaningful remediation.

  This framework should clearly define roles and responsibilities, specify the tools used for monitoring, and outline communication protocols. Incorporating these elements into a formal procedure, such as one documented within the organization's audit manual, helps maintain consistency. Both auditors and auditees must be well-versed in this procedure to support seamless execution.

- **Evaluation criteria**: After an audit report is issued, organizations typically formulate action plans to address recommended improvements. In alignment with professional standards, auditors are tasked with tracking the progress of these plans and regularly updating both management and the audit committee.

To perform this effectively, auditors should apply well-defined evaluation criteria that guide the information needed to assess each recommendation. This assessment must tie directly into the organization's wider governance, risk management, and internal control functions to ensure that the full value of the audit is realized.

- **Reporting**: Even though both auditors and management recognize that audit follow-up is a core responsibility, a lack of clear evaluation criteria can result in reporting that is disconnected from governance and control frameworks.

  To bridge this gap, internal audit teams should collaborate with management to establish a shared understanding of the evaluation benchmarks and tailor reports to reflect the organization's unique priorities. The frequency and format of reporting should be agreed upon and integrated into the audit team's communication plan to ensure transparency and accountability across all levels.

Thorough follow-up procedures are essential to the effectiveness of any audit. After the initial audit concludes, it becomes critical to verify that recommended actions are not only being implemented but are delivering the intended results. This stage transforms audit findings into meaningful change, marking the point at which the audit's impact is truly realized.

Progress monitoring requires a structured and ongoing process, one that includes routine status checks, updates, and periodic reevaluation. A simple handoff of recommendations is not enough; auditors must maintain close collaboration with the auditee, helping navigate challenges, adapt strategies, and ensure objectives stay on track. This ongoing dialogue often includes multiple stakeholders, each bringing a distinct set of priorities to the table. For example, a financial controller may focus on reducing costs, while a department leader may emphasize streamlining operations. Aligning these varying perspectives is key to creating a well-rounded and successful follow-up process.

ISO 20000 certification process

Any ISO certification offers value that goes far beyond simply obtaining a certificate. It reflects an organization's dedication to globally accepted standards, a culture of continuous improvement, and operational excellence. Achieving certification builds credibility and inspires trust among stakeholders, including customers, regulators, and business partners, by verifying adherence to international benchmarks. It also enhances competitiveness, often serving as a prerequisite for entering new markets, securing government contracts, or forming strategic alliances with larger enterprises.

Moreover, ISO certification often aligns with legal and regulatory requirements, helping demonstrate compliance and reducing the likelihood of fines or legal issues. It fosters greater customer satisfaction by reinforcing quality consistency and responsiveness to client needs, while simultaneously strengthening governance and encouraging a performance-driven culture.

Internally, certification promotes employee engagement by clarifying processes, encouraging training, and driving improvement, all of which reduce uncertainty and support a culture committed to excellence. At its core, the ISO methodology is built on the PDCA cycle, creating a mindset focused on ongoing enhancement and adaptability.

The ISO 20000 certification audit is a structured process carried out by an accredited **certification body (CB)** to verify whether an organization's **service management system (SMS)** meets the standard's requirements. Let us look at the steps in detail:

1. **Organizational pre-audit preparation**: Before external auditing begins, the organization must lay a solid foundation.

   a. Familiarize with ISO 20000 standard requirements in detail.

   b. Conduct a gap analysis internally (or with expert guidance) to detect discrepancies between current practices and standard expectations.

   c. Develop or refine the SMS to address identified gaps, establishing documented policies, processes, roles, and controls.

   d. Perform internal audits to ensure conformity and uncover any unresolved issues prior to external review.

   e. Hold management reviews to evaluate SMS effectiveness and ensure top-level oversight and commitment.

   f. Gather evidence such as documented processes, audit results, and review records to prove compliance.

2. **Stage 1 audit, documentation and readiness review**: The first formal check by the CB focuses on preparedness.

   a. Review SMS documentation, including policies, internal audit results, and process descriptions.

   b. Confirm the scope of certification.

   c. Interview key personnel to understand SMS implementation.

   d. Evaluate readiness for stage 2 and identify gaps needing correction.

   e. Deliver a stage 1 audit report, listing observations and non-conformities that must be addressed beforehand.

3. **Stage 2 audit, main certification assessment**: This in-depth evaluation confirms the SMS is effective and operational.

   a. Conduct on-site assessments (or remote as agreed) to observe practices and verify evidence.

   b. Interview staff across functional areas to gauge awareness and execution.

   c. Verify process implementation, focusing on real-world service delivery.

   d. Evaluate continual improvement efforts, including response to previous audit findings.

   e. Apply sample testing of documentation and activities.

   f. Issue a stage 2 audit report, highlighting any major or minor non-conformities requiring remediation.

4. **Certification decision and issuance**: Once remediation is complete, the CB reviews all evidence.

   a. Evaluate audit findings and corrective actions through an independent review panel.

   b. Grant certification if requirements are fulfilled. The ISO 20000 certificate is valid for three years.

5. **Surveillance audits (ongoing monitoring)**: Annual audits ensure continued compliance and effectiveness.

   a. Verify SMS consistency and responsiveness to improvement opportunities.

   b. Focus reviews on high-risk areas, past issues, and operational maturity.

   c. Maintain certification if no major issues are found and minor ones are quickly addressed.

6. **Re-certification audit (after 3 years)**: A full reassessment validates long-term commitment and system resilience.

   a. Conduct a deep dive into the SMS, similar to stage 2.

   b. Tailor depth based on system maturity, stability, and historical performance.

   c. Renew certification for another three years if compliance is confirmed.

Continuous improvement through PDCA happens throughout all phases. The PDCA methodology is embedded, ensuring that the organization's service management continually evolves to meet new challenges and expectations.

Conclusion

In summary, the culmination of an IT audit, from its early planning and data-gathering stages to the final reporting, reaches its most critical and transformative phases in the analysis of audit findings and the delivery of an actionable audit report. Far from being procedural formalities, these stages are where raw data is distilled into strategic insight and operational direction. A thorough analysis goes beyond surface-level observations to uncover the root causes of deficiencies, evaluate their potential business impact, and prioritize them based on risk and relevance. This process ensures that the audit remains focused on addressing the most significant threats to the organization, rather than becoming mired in less critical issues that could dilute its effectiveness.

The audit report, when thoughtfully crafted, becomes the vehicle for communicating this intelligence. Rather than simply listing problems, it presents clear, structured, and actionable recommendations, explaining what needs to be addressed, why it matters, and how remediation can be achieved. In doing so, the report becomes a decision-making tool, enabling leadership to allocate resources wisely and implement meaningful improvements. It bridges the divide between technical findings and strategic governance, turning audit results into actionable change. Ultimately, the value of an IT audit is not defined by the volume of issues it identifies, but by the positive transformation it enables. When findings are analyzed with depth and audit reports are delivered with clarity and purpose, audits evolve from routine assessments into catalysts for stronger governance, reduced risk, and lasting organizational resilience in an ever-changing digital landscape. As we saw in the previous subsection, ISO's global recognition means that the ISO certification serves as an international badge of professionalism, helping organizations elevate their reputation and expand their reach across borders.

Successfully completing a stage 2 audit marks a major achievement, signaling that the organization's SMS meets the requirements of ISO certification. However, this accomplishment is not the end; it is the launch point for an ongoing commitment to excellence. What follows is an intensive cycle of reviewing and resolving audit findings, participating in regular surveillance audits, performing internal evaluations, and continuously refining the SMS. These efforts are essential not only to preserve certification but also to drive sustained improvements in service quality and operational performance.

In the next chapter, we will conclude the IT audit process: the scope definition, the pre-audit phase, the during-audit phase, and the after-audit phase.

Join our Discord space

Join our Discord workspace for latest updates, offers, tech happenings around the world, new releases, and sessions with the authors:

https://discord.bpbonline.com

CHAPTER 23
Evolving with the Audit Landscape

Introduction

Information technology (IT) audits have transformed from routine compliance checks into powerful strategic tools. Today, they help organizations protect digital assets, enhance operational performance, and ensure that technology initiatives align closely with business objectives. An IT audit is defined as a systematic evaluation of an organization's IT infrastructure, policies, and operations, aimed at ensuring security, efficiency, and regulatory compliance. The audit process typically includes planning, risk assessment, control evaluation, vulnerability testing, reporting, and follow-up actions. Depending on the organization's needs, audits may focus on areas such as systems and applications, network security, compliance standards, data integrity, or disaster recovery planning.

The benefits of IT audits are wide-ranging. They help organizations mitigate risk by identifying and addressing vulnerabilities before they become serious threats. They also support regulatory compliance by ensuring alignment with standards such as the **General Data Protection Regulation (GDPR)**, **Health Insurance Portability and Accountability Act (HIPAA)**, or the **International Standards Organization (ISO)**, etc., thereby reducing the risk of penalties and reputational harm. Audits can reveal inefficiencies within systems and workflows, which in turn lead to cost savings and improved productivity. Additionally, they provide strategic insights that support informed IT investment and digital transformation efforts. By demonstrating accountability and transparency, IT audits also help build confidence among customers, partners, and regulatory bodies.

Structure

The chapter covers the following topics:

- Key concepts

- Core of IT auditing

- ITIL compliance

- ISO 9001, ISO 27001, ISO 20000 compliance

- ISACA IT audit framework and COBIT

Objectives

By the end of this chapter, readers will possess a comprehensive understanding of IT auditing, beginning with its foundational principles, objectives, and how it differs from other audit types, such as financial or operational audits. They will grasp the integral role IT plays in business governance, recognizing the importance of sound IT controls and governance practices in supporting organizational performance and managing risks. Readers would have been equipped to design and execute IT audits, using risk-based approaches to perform fieldwork, collect audit evidence, and evaluate control effectiveness in key areas like cybersecurity, data integrity, access controls, and change management. Readers will learn how to write clear, actionable audit reports that translate technical findings into meaningful, business-relevant insights and recommendations. They will also gain awareness of emerging risks stemming from advances in cloud computing, **artificial intelligence** (**AI**), privacy regulations, and digital transformation, along with how these trends are reshaping IT audit practices. Ultimately, readers will evolve into strategic advisors, moving beyond a compliance mindset to add value, foster innovation, and strengthen resilience across the enterprise.

Key concepts

In today's digital economy, business success is tightly interwoven with the strength and reliability of IT. This book has explored how IT process controls, when properly aligned with business mandates, serve not just as technical safeguards but as strategic assets, driving resilience, operational excellence, and competitive advantage. Our examination of business-mandated IT controls has consistently highlighted the central theme of IT controls that are deliberately shaped by business goals and risk priorities, offering far more than compliance; they become enablers of long-term value and sustainability.

An effective IT audit is far more than a technical review; it is an exercise in understanding how IT underpins the organization's broader strategic objectives. Throughout this book, we have emphasized that IT controls must reflect the needs and language of the business. This requires collaboration between business process owners and IT stakeholders to define control requirements that serve governance, not just technology. The most impactful IT audit work arises when auditors act as translators, bridging the technical with the strategic, and ensuring that control evaluations speak directly to business risk and performance.

Several key takeaways emerged throughout our deep dive into business-driven IT process controls. A top-down, risk-based mindset was found to be essential. Audits must begin with a clear grasp of business priorities and the risks that threaten them. This ensures focus on what truly matters. Cross-functional collaboration is critical. Effective control environments are built through cooperation between IT, business units, risk management, and audit teams, breaking down silos and aligning perspectives. Beyond compliance lies value addition provided by audits. While regulatory adherence remains a core obligation, the real power of IT controls is in enabling better decisions, safeguarding critical assets, improving data integrity, and increasing agility. The threat landscape is constantly changing. With emerging technologies, AI, evolving cyber risks, and regulatory shifts, organizations must adapt continuously. Auditors must stay current to remain effective. Leveraging automation, data analytics, and technology-enabled audit tools transforms traditional methods, enhancing accuracy, reducing effort, and uncovering deeper insights.

Core of IT auditing

The audit of IT operations and **IT service management** (**ITSM**) offered a thorough evaluation of the organization's technology governance, risk management practices, and control environment. The primary aim was to assess how effectively, efficiently, and compliantly IT processes and services are functioning in alignment with established frameworks, internal policies, and industry best practices.

The audit highlights several positive aspects of the current IT operations and ITSM framework. These strengths often include a strong commitment from leadership to IT governance and service quality, well-documented procedures for essential IT processes such as incident and change management, and a capable, engaged IT team that understands its responsibilities. The organization also has to make effective use of ITSM tools to support service delivery and maintain mechanisms to regularly review and update certain IT security controls.

Despite these strengths, the audit identifies several areas where enhancements are needed to improve the maturity, resilience, and effectiveness of IT operations and service management. Common recommendations include:

- Optimizing incident and problem management processes to improve resolution times and prevent recurring issues.

- Strengthening change management controls to limit unauthorized changes and reduce the risk of service disruptions.

- Enhancing IT security through regular vulnerability scans, penetration testing, and stronger access controls.

- Developing a more robust and regularly tested disaster recovery and business continuity plan.

- Improving performance metrics and reporting to better monitor service delivery and uncover bottlenecks.

- Increasing user awareness and training on IT policies and security best practices.

- Reviewing and updating **service level agreements (SLAs)** to better align with evolving business needs and service capacities.

The organization shows a foundational commitment to strong IT operations and service management. By addressing the areas identified for improvement, it can significantly strengthen its ability to deliver secure, reliable, and business-aligned IT services. Prioritizing these recommended actions will not only help mitigate risks and optimize resources but also support the company's broader strategic goals.

Ongoing audits and proactive monitoring will be critical to maintaining compliance, adapting to technological change, and fostering a resilient, forward-thinking IT environment that supports innovation and operational excellence.

The role of the IT auditor has evolved dramatically. No longer confined to compliance checklists, auditors are now positioned to offer strategic guidance. By focusing on business-mandated controls, they help organizations understand not only whether controls are in place but also whether those controls meaningfully contribute to business performance, risk management, and strategic alignment. This expanded role demands more than technical skills. It requires auditors to cultivate business fluency, engage stakeholders effectively, and deliver insights that are actionable and relevant to leadership.

Establishing and maintaining effective IT process controls is not a one-time effort; it is an ongoing commitment. Organizations must remain vigilant, continuously evaluating and refining their control frameworks in response to new risks, innovations, and business shifts.

For IT auditors, the road ahead will demand cultivating the following aspects:

- Lifelong learning, to stay ahead of fast-paced technological and regulatory developments.

- Embracing emerging tools, including AI, automation, and advanced analytics, to modernize audit practices.

- Deepening business understanding, especially within the industry-specific context in which IT operates.

- Championing a culture of controls, where governance and accountability are embraced across all levels of the enterprise.

By adhering to these principles, organizations can reframe IT process controls not as constraints, but as foundational elements of growth, trust, and competitive edge. The insights derived from auditing business-aligned IT controls will continue to play a vital role in protecting assets, ensuring service continuity, and fueling strategic success in an increasingly digital world.

In the context of IT audits, maintaining clear segregation of duties is vital for integrity and consistency. Those responsible for selecting audit subjects should operate independently from auditors conducting the assessments, and entirely separately from personnel involved in resolving disputes or implementing remediation. This separation safeguards objectivity, reinforces the ethical foundation of the audit process, and ensures that compliance is upheld in a fair and consistent manner. Certain audit scenarios, particularly those involving high-risk findings, policy implications, or legal exposure, may require elevated supervisory review to confirm that procedures align with organizational policy and statutory obligations.

Organizationally, IT audit teams are best structured regionally to ensure coverage across distributed operations, while maintaining centralized oversight from headquarters. Auditors typically report to team leaders, who in turn report to audit managers and up the chain to central governance authorities. The ideal team size and reporting structure may differ across countries or industries, depending on the complexity of systems, volume of audits, and maturity of IT governance practices. Establishing this layered, transparent structure not only improves accountability but also strengthens the credibility and effectiveness of the IT audit function.

ITIL compliance

Compliance with the ITIL significantly strengthens IT audit conclusions by offering a structured and proven framework for ITSM. Organizations that follow ITIL principles enable auditors to more accurately evaluate the effectiveness, efficiency, and control of IT processes. This leads to audit findings that are not only more robust but also more actionable and aligned with best practices.

ITIL compliance positively influences IT audits across several dimensions:

- **Standardization and process consistency**: ITIL introduces standardized processes and terminology across ITSM functions such as incident, problem, and change management. When these processes are consistently implemented and documented, auditors are better equipped to assess operations against internal standards and external benchmarks, reducing ambiguity and enhancing the reliability of audit conclusions.

- **Stronger documentation practices**: A cornerstone of ITIL is thorough documentation, covering SLAs, operational workflows, configuration records, and change logs. This level of documentation supports auditors in tracing control execution, verifying compliance, and understanding how IT services are delivered and managed.

- **Improved control environment**: ITIL promotes robust controls throughout the IT service lifecycle. Key examples include change management, incident and problem management, security management, etc.

- **Enhanced risk management**: By embedding risk identification and mitigation into service management, ITIL helps organizations proactively manage IT-related risks. Auditors can use this risk-conscious approach to focus their efforts on high-impact areas and rely on the organization's existing risk mitigation strategies as part of their own assessments.

- **Clear accountability and role clarity**: ITIL defines roles and responsibilities for all ITSM functions. This transparency makes it easier for auditors to evaluate control ownership, identify breakdowns, and recommend improvements with confidence.

- **Commitment to value and continuous improvement**: ITIL emphasizes the delivery of business value and ongoing service improvement. Auditors can assess not only compliance and control maturity, but also the organization's capacity to adapt and evolve its IT services to meet changing business needs.

Thus, it can be seen that ITIL compliance enhances the quality and impact of IT audits by introducing structure, consistency, and clarity across ITSM processes. It enables auditors to conduct more efficient, risk-focused assessments and deliver insights that are not only technically sound but strategically aligned with the organization's objectives.

Integrating ITIL compliance into the scope of IT audits offers numerous advantages that directly impact audit findings:

- **Increased assurance and audit credibility**: When an audit concludes that IT processes align with ITIL, it reassures stakeholders that services are managed according to globally recognized standards, strengthening the reliability of the audit report.

- **More targeted and actionable recommendations**: Auditors can deliver recommendations grounded in a well-established framework, referring directly to specific ITIL processes. For instance, guidance like enhancing the change approval process per ITIL best practices offers clear direction rather than generic suggestions.

- **Deeper root cause analysis**: ITIL's structured approach to problem management helps uncover the root causes behind recurring issues. This enables audit conclusions to address systemic problems, not just isolated incidents, leading to more sustainable corrective actions.

- **Effective performance benchmarking**: With ITIL as a reference point, auditors can measure the maturity of IT processes and identify where improvements are needed. Audit findings can clearly articulate performance gaps relative to best practices.

- **Stronger alignment with business goals**: ITIL promotes a focus on delivering business value, and audits grounded in this framework can evaluate how well IT supports strategic objectives, helping organizations shift from reactive compliance to proactive value creation.

- **Audit efficiency and cost savings**: Organizations with mature ITIL adoption typically have well-documented, well-controlled environments. This readiness simplifies audit planning and evidence gathering, potentially reducing the time and resources required for audit execution.

ITIL compliance provides a clear, structured, and industry-aligned foundation for IT operations. For auditors, it means more consistent processes to evaluate, clearer documentation to verify, and more meaningful insights to deliver. Ultimately, audits that incorporate ITIL principles produce findings that are not only credible and insightful but also highly relevant to organizational improvement, risk reduction, and strategic alignment.

ISO 9001, ISO 27001, ISO 20000 compliance

We saw how ISO 19011, titled *Guidelines for Auditing Management Systems*, plays a pivotal role in IT audits by offering a standardized, systematic approach to auditing. Though it is a guidance document rather than a certifiable standard, it underpins the audit methodologies used across various ISO frameworks, including ISO 27001 for information security management, ISO 20000 for ITSM, and ISO 9001 for quality management, all of which are highly relevant to IT environments.

ISO 19011 lays out a uniform process for planning, executing, and following up on audits. For IT audits, this leads to consistency regardless of the domain, namely cybersecurity, infrastructure, and application controls, where auditors can apply a common methodology. This also ensures efficiency through application of a shared framework, reducing redundancy and helping streamline audit execution, saving both time and effort.

The standard introduces seven key principles that form the ethical and procedural foundation of any audit, like integrity, fair presentation, due professional care, confidentiality, independence, evidence, and risk-based approaches, etc.

ISO 19011 outlines the skills and qualifications auditors should possess. In IT contexts, this includes proficiency in areas such as cybersecurity, data privacy, ITSM frameworks, and relevant technologies, and also commitment to continuous professional development, ensuring auditors stay current with evolving threats and best practices.

The standard guides building and maintaining an effective audit program, including clearly defining audit objectives, scope, and criteria, allocating appropriate resources and scheduling, and ongoing monitoring and improvement of the audit program itself.

ISO 19011's broad applicability allows it to serve as a unified auditing guide for multiple management systems. For IT audits, this means the following:

- **Integrated audits**: Organizations can evaluate ISO 27001, ISO 20000, and ISO 9001 requirements together in a single audit cycle.

- **Operational synergy**: Auditors can assess the interdependencies between quality, security, and service management, providing a holistic view of IT performance and risks.

By aligning with ISO 19011, IT audits become more structured and defensible, more strategic, and globally recognized. Adherence to an internationally accepted auditing standard lends authority and trustworthiness to audit results.

In essence, ISO 19011 is far more than a generic auditing guide; it is a practical blueprint for conducting high-quality, risk-aware, and business-relevant IT audits. Its principles and methodology help ensure IT audits are not only efficient and consistent but also truly value-adding. By adopting ISO 19011, organizations and auditors elevate IT audits from procedural checks to strategic instruments that drive continuous improvement, bolster risk management, and strengthen overall governance in today's complex digital environment.

This book has explored the critical role of IT audits in supporting compliance with ISO 9001, ISO 27001, and ISO 20000, three foundational standards that collectively shape the pillars of modern IT governance. Through detailed examination of each standard's unique requirements, practical audit techniques, and real-world implications, we have uncovered a deeper insight: these frameworks are not just individual certifications, but components of a unified strategy for achieving sustainable IT excellence.

Compliance with these ISO standards is not simply a matter of meeting requirements; it is a transformative journey that reshapes how organizations approach quality, security, and service delivery at a strategic level:

- ISO 9001 cultivates a culture of quality, focusing IT activities on customer satisfaction, consistent processes, and continuous improvement. It ensures that IT operations are built around delivering measurable value.

- ISO 27001 protects the organization's information assets through structured risk management, securing the confidentiality, integrity, and availability of data—a foundation for trust and operational resilience.

- ISO 20000 brings discipline and structure to ITSM, aligning IT services with business needs while promoting efficiency, reliability, and improvement.

Rather than treating these standards as separate tracks, this book has shown the value of integrating them into a cohesive management system in carrying out ITSM activities. Due to the high-level structure shared across all ISO standards, this integration is both natural and beneficial.

When audits are conducted with this unified perspective, organizations realize greater strategic, operational, and compliance value through the following:

- Comprehensive risk oversight allows for integrated management of quality, security, and service risks, resulting in more effective controls and business continuity.

- Process efficiency and synergy emerge as overlapping requirements are harmonized, reducing duplication and streamlining audit and operational efforts.

- Stronger strategic alignment is achieved as IT functions are assessed not only for compliance but for how well they support organizational goals and deliver business value.

- Greater stakeholder confidence is earned by demonstrating rigorous, multidimensional compliance across key operational domains.

- A culture of continuous improvement is embedded into the organization, turning audits into opportunities for learning, adaptation, and innovation.

For IT auditors, the integrated approach described in this book elevates your role beyond compliance verification. You become trusted advisors, guiding organizations toward greater maturity, resilience, and performance. Your insights into how these standards intersect will help organizations not only meet regulatory and operational expectations but exceed them.

As digital ecosystems grow more complex and expectations for IT governance intensify, the relevance of ISO 9001, ISO 27001, and ISO 20000 will only increase. By embracing these standards holistically and applying the audit principles discussed here, organizations can build future-ready IT environments, ones that are secure, high-performing, customer-focused, and continuously evolving. In the end, the path to IT excellence is not paved by compliance alone, but by integration, intention, and insight. That journey begins and converges here.

ISACA IT audit framework and COBIT

ISACA's **Information Technology Assurance Framework (ITAF)** offers a globally accepted foundation for conducting IT audits in a structured and principled manner. It equips audit and assurance professionals with essential standards, guidelines, and tools, ensuring that audits are executed with professionalism, ethical integrity, and technical rigor. By following ITAF, organizations can achieve audit results that are credible, actionable, and aligned with international best practices.

The framework is organized into three tiers of guidance. First, the IT audit and assurance standards are the mandatory controls, which serve as the bedrock for ethical behavior, competence, objectivity, and proper audit execution. These standards cover core areas such as general conduct, engagement performance, and result reporting. Second, the IT audit and assurance guidelines offer non-mandatory but highly practical advice on implementing the standards. These guidelines include interpretive support, best practices, and procedural insights. Lastly, the tools and techniques component features resources like audit programs, reference materials, and the COBIT framework to help auditors tailor their methodology to the context and domain of the audit.

To conduct an audit using ITAF, practitioners begin by defining the audit scope and objectives, performing a thorough risk assessment, and crafting an audit engagement plan. During the fieldwork phase, auditors collect and evaluate evidence through interviews, document reviews, system observations, and control testing. Findings are categorized as strengths, weaknesses, or improvement opportunities, and must be supported by verifiable evidence and assessed with objectivity and professional care. The reporting phase focuses on creating a clear, actionable audit report. It includes an executive summary, detailed findings, risk implications, and targeted recommendations, alongside management's response and commitment to remediation. Communicating results to stakeholders is vital, followed by ongoing follow-up to ensure that corrective actions are implemented and risks are effectively addressed. Ultimately, ISACA's ITAF ensures a reliable and repeatable audit process that strengthens organizational control environments, supports governance objectives, and reinforces compliance initiatives.

COBIT as an IT audit framework

COBIT was developed by ISACA, formerly known as the **Information Systems Audit and Control Association**. The IT audit framework based on COBIT offers a thorough and structured approach to evaluating IT governance and management practices within an organization. COBIT is not merely an audit tool but a comprehensive governance and management framework for enterprise information and technology. For IT auditors, COBIT serves as a powerful resource, providing detailed control objectives, structured processes, and performance indicators that enable a meaningful assessment of how well IT aligns with business goals, mitigates risks, and creates value.

COBIT, the latest iteration of the framework, is especially effective for IT audits. It introduces the Goal Cascade, which connects stakeholder needs to enterprise goals, alignment goals, and finally to specific governance and management objectives. This layered structure helps auditors contextualize IT controls within broader business priorities. The framework includes 40 governance and management objectives, categorized under domains such as **Evaluate, Direct and Monitor (EDM)**; **Align, Plan and Organize (APO)**; **Build, Acquire and Implement (BAI)**; **Deliver, Service and Support (DSS)**; and **Monitor, Evaluate and Assess (MEA)**. Each objective is linked to specific processes and activities, allowing for detailed and targeted audit assessments.

COBIT also defines the components necessary for a functioning governance system, ranging from organizational structures and information flows to culture, policies, services, and applications. These elements give auditors a lens through which to examine the overall health and maturity of IT governance. Design factors within the framework allow for customization based on the organization's size, industry, strategy, and risk appetite, ensuring audits remain contextually relevant.

Conducting an IT audit using COBIT typically begins with a planning phase. Auditors must first understand the organization's strategic and IT-specific context. Using the Goal Cascade, they identify relevant enterprise and alignment goals, which guide the selection of COBIT's governance and management objectives most applicable to the audit scope. These selected objectives inform specific audit goals, define the audit boundaries, and help assess potential risks. A detailed audit program is then developed, incorporating the control practices and activities from COBIT relevant to the selected objectives.

During execution, auditors gather evidence through interviews, documentation reviews, observations, and control testing. They assess both the design and operational effectiveness of controls and evaluate the maturity of IT processes in comparison to COBIT's guidance. Any gaps or deficiencies are identified and linked directly to specific COBIT objectives, ensuring findings are clear, actionable, and aligned with recognized best practices.

The final phase involves reporting. Auditors document their findings in a comprehensive audit report that includes the audit scope, objectives, and criteria based on COBIT. It outlines identified issues, evaluates their risk implications, and offers recommendations grounded in COBIT practices. The report also includes responses from management and provides an overall assessment of IT governance effectiveness. Ongoing follow-up ensures that corrective actions are implemented, fostering continuous improvement.

By adopting COBIT as an audit framework, IT auditors can deliver insights that go beyond compliance. They help organizations strengthen their governance posture, enhance process maturity, and ensure IT initiatives are strategically aligned with business needs. COBIT's structured and flexible nature makes it an indispensable tool for delivering audits that are both rigorous and business-relevant.

In a rapidly evolving digital landscape, characterized by increasing cyber threats and tightening data regulations, IT audits have become essential rather than optional. They enable organizations to stay ahead of security risks, build resilient IT environments, and make decisions based on up-to-date, accurate assessments of their systems. Ultimately, an effective IT audit is not a one-time task but a continuous commitment to strong technology governance. Organizations that prioritize regular, thorough audits place themselves in a stronger position to succeed in an increasingly competitive, compliance-oriented, and security-conscious environment.

In the context of IT auditing, noncompliance can be addressed through three key categories of treatment strategies: preventative, facilitative, and enforced compliance. IT audit programs, particularly those that delve deeply into critical control failures or systemic breaches, typically fall under the enforced compliance category. These audits serve as a corrective mechanism, investigating and validating whether controls are functioning as intended and highlighting areas of serious non-adherence.

However, achieving and sustaining compliance in an IT environment requires more than audit enforcement alone. Preventative measures, such as robust training, well-structured governance frameworks, and automated controls, help mitigate risks before they arise. Facilitative actions, including guidance, toolkits, and real-time monitoring, support teams in implementing controls effectively and navigating complexities.

An optimal compliance strategy in IT relies on a balanced combination of these approaches. While audits and investigations play a critical role in detecting and correcting issues, long-term resilience is cultivated through proactive and supportive measures that embed compliance into daily operations.

Conclusion

This book has explored the essential principles, practices, and frameworks that shape the modern landscape of IT auditing. From dissecting governance models and control environments to applying globally recognized standards, we have examined how these tools equip IT auditors to deliver meaningful assurance and insight. In a world where technology is deeply embedded in every aspect of businesses, we have seen how the IT auditor's role has grown far beyond compliance checks.

Today's auditors need to be strategic partners, translating technical risk into business context, supporting innovation with integrity, and strengthening organizational resilience. By harnessing structured frameworks, embracing a risk-based mindset, and integrating tools for automation and analytics, IT auditors can transition from procedural reviewers to proactive enablers of value. Their assessments can inform strategy, shape controls that matter, and foster trust across the enterprise. The modern IT environment is dynamic, layered, and high-risk. As auditors, your ability to interpret risks, evaluate controls, and communicate insights in a clear and actionable way is crucial. The techniques covered in this book, from risk-based scoping and control testing to integrated audit planning and reporting, equip you to deliver audits that matter.

Moving forward, your role is both analytical and advisory. By combining technical insight with business awareness and by embracing continuous learning and emerging tools like analytics and automation, you can elevate audit quality while driving forward-looking change. At its core, IT audit serves as a lens into risk, a driver of accountability, and a catalyst for continuous improvement. With the knowledge and techniques shared throughout this book, auditors are equipped not only to assess but to lead, guiding organizations with confidence and clarity through the complexities of digital transformation.

Join our Discord space

Join our Discord workspace for latest updates, offers, tech happenings around the world, new releases, and sessions with the authors:

https://discord.bpbonline.com

Index

www.ingramcontent.com/pod-product-compliance
Lightning Source LLC
Chambersburg PA
CBHW061741210326
41599CB00034B/6755